Windows 3.0

A Self-Teaching Guide

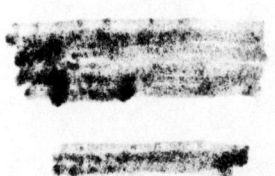

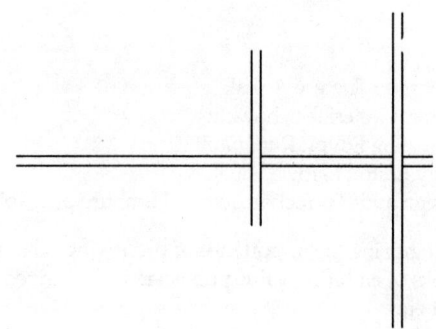

Windows 3.0
A Self-Teaching Guide

Keith Weiskamp
Saul Aguiar

John Wiley & Sons, Inc.
New York • Chichester • Brisbane • Toronto • Singapore

Publisher: Therese A. Zak
Editor: Katherine Schowalter
Managing Editor: Ruth Greif
Copy Editor: Pamela Dillehay
Design and Production: Lenity Himburg and Rob Mauhar, The Coriolis Group

Recognizing the importance of preserving what has been written, it is a policy of John Wiley & Sons, Inc. to have books of enduring value published in the United States printed on acid-free paper, and we exert our best efforts to that end.

Ami Professional is a registered trademark of Samna Corporation
Corel Draw is a registered trademark of Corel Systems Corporation
Crosstalk for Windows is a registered trademark of Digital Communication Associates, Inc.
Hayes is a registered trademark of the Hayes Microcomputer Products, Inc.
Hercules is a registered trademark of Hercules Computer Technology
IBM, IBM PC, PS/2, and PC-DOS are registered trademarks of International Business Machines, Inc.
Logitech Mouse is a registered trademark of the Logitech Corporation
Microsoft, MS-DOS, Microsoft Word, Microsoft Excel, Microsoft Network, and Microsoft Windows are registered trademarks of the Microsoft Corporation
Novell Network is a registered trademark of Novell Corporation
3Com Plus Open LAN Manager and 3Com 3Plus Share are registered trademarks of 3Com Corporation
PageMaker is a registered trademark of Aldus Corporation

This publication is designed to provide accurate and authoritative information in regard to the subject matter covered. It is sold with the understanding that the publisher is not engaged in rendering legal, accounting or other professional service. If legal advice or other expert assistance is required, the services of a competent professional person should be sought. FROM A DECLARATION OF PRINCIPLES JOINTLY ADOPTED BY A COMMITTEE OF THE AMERICAN BAR ASSOCIATION AND A COMMITTEE OF PUBLISHERS.

Copyright © 1991 by John Wiley & Sons, Inc.
All rights reserved. Published simultaneously in Canada.

Reproduction or translation of any part of this work beyond that permitted by section 107 or 108 of the 1976 United States Copyright Act without the permission of the copyright owner is unlawful. Requests for permission or further information should be addressed to the Permission Department, John Wiley & Sons, Inc.

Library of Congress Cataloging-in-Publication Data

Weiskamp, Keith.
    Windows 3.0 : a self-teaching guide / Keith Weiskamp, Saul Aguiar.
       p.   cm.
       Includes index.
       ISBN 0-471-52954-0
       1. Microsoft Windows (Computer programs)   I. Aguiar, Saul.
II. Title.   III. Title: Windows three-point-zero.
    QA76.76.W56W45   1991
    005.4'3—dc20   90-48606
                                                                          CIP

Printed in the United States of America
91 92 10 9 8 7 6 5 4 3 2 1

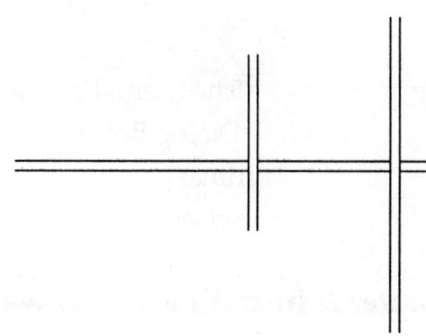

Contents

Preface — **xvii**
    Who Should Read This Book — xviii
    What You'll Need — xviii
    A Quick Look Inside — xviii
    Contacting the Authors — xx
    Acknowledgments — xx

Chapter 1: Getting Started — **1**
    Why Windows? — 1
        Breaking the Barriers — 4
    What's Available — 4
    Understanding Operating Modes — 7
    What You Will Need — 8
    The Windows Quick Tour — 9
        A Look at the Mouse — 9
        Windows — 10
        Icons — 11
        Scroll Bars — 13
        Title Bars — 14
        Positioning and Sizing Windows — 15

The Menu Bar and Drop-Down Menus	16
Dialog Boxes	18
Summary	18
Exercises	18

Chapter 2: Installing Windows — 19

Getting Started	20
What You Need to Know	20
Installing a Printer	23
Beginning the Installation	23
The Installation Process	24
Non-Windows Applications	28
Installation Side Effects	29
Changing Your Installation	29
Starting Windows	31
Options for Starting Windows	32
Starting Windows with an Application	33
Quitting Windows	34
Using the Help System	35
Introducing the Help Menu	36
Using the Help Buttons	38
Searching for Help Information	38
If You Need More Help	39
Printing Help Information	39
Summary	40
Exercises	41
What If It Doesn't Work?	42

Chapter 3: Building Your Windows Skills — 43

Starting with the Desktop	44
What's in a Window	44
Scrolling Windows	46
Changing a Window's Size	48

Moving a Window	51
Converting a Window to an Icon	52
Tips for Working with Multiple Windows	53
Selecting an Application Window	55
Selecting Windows with the Keyboard	56
Closing a Window	56
Icons	57
Selecting and Moving Icons	59
Activating an Icon	60
Accessing Menus	60
Working with Special Menu Commands	62
Using the Control Menu	63
Accessing the Control Menu for Icons and Dialogs	65
Mastering Dialog Boxes	65
Selecting Dialog Options	66
Using Warning Dialog Boxes	67
Command Buttons	68
Check Boxes	68
Using Menu Option Dialogs	70
Option Buttons	71
Using Text Boxes	71
Using List Boxes	72
Drop-Down List Boxes	73
Closing Dialogs	74
Summary	74
Exercises	74
What If It Doesn't Work?	75

Chapter 4: Introducing the Program Manager — 77

The Program Manager—A Close Look	77
A Closer Look at Group Windows	81
Working with the Keyboard and the Mouse	82
Control Menu Options	84

Working with the Menu System	85
The File Menu	85
The New Command	86
Creating a Program Group	87
Creating a Program Item	89
Including a Document with a Program Item	90
The Open Command	91
Editing a Program Item	91
The Copy and Move Commands	92
Moving Program Items and Group Windows with the Mouse	93
Using the Delete Command	94
The Properties Command	94
The Run Command	96
Activating an Application with the Mouse	96
Exiting Windows	96
Using The Options Menu	97
Auto Arrange	97
Minimize on Use	98
The Window Menu	98
Cascade and Tile Options	98
The Arrange Icons Command	98
Group Selection	100
The Help Menu	100
Help Menu Options	101
About the Program Manager	102
Summary	103
Exercises	103

Chapter 5: Putting Windows to Work — 105

Writing a Document	105
Editing Your Document	108
Saving Your Document	111
Printing Your Document	114

Exiting Write	115
Creating a Small Index File Using Cardfile	116
Starting a Cardfile	119
Setting an Alarm Using Calendar	120
Summary	122
Exersises	122
What If It Doesn't Work?	124

Chapter 6: The Control Panel — 125

Overview of the Control Panel	125
Starting the Control Panel	127
Selecting Colors	128
Creating Your Own Color Scheme	130
Creating Custom Colors	131
Setting the Date and Time	133
Setting the Desktop	134
Creating Your Own Desktop Pattern	135
Using Wallpaper	136
Setting the Cursor	138
Controlling Icon Spacing	139
Setting Border Widths	139
Selecting Fonts	140
Removing Font Files	141
Adding Fonts	142
International Settings	143
Setting the Date Format	144
Setting the Time Format	145
Setting the Currency and Number Format	146
Setting the Keyboard	147
Setting the Mouse	147
Setting Network Options	149
Setting Ports	149
Installing Printers	152

  Removing an Installed Printer   154
 Setting Sound   154
 Setting 386 Enhanced Mode Options   155
 Summary   156
 Exercises   156
  What If It Doesn't Work?   157

Chapter 7: The File Manager   159

 DOS Directory Basics   159
 Directory Requirements   161
 Introducing the File Manager   163
  Starting the File Manager   163
  A Quick Look at the File Manager   163
  Using the Directory Tree Window   165
 Viewing a Directory   167
  Opening Multiple Directory Windows   168
 Navigation Shortcuts   169
 Determining File and Directory Information   171
  Finding the Size of a File   171
  Viewing File Information   172
  Viewing Files by Categories   174
  Sorting and Excluding Files   174
  Using a Filter   175
 Selecting Files and Directories   177
 Moving Files and Directories   178
 Copying Files and Directories   181
 Deleting Files and Directories   183
 Searching for Files and Directories   185
 Creating and Deleting Directories   187
 Renaming Files and Directories   187
 Changing File Attributes   190
 Launching Applications   190
 Printing Files   191

Performing Disk Maintenance	193
Copying Disks	193
Formatting Disks	194
Summary	196
Exercises	196
What If It Doesn't Work?	197

Chapter 8: The Print Manager — 199

The Problem with Printing	199
How Print Manager Works	200
Selecting Print Manager	200
Starting Print Manager	202
Working with the Queue	203
Using Multiple Printers	203
The Options Menu	204
Print Manager Messages	205
Using a Network	205
The View Menu	206
Intercepting Print Jobs	207
Summary	209
Exercises	209
What If It Doesn't Work?	209

Chapter 9: Working with Non-Windows Applications — 211

Running Non-Windows Applications	211
Options and Limitations	212
The DOS Prompt Application	213
Creating Your Own Built-In Applications	215
Moving a Program Icon	217
Deleting an Icon	218
Modifying an Icon	218
Working with PIFs	219
Using the PIF Editor	220

Non-386 Enhanced Mode	222
386 Enhanced Mode	223
Advanced PIF Options	225
A Custom Directory Program	228
Basic DOS Commands	230
Summary	232
Exercises	233
What If It Doesn't Work?	233

Chapter 10: Using Desktop Accessories — 235

Working with Clock	235
Using the Notepad	236
Starting Notepad	237
Opening an Existing Text File	238
Editing Text	239
Basic Navigation Keys	240
Using the Word Wrap Feature	240
Searching for Text	240
Setting Up a Page	241
Printing a File	242
Using the Time/Date Feature	243
Using Multiple Files	243
Using the Calendar	243
Starting Calendar	243
Changing the Calendar Format	244
Selecting an Appointment Date	245
Setting Time Slots	246
Marking Special Days	248
Setting an Alarm	248
Alarm Options	250
Creating and Saving Calendars	251
Printing a Calendar	252
Working with Calculator	253

Starting the Calculator	253
Setting up and Using Your Keyboard	253
Performing a Calculation	255
Working with Memory	256
Using Calculated Results	256
The Scientific Mode	257
Using Number Systems	257
Performing Statistics	258
Using Cardfile	258
Starting Cardfile	259
Creating a Card System	259
Adding Additional Cards	261
Deleting Cards	262
Editing Options	262
Restoring a Card	262
Pasting a Picture	262
Saving, Opening, and Merging a Card Set	263
Tips for Viewing Cards	264
Searching for a Card	264
Using a Calling Card	265
Summary	265
Exercises	266
What If It Doesn't Work?	267

Chapter 11: Working with Desktop Applications — 269

Notes about Using Paintbrush	270
Starting Paintbrush	270
Basic Techniques	271
Defining a Drawing Region	271
Introducing the Paintbrush Tools	272
Selecting Drawing Tools and Colors	273
The Closed Shapes and Standard Tricks	274
Using The Roller Tool	276

      Drawing Tips   279
      Using the Polygon Tools   279
      The Eraser Tools   280
      Using the Color Eraser   281
      Drawing Lines and Curves   282
      Selecting a Brush Shape   284
      The Airbrush Tool   286
      Scissors and Pick   287
      The Text Tool   288
Using Write   291
      Starting Write   291
      Using the Ruler   291
      Setting up A Document   293
      Formatting Paragraphs   294
      Placing Tabs   294
      Line Spacing   296
      Paragraph Alignment   296
      Indenting Paragraphs   297
      Setting Page Breaks   298
      Creating Headers and Footers   299
      Using Fonts and Styles   300
      Combining Text and Graphics   302
      Saving Files   304
Using Terminal   304
      Starting Terminal   304
      Setting Up Communication Parameters   305
      Setting up Your Terminal   307
      Selecting a Modem   308
      Selecting a Number   308
Making the Call   309
      What If You Can't Connect   309
Transferring a File   310
Receiving a File   310

Disconnecting	311
Saving Terminal Settings	311
Summary	311
Exercises	311
What If It Doesn't Work?	313

Glossary 315

Index 323

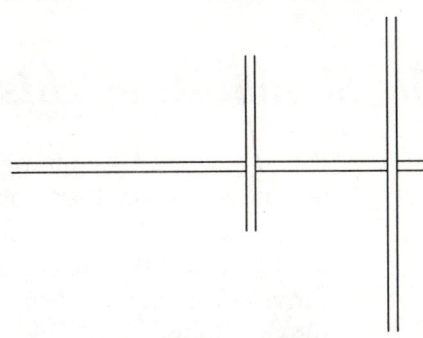

Preface

With the release of Microsoft Windows 3.0, your PC just became much easier to use. In the past, using the PC involved memorizing a number of cryptic DOS commands. Windows, on the other hand, adds a rich, full-powered graphical interface to your computer so that you can get your work done easier and faster. In addition, the new Windows allows you to take advantage of the more advanced memory management capabilities of 286 and 386 PCs. This means that you can run multiple applications at the same time and easily switch between them without returning to the DOS prompt.

To help you learn how to use Windows 3.0, *Windows 3.0: A Self-Teaching Guide* provides a practical "hands-on" approach. Here are some major highlights of this book:

- Emphasizes the learn-by-doing approach to performing file management and DOS operations
- Incorporates self-checks throughout the book to help you learn at your own pace
- Provides special chapters to help you install Windows and develop your basic skills
- Covers the key components of Windows including the Program Manager, File Manager, Print Manager, and the Control Panel
- Provides coverage of the useful desktop applications and accessories
- Explains how operations can be performed with both the keyboard and the mouse

Who Should Read This Book

If you're currently running Windows 3.0 or you're planning to upgrade from an earlier version, then you've come to the right place. If you take a minute a look through this book you'll see that each chapter provides a number of illustrations and visual cues to help you master Windows. All of the examples provided are designed to help you perform useful operations from managing files to running applications. If you're the kind of person who likes to learn at your own pace, you'll especially benefit from the self-checks that are provided in each chapter.

What You'll Need

To use this book you'll need Windows 3.0, MS-DOS 3.1 or later, as well as an IBM PC XT, AT, PS/2, or compatible computer system. Windows is designed to run on a number of different types of PCs from XTs to 80386 computers. Of course, you'll get the best performance by using a higher-performance PC such as an 80386. You'll also need a hard disk with 6 to 8 megabytes of free space, and a monitor that is supported by Windows. Because the graphical interface of Windows is especially designed to work with a mouse, we highly recommend that you add one to your system if you don't currently have one installed.

A Quick Look Inside

This book progresses from the basics to more advanced topics—in a way that lets you put previously learned skills to use quickly. In each chapter, you'll find a set of self-checks to help you review the material that has been presented. We've also included special tips throughout the book to point out important techniques for using Windows.

Chapter 1: *Getting Started* covers the basics of running Windows—including the operating modes supported, what equipment is needed, and what basic operations Windows performs. The second half of the chapter presents a quick tour to help you get started using the interface components such as the mouse, windows, icons, menus, and dialog boxes.

Chapter 2: *Installing Windows* shows you how to easily install and start up Windows. You'll learn how to use the installation program to select the hardware that is provided with your computer system. You'll also learn how to access and use the powerful built-in help system.

Chapter 3: *Building Skills* presents the basic techniques for using the major Windows components including application and document windows, icons, menus, and dialog boxes. This chapter serves as a useful reference guide that you'll want to refer to whenever you need to brush up on a basic technique for using the Windows interface.

Chapter 4: *Introducing the Program Manager* shows you how to use the heart of the Windows environment. The Program Manager is the main window that allows you to run and organize your applications.

Chapter 5: *Putting Windows to Work* presents a hands-on introduction to three of the more useful Windows applications—Write, Cardfile, and Calendar. The goal of this chapter is to show you how to use these applications to perform some useful operations such as creating a document and setting an alarm.

Chapter 6: *The Control Panel* covers the basic techniques for using the Control Panel for customizing your Windows working environment. Some of the topics covered include selecting colors, setting the system date and time, selecting fonts, installing printers, and setting up the mouse and keyboard.

Chapter 7: *The File Manager* shows you how to use the File Manager application to manage your DOS files. Here you'll learn a variety of techniques for performing file- and directory-related operations such as viewing directories, moving, copying, and deleting files, searching for files, and renaming files and directories.

Chapter 8: *The Print Managers* explores the Windows application that allows you to control how your documents are printed.

Chapter 9: *Working with Non-Windows Applications* shows how setup non-Windows applications so that they can be run in the Windows environment. You'll learn how to use the PIF editor to customize your applications for Windows.

Chapter 10: *Using Desktop Accessories* presents the major built-in accessories including Clock, Notepad, Calendar, Calculator, and Cardfile..

Chapter 11: *Working with Desktop Applications* covers the basic techniques for using the Windows applications Paintbrush, Write, and Terminal.

Glossary provides definitions for all of the Windows- and DOS-related terms used in this book.

Contacting the Authors

After working through this book, you might want to correspond with the authors. We'd like to encourage you to do so by using electronic mail or U.S. Mail. The quickest way to reach us is through the CompuServe Information Service. (The ID is 72561,1536 for Keith Weiskamp.) You can reach us by mail at 3202 E. Greenway, Suite 1307-302, Phoenix, AZ 85032.

Acknowledgments

We would like to thank everyone who helped in the preparation and production of this book. We are indebted to Rob Mauhar for his excellent design and typesetting work. Lenity Himburg deserves special credit for her indexing work. Finally, we would like to thank Katherine Schowalter for taking on this book, Ron Pronk for his valuable suggestions, and Ruth Greif who kept us on schedule.

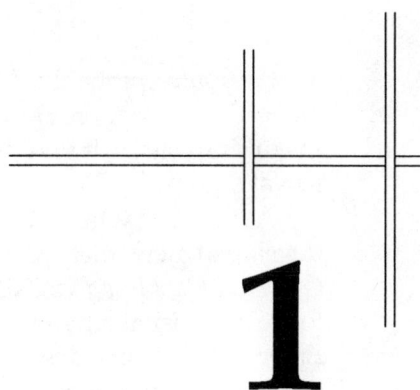

1

Getting Started

Welcome to the Microsoft Windows 3.0 environment. In this book we'll show you what Windows 3.0 can do and how to use it most effectively. First, to better understand the advantages of using Windows 3.0, you must understand some of the problems it's designed to solve.

We'll start by discussing some of the reasons why Windows 3.0 was created to be a powerful enhancement to DOS. Next, we'll discuss the basic components of Windows, including the following:

- Graphical User Interface (GUI)
- The basic features of Windows
- Windows' operating modes
- The hardware and software needed to run Windows
- The applications provided with Windows

Why Windows?

A complaint that has dogged the PC industry for years is that methods provided for the user and the computer to communicate are too cryptic. Computer languages and commands were devised by people who were very familiar with the internal operation of these machines. As personal computers (PCs) became more available and affordable, more nontechnical people began to use them and needed a simpler, more intuitive way to control the PCs.

As you're probably aware, the first operating system for the IBM PC was DOS. This system provided the features that most users needed, but it had two major drawbacks: It was difficult to use, and it allowed only one program to be run at a time.

At the time when PCs were rapidly evolving, a small group of researchers developed new methods for controlling computers based on the idea of a *Graphical User Interface* (GUI). The idea behind the development of a GUI was to create a visual environment that the computer user could easily understand. Enter the electronic desk (Figure 1.1), where multiple files and programs could be opened at the same time. Here the computer screen looks like your average desk, where everything is at your finger tips.

With the electronic desk, you don't need to memorize cryptic commands, such as COPY A:*.* B:. Instead, all operations are initiated by selecting symbols, called *icons*, that each represent a particular operation. Also multiple programs can reside within the computer's memory at the same time, so a particular task can be suspended while another is activated. The ability to hold

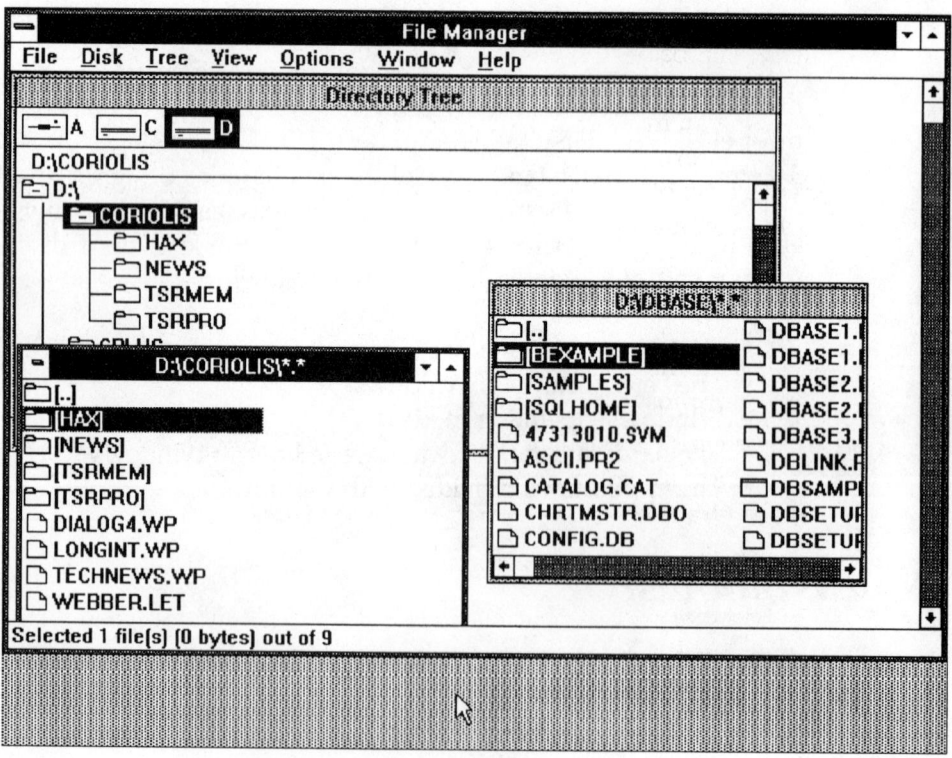

Figure 1.1. The Electronic Desk

several programs at once saves you from wasting time continuously loading and quitting programs. After all, you wouldn't want to have to put away the papers on your desk every time the phone rang, or a fellow worker stopped by to ask you a question.

For many years, these concepts were implemented only in experimental computers at research facilities. Why? The GUI required fast microprocessors, fast disk drives, a lot of memory, and high-quality displays. Finally, in the mid-1980s, the Apple Macintosh series of computers broke with tradition by using a GUI. Today several GUI products are available on the market for the IBM PC and compatibles. In fact, this interface is becoming so common that it's getting harder to find a PC that displays a C> prompt.

Microsoft Windows 3.0 is designed to provide a high-quality GUI in the IBM-compatible PC world. Once installed, it is extremely easy and intuitive to use. Most applications programs for Windows 3.0 follow a certain appearance and design philosophy, resulting in a user-friendly environment where things are done consistently within different programs. Whether you're running a word processor, a spreadsheet, or a database, the basic techniques for performing tasks (such as opening, closing, and printing files) are the same. Once you learn the basics, you won't have to search through manuals for commands. Windows 3.0 also allows multiple applications to be resident at the same time so you can move quickly from one program to another (and in some instances, move information from one application to another). Finally, Windows 3.0 provides a set of special applications that let you write documents, create pictures, and even maintain an electronic equivalent of a card index file.

This book provides a number of self-checks (like the one shown here) in each chapter to help you test your skills as you progress. We call this the "learn-by-doing approach."

1. For your first self-check, take a moment to find out some of the applications that are available for Windows 3.0.
2. Do you need to use DOS to run Windows?

1. Here are some examples: Microsoft Word, Microsoft Excel, Ami Professional, Crosstalk for Windows, PageMaker, and Corel Draw.
2. Yes. Windows is not its own operating system. It serves as an interface to DOS. You can execute all of the DOS commands from inside Windows.

Breaking the Barriers

The most unique feature about Windows 3.0 is that it can take advantage of all your computer's memory. (If you're familiar with older versions of Windows, you're probably aware that they could not break the DOS 640K barrier.) The improvement in memory access means you can work more efficiently. In fact, if you use a computer with 1Mb of memory or more, you can load multiple applications simultaneously and switch between them. If you use a 386-based computer, you can even run multiple applications at the same time. This feature is called *multitasking*.

Windows 3.0 also sports a whole new look. When you first see the new Windows environment, you'll discover visually appealing icons, 3-D buttons, new colors and fonts, and easy-to-use dialog boxes, menus, and windows—all provided to create an attractive and easy-to-use system.

What's Available

The heart of Windows 3.0 is a control window called the *Program Manager*. Because of the importance of this component, we've devoted an entire chapter to it (see Chapter 4). From this window, you can run other Windows applications to perform operations from managing your files to setting up your working environment. As Figure 1.2 shows, the Program Manager provides a window at startup, called Main, and a set of icons that represent Windows applications. The Main window contains the following components:

- File Manager
- Control Panel
- Print Manager
- Clipboard
- DOS Prompt
- Windows Setup

The powerful *File Manager* application lets you perform disk-maintenance operations (moving or deleting files, searching for files or directories, renaming files, and so on). The *Control Panel* lets you enable or disable a large variety of options associated with the Windows environment. These include selecting the colors of the parts of the Windows screens, setting the speed of mouse travel, selecting Date and Time formats, and so on.

The *Print Manager* schedules and controls output to the printer. It lets you "send" a job to the printer and then resume work in an application program. The Print Manager saves the data to be sent to the printer in temporary stor-

Getting Started

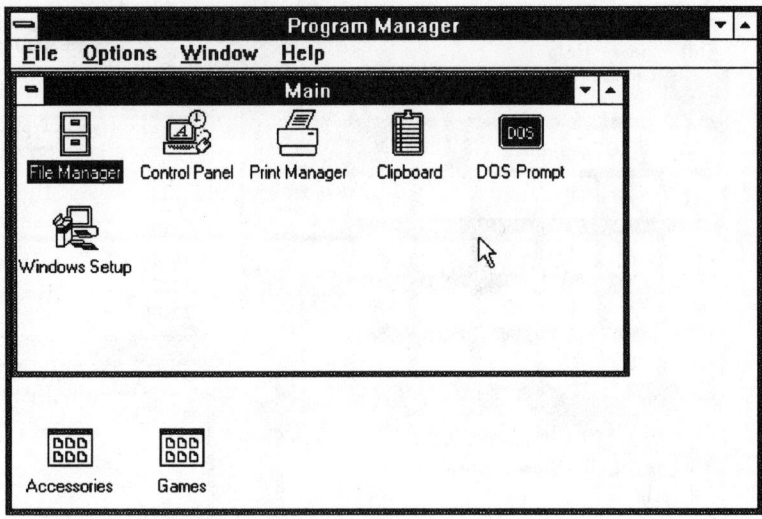

Figure 1.2. The Program Manager

age, and provides the data to the printer at the rate that the printer wants.

The *Clipboard* is a temporary storage area that you use to transfer information between Windows applications. The Clipboard is always available so that you can cut or copy information from an application, store the information in the Clipboard, and transfer the information later from the Clipboard to another application. The *DOS Prompt* accesses the DOS command interpreter so you can easily execute DOS commands. When this feature is activated, you can type in the name of any MS-DOS command or a non-Windows application. The last component in the Main group, the *Windows Setup*, lets you configure your Windows environment.

As part of the Windows environment, you also receive a group of special applications that perform typical PC-oriented tasks. These include a word-processor program (called Write) and a drawing program (called Paintbrush). You also receive a simple database program (called Cardfile), an electronic Calendar that can sound an alarm, and a Calculator that allows you to transfer results of calculations to other programs. You also get a Notepad program that you use to save information temporarily and a Terminal program that automatically dials telephone numbers and transfers files to or from another modem-equipped computer. (Your computer must be equipped with an internal modem card to use the auto-dialing features.) You can also use the Terminal program to transfer files between two computers using a simple RS-232 connection. (This will be discussed in greater detail later.) These different applications are shown in Figures 1.3 and 1.4.

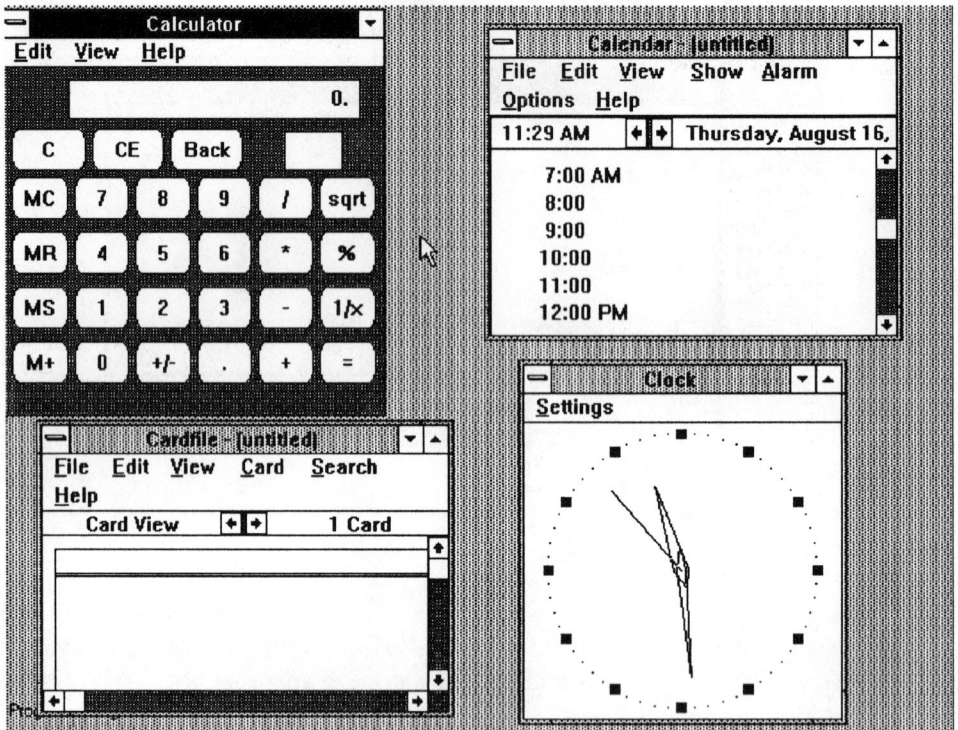

Figure 1.3. Windows Applications: Calculator, Calendar, Cardfile, and Clock.

Windows 3.0 also provides a Clock program that displays the system time. In addition, a specialized program called Recorder lets you record your commands for reuse. Another specialized program, called PIF Editor, tells Windows how to allocate resources for running non-Windows applications. In case you need a break from the daily grind, Windows even provides two games: Solitaire, the card game; and Reversi, which resembles a simplified version of Go.

Windows also includes provisions to run most programs that run under DOS. This extremely important feature allows you to transition over time from programs that you've used for years to new Windows-compatible applications software.

Many third-party software developers have already converted their best-selling programs to run under Windows and many others have announced that they are doing so. The availability of applications for the Windows environment is expected to increase rapidly in the next few years.

Getting Started

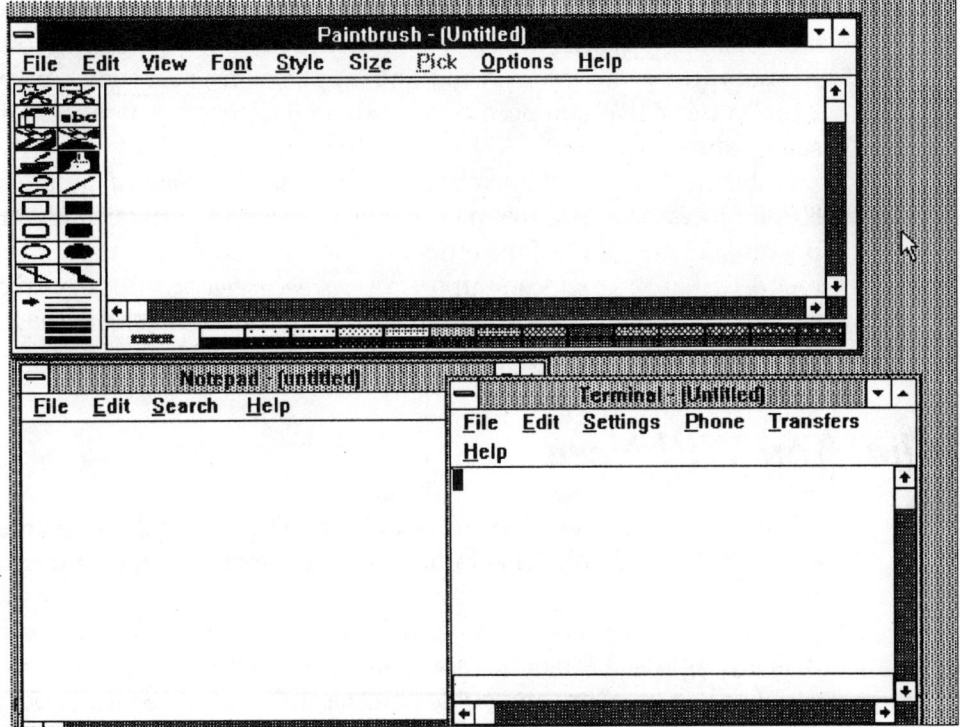

Figure 1.4. Windows Applications: Paintbrush, Notepad, and Terminal.

Understanding Operating Modes

In order to install and make full use of Windows, you need to know about the operating modes that it supports. With earlier releases of Windows, special versions of the program were introduced to support different hardware platforms. For example, if you used a PC with a 80386 processor, you needed Windows 386. Fortunately, Windows 3.0 has integrated the different operating modes into one product.

The operating modes that Windows 3.0 supports come in three flavors: real mode, standard mode, and 386 enhanced mode. *Real mode* is the basic mode designed for the standard 8088 PCs. It's the most compatible mode with previous versions of Windows, and is the only mode that can be used with PCs that have less than 1Mb of memory. The disadvantage of using this mode is that it restricts you from taking advantage of the new memory-management features of Windows 3.0.

The second level of operating modes is the *standard mode*, which is the normal operating mode. When you run this mode, you can access extended memory (up to 16Mb), load multiple applications, and switch between them. Keep in mind that you need a PC with an 80286 or 80386 processor to run the standard mode.

The most powerful operating mode is the *386 enhanced mode*. You'll need a 80386 processor to run this mode, which is designed to take advantage of the power and flexibility of the 80386. One of the more important features of this mode is that it provides support for *virtual memory*. With a virtual memory system, a computer can access more memory than it actually has, which lets you run very large programs and run multiple programs simultaneously.

What You Will Need

Windows 3.0 is designed to run on XT and AT-class machines that use the Intel 8088, 80286, 80386 or 80486 family of microprocessors (or their equivalent). It prefers 386/486 processors becaus these have advanced memory-management hardware features not available on the 80286. Windows also expects a hard disk and at least 2 Mb of memory, and works with the Microsoft mouse (either serial or bus-type) or compatible hardware. (Windows 3.0 can operate without a mouse and be controlled through keyboard commands, but the use of a mouse adds significantly to the friendliness of the Windows environment.)

1. Take a few minutes to review the requirements for running Windows. If you use a PC with an 80286 processor, how much memory can you access? How much memory can you access with an 80386 PC?
2. How much hard disk space does Windows require?
3. Do you need to install a mouse in order to run Windows?
4. What are the differences between the real mode, the standard mode, and the 386 enhanced mode?

1. *Up to 16Mb can be accessed by both processors.*
2. *6Mb to 8Mb of free disk space are needed.*
3. *No. However, you'll find that a mouse greatly enhances Windows' ease of use.*
4. *Real mode is the basic mode that simulates the operation of the 8088 processor. Standard mode is designed for the 80286 processor, and the 386 enhanced mode is designed to take advantages of the memory-management features of the 80386.*

The Windows Quick Tour

To really get started with Windows, you should familiarize yourself with several of its basic components, such as the mouse, the menus, the icons, and the windows themselves. Use the quick tour of these components in this last section to prepare yourself to start using Windows. (Chapter 3 provides more detailed information about working with these components.) Let's start with the mouse.

A Look at the Mouse

To best utilize the Windows 3.0 environment, you should understand the function and the use of the mouse. As you slide your mouse around your desk, notice that the standard *mouse pointer*, a single arrow, moves in the same direction on the screen. To select an object or a menu, simply move the mouse pointer (also called the *mouse cursor*) on top of the object. Next, press the left mouse button while the mouse cursor is over the object. The process of moving the mouse cursor to a position and pressing the left mouse button is called *clicking an object*. We will use this term throughout the book.

On certain occasions you may wish to move an object. To do so, move the mouse cursor to the object, press the left mouse button, and hold the button down while you move the mouse cursor to the new location. This action is called *dragging an object*, because you seem to drag it across the screen.

You can also activate commands by placing the mouse pointer over an icon, a button, or a menu item and then pressing the mouse button twice in quick succession. This technique is called *double-clicking the mouse*. In many situations, a double-click corresponds to the process of using the keyboard to highlight an item and pressing the Enter key.

The standard mouse cursor (arrow) isn't the only pointer you'll encounter while using Windows. In fact, eight types of mouse pointers are provided, as shown in Figure 1.5. The pointer displayed corresponds to the task that you are currently performing. For example, if you are waiting for a task to finish, the hourglass pointer displays. In this respect, the mouse pointer serves as a useful visual cue.

Tip | Windows is designed to work with both the mouse and the keyboard. If you don't have a mouse installed, you can still operate Windows (although the mouse is the preferred input device). As we present different techniques for using the mouse to perform Windows operations, we'll also show you how to use the keyboard.

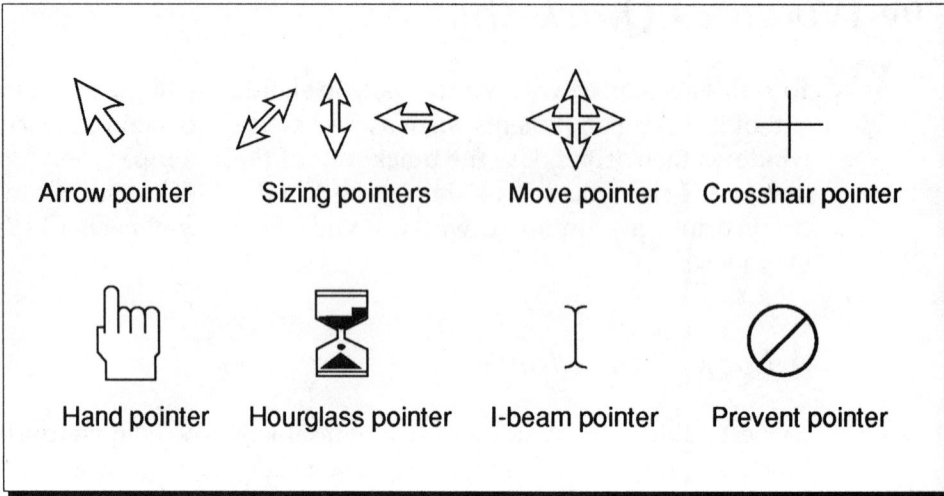

Figure 1.5. Mouse Pointers

Windows

In general, a *window* is a rectangular section of the screen that represents a means of communication between you and a task. Every application that you run has its own corresponding window. As Figure 1.6 shows, an application window contains four main components: a frame, a title bar, a Control menu, and a menu bar. The *frame* defines a window's edge, and the *title bar* displays the window's title. The *Control menu* provides a set of options for manipulating a window. This menu is typically used to perform tasks such as changing the size of a window, moving the window, and closing the window. The *menu bar* provides the menus for controlling the application.

The window displayed in front or on top of other windows is called the *active window*. The active window represents the task currently responding to the commands from the user. The active window can also be recognized because its title bar is highlighted, while the title bars for the other tasks are the same color as other parts of the window. To activate a different window, simply move the arrow associated with the mouse to a location anywhere in the window to be activated (excluding the size buttons in the window's top-right corner), and press the left mouse button. When a new window is activated, the previously active window moves into the background and its title bar is removed.

In Chapter 3, we'll present a number of different techniques for processing windows using the keyboard and the mouse.

Getting Started 11

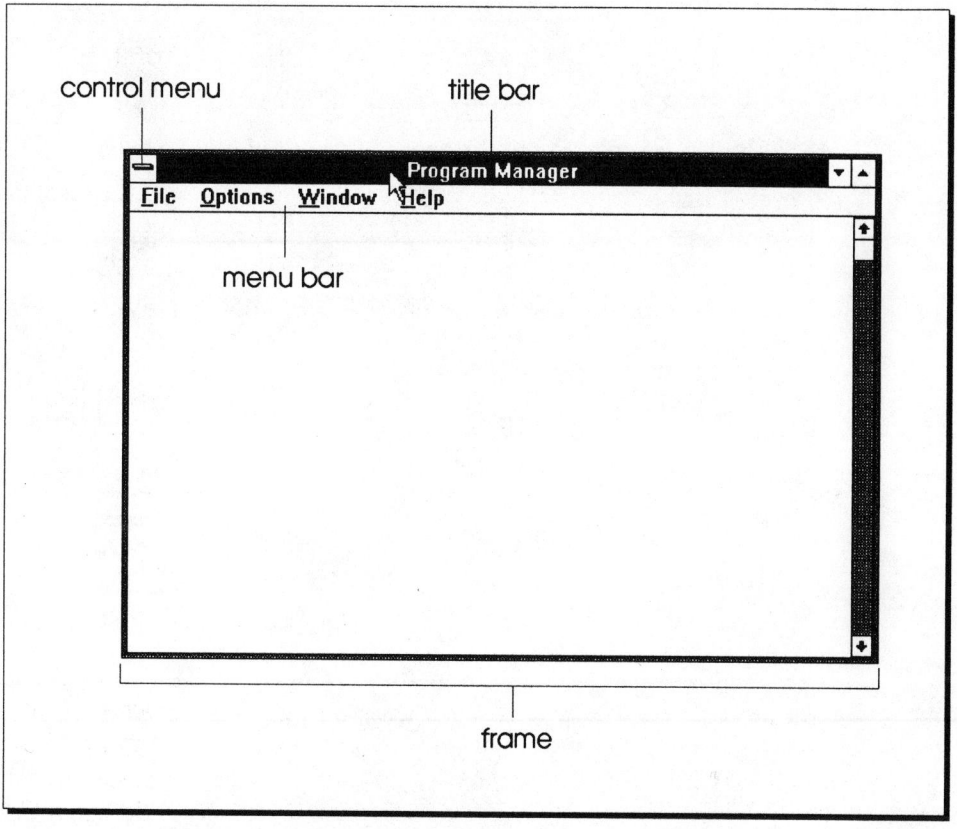

Figure 1.6. Basic Components of a Window

Tip By default, an active window is displayed with a blue title bar. An inactive window is displayed with a white title bar.

Icons

An *icon* is a small picture that represents some task or operation. Figure 1.7 illustrates the icons associated with the standard tools provided with Windows. Any of these tasks or programs can be activated by using the mouse to double-click on them. If you click the mouse button once, a pop-up menu appears that lets you alter the appearance and the location of the icon.

You can arrange your desktop by moving icons around so that they display in a different order. To move an icon, click on the icon and drag it to a new location.

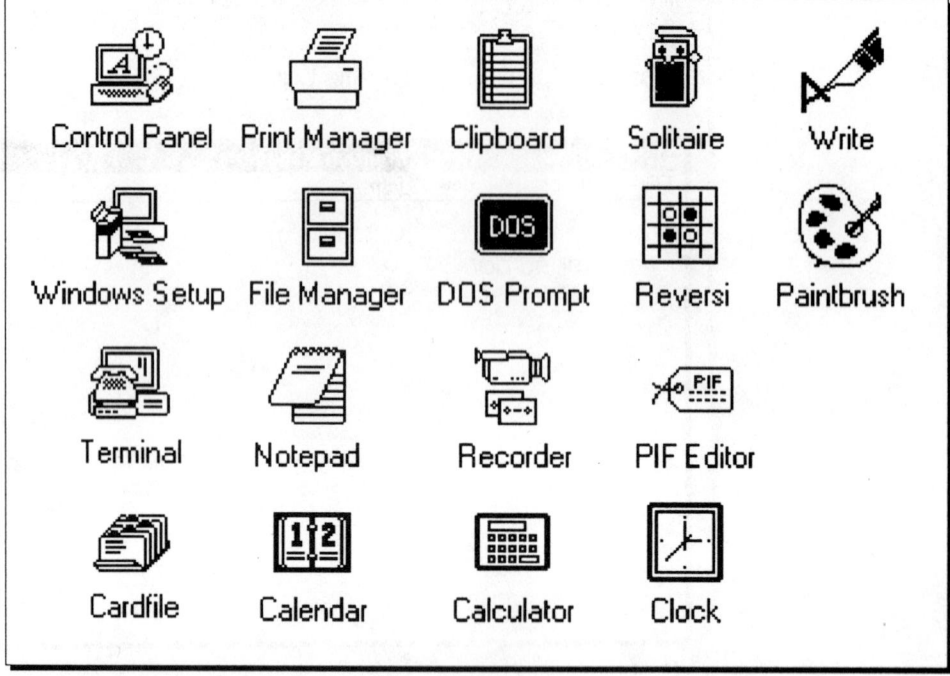

Figure 1.7. Windows Icons

1. What mouse pointer does Windows display to indicate that a window can be moved?
2. Practice moving an object such as a window with the mouse.
3. How can you tell which task is assigned to a window?
4. What is the difference between clicking the mouse and double-clicking the mouse?

1. *The move pointer that contains four arrows (up, down, left, and right).*
2. *To move an object, first select it by positioning the mouse pointer on it. Click the left mouse button and drag the mouse while the left button remains pressed.*
3. *The window's title indicates which task is assigned to the window. For example, when you run the File Manager application, the window displayed has the title shown in Figure 1.8.*
4. *A single click selects (highlights) an item. A double-click activates a command (performs an action).*

Getting Started

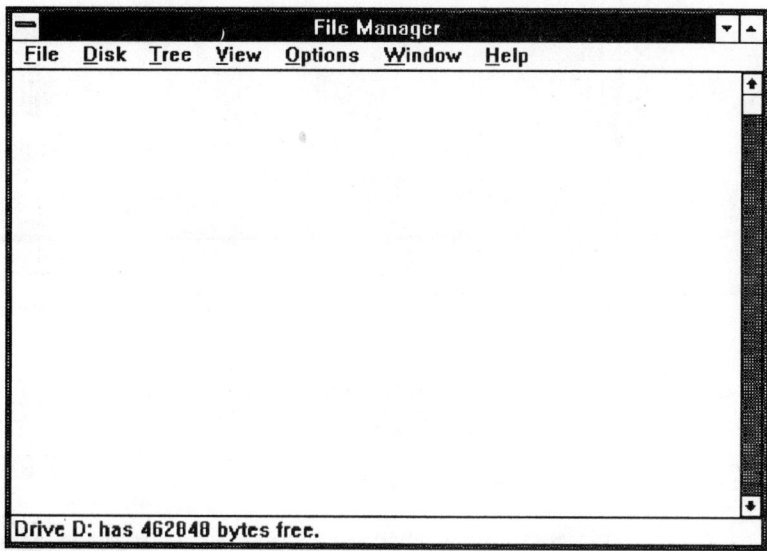

Figure 1.8. The File Manager Window

Scroll Bars

Most Windows applications provide for scroll bars along the bottom and the right side of a window. If you position the mouse arrow over one of the small boxes that indicates either up and down or left and right, and then you hold down the left mouse button, you can scroll around what appears to be a larger area behind the window. These small boxes, called *scroll arrows*, act like buttons that can be pressed to move the information in the window. Scrolling allows you to view a document or a picture that is much larger than the screen or the window (Figure 1.9).

Scroll through a window and notice that a small box appears to slide on a rectangular slot. This square, called the *scroll box*, indicates the approximate location of the current window in the full document. For example, if the scroll box for the up/down scroll bar is positioned at the very top of the slot, you are viewing the top of the document or the picture. As you press the down arrow, the scroll box will slowly move down the slot, until it rests at the bottom when you reach the bottom of the document or the picture. To move immediately to the middle or the end of a large document, place the mouse arrow over the scroll box, press the left mouse button, and drag the mouse (and the scroll box with it). As you move the scroll box, notice that the screen jumps through the various parts of the document or the picture. When you reach the desired general area, release the left mouse button to let go of the scroll box. If the

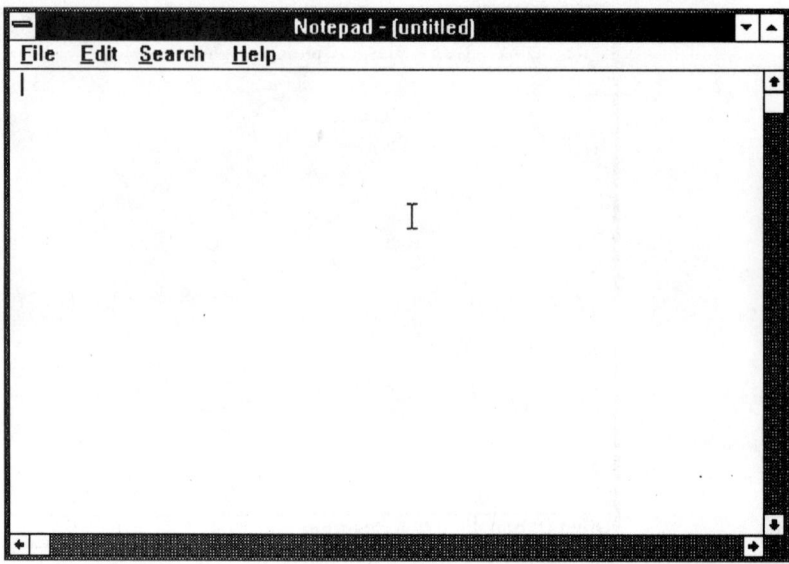

Figure 1.9. A Window with Scroll Bars

placement isn't exactly what you want, use the up/down scroll arrows to fine-tune it. (If your document is so short that it can be viewed completely within the window, an up/down scroll bar will not appear.) After you've used Windows a while, you will develop an intuitive feel for the size of a document by noting the speed with which the scroll box moves when you press the scroll arrows. The scroll box will move quickly through a short document (it may even appear to jump), and may barely move while you press the scroll arrows when a document is very large.

All of the information just presented about up/down scrolling also applies to a left/right scroll box and scroll arrows. (If a document or a picture is no wider than the width of the window, the left/right scroll bar will not appear.)

Title Bars

Figure 1.10 illustrates a typical screen with several windows. You can tell the function or application of each window at a glance because of the title bars along the top of the window. (This aspect of Windows shows how the program provides a consistent and friendly interface to the user. If the title bars were not present, you would have to identify the application in each window by looking at the contents of the window. If a window in the background was covered by other windows, you would have to make that window active by bringing it

Getting Started

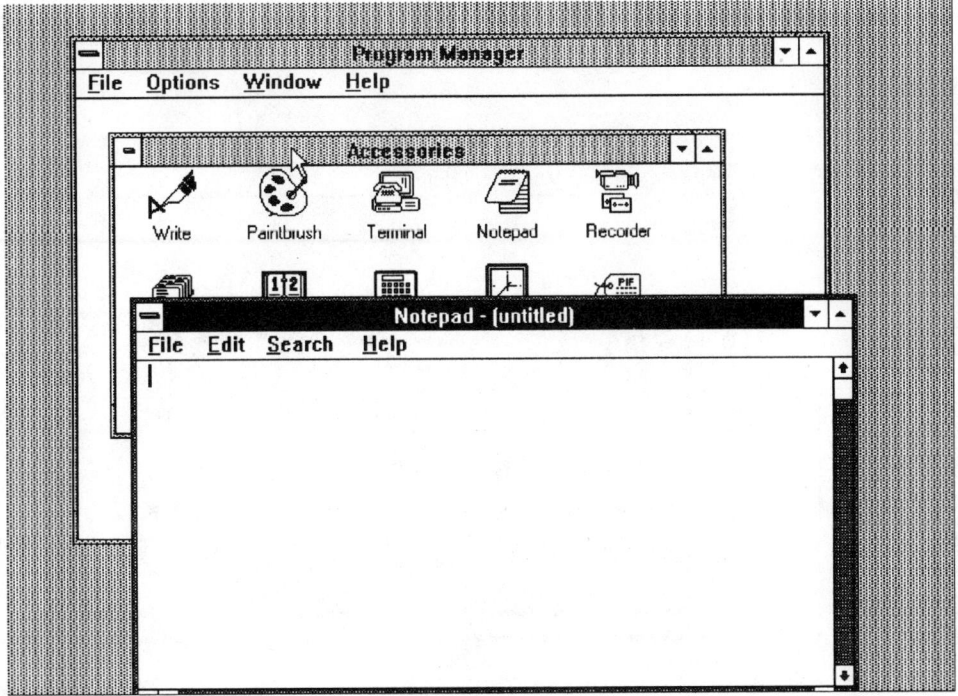

Figure 1.10. The Desktop with Multiple Windows

up to the front so that you could figure out what it was doing.) As we mentioned earlier, the title bar of the active window is highlighted. This is useful when two windows appear side by side.

Positioning and Sizing Windows

When you move the mouse cursor to the border of the active window, the arrow changes from its usual shape to either a diagonal, horizontal, or vertical two-headed arrow. When this occurs, you can resize the window by pressing the left mouse button and dragging the boundary in the desired direction. You can also use the *sizing boxes* (also called *sizing icons*) located at the top-right corner of each window (Figure 1.11). When you locate the mouse cursor over the box that points up and press the left mouse button, the window grows larger. When you select the box with the down arrow and press the left mouse button, the window becomes smaller. If your window has a sizing box with both an up arrow and a down arrow, select that box to adjust the window back to its original size.

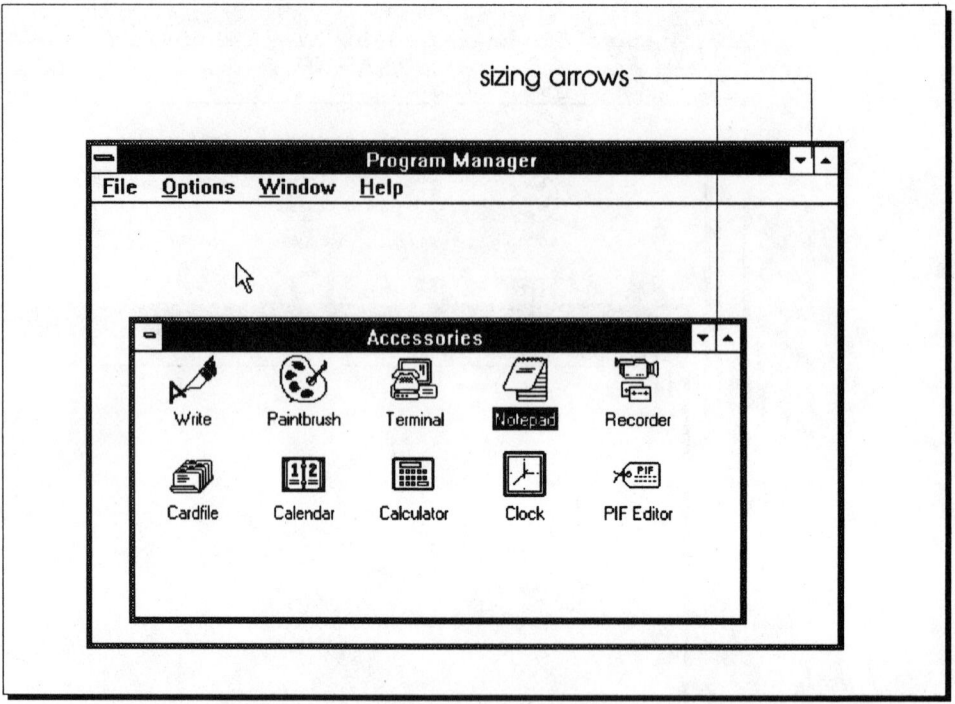

Figure 1.11. Windows with Sizing Arrows

Positioning a window is very easy to do; place the mouse cursor anywhere inside the title box of the window, press the left mouse button, and drag the window in the desired direction. When the window is positioned at the desired location, release the mouse button.

The Menu Bar and Drop-Down Menus

The last major component of a typical window is the menu bar. As you can see in Figure 1.12, the *menu bar* provides several categories of actions that can be taken within that window. Move the mouse cursor to one of the items on the menu bar, press the left mouse button, and watch the item expand into a *drop-down menu*. Select one of the items on this menu by moving the mouse cursor to the item and clicking on it.

Drop-down menus can contain several types of entries. For example, you may see information along the right-hand side of the entry, such as Alt+F4, which in this case means that the particular option can be selected when you are in that window by pressing the Alt key and the F4 function key at the same

Getting Started

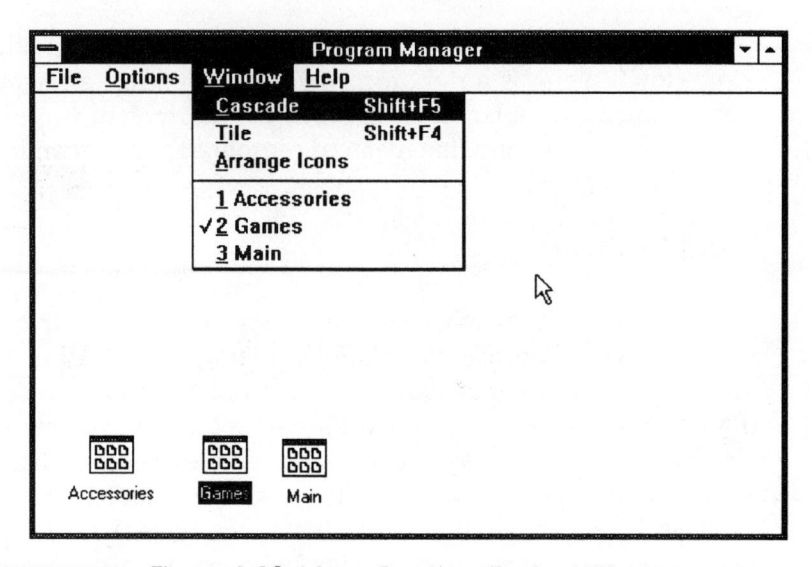

Figure 1.12. Menu Bar for a Typical Window

time. This is called a *keyboard shortcut sequence*. Keyboard shortcuts can be invoked at any time when you're in the window, even if the drop-down menu isn't visible.

Sometimes you'll see items displayed at half-intensity in a drop-down menu (Figure 1.13). The options represented by these items aren't currently available. (If you select any of these options, Windows ignores your request.)

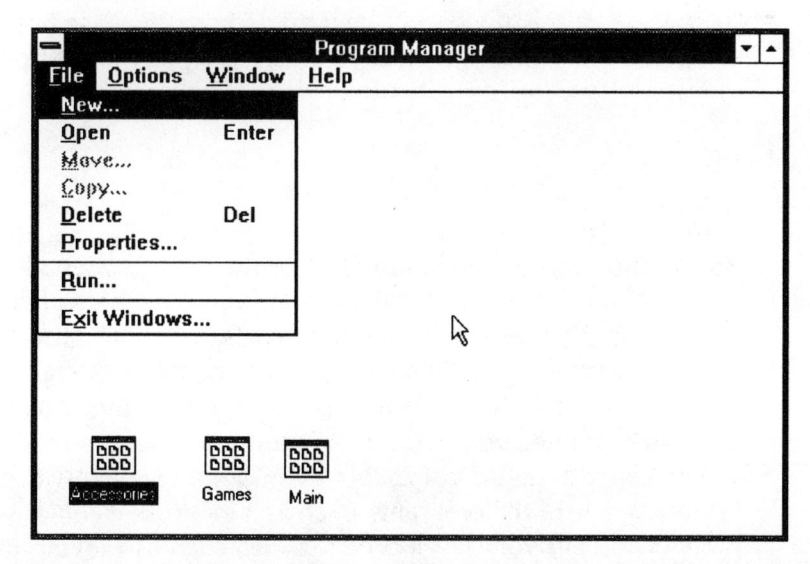

Figure 1.13. A Menu with Items Displayed at Half-intensity

Windows 3.0 also allows *cascading menus*. Notice that another option in the drop-down menu is a right arrow. When you select an item in this menu, a second menu of suboptions appears to the right of the drop-down menu. Select suboptions from that menu to complete the command.

Dialog Boxes

Dialog Boxes appear whenever you need to make multiple selections associated with an action. The most familiar dialog box is the one that appears each time you select the Exit Windows option in the File drop-down menu in the Program Manager. It requests confirmation that you want to exit the Windows environment, and also asks if you want to save the setup changes you've made to the Windows environment. If the small square box contains an X, the changes will be saved, if the small box is empty, the changes will not be saved. Alternate between the two options by clicking on the box with the mouse. Make your selection and exit Windows by clicking on the large box.

Summary

In this chapter you've learned why Windows was developed and how it provides a useful interface to DOS, the PC's operating system. You've also learned about the basic components that Windows provides including icons, windows, menus, and dialog boxes.

In the next chapter, we'll step through the process of installing Windows.

Exercises

These exercises are provided to help you review the material covered in this chapter and prepare you to install Windows.

1. Take a few minutes to review the hardware installed in your computer. If you don't know the type of PC you have (8088, 80286, or 80386), consult your owner's manual. Make a list of your computer's components, such as a mouse, printer, video board, monitor, printer, and so on.
2. If you have a mouse installed but you don't know how to use it, practice by running one of the programs, such as a game, that comes with your mouse. This will help you develop basic skills, such as moving the mouse cursor, selecting objects, and dragging them.

2

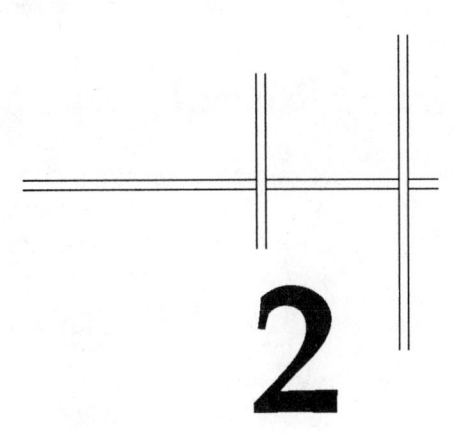

Installing Windows

Believe it or not, installing Windows is the most challenging part about working with this powerful GUI. As you've seen, one of the big advantages of Windows is its ease of use. Another key advantage is that it allows you to integrate the important resources available to your PC. For example, you can print a file with the Print Manager while you're creating a picture with the Paintbrush.

To perform so many tasks at once, Windows must know about the capabilities of your PC hardware. In order to answer the questions about your PC setup, you may first have to spend a few minutes searching for the information. This chapter will explain the questions that Windows asks during the setup process and some of the key issues about the available options.

We will cover these topics:

- How to choose the correct Windows software for your system
- What information you need in order to successfully install Windows
- How to install Windows
- How to start and exit Windows
- How to use the help system

Tip If you've already installed Windows, move ahead to Chapter 3, which discusses the basic skills you need for using Windows.

Getting Started

Before you open the Windows package, examine the top-right corner of the front of the box for information about the type of software in the box. For example, you might see "For DOS Systems" and diskette information, such as "5 1/4-inch 1.2Mb" or "3 1/2-inch 1.44Mb." If this information doesn't match the needs of your system, DON'T OPEN THE PACKAGE; return it to your vendor and get the correct version. If your system only has 360Kb floppies, you need to either copy the high-density disks to low-density disks, or request the lower-density diskettes from Microsoft directly. (Use the order form in the Windows package to obtain them free with your proof-of-purchase). A third alternative is to add a high-density drive to your system, but this can get complicated and expensive.

If your Windows package is the correct version for your computer system, open the package and find a sealed envelope containing the diskettes and a manual called *Microsoft Windows User's Guide*. The installation procedure assumes that you've booted-up your system with a version of DOS that is either 3.0 or later. Windows insists on the newer versions of DOS because it needs the added features supported by those versions. If you run DOS versions 1.x or 2.x, upgrade DOS first before installing Windows.

☑ Execute the VER command at the DOS prompt. Which version of DOS are you running?

This command displays the DOS version information in the format:

MS-DOS Version 3.30

What You Need to Know

Unless you know a great deal about your PC, you'll need to do some research. The Windows Setup program asks you for the following information:

- The type of PC you have
- The type of display adapter and monitor in your system
- The type of printer you have and which port it's connected to
- The type of mouse you have (if any)

- The name of the directory where you want the Windows files stored
- Information about a PC network, if you're connected to one
- Information about your keyboard, and so on

You'll find most of this information by searching the owner's manuals that came with your PC. If you don't have this documentation, you may need to do a bit of detective work. For example, Windows needs to know the type of display adapter card in your system because different display cards provide different capabilities. A PC with a CGA display has serious limitations compared to a display using EGA or VGA technology. The following display combinations are supported by the initial release of Windows 3.0 (subsequent releases may support additional combinations):

- 8514/a
- CGA
- Compaq Portable Plasma
- EGA
- Hercules Monochrome
- Olivetti/AT&T Monochrome or PVC Display
- QuadVGA, ATI VIP VGA, 82C441 VGAs
- VGA
- VGA with Monochrome display
- Video Seven VGA with 512K

If you have a typical PC with a color display and you don't know which display adapter card is installed, try selecting CGA. (Most EGA and VGA cards are compatible with the simpler CGA standard.) This option will allow you to proceed with the installation. Unfortunately, the CGA option is also the most limited in terms of graphics capability, so change this installation selection as soon as possible if you have a higher-capability display (more about this later).

Windows also needs to know the type of keyboard so that it can properly interpret keyboard commands. The following models are supported by release 3.0 of Windows:

- All AT type keyboards (84-86 keys)
- AT&T '301' keyboard
- AT&T '302' keyboard
- Enhanced 101 or 102 key U.S. and Non-U.S. keyboards
- Hewlett-Packard Vectra keyboard (DIN)
- Olivetti 101/102 A keyboard

- Olivetti 83 key keyboard
- Olivetti 86 key keyboard
- Olivetti M24 102 key keyboard
- PC-XT 83 key keyboard
- PC-XT-type keyboard (84 keys)

Windows Setup also asks about the type of mouse on your system. The supported types are:

- HP Mouse (HP-HIL)
- Logitech bus or PS/2-style
- Logitech serial mouse
- Microsoft or IBM PS/2
- Mouse Systems (or VisiOn) connected to COM1:
- Mouse Systems (or VisiOn) connected to COM2:
- No mouse or other pointing device
- Olivetti/AT&T Keyboard Mouse

Lastly, Windows 3.0 asks if your PC is connected to a PC network. Networks allow several PCs to share expensive resources, such as laser printers, and to share information between the PCs. The PCs are usually interconnected via cabling similar to that used by cable TV systems. These cables connect to special interface cards installed in each PC. Only a small percentage of PCs are connected to networks at this time, but Microsoft has made certain that Windows 3.0 will be as attractive as possible to the business community by integrating network communications into the Windows environment. If you're not connected to a network, simply select (or affirm) the option "No Network Installed." If you use a PC network, Windows asks you to select from the following list:

- 3Com 3+Open LAN Manager (XNS only)
- 3Com 3+Share
- Banyan VINES 4.0
- IBM PC LAN Program
- LAN Manager 1.x (or 100% compatible)
- LAN Manager 2.0 Basic (or 100% compatible)
- LAN Manager 2.0 Enhanced (or 100% compatible)
- Microsoft Network (or 100% compatible)
- No Network Installed
- Novell Network 2.10 or above, or Novell Network 386

Installing a Printer

The page called "Microsoft Windows Version 3.0 Hardware Compatibility List" (provided with the Windows package) lists the printers, the displays, and the mice supported by Windows. Windows also supports a variety of dot-matrix printers and a large number of inkjet/laser printers, but ignores letter-quality, daisy-wheel printers (which are still prevalent in small office environments).

If your printer is not listed and you can't identify a compatible one made by a different manufacturer, select the Generic Printer option. This option may not allow you to use your machine to its full capability (superscripts, subscripts, etc.), but you can still print normal text.

If your printer is connected to a parallel port, it's most likely connected to the LPT1: port. Use this command to verify that the printer is connected to that particular port:

PRINT/D:LPT1 AUTOEXEC.BAT

The AUTOEXEC.BAT is a small file often found in the root directory of the system disk. (If you don't have this file in your system, substitute the name of any small ASCII file. This command sends the file to the specified output port. Your printer must first be powered-up and set ON-LINE for this test to work. If the printer does not respond to the command, repeat the commands, replacing LPT1 with each of the following in turn until the printer responds:

LPT2, LPT3, COM1, COM2, COM3, or COM4

You can also investigate the mode of the various ports by using the MS-DOS MODE command. (See your *MS-DOS User's Guide* for details.)

Beginning the Installation

To install Windows, follow these simple steps:

1. Insert the diskette marked "Disk 1" into the appropriate drive.
2. Define that diskette drive as the default drive by typing the letter of the drive, followed by a colon(:). For example, to use drive A, type in A:.
3. Press the Enter key.
4. Type the command

    SETUP

    and press the Enter key.

From this point on, the Windows SETUP program takes over and guides you through the installation process with detailed explanations. We'll describe this process in the next section.

Tip

Before beginning the installation, make sure your hard disk has enough free memory space. (You need 6 to 8Mb available to install Windows.) Run the following DOS command:

CHKDSK

This command displays the information shown in Figure 2.1.

The Installation Process

The SETUP installation process starts with the screen shown in Figure 2.2. This screen offers three choices:

1. You can get more help on the setup process.
2. You can install Windows.
3. You can exit the installation process.

```
17:39:30 ··· Mon   9-10-1990 ··· D:\WINDOWS
D>chkdsk

 42098688 bytes total disk space
     4096 bytes in 1 hidden files
   495616 bytes in 116 directories
 40497152 bytes in 2487 user files
    49152 bytes in bad sectors
  1052672 bytes available on disk

   655360 bytes total memory
   541424 bytes free

17:39:46 ··· Mon   9-10-1990 ··· D:\WINDOWS
D>
```

Figure 2.1. Using the CHKDSK Command

Installing Windows

```
Windows Setup

    Welcome to Setup.

    The Setup program for Microsoft Windows Version 3.00 prepares Windows
    to run on your computer. Each Setup screen has basic instructions for
    completing a step of the installation. If you want additional
    information and instructions about a screen or option, please press
    the Help key, F1.

    To learn how to use Windows Setup, press F1.

    To install Windows on your computer now, press ENTER.

    To exit Setup without installing Windows, press F3.




ENTER=Continue   F1=Help   F3=Exit
```

Figure 2.2. The First SETUP Screen

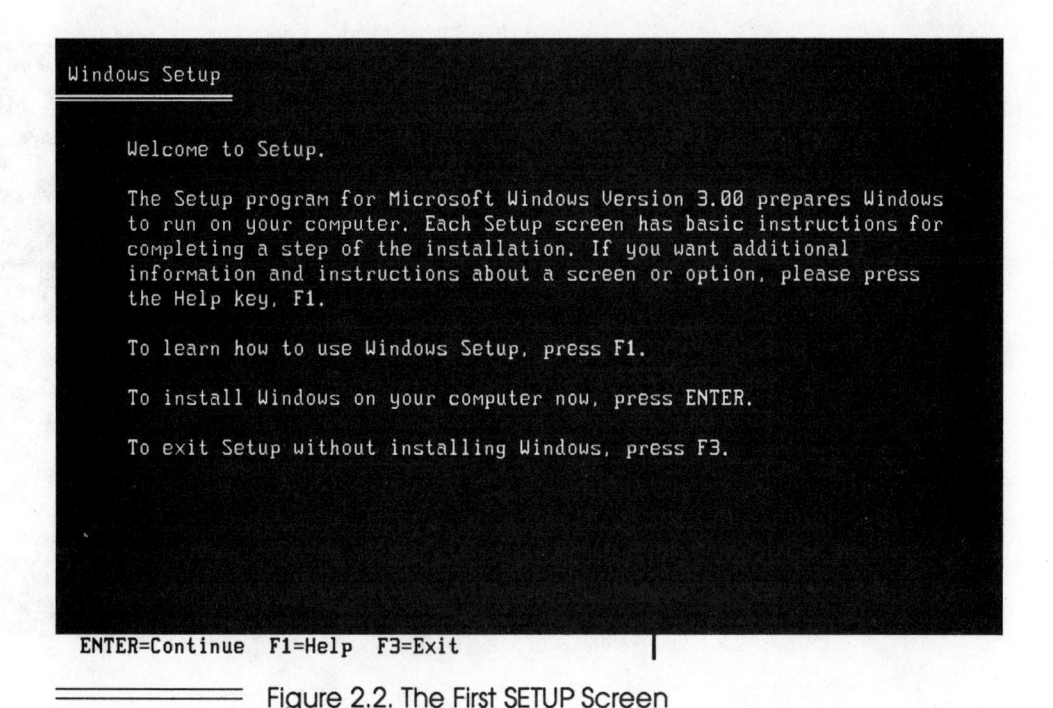

Press the Enter key to start the installation process. The next screen, shown in Figure 2.3, asks you to enter the drive and directory where you want to install Windows. By default, the drive C and the directory \WINDOWS are selected. To change this information, use the arrow keys, backspace or the Delete (or Del) key to erase the text and type in the new information. When you're done, press the Enter key.

The third screen (Figure 2.4) asks you to verify your computer equipment. Make sure that you double-check each item and change any incorrect ones. For example, if your system has a mouse but the Mouse category lists the text "No mouse or other pointing device," highlight this section and press the Enter key to view the available options. When you're done with this screen, highlight the No Changes row and press the Enter key.

The SETUP program will now copy several files to your hard disk. This operation takes a few minutes. After the files have been copied from Disk 1, you'll see the screen in Figure 2.5, which asks you to enter another disk. Put the requested disk (Disk 2) into the drive and press the Enter key.

Your screen will soon change to a Windows-like screen and then display the Windows Setup dialog box with three options:

- You can set up printers.

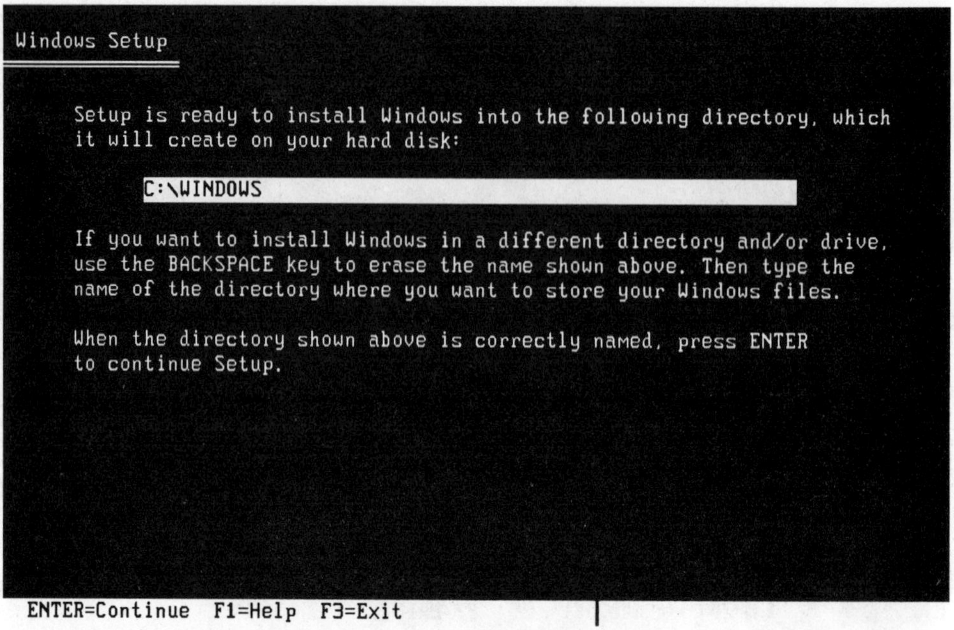

```
Windows Setup

    Setup is ready to install Windows into the following directory, which
    it will create on your hard disk:

        C:\WINDOWS

    If you want to install Windows in a different directory and/or drive,
    use the BACKSPACE key to erase the name shown above. Then type the
    name of the directory where you want to store your Windows files.

    When the directory shown above is correctly named, press ENTER
    to continue Setup.




ENTER=Continue   F1=Help   F3=Exit
```

Figure 2.3. The Second SETUP Screen

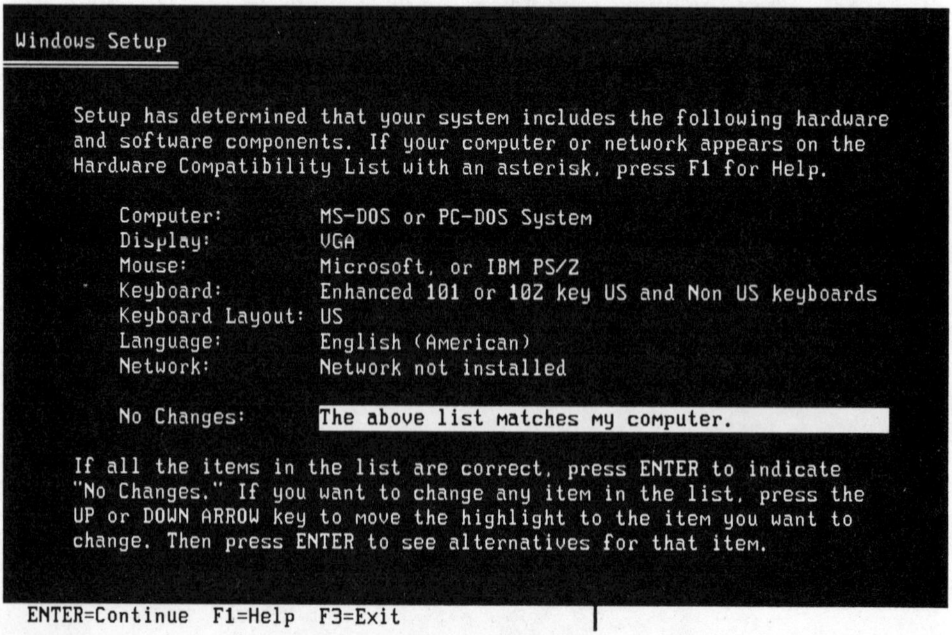

```
Windows Setup

    Setup has determined that your system includes the following hardware
    and software components. If your computer or network appears on the
    Hardware Compatibility List with an asterisk, press F1 for Help.

        Computer:           MS-DOS or PC-DOS System
        Display:            VGA
        Mouse:              Microsoft, or IBM PS/2
        Keyboard:           Enhanced 101 or 102 key US and Non US keyboards
        Keyboard Layout:    US
        Language:           English (American)
        Network:            Network not installed

        No Changes:         The above list matches my computer.

    If all the items in the list are correct, press ENTER to indicate
    "No Changes." If you want to change any item in the list, press the
    UP or DOWN ARROW key to move the highlight to the item you want to
    change. Then press ENTER to see alternatives for that item.


ENTER=Continue   F1=Help   F3=Exit
```

Figure 2.4. The Third SETUP Screen

Installing Windows

```
Windows Setup

    Please insert the: Microsoft Windows 3.0 Disk #2

    If the files on this disk can be found at a different location,
    enter a new path to the files in the prompt below.

        ┌─────────────────────────────────────┐
        │A:                                   │
        └─────────────────────────────────────┘




  ENTER=Continue   F1=Help   F3=Exit        │ Copying : vgalogo.rle
```

Figure 2.5. The Fourth SETUP Screen

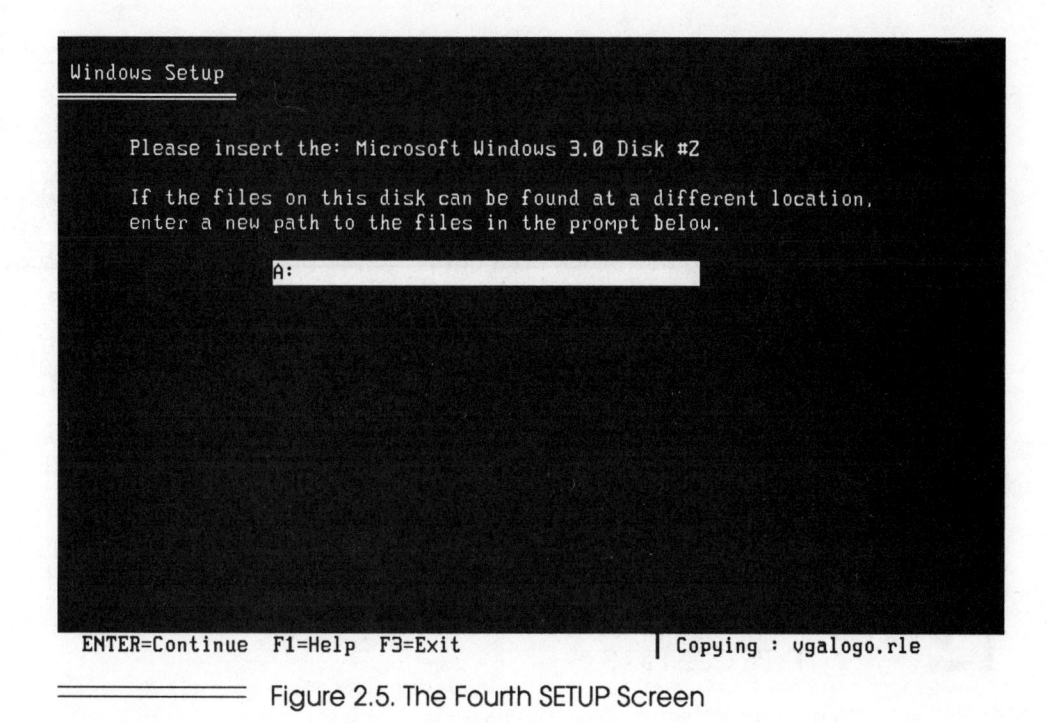

- You can set up applications already on hard disk.
- You can read on-line documents.

By default, all three options are selected. If you don't want to continue the installation process with one or more of these options, disable the option by clicking on its checkbox. To continue, select the Continue button.

The installation program will ask you to enter each of the other three disks in turn, and will continue to copy all of the files required to operate Windows. A status bar shows you its progress.

Next, the program displays a window with three options for modifying your CONFIG.SYS file:

- All modifications will be made for you.
- You can review and edit changes, before modifications are made.
- You can make the modifications later.

At this point, the installation program needs to modify your CONFIG.SYS file, which contains the configuration information for your PC. If you don't know much about your PC, let Windows change your system files itself.

If you are concerned about letting Windows change your system configuration files, select the second option to open a window containing two scroll boxes. One box shows how the configuration file looks before it's modified. The second box shows how the file looks after it's modified.

Scroll up and down the file and decide for yourself whether the proposed changes will adversely affect your computer's operation. If you find the changes acceptable, click on a button to perform the file update. With the first two options, Windows renames your configuration files to a different name so that you can reverse the operation later. (The third option is designed for PC experts who want to get involved in the details of the installation. Most users will find the first two options acceptable.)

After you let Windows change the system configuration files, you will view a final window. Use the buttons in this window to return to DOS, or to restart the Windows installation process.

✔ Execute the command:

   TYPE CONFIG.SYS

Which information is displayed?

You will see information such as:

   DEVICE=C:\HIMEM>SYS
   BUFFERS=20
   FILES=40

This type of information is stored in the CONFIG.SYS file.

Non-Windows Applications

After the SETUP program has installed all of the Windows files, it searches for non-Windows programs compatible with the Windows environment. A new window appears and asks you which disk drives or directories it should search. After the search is completed, another window appears that contains two scroll boxes. The left scroll box lists the programs found by SETUP. Select the programs that you want to install in the Windows environment by clicking on the individual names. If you select a program by mistake, cancel the selection by clicking on it a second time. Each time you select a program, the program name becomes highlighted.

When you have completed your selections, press the Add-> button (between the scroll windows) to install these programs. (The program names will move to the right-hand window.) Next, press the OK button at the bottom of the window to exit from that operation. If you don't want to install any programs now, simply press the OK button on the screen when you reach the window containing the two scroll boxes. If the right-hand scroll box is empty, no programs are installed. You can easily install applications later by using the Windows Setup application under the Main applications group. This topic is covered later in this chapter.

Installation Side Effects

Depending on your system resources, SETUP may perform actions that you do not want. The most noticeable of these actions affects how your hard disk is used. Most modern operating systems use variations of a technique known as *virtual memory*—when a computer needs more memory than is physically available, it saves some of the unneeded program areas in a temporary file on a disk drive. This trick allows Windows to act as if it had many megabytes of computer memory available even though only 1 or 2 Mb of real memory are actually available.

This scheme has some drawbacks. First, it can use several additional megabytes of storage on your hard disk. (The Windows software alone uses up several megabytes for program files.) If you have a 20Mb hard disk, you could lose almost half of your disk storage to Windows alone. Another disadvantage is execution speed. If your disk and/or microprocessor are slower than average, you may find yourself waiting during these memory-swapping operations. If you have a reasonably fast computer with an 80286 (or better) microprocessor, you may not notice any problems.

Changing Your Installation

If you've made a wrong selection, you won't have to redo the entire procedure from scratch. Although this may be necessary under some scenarios (such as when you upgrade from an older version of Windows to a newer one), Windows 3.0 provides a program to make installation changes even after the system has been used for some time, called Windows Setup.

To use this feature, double-click on the Windows Setup icon in the Main window, as shown in Figure 2.6. (If you don't have a mouse, use the arrow keys to highlight the icon and then press the Enter key.) Figure 2.7 shows the start-up window for Windows Setup. Use this application to modify the Windows configuration, or to install additional applications.

Use the first option to modify the Windows configuration when you upgrade your hardware. For example, you might change your CGA display hardware to VGA or you may add a PC network card.

Open the Options menu by clicking on the Options item or pressing Alt+O. To modify the configuration, select the Change System Settings... command. The dialog box in Figure 2.8 appears. Notice that pulldown boxes are displayed for the display, the keyboard, the mouse, and the network. Click on the down scroll arrow to the right of a particular group, and open the menu to view several entries at once. Use the scroll arrows to view all possible options. Make your selection by clicking on the option.

After you've made your configuration selections, click on the OK button in the dialog box to tell Windows to reconfigure itself. This step is much faster than going through the entire Setup procedure again. If you use this feature, keep the installation disks available, because Windows will ask you to put them into a disk drive so that it can obtain the required files to change the configuration.

If you select the Windows Setup option to install an additional application, a new window will request more information, such as the location of the application file.

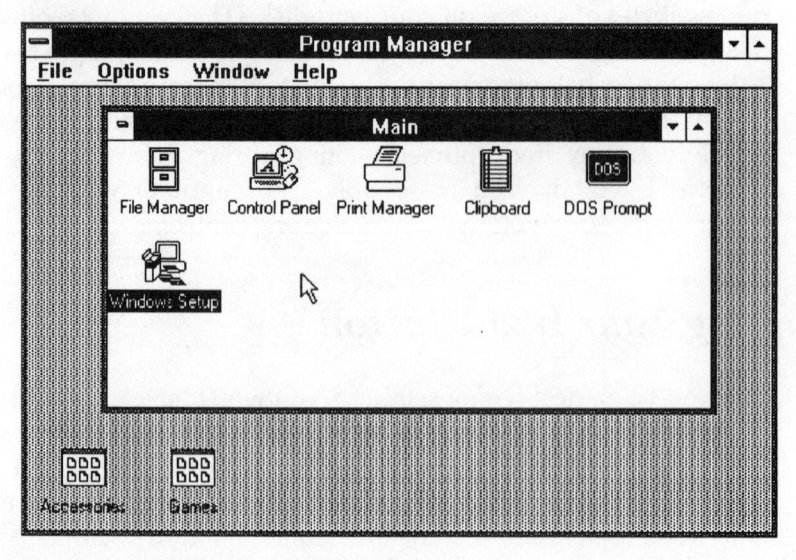

Figure 2.6. Selecting the Windows Setup Icon

Installing Windows

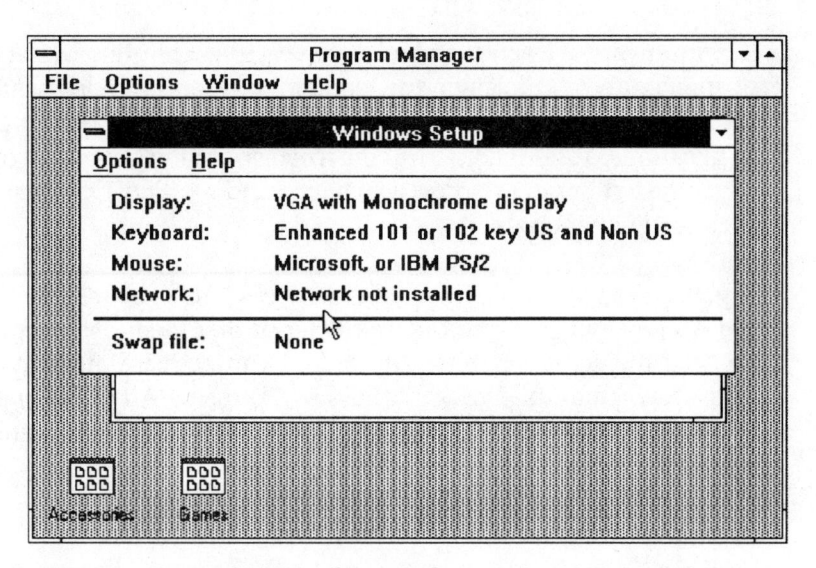

Figure 2.7. The Startup Screen for Windows Setup

You don't need to install an application that stays within the 640K memory limits imposed by DOS. Instead, you can invoke the program through the DOS option in the Main applications group. (This will be discussed in detail later.)

Starting Windows

Before you can start up Windows, your PC must first successfully boot-up its Disk Operating System software. When the DOS prompt appears (it will look similar to C>), invoke the Windows environment by moving to the directory that contains the Windows files and entering the command:

WIN

Figure 2.8. The Change System Settings Dialog Box

If Windows has been installed correctly, the Program Manager window appears (Figure 2.9). This window contains a second window, called Main, which displays icons for each of the internal applications. To access one of these applications, double-click on the corresponding icon. To open one of the menus listed in the Program Manager window (File, Options, Window, Help), click on the menu item.

Tip If you don't have a mouse, you can access a menu bar item by holding down the Alt key and pressing the first letter of that menu item. For example, select the File menu by pressing Alt+F. You can activate an icon by pressing the arrow keys until the icon is highlighted, pressing Alt+F to open the File menu, and then pressing O to choose the Open command in the menu.

Options for Starting Windows

When the WIN command is executed, Windows automatically determines whether it should start in the real, standard, or 386 enhanced operating mode. If you want to use a mode other than the default mode, call up the WIN command and specify an option. Three options are supported:

    WIN/R
    WIN/S
    WIN/3

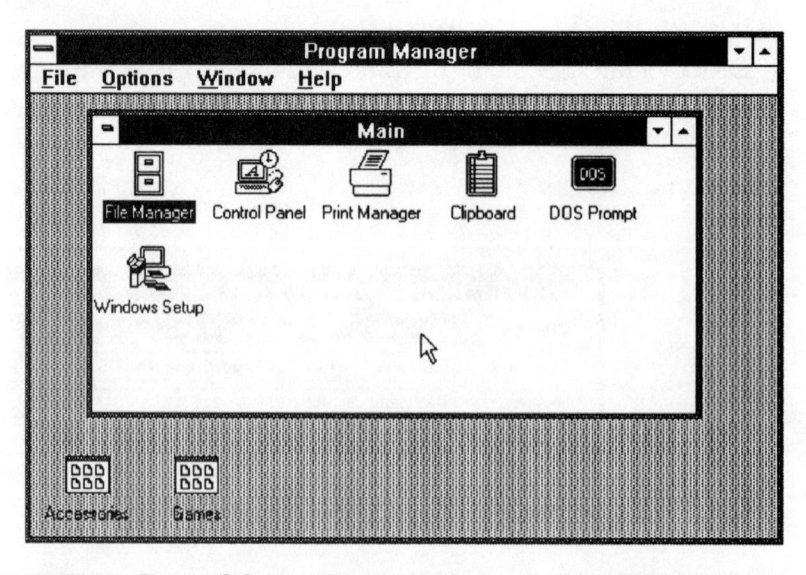

Figure 2.9. The Program Manager Startup Window

Installing Windows

The first command invokes Windows in real mode, the second command invokes Windows in standard 286 mode, and the third command invokes Windows in the 386 enhanced mode. Recall from Chapter 1 that the real mode is the most restricted mode, and the 386 enhanced mode is the most powerful. If you have an AT-class system with an 80286 microprocessor, you must run in either WIN/R or WIN/S mode. If your system uses either an 80386 or 80486 microprocessor, select WIN/3 to use Window's advanced memory-management and task-scheduling features.

The Windows installation procedure recommends that you may wish to locate all of the Windows files in a directory called WIN30. If you followed this advice and created a directory by that name off the root directory, move to that directory by entering:

    CD C:\WIN30

To invoke Windows 3.0 after the DOS boot process, type these two lines:

    C>CD C:\WIN30
    C>WIN/?

where the question mark represents whichever Windows mode you wish to use (r, 2, or 3). To enter Windows 3.0 automatically whenever the machine is powered-up, append the previous two commands to the end of the AUTOEXEC.BAT file (which is usually present in the root directory). The computer will complete its normal cold-start procedure, and then automatically invoke Windows. Once you enter Windows 3.0, you will probably never exit the program except to power-down your machine.

Starting Windows with an Application

You can specify a command to start Windows and tell it to automatically run an application. As an example, the following command starts Windows and executes Aldus' PageMaker (which is stored in the directory COMP):

    WIN \COMP\PM

---

1. Which command do you use to run Windows in the 386-enhanced mode on an AT with an 80286 processor?
2. Start up Windows. Which operating mode has been selected?
3. Which command is required to start Windows and load the application Microsoft Excel? (Assume that Excel is in the directory C:\WS.)

1. The command to select this operating mode is WIN/3. This command doesn't work, however, with a PC that has the 80286 processor.
2. Open the Help menu in the Program Manager window and select the About Program Manager command. Which mode is Windows using?
3. WIN C:\WS\EXCEL

Quitting Windows

Windows can be terminated using a number of different techniques, but you must use the Program Manager window to exit Windows.

The quickest way to exit Windows is to press Alt+F4. This action brings up a simple dialog box which contains three items. Select the first item, Save Changes, to save the current configuration of the Program Manager so it remains the same the next time Windows is used. Then select the OK button to exit Windows.

To exit Windows by using the mouse, either open the File Menu and select the Exit Windows... command, or open the Control menu and select the Close command. To access the Control menu, select the small box in the upper-left corner of the Program Manager window (Figure 2.10).

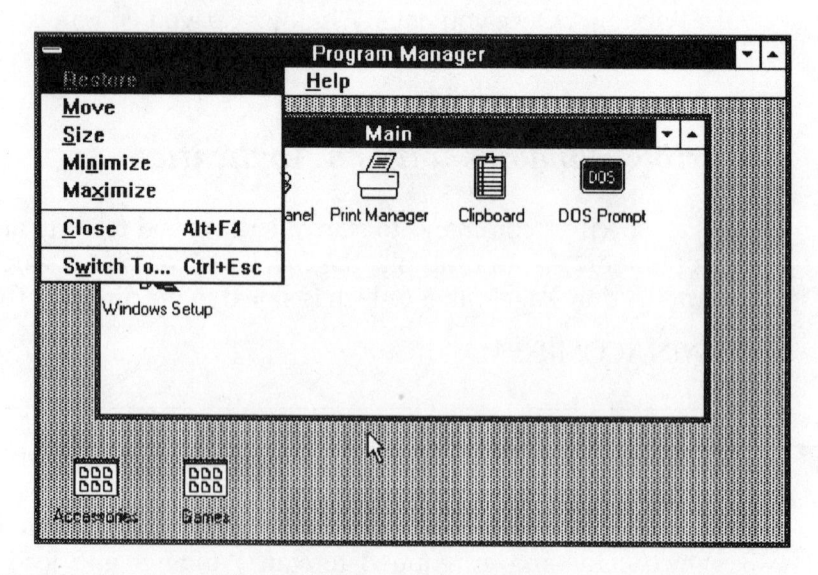

Figure 2.10. The Program Manager's Control Menu

Tip You can access the Control menu from the keyboard by pressing Alt+ Spacebar.

---

1. Practice starting up Windows in the real mode, opening the File menu, and exiting Windows.
2. Open the Control menu. Which options are provided?
3. Why are some of the menu items dimmed, and other items highlighted?

---

1. *Start Windows by issuing the command WIN/R. Select the File option in the Program Manager with the mouse, or press Alt+F. While the File menu is open, select the Exit Windows... option to exit Windows.*
2. *The options are Restore, Move, Size, Minimize, Maximize, Close, and Switch To...*
3. *The dimmed items are currently disabled. The highlighted items can be selected. Windows automatically dims certain items because the tasks they correspond to are unavailable.*

Using the Help System

Now that you have Windows up and running, you need to learn how to access the help system. The comprehensive Windows help system can help you perform a variety of tasks, from using the Program Manager to running Windows applications such as Paintbrush. You can perform these tasks and more using the help system:

- View Help for the special Windows commands
- Examine the keyboard combinations for controlling Windows
- View the instructions for running the different Windows applications
- Search for Help information
- Quickly view the available Help topics by using the index option
- Place a bookmark so that you can easily return to a Help topic

The Help information is provided in different ways. The standard way to access Help is to use the Help menu that displays with each application window. The flexible Help system is context-sensitive, so only the Help information for the current window displays. You can also access Help information when using a dialog box by clicking a help button.

Tip | Here's a quick method for displaying the Help topics for an application: While the application window is active, press F1. This key is a *hot key* for activating the Help system.

Introducing the Help Menu

Let's take a tour of the Help system by way of the Help menu. Start Windows to bring up the Program Manager's window. (Recall that this window is always the first one that appears when Windows starts.) Next, select the Help menu that appears with this application. (Remember that you can press Alt+H to display the help menu.) You should see the menu shown in Figure 2.11, which lists eight options. (A description of these options is provided in Table 2.1.) The name of each of the first five options is the same in each application's Help menu. The last option's name is specific to the application. (For example, this entry is called About File Manager... in the Help menu shown in Figure 2.11.)

To see how useful the help system is, let's investigate a few of the options. First, select the Index option with the mouse or the keyboard. You'll see the Help window shown in Figure 2.12. You can move, resize, scroll, and close this window. (We'll explain the basic techniques for controlling windows in the next chapter.)

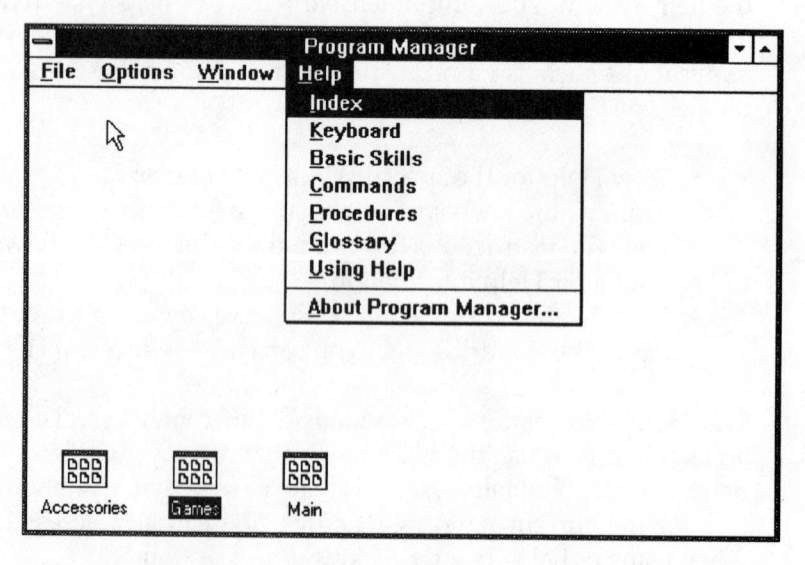

Figure 2.11. The Help Menu

Installing Windows

Table 2.1. The Help Menu Options

Option	Description
Index	Provides a comprehensive list, in alphabetical order, of help topics available for the current application.
Keyboard	Provides the set of available keyboard commands.
Basic Skills	Provides information about the basic skills for using Windows.
Commands	Describes each command provided with the application.
Procedures	Describes the basic steps for using the application's features.
Glossary	Provides a glossary of Windows terms.
Using Help	Provides help information on the help system.
About (application)	Lists background information about the running application.

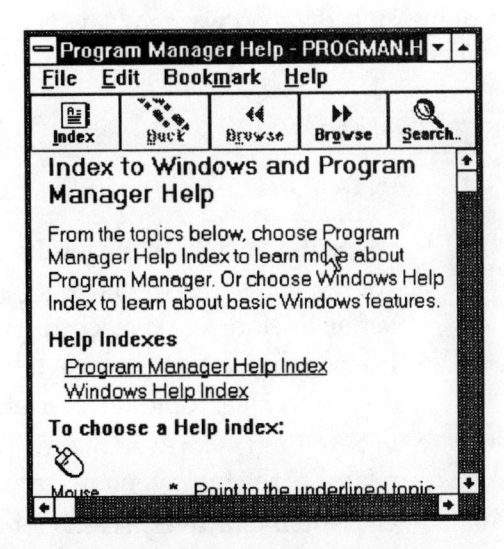

Figure 2.12. The Help Index Option

Tip A help window can be turned into an icon for easy selection at any time while you are running an application. To create the icon, open the help window's Control menu by clicking on the small rectangle in the upper-left corner of the window, or press the Alt key and the comma (,) key. Then, select the Minimize option from the menu.

As Figure 2.12 shows, the Index Help window lists all of the help topics for the Program Manager. Scroll through this window to the topic you want, and double-click on the topic to select it. If you're using the keyboard, highlight the topic using the Tab key and then press the Enter key.

Using the Help Buttons

Notice a set of five special menu buttons at the top of each Help window (directly below the menu bar). These buttons, described in Table 2.2, are provided to help you navigate through the Help system. Whenever one of the buttons is displayed (without being dimmed), you can select it.

Searching for Help Information

One of the more important features of the Help buttons has to do with searching for Help information. This feature is especially handy if you already know the name of the topic that you want to view help on. Let's investigate how this feature works.

Table 2.2. The Help Control Buttons

Button	Description
(Index)	Displays the Help Index for the current application.
(Back)	Allows you to display Help topics that were displayed before the Index was reached.
(Browse) «	Lets you move backward and display the previously displayed Help topics in a series.
(Browse) »	Lets you move forward and display the next Help topics related to the topic you are currently viewing.
(Search)	Lets you interactively search for a topic by entering a keyword or a phrase.

Assume that you're using the Program Manager and you want to get help on a certain topic. Select the Search button by clicking on it or pressing Alt+S. The Search dialog box shown in Figure 2.13 appears and provides a text field where you can type in the name of a topic to search for. In this case, we've typed in the text "active window."

If You Need More Help

If you have difficulties using Help at any time, select the Using Help option in the Help menu. This option brings up the Help window shown in Figure 2.14.

Printing Help Information

You can print the Help information displayed in a window for future reference through a simple two-step process.

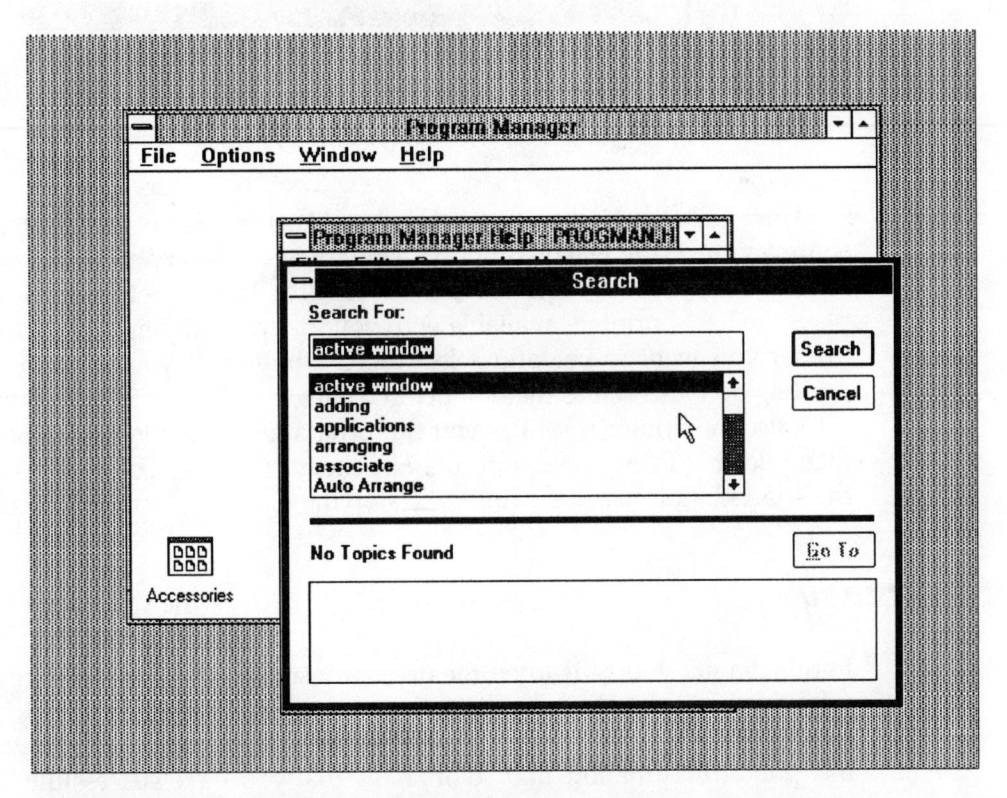

Figure 2.13. The Help System's Search Dialog Box

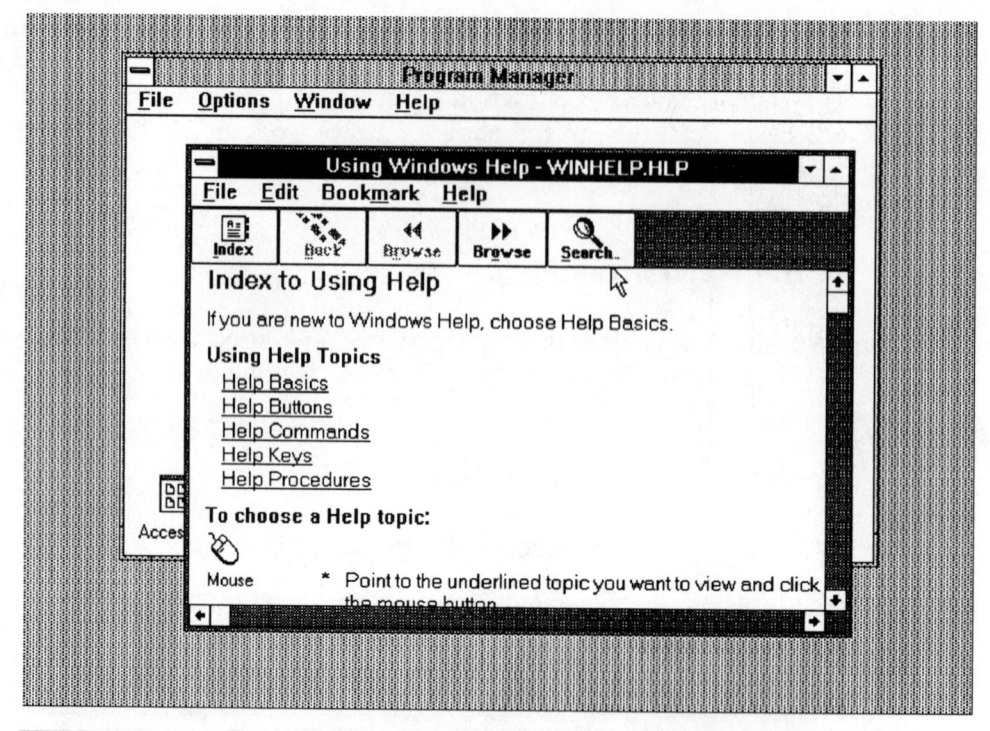

Figure 2.14. The Using Windows Help Window

First, make sure your printer is properly set up. Select the Printer Setup... command from the File menu provided with one of the Windows applications, such as Notepad. As Figure 2.15 illustrates, the Printer Setup dialog box displays the list of printers available with your system. Highlight the name of the printer you want to use and select the OK button. If you want to set other printing options such as the number of copies, click on the Setup... button.

Once the printer is set up, you can print a topic by selecting the topic and then selecting Print Topic from the File menu. A dialog box notifies you that the selected topic is being printed. To stop the printer, select the Cancel button.

Summary

In this chapter you've learned the necessary steps and information to successfully complete the Windows installation process. You've provided basic PC information, such as type of display, desired disk directory for the Windows file, printer information, and so on. Now that you have successfully installed Windows, you're ready to experiment with it.

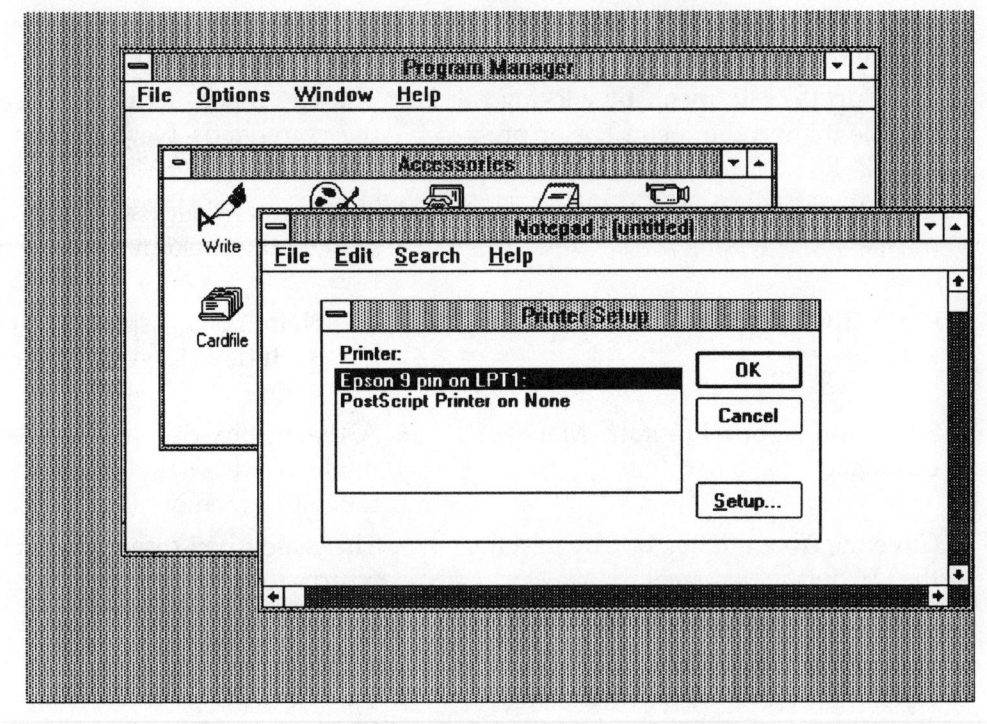

Figure 2.15. The Printer Setup Dialog Box.

You've also exited Windows by using a few different techniques, and then explored the Help system.

In the next chapter, we'll cover the basic techniques for using the components of Windows: the icons, the menus, the windows, and the dialog boxes.

Exercises

Use these exercises to review some of the basics of running Windows after you've successfully installed the software.

What You Should Do	How the Computer Responds
1. Move to the directory where Windows is installed, by executing the DOS CD (Change Directory) command: CD \WINDOWS	1. If your system uses the directory name as the DOS prompt, you can tell you're in the correct directory; otherwise, execute the DIR command to verify the directory.

2. Start up Windows by typing WIN and pressing the Enter key.

2. The Program Manager window will appear on the desktop.

3. Open up the File menu by clicking on the File item in the menu bar or pressing Alt+F.

3. The File menu is displayed containing the commands New..., Open, Move..., and so on.

4. Close the File menu by clicking outside the menu or pressing the Esc key.

4. The menu will close. If you press the Esc key, the cursor remains on the menu bar.

5. Open the Help menu by pressing Alt+H.

5. The Help menu displays with the commands Index, Keyboard, Basic Skills, and so on.

6. Select the About Program Manager... command.

6. A dialog box displays to show which mode Windows is running in and how much free memory is available.

7. Close the About dialog box by selecting the OK button.

7. The dialog box disappears and control returns to Help menu.

8. Close the Help menu.

8. Control returns to the Program Manager window.

9. Open the Control menu by clicking the upper-left corner of window or pressing Alt+Spacebar.

9. The Control menu for the Program Manager displays.

10. Select the Close command to exit Windows.

10. The Exit Windows dialog box displays.

11. Select the OK button in the Exit Windows dialog box.

11. Windows quits and control returns to the DOS prompt.

What If It Doesn't Work?

1. If Windows won't run, make sure you've installed it correctly by following the installation procedures presented in this chapter.
2. If you suspect that Windows is installed correctly, make sure you're in the directory where it's installed or the DOS path is set correctly.
3. If you've installed a mouse but the mouse isn't operating, you can use the keyboard to perform the basic Windows navigating commands. After you exit Windows, verify that your mouse is a Microsoft-compatible mouse and that it's installed correctly.

3

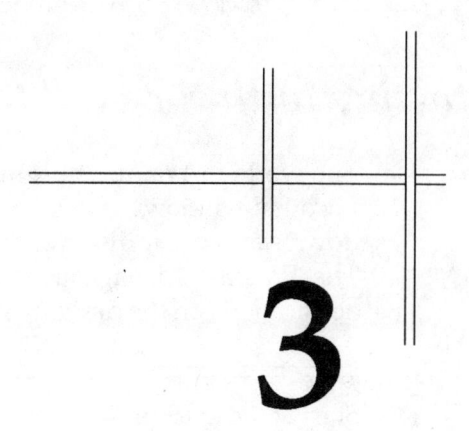

Building Your Windows Skills

The real advantage of using Windows is that it allows you to communicate easily with your computer. In fact, you'll find that you only need to learn a few basic techniques in order to perform a variety of operations, from opening windows to selecting dialog boxes. Before you start using the basic Windows features, such as the Program Manager and the File Manager, you need to develop your basic skills for working with windows, menus, dialog boxes, and control menus.

This chapter will show you how to use the mouse and the keyboard to navigate in the flexible Windows environment. Along the way, we explain all of the basic terms and concepts that you need to know to successfully use Windows. Whenever you have difficulty performing an operation, such as moving or resizing a window, refer back to this chapter.

This chapter will tell you how to:

- Use the Windows desktop
- Work with windows and menus
- Use scroll bars to view data in windows
- Work with icons
- Use control menus to move, resize, and close windows
- Work with dialog boxes
- Use interface features such as check boxes, option buttons, text boxes, and list boxes

Starting with the Desktop

The world of Windows begins with the *desktop*—the place where all of the application windows, menus, icons, and dialog boxes are displayed. When Windows starts up, it displays the Program Manager application on the desktop. The Program Manager is the main application, but you can open up other applications on the desktop at any point during your Windows session.

Start at the DOS prompt. Make sure you are in the directory where Windows is installed.
1. Start Windows.
2. What are some of the components on the desktop?
3. Close the Program Manager window by pressing Alt+F4. What happens to the desktop?

---

1. *Type in WIN and press the Enter key.*
2. *The major component is the Program Manager, which is represented as a window. You should also see a set of icons at the bottom of the Program Manager's window. These icons represent the applications selected during Windows Setup, and include Windows Applications, Accessories, Non-Windows Applications, and Games.*
3. *By closing this window, you are effectively shutting down Windows (the desktop).*

What's in a Window

Windows divides the desktop into rectangular screen regions, called *windows*. These windows are used to run applications, such as Microsoft Excel and Word, and to display the documents used with these applications. Windows are much more flexible and powerful than the standard DOS screen, and they're easy to use.

Only two kinds of windows are provided: *application windows* and *document windows*. Application windows are used to run applications, and document windows display the documents associated with applications. As Figure 3.1 shows, an application window consists of a title bar, a menu bar, a frame, and optional scroll bars. The Program Manager window introduced earlier is an example of an application window.

A document window looks different than an application window because it does not have a menu bar. Instead, it displays the data associated with an

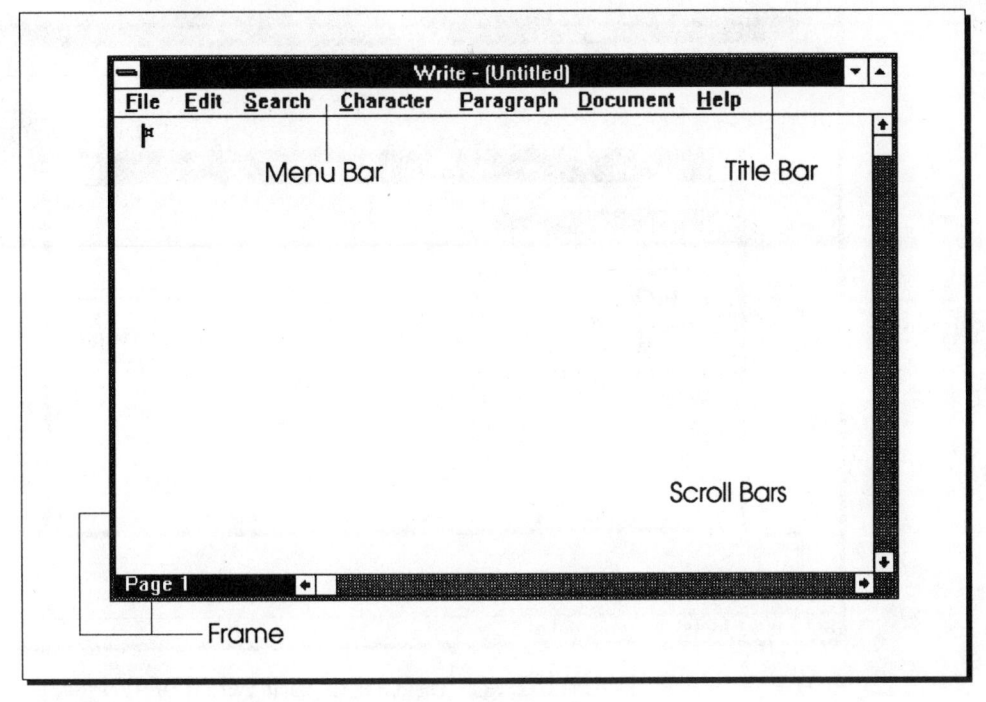

Figure 3.1. An Application Window

application. For example, if you use a word processor application, such as Write, to create a document named Budget, the text that you compose displays in an application window named Budget.

Figure 3.2 shows a sample document window created by the File Manager application. Notice that the menu bar is missing: in the File Manager's application window, all of the commands to control the application are provided with the menu.

1. Double-click on the Accessories icon from the Program Manager application window. What type of window is displayed?
2. Select the Notepad icon displayed in the Accessories window. What menu items appear in the window's menu bar?
3. Click on the small rectangle in the upper-left corner of the Notepad window. What happens?
4. Click on the lower-right corner of the Notepad window. What happens?
5. Click on the frame of the Notepad window and try to drag it off the screen. What happens?

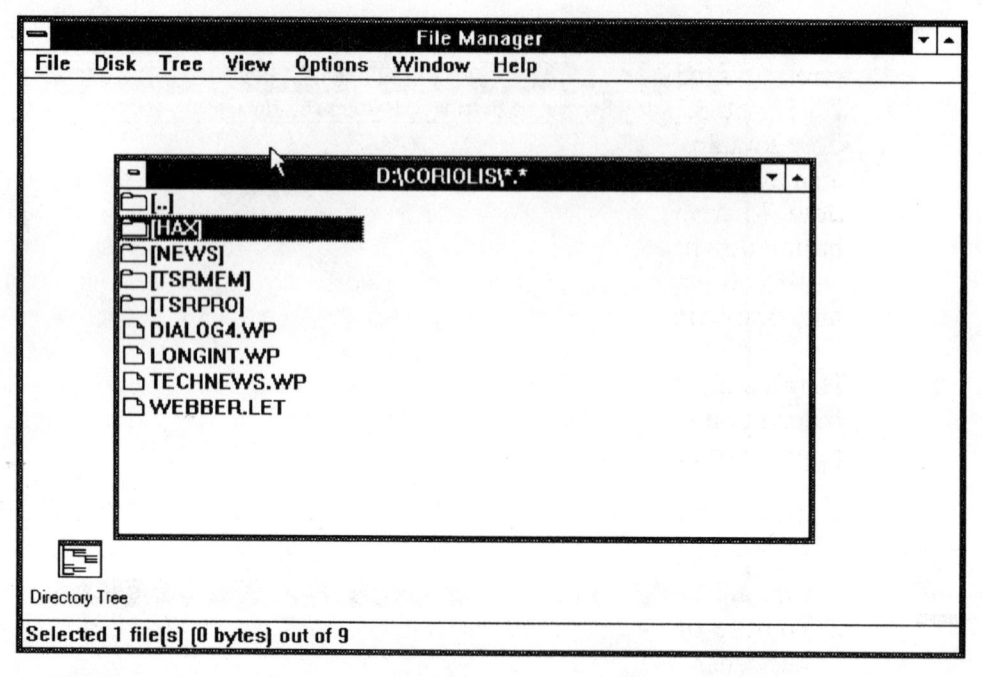

Figure 3.2. Sample Document Window

6. When multiple windows are displayed, how can you tell which window is the active window?

---

1. *A document window; the window doesn't have a menu bar.*
2. *File, Edit, Search, and Help.*
3. *The Control menu from the window (application) appears. This menu provides the basic commands for processing the window.*
4. *The cursor changes to a diagonal double-headed arrow so you can move the window.*
5. *The window can be dragged off the edge of the screen.*
6. *The active window is displayed on top of all the other open windows.*

Scrolling Windows

If you're an experienced DOS user, you're probably well aware of the frustration of performing a command, such as DIR, and seeing your data pass by on the screen before you have a chance to read it. With Windows, you don't have

Building Your Windows Skills

to worry about this problem because many of the windows provide special scroll bars to help you view your data.

Figure 3.3 shows a window with labeled scroll bars. Notice that the window contains a horizontal and a vertical scroll bar. The scroll bar track contains a small box, called a *slider* or *scroll box*, which is used to quickly scroll a window. To move the slider, position the mouse pointer on it, hold the mouse button down, and drag the slider.

If you want to scroll the window vertically one line at a time or horizontally one character at a time, use the up, down, right, or left scroll arrows.

Tip Here's a quick method for scrolling a window, one screen at a time: Click the mouse pointer directly above or below the slider. You can also use this technique to scroll the window horizontally.

1. Which mouse action is required to quickly scroll to the end of a window? Can this be done from the keyboard?
2. Point to one of the scroll arrows and hold the mouse button down. What happens?
3. How can you tell when you have scrolled to the middle of a window? How about the end of a window?
4. Which other key sequences can you use to scroll the window?

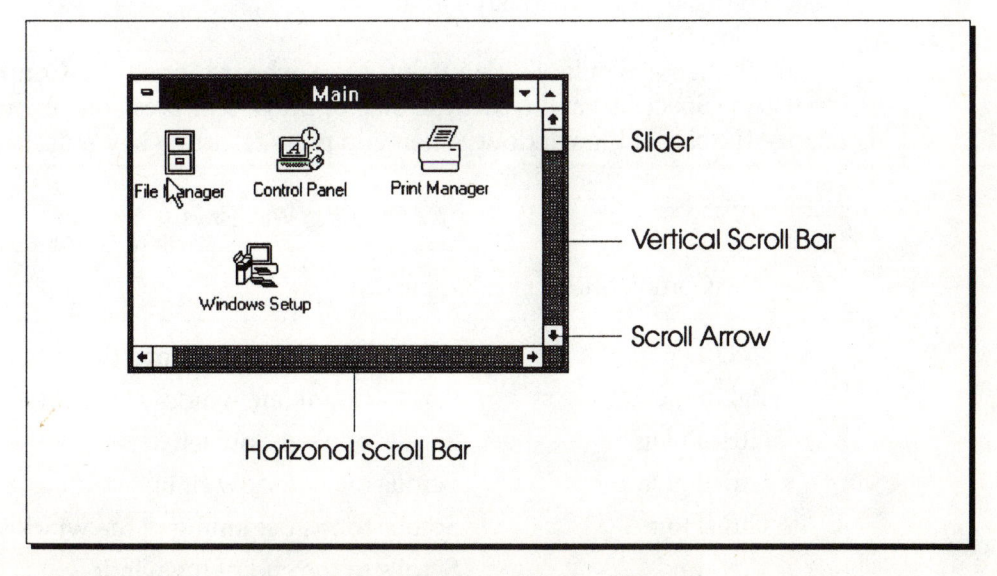

Figure 3.3. A Window with Scroll Boxes

1. *Drag the vertical slider to the bottom of the window. Press Ctrl+End on the keyboard.*
2. *The window continues to scroll until you release the mouse button.*
3. *When you've scrolled to the midpoint of a window, the vertical slider is positioned in the middle of the window. The vertical slider moves to the bottom of the window when you have scrolled to the end.*
4. *The key sequences supported for scrolling windows are listed in Table 3.1.*

Changing a Window's Size

What can you do if you need more space on your desktop to view multiple windows? This problem is easy to solve because you can change the size of a window using the mouse or the keyboard.

Move the mouse pointer to any part of the window frame: top, bottom, left, or right. Depending on where you move the pointer, it will change to show how the window can be resized. In each case, the pointer will display with two heads. The following three pointer types appear in Figure 3.4:

- *Vertical pointer heads* show that the window's height can be changed.
- *Horizontal pointer heads* show that the window's width can be changed.
- *Diagonal pointer heads* show that both the width and the height can be changed simultaneously.

To change a window's size using the keyboard, open the Control menu (press Alt+Spacebar) and select the Size option. Next press the arrow keys to change the size of the window. When you press an arrow key, a dashed outline

Table 3.1. Keys for Scrolling Windows

Key Combinations	Operation
PgUp	Scrolls up one window at a time
PgDn	Scrolls down one window at a time
Ctrl+PgUp	Scrolls one window left
Ctrl+PgDn	Scrolls one window right
Ctrl+Home	Scrolls to the beginning of the window
Ctrl+End	Scrolls to the end of the window

Building Your Windows Skills

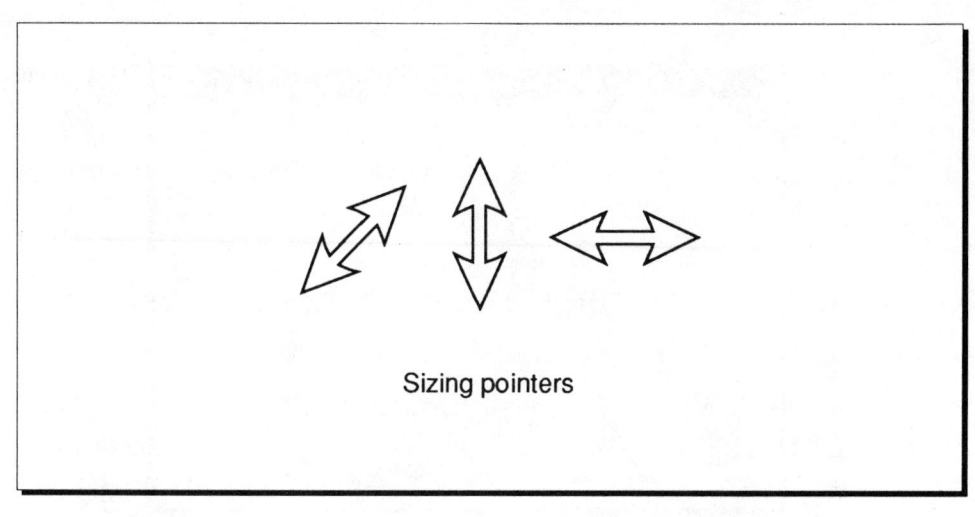

Figure 3.4. Pointer Types for Window Sizing

shows you the actual size and location of the window while it is being resized. When you're done, press the Enter key to save the window's new size.

Tip | To change both the horizontal and the vertical dimensions of a window from the keyboard, select the Size command and press two arrow keys simultaneously to select a corner. For example, press the up arrow and the right arrow to select the top-right corner of the window. Next, press the right arrow to stretch the window to the right, or the up arrow to stretch the window upwards. Remember to press the Enter key when you finish resizing the window.

In addition to changing a window's size by moving its frame, you can quickly expand a window so that it takes up the full desktop. This technique, called *maximizing a window*, can be performed in one of two ways:

1. Click on the up arrow button (Maximize button), as shown in Figure 3.5.
2. Select the Maximize command from the window's Control menu.

In either case, first make sure the window you want to maximize is currently selected. (We'll explain how to select windows shortly.)

After a window has been enlarged, a new button appears in the upper-right portion of the window. As Figure 3.6 shows, this button is called the *Restore* button. You can click on it to restore an enlarged window to its previous size. (You can also restore the window's previous size by selecting the Restore command from the Control menu.)

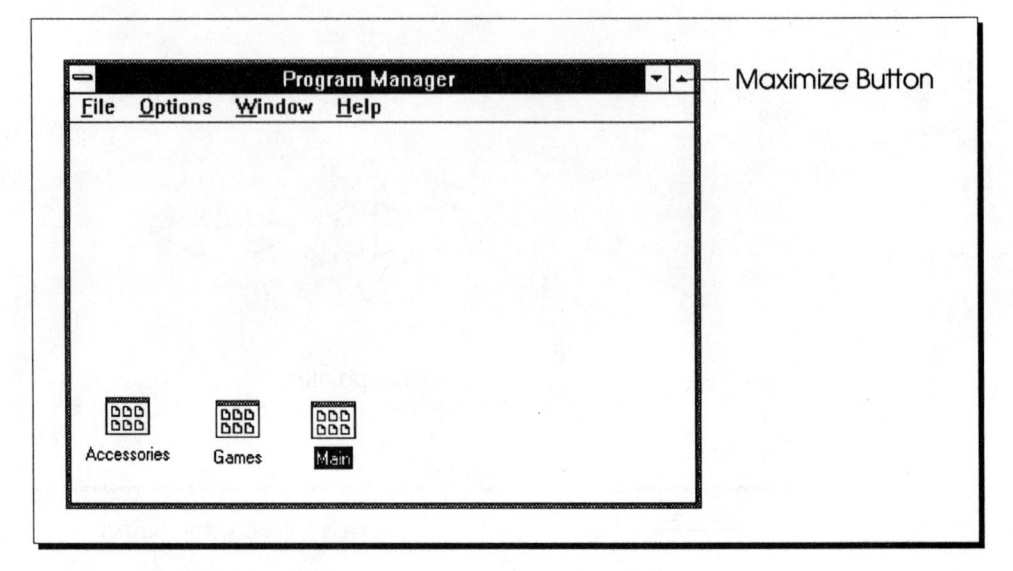

Figure 3.5. Using the Maximize Button

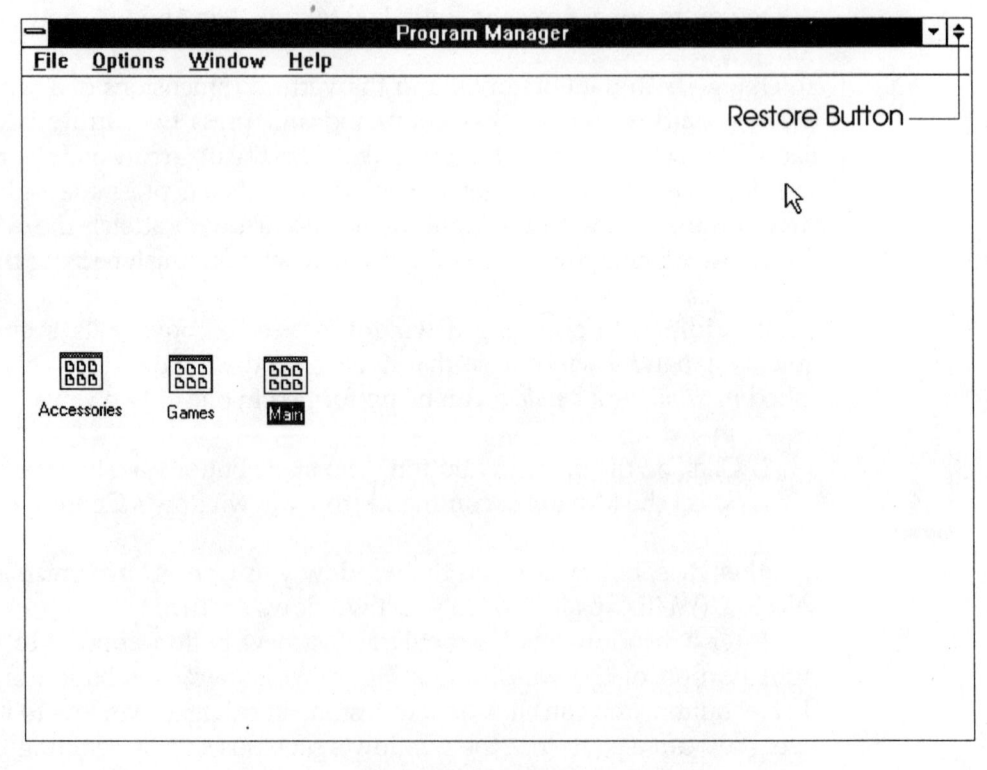

Figure 3.6. The Window Restore Button

1. Click the mouse on the lower-right corner of a window. What type of pointer is displayed?
2. Can a window be sized larger than the screen?
3. Open the Control Panel application by clicking on the Control Panel icon. (This icon is located in the Main window.) What happens if you try to resize the Control Panel window?
4. Press the Esc key while resizing a window. What happens?

1. *A diagonal pointer.*
2. *No.*
3. *The window has a fixed size and cannot be changed.*
4. *The resizing operation is canceled, and the window returns to its previous size.*

Moving a Window

No matter what application you run in Windows, you'll want to move application and document windows around on the desktop to easily view more than one window. Fortunately, moving a window is even easier than changing a window's size. To quickly move a window, drag the title bar at the top of the window until the window reaches the position you want, and release the mouse button.

From the keyboard, open the Control menu (press Alt+Spacebar) and select the Move command. Move the window with the arrow keys in the same way you use these keys to change a window's size. When you finish moving the window, press the Enter key to anchor it.

1. Open the Notepad application, select the Move command from the Control menu, and move the window with one of the arrow keys. What happens if you try to use the window before pressing the Enter key?
2. Try to move a window off the screen. What happens?

1. *The window returns to its previous position. (The Move operation is canceled.)*
2. *The window moves off of the desktop.*

Converting a Window to an Icon

When windows are opened, they are always displayed with a title, a frame, optional scroll bars, and so on. Although you can open multiple windows and move them around to make your desktop a more productive environment, you may find that the desktop becomes cluttered with windows. Of course, you can always close the windows not currently in use; however, if you plan to use them later, you'll have to open them again.

To help you manage the desktop, Windows lets you convert a window to an icon. You can select the icon later to activate the window. The best part about this feature is that when an application window is converted to an icon, the application is still running in memory.

Follow these steps to convert a window to an icon:

1. Select the window using the mouse or the keyboard.
2. Click on the down arrow button (Minimize button) in the upper-right corner. (The Minimize button is directly to the left of the Maximize button. See Figure 3.7.) If you're using the keyboard, select the Minimize command from the Control menu.

After a window is converted to an icon, the icon appears at the bottom of the screen. Use the mouse or the keyboard to select the icon and move it around. To bring the window up, double-click the icon, or highlight it, press Alt+Spacebar to bring up the Control menu, and select the Restore command.

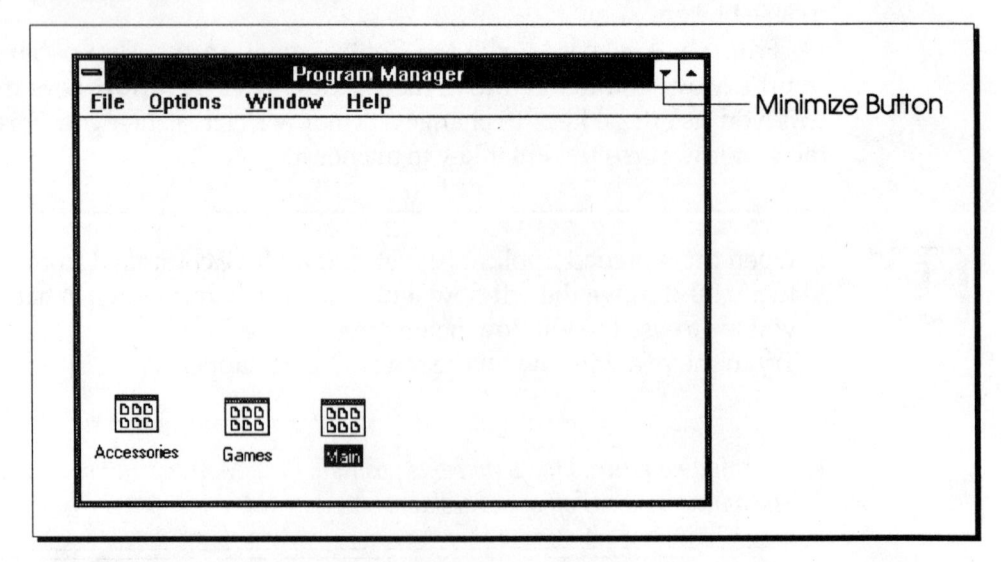

Figure 3.7. The Minimize Button

> ✓ Open the Notepad application, and enlarge the window to its full size by pressing the Maximize button. Try to convert the window to an icon by clicking the Restore button.

You can't minimize a window that has been enlarged in this way. Before minimizing a window, you must either restore the window to its previous size by clicking the Restore button, or select the Restore command from the window's Control menu.

Tips for Working with Multiple Windows

More than likely, you'll want to display multiple windows on your desktop at the same time. After all, you can use multiple windows to transfer data between applications (such as Microsoft Word and Excel), edit multiple documents at the same time, and perform other useful operations. The key to working with multiple windows is to always know where your windows are and which window is currently selected.

To help you manage your application windows, the Program Manager provides the Cascade and Tile commands, which are listed with the Window menu (Figure 3.8). The Cascade command overlaps the windows so that each window's title bar is visible (Figure 3.9). The Tile command displays the windows in a smaller size, arranged as if they were tiles (Figure 3.10). This format lets you view all of the open windows simultaneously.

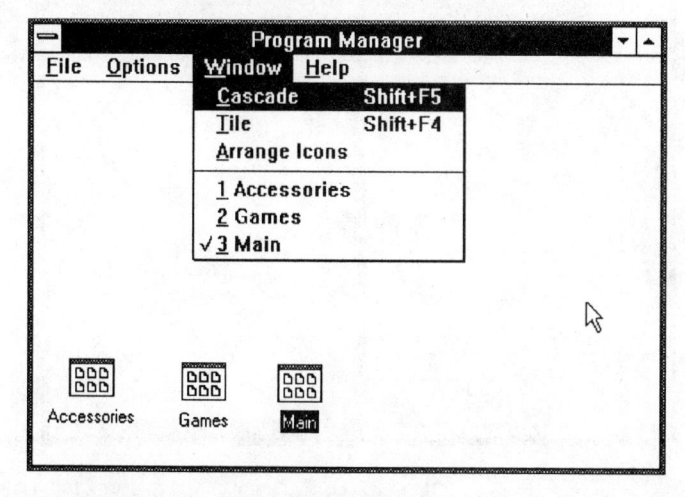

Figure 3.8. The Window Menu

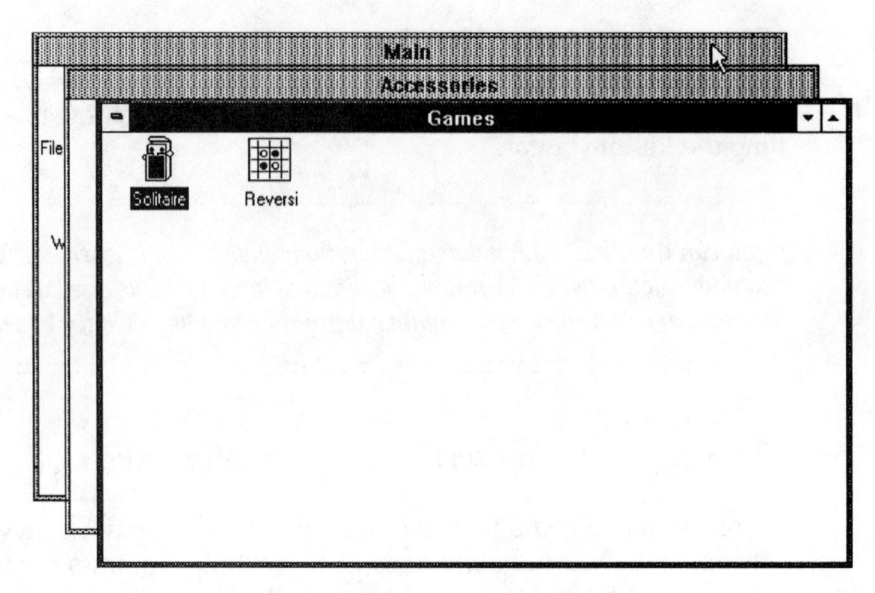

Figure 3.9. Windows Displayed with the Cascade Format

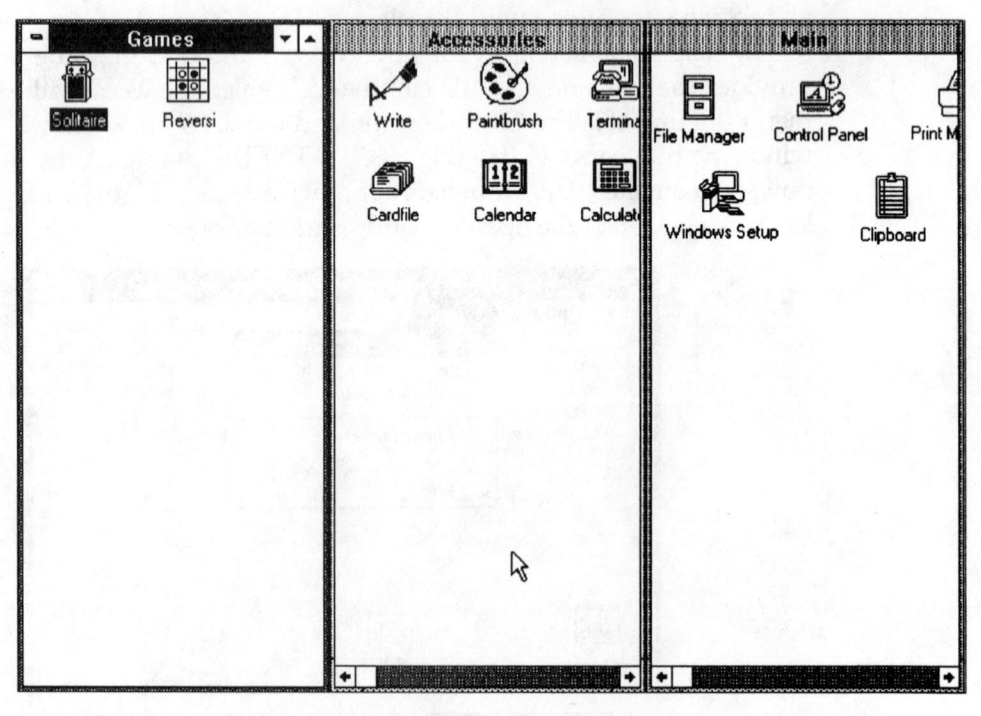

Figure 3.10. Windows Displayed in the Tile Format

Selecting an Application Window

Before you can use an application such as Microsoft Excel or Word, you must first select its window by clicking on it with the mouse.

Windows provides a useful controller, called the *Task List*, to help you select an application window from the keyboard. The Task List lists all of the applications open on the desktop. Figure 3.11 shows a Task List window with a number of open applications. Notice that several options are provided: You can select a new task, end a task, and cascade or tile application windows.

To open the Task List, double-click anywhere on the desktop. As an alternative, select the Switch To command from the Control menu. Once the Task List is opened, you can select a new application by double-clicking on the application's name. From the keyboard, use the arrow keys to highlight the application and select the Switch To button by pressing Alt+S.

Tip || This keyboard shortcut displays the Task List: Press Ctrl+Esc.

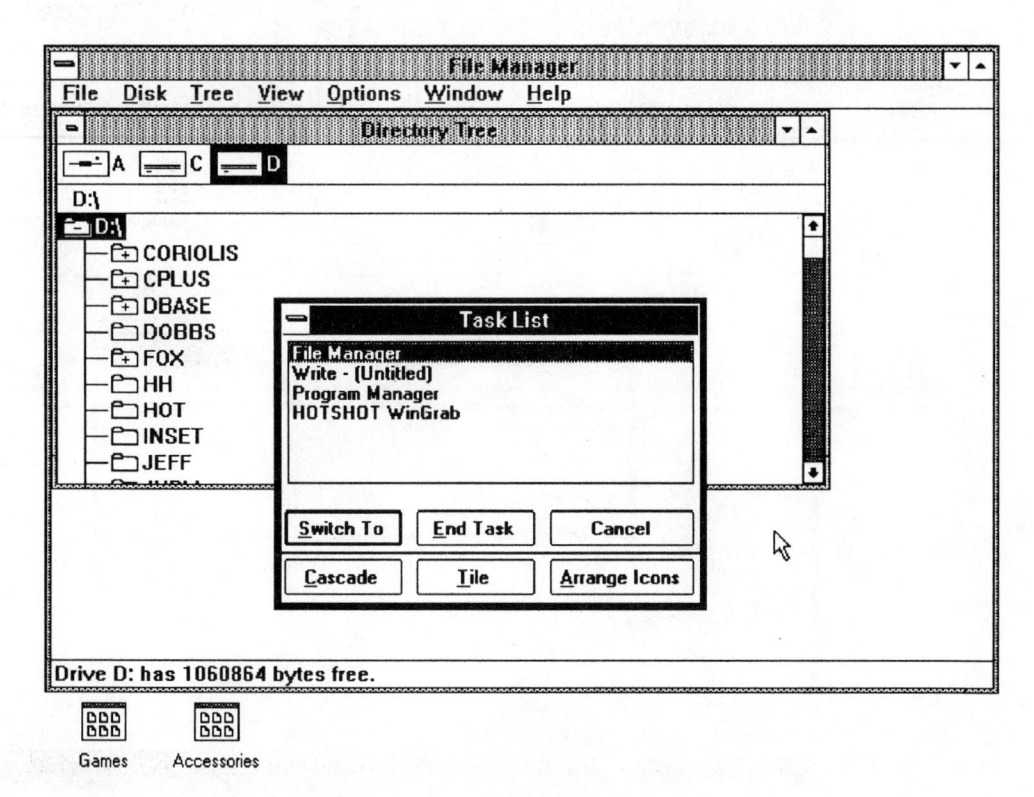

Figure 3.11. The Task List Window

Selecting Windows with the Keyboard

Using the mouse to select a window as the active window is relatively easy, as long as you know where the window is. Selecting a window from the keyboard is a little trickier: If the window you want is covered by another window, you need to cycle through the windows displayed on the desktop. You can do so in one of two ways: to cycle through for application windows, press Alt+Esc. To cycle through document windows, press Ctrl+Tab.

Closing a Window

When you're finished using a window, you can close it by selecting the Exit command from the window's File menu. This action terminates the application and closes the opened files associated with that application. You can also close a window by selecting the Close command from the Control menu. In either case, a dialog box displays (Figure 3.12) if you try to close a document window that you've changed but not yet saved.

Tip | As a shortcut, double-click on the window's Control menu to close the window.

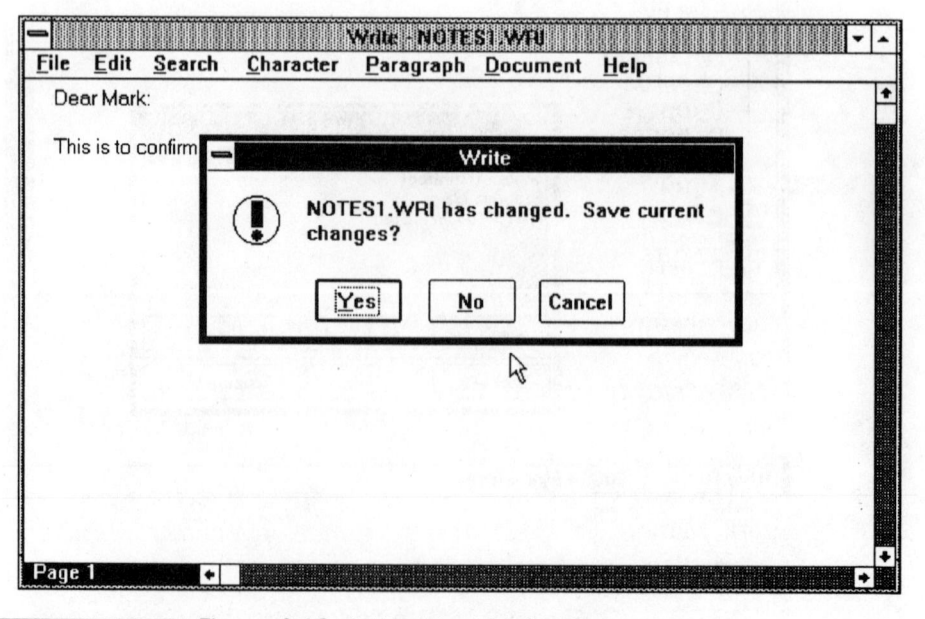

Figure 3.12. A Warning Dialog Box

1. Move the mouse to the right edge of a window. Which cursor is displayed?
2. What is the difference between the Size and Move options provided in the Control menu for each application window?
3. Open a few document windows. What happens when you press Ctrl+F6?
4. What happens when you double-click on the desktop?
5. Which key do you press to cancel moving or resizing a window?
6. True or false? Document windows usually contain menus.

1. *The right and left double-headed arrow.*
2. *The Size option is used to resize a window, and the Move option is used to move a window.*
3. *The Windows program will cycle through the document windows.*
4. *The Task List is displayed.*
5. *The Esc key.*
6. *False.*

Icons

If you've ever used a Macintosh computer, you already know how useful icons can be. Windows uses icons to represent three types of objects: an application, a document, and a program item (Figure 3.13). You can select the icons with the mouse or the keyboard and move them around.

Application icons are displayed on the desktop outside of the window borders. Windows doesn't allow you to put this type of icon into another window. As you've seen, application icons are created by minimizing a window. Figure 3.14 shows the application icons provided with Windows.

Document icons represent the documents associated with an application. They always appear at the bottom of the application window that they're assigned to. For example, if you use the application Write, you open a document window called Text1, and then you minimize this window, an icon called Text1 will display at the bottom of the Write window. When you activate a document icon, a document window displays.

The last type of icon, the *program item icon*, is used exclusively by the Program Manager. These icons, such as the Paintbrush, the Cardfile, and the Clock, display in group windows. They can be moved between group windows, but they can't be moved out of the Program Manager window.

Figure 3.13. The Three Types of Icons

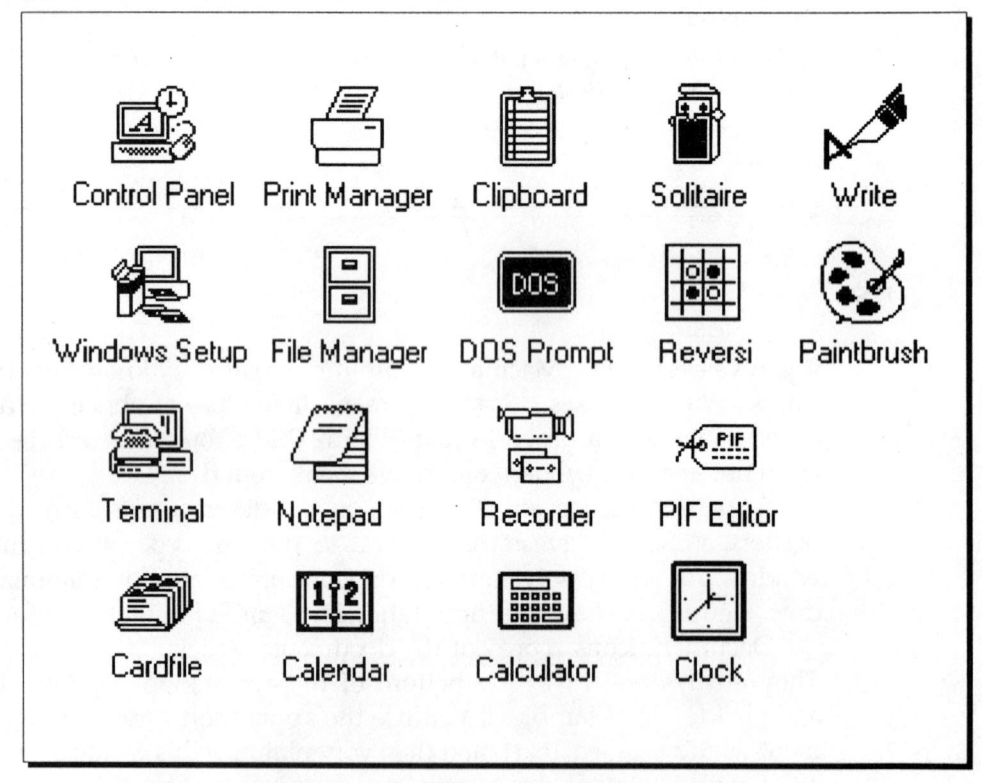

Figure 3.14. Windows Application Icons

1. Try to drag an application icon, such as the Calendar, inside a window. What happens? What happens if you move the window?
2. What type of icon is the Terminal?

1. *The application icon moves into the window, but it still resides on the desktop. If you move the window, the icon will not move with it.*
2. *A program item icon.*

Selecting and Moving Icons

There's a subtle but important difference between selecting an icon and activating it. When you select an icon, it becomes highlighted and you can move it, activate it, or access its Control menu. When you activate an icon, on the other hand, you open the application, and the application window appears.

To select an icon using the mouse, click on the icon. To use the keyboard, press Alt+Esc to select an application icon, or press Ctrl+Tab to select a document icon. (Each time you press Alt+Esc or Ctrl+Tab, a different application icon or document icon is selected.)

Once you select an icon, you can move it by dragging it with the mouse. If you don't have a mouse, access the icon's Control menu by highlighting the icon and pressing Alt+Spacebar for an application icon or Alt+Hyphen (-) for a document icon. After the Control menu appears, select the Move command and position the icon using the arrow keys. (This technique is the same one you used for moving a window.)

Tip — To neatly arrange the icons on the desktop, open the Task List by double-clicking anywhere on the desktop or pressing Ctrl+Esc. Select the Arrange Icons button, as shown in Figure 3.15.

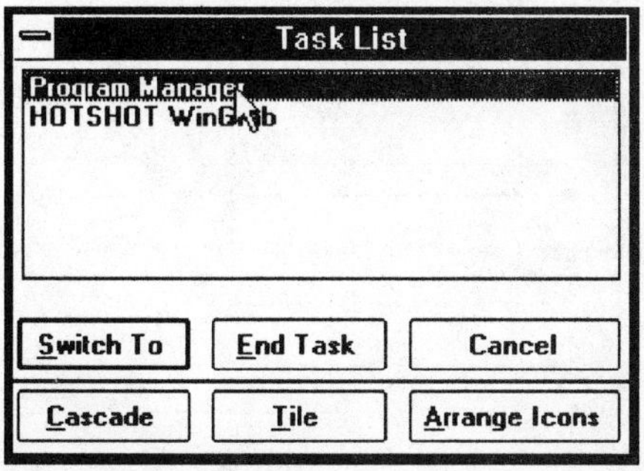

Figure 3.15. Using the Task List Window

Activating an Icon

The easiest way to activate an icon is to double-click it. The mouse pointer changes to an hourglass while the application is loading. If you're using the keyboard, select the icon and press the Enter key.

---

1. Drag an icon with the mouse. How does the mouse pointer change?
2. Select an application icon, such as Write, and press Alt+Spacebar to display the icon's Control menu. Which commands are provided with the menu?

---

1. *The mouse pointer changes to an outline of the icon being moved.*
2. *Restore, Move, Size, Minimize, Maximize, Close, Switch To..., and Next.*

Accessing Menus

In addition to selecting icons to open an application, you'll perform operations in Windows by selecting commands from menus. Each application window has its own set of menus, which are grouped in a *menu bar system*. Figure 3.16 shows the two key components of a menu bar system: a *menu bar*, and a *pull-down menu* associated with each menu bar entry.

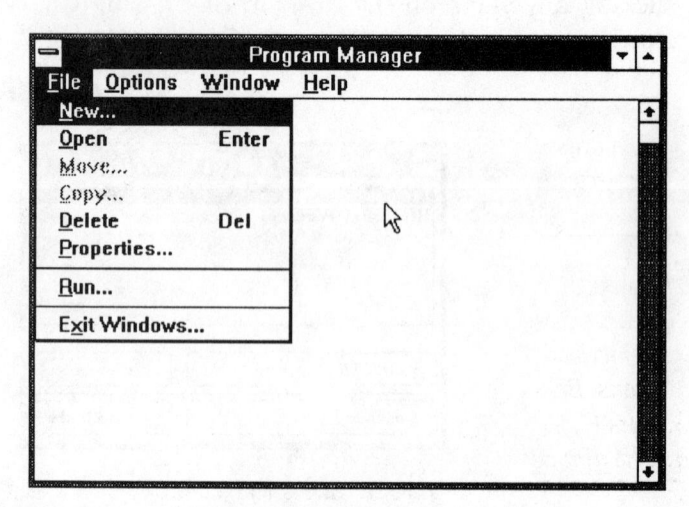

Figure 3.16. A Menu System

Building Your Windows Skills

The menu bar is used to open a specific menu, and the pull-down menu lists the commands associated with a menu bar entry. Using a mouse, you open a pull-down menu by clicking on a menu bar entry. For example, to open the File menu in the Program manager you click on the File item. You don't have to hold the mouse button down to keep the menu open. When the menu is open, select a command by clicking the mouse pointer on the command's name.

To open a menu from the keyboard, press Alt or F10 to select the menu bar. Next, use the arrow keys to highlight the menu entry, and press the Enter key.

Here are some tips for using menus and selecting commands:

- To close a menu and return to the current application, press Alt or F10.
- To close a menu but remain on the menu bar, press the Esc key on the keyboard.
- Menu commands with underlined letters can be selected by pressing the Alt key and the key for the underlined letter.
- Some menu commands provide shortcut keyboard options so that you select them without opening the menu.
- Sometimes a menu command name will change because of the context in which a menu is being used. The Undo command is one example.

---

1. Open the Options menu within the Program Manager window. Which commands does it provide?
2. Activate the Accessories icon to open the Accessories window. Now open the Window menu to see the commands available. Which command has a checkmark?
3. Which two keys do you press to open the Program Manager's File menu?
4. Why are some menu commands dimmed?
5. Which shortcut key do you press to activate the Cascade command in the Program Manager's Window menu?

---

1. *To open the Options menu, click on the Options item, or press Alt+O. The commands listed are Auto Arrange and Minimize on Use.*
2. *To activate the Accessories icon, double-click on it. The commands are Tile, Arrange Icons. Below the dividing line, you'll find the window names Main and Accessories.*
3. *Alt+F.*
4. *The dimmed menu commands represent the commands that are currently disabled.*
5. *Shift+F5.*

Working with Special Menu Commands

Usually, when you select a menu item, Windows performs a command. Some menu items are displayed differently because they perform functions other than simply activating a command. For example, we've already seen that a dimmed item represents a command that is currently unavailable. The other three types of menu items include a menu item with ellipses (...), a menu item with a checkmark, and a menu item with a right-pointing triangle.

A menu item with ellipses indicates that a dialog box appears when the command is selected. Figure 3.17 shows the dialog box that appears when the Move... command is selected from the Program Manager's File menu. The dialog box appears because Windows needs more information from the user in order to carry out the command.

When a checkmark appears next to a menu item, as shown in Figure 3.18, the command is active. You'll see this feature whenever you work with menus containing commands with on and off settings, such as the Paragraph menu provided with the Write application. For example, when the Left command in the Paragraph menu has a checkmark, the left alignment style is currently selected.

When a triangle appears next to a command, the command represents a *cascading* menu. When you select that command, a second level of menus is displayed.

---

1. Open the Program Manager's File menu. Which menu items have ellipses?
2. If a menu command is dimmed, how can you select it?
3. Which Program Manager window provides checkmark options?

---

1. *To open the Program Manager's File menu, click on the File item in the menu bar, or press Alt+F. These menu items have ellipses:*

    New, Move, Copy, Properties, Run, Exit Windows

2. *You need to perform another command (such as open a file) or select something (such as mark a paragraph) to undim the command. For example, if you are using an application such as Write, and you want to select the Save command from the File menu, you must open a file using the Open... command before you can select the Save command.*
3. *The Window menu.*

Building Your Windows Skills

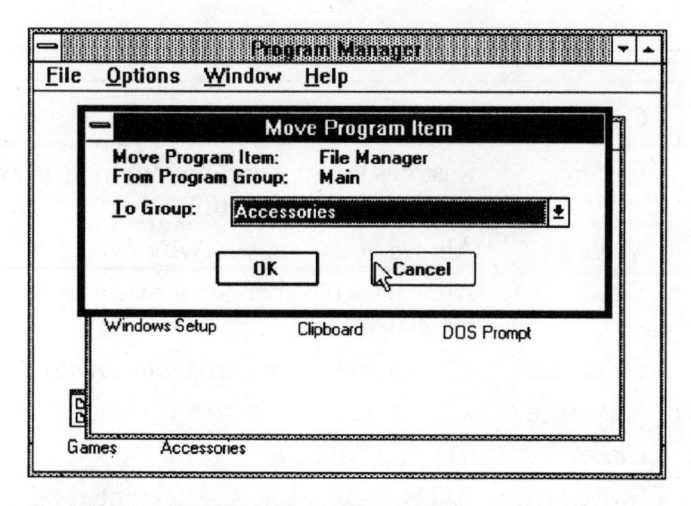

Figure 3.17. The Move Program Item Dialog Box

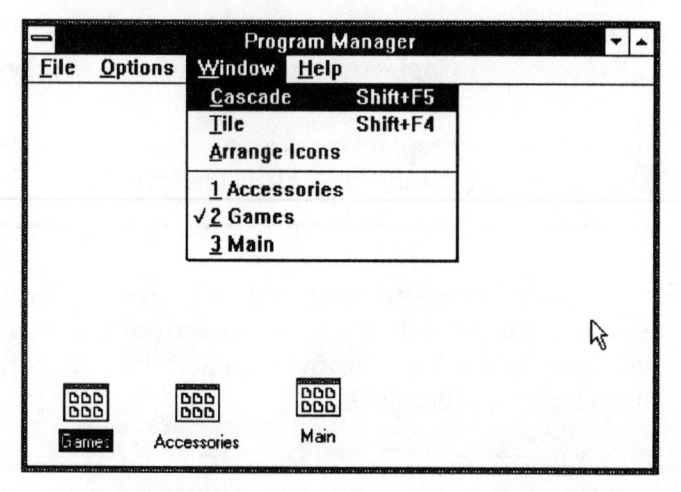

Figure 3.18. Menu Showing an Active Command

Using the Control Menu

The Control menu is represented by the small rectangle in each application window. This menu is common to all applications, and it always contains the set of commands listed in Table 3.2.

As we've seen, the easiest way to access the Control menu for a window is to click on the Control menu box icon. Remember to click only once—if you double-click, you'll close the window.

Table 3.2. The Control Menu Commands

Command	Description
Restore	Restores the current window to its previous size after it has been enlarged or shrunk.
Move	Allows you to move a window by using the arrow keys.
Size	Allows you to change the size of a window by using the arrow keys.
Minimize	Allows you to convert a window to an icon.
Maximize	Allows you to enlarge a window to its maximum size.
Close	Closes a window.
Switch To...	Allows you to select a different application from the Task List.
Next	Allows you to switch among document windows and icons.
Paste	Copies text from the Clipboard to the current document window.
Edit	Displays a cascading menu with additional editing commands (only available with the 386 Enhanced mode).

If you're using the keyboard, select the application window and press Alt+Spacebar. After the menu opens, activate commands by highlighting them with the Up and Down arrow keys and then pressing the Enter key. To close the menu, press the Alt key.

1. Select the Notepad application icon.
2. Open Notepad's Control menu. What commands are available?
3. Which command in the Control menu displays a dialog box when selected?
4. Which keyboard shortcut activates the Close command in the Control menu?

1. Click once on the Notepad icon. (Don't double-click, or you'll start the application.)
2. Press Alt+F4. The commands listed in the Control Menu are Restore, Move, Size, Minimize, Maximize, Close, and Switch To.
3. Switch To...
4. Alt+F4.

Building Your Windows Skills

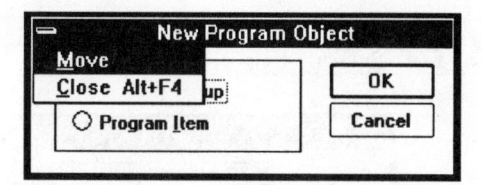

Figure 3.19. The Control Menu for a Dialog Box

Accessing the Control Menu for Icons and Dialogs

Windows provides a Control menu for icons and dialog boxes, as well as for windows. As Figure 3.19 shows, the Control menu for dialog boxes is typically much shorter. You can easily open the Control menu for either type of object by using the procedure we just discussed for accessing a window's Control menu. In the case of an icon, simply click the mouse on the icon once, or highlight the icon with the keyboard and press Alt+Spacebar. For a dialog box, click the Control menu box displayed in the upper-left corner, or press Alt+Spacebar.

Mastering Dialog Boxes

In addition to windows and menus, the other key ingredient to the Windows environment is dialog boxes. Windows uses dialog boxes to request and provide important information.

Dialog boxes are typically displayed as warning messages or linked with menu commands. For example, when you exit Windows, a special dialog box asks if you want to save the changes you made during your Windows session. As an example of a menu option dialog, when you select the Open... command from the Notepad application's File menu, a dialog box asks you to enter the directory and the filename for the file you wish to open (Figure 3.20).

The techniques for controlling dialog boxes are easy to learn because dialog boxes and windows share some common features. For example, all dialog boxes provide Control menus to help you close and move them.

1. Select the Move... command from the Program Manager's File menu. What is the name of the dialog box that is displayed?
2. Click on the title bar of the dialog box and drag the mouse. What happens?
3. While the dialog box is open, press the Tab key. What happens?
4. Can you change the size of a dialog box?
5. Can you minimize a dialog box?

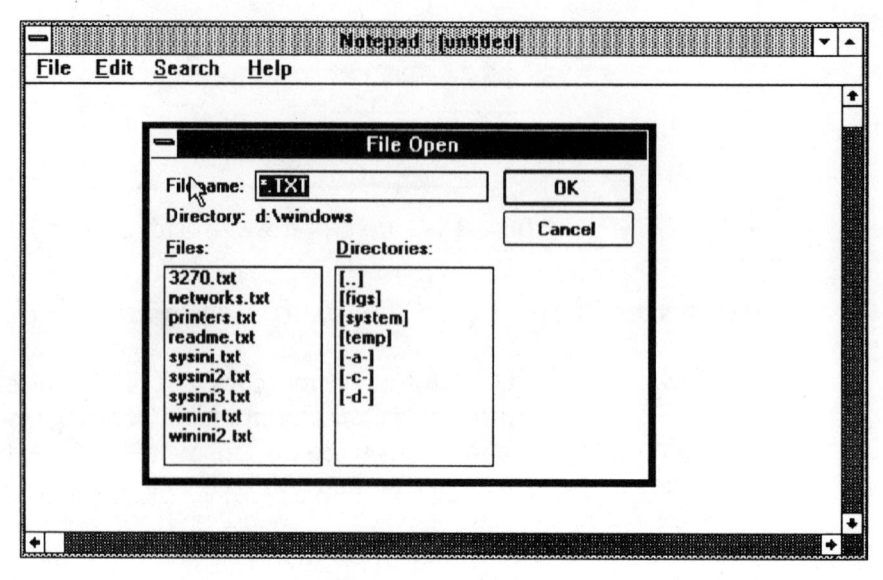

Figure 3.20. File Open Dialog Box

1. *Move Program Item.*
2. *The dialog box moves.*
3. *One of the items in the dialog box is selected.*
4. *No.*
5. *No.*

Selecting Dialog Options

Before we explore the different types of dialog boxes and the dialog box options, let's look at how you select the items in a dialog box.

Only one item in a dialog box, whether it's a text box, a button, or a menu list, can be active at a time. This item will either be highlighted, outlined with a dashed line, or contain a blinking cursor. Before you can work with an item, you must select it. If you're using the mouse, simply click on the item. With the keyboard, either press the Tab key to move the selection in a forward direction, or press Shift+Tab to move the selection backwards. You can also select an item that has an underline by pressing the Alt key and the key for the letter. For example, in the File Open dialog box shown in Figure 3.21, press Alt+F to select the Files list menu.

Building Your Windows Skills

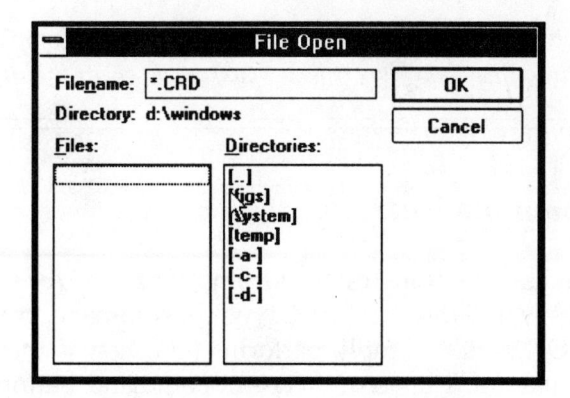

[Figure: File Open dialog box with Filename "*.CRD", Directory "d:\windows", Files list, Directories list showing [..], [igs], [system], [temp], [-a-], [-c-], [-d-], and OK/Cancel buttons]

Figure 3.21. Selecting the Files Menu

1. Open the Write application.
2. Select the Open... command from the Write application's File menu. Which item is highlighted when the dialog box first appears?
3. Select the Print... command from the File menu. Which item is highlighted when the Print dialog displays?
4. How can you select the Draft Quality check box using the keyboard?

1. *Double-click on the Write icon. (This icon is stored in the Accessories window.)*
2. *The Filename text box.*
3. *The Copies text box.*
4. *Press Alt+D.*

Using Warning Dialog Boxes

The warning dialog boxes are the easiest to use because they provide only a few options. This dialog box contains two types of selection items: command buttons and a check box.

In addition to the Exit Windows dialog box, what other three warning dialog boxes does Windows use?

The Notepad warning dialog box, the Format Complete dialog box, and the Error Deleting File dialog box (the last two are associated with the File Manager application).

Command Buttons

Command buttons carry out an operation. As you work more with dialog boxes, you'll discover three types of command buttons. The first type, such as the OK button, simply performs an action without requiring any additional information. The second type of command button, which is marked with ellipses (...), opens another dialog box. Finally, the command buttons marked with the symbols >> expand the current dialog box by presenting more information that doesn't fit in the dialog box.

Tip When a command button is dimmed, you can't select it.

Check Boxes

Check boxes are different from command buttons because they don't actually initiate an operation. The check box options in a dialog box are grouped by category. Figure 3.22 shows the Terminal Preferences dialog box displayed by the Terminal application. Notice the two groups of check boxes: Terminal Modes and CR -> CR/LF. In each group, you can select as many of the check

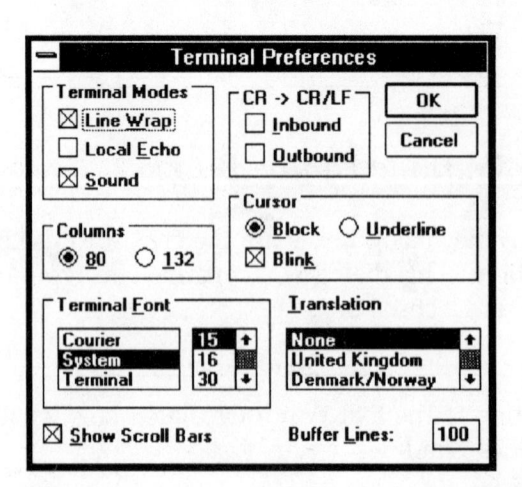

Figure 3.22. The Terminal Preferences Dialog Box

Building Your Windows Skills

boxes as you want. When an item is selected, an X appears in the box. If an item is dimmed, you can't select it.

To select a check box with the mouse, click on the check box. To use the keyboard, highlight the item by pressing the Spacebar. The highlighted item is enclosed by a dashed box. To place or remove a check mark, press the Spacebar.

Tip — You can select check box items that contain an underlined letter by pressing the Alt key and the key for the underlined letter. For example, you can select the Left Margin option in Figure 3.23 by pressing Alt+L.

1. Start the File Manager application by double-clicking on the File Manager icon in the Main group window. Next, select the Change Attributes... command in the File menu. What check boxes are provided?
2. Which keyboard shortcut selects the Hidden check box?
3. Which check box is highlighted when the Change Attributes dialog box first opens?
4. True or false? Check boxes are represented with either a square or a circle.

1. *Read Only, Archive, Hidden, and System.*
2. *Alt+H.*
3. *Read Only.*
4. *False. Check boxes are represented with a square, and option buttons are represented with a circle.*

Figure 3.23. The Page Layout Dialog Box

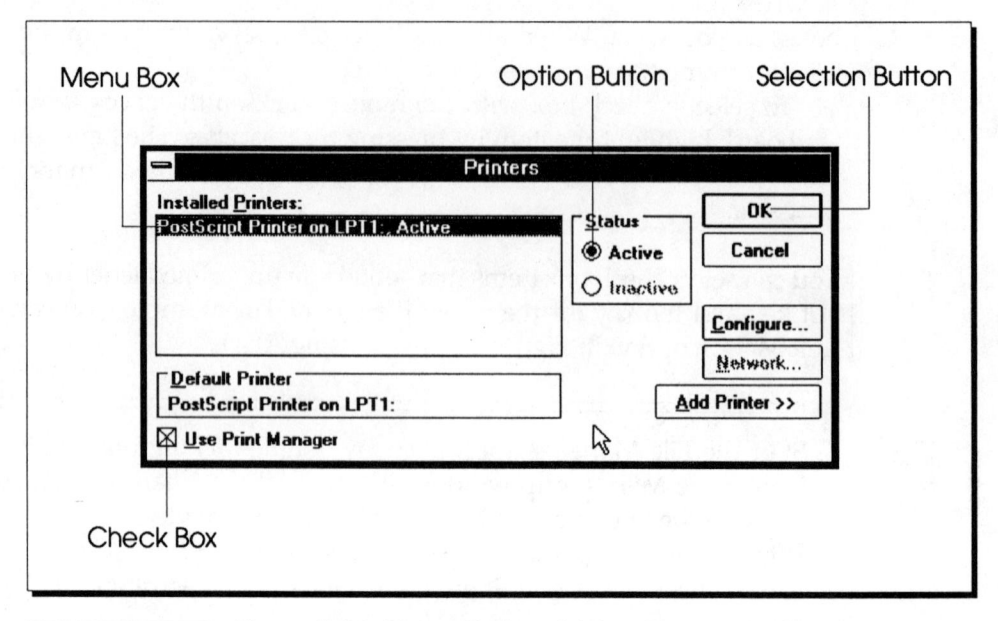

Figure 3.24. Menu Option Dialog Box

Using Menu Option Dialogs

Figure 3.24 shows a typical menu option dialog box with its components labeled. Notice that these dialogs are much more complex than simple warning dialogs. In addition to selection buttons and check boxes, they contain other selectable objects, such as option buttons, list boxes, text boxes, and menu boxes.

An *option button* is similar to a check box but only one option button in a group can be selected. A *list box* provides you with a list of choices that you select, using the mouse or the keyboard. A *text box* is a single-line rectangular box where you type in information, such as a filename. A *menu box* is a single-line rectangular box that displays a menu. It's also called a *drop-down list box*.

1. Which menu commands in the Program Manager's File menu produce menu option dialog boxes?
2. Open the Properties dialog box (select the Properties... command). Which text boxes do you see?
3. Which dialog box accessible from the Program Manager provides a list box?
4. True or false? The Save Changes option in the Exit Windows dialog box is an option button.

Building Your Windows Skills

1. *New, Move, Copy, Properties, Run, and Exit Windows.*
2. *Description and Command Line.*
3. *The Task List.*
4. *False; it's a check box.*

Option Buttons

Option buttons are different from check boxes because they represent a set of one or more options where you can select only one of the options. Figure 3.25 shows a dialog box with option buttons. Notice that only one option in the group can be selected, and the selected option contains a black dot.

1. What's the difference between a check box and an option button?
2. How can you select an option button from the keyboard?

1. *In a check box, you can select multiple options. An option button is mutually exclusive—you can select only one option at a time.*
2. *Either press the Alt key and the key that corresponds to the underlined letter, or press the Tab key to move to the option group and then use the arrow keys to select the option button.*

Using Text Boxes

Text boxes provide an interactive prompt so that you can type in text, such as a filename or a date. The text that you type is used by the dialog box to perform its operation.

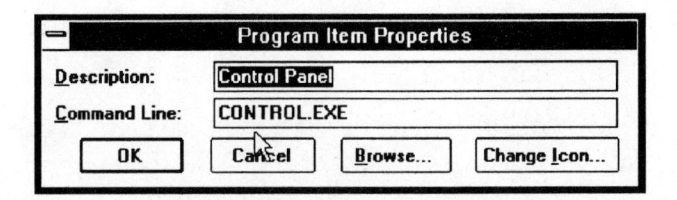

Figure 3.25. Dialog Box with Option Buttons

You type text into a text block in the same way you type text into a window. You can use any of the cursor positioning keys as well as the Delete and Insert keys. You can also use the mouse to select text. To select the entire text block, click and drag the mouse inside it. To select text from the keyboard, hold down the Shift key and press the right or left arrow keys to select the region of text.

When text is highlighted in a text box, you can delete the text by pressing the Delete key or the backspace key.

---

1. Select the Run... command from the Program Manager's File menu. Type in the text Write in the Command Line text box, and double-click the mouse inside the box. What happens?
2. Open a dialog box that has a text box containing text. How is the text formatted when the dialog box opens?

---

1. *The entire text box is selected.*
2. *The text is highlighted.*

Using List Boxes

A list box functions like a menu because it provides the names of options that can be scrolled and selected using the mouse. Figure 3.26 shows the Open dialog box associated with the Notepad application's File menu. This dialog box contains two types of list boxes: scrollable and nonscrollable. The scrollable list boxes can be operated using the same techniques for scrolling windows.

To select an item in a list, either double-click on the item, or highlight it by clicking once and then choose the appropriate command button. For example, to open a file with the File Open dialog box, click on the desired filename in the Files list, and then click the OK button. Remember that if the item you want is not listed, click the scroll arrows or move the arrow keys to locate the item.

To select an item from the keyboard, move the arrow keys or press the key for the first letter of the item. Select the highlighted item by pressing the Enter key.

Tip — Some list boxes allow you to select multiple items at once. To do so, either click on each item that you want, or highlight the item using the arrow keys and press the Spacebar. You can also deselect items by clicking on them or pressing the Spacebar.

Building Your Windows Skills

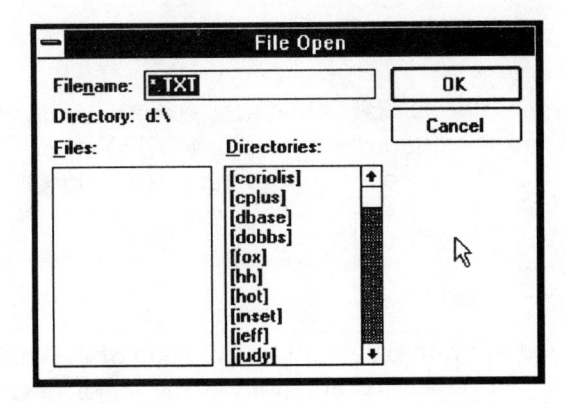

Figure 3.26. Dialog Box with List Boxes

Drop-Down List Boxes

In addition to the standard list boxes, some dialogs provide a variation called *drop-down list boxes*. (Figure 3.27 shows an example.) To activate the drop-down list box, click the arrow at the right of the box. You can then drag the scroll box to select an item.

To open a drop-down list box from the keyboard, press Alt+Down arrow. Use the up and down arrow keys to highlight the item and press the Enter key.

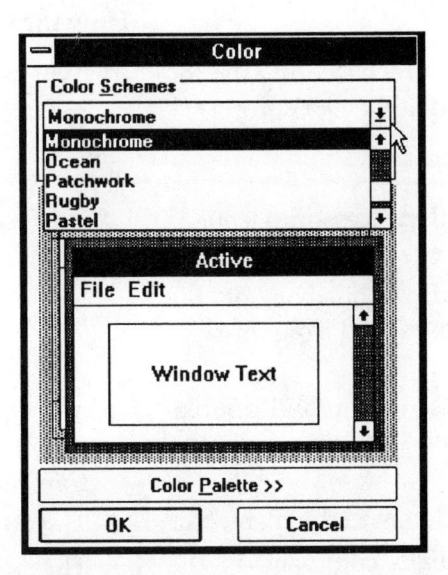

Figure 3.27. A Drop-Down List Box

Closing Dialogs

There are two basic methods for closing a dialog box. If you don't want to carry out the options you've selected, select the Cancel button. To accept the options and carry out the command, select the OK button.

Summary

This chapter completes our examination of the basic techniques for using Windows. You've learned about all of the major interface components, including windows, icons, menus, and dialog boxes. You'll find yourself returning to this chapter whenever you need to brush up on the basic techniques for using Windows.

In the next chapter, you'll use the heart of Windows—the Program Manager.

Exercises

The following exercises are provided to help you practice using the major components of Windows. (They're designed to be used with the mouse.)

What You Should Do	How the Computer Responds
1. Start up Windows by executing the following command at the DOS prompt: WIN	1. Windows loads and you see the Program Manager and Main windows.
2. Double-click on the Accessories icon.	2. The Accessories windows open and a set of application icons appears.
3. Click on the window's title bar, hold the mouse button down, and drag the window to the right.	3. The window moves to the right.
4. Release the mouse button and double-click on the Cardfile icon.	4. The Cardfile application loads and displays a window with the title bar Cardfile - (Untitled).
5. Click on the Card item in the menu bar.	5. The Card menu displays.
6. Select the Autodial... command in the Card menu.	6. The Autodial dialog box displays.

7. Click on the Control menu icon in the upper-left corner of the dialog box.
8. Press Alt+F4.
9. Click on the Use Prefix check box.
10. Click on the Pulse option button in the Dial Type group.

11. Click the Cancel button.

12. Minimize the Cardfile application by selecting the down arrow icon in the upper-right corner.
13. Double-click on the Cardfile icon.
14. Exit Cardfile by selecting the Exit command from the File menu.
15. Point at the left border of the Accessories window.
16. Drag the border to the right.
17. While holding down the mouse button, press the Esc key.
18. Press Alt+F4.
19. Select the Exit Windows... command in the Program Manager's File menu.
20. Select Cancel.

7. The Control menu for the dialog box displays.
8. The Control menu disappears.
9. An X appears in the empty check box.
10. The Tone option button becomes deselected, and a black dot appears in the Pulse option button. Recall that only one option button can be selected in a group.
11. The dialog box disappears, and the options you selected aren't saved.
12. The Cardfile application turns into an icon, and control returns to the Program Manager.
13. The Cardfile application restarts.
14. Cardfile terminates; control returns to the Program Manager.
15. The mouse cursor changes to a two-headed arrow.
16. The size of the window changes.
17. The window returns to its previous size.
18. The Accessories window closes.
19. The Exit Windows dialog box is displayed.
20. Control returns to the Program Manager.

What If It Doesn't Work?

1. If Windows doesn't load, make sure it's been installed correctly.
2. If the Accessories icon doesn't appear, make sure that these applications were installed by the installation process (see Chapter 2).

4

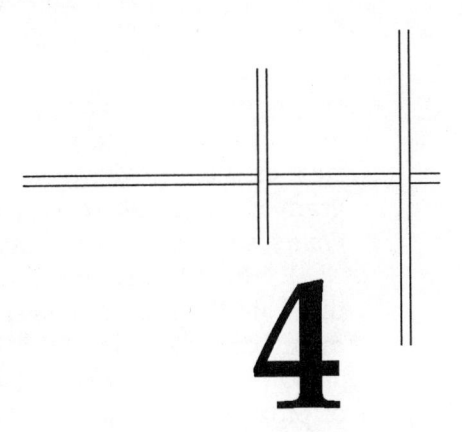

Introducing the Program Manager

Now that you've successfully installed Windows and learned the basic skills for controlling the program, you're ready to put it to work. When Windows starts, the first useful window that opens is the Program Manager. You can think of the Program Manager as your portal into and out of the Windows environment.

This chapter explores what the Program Manager can do for you and covers these major topics:

- The basic components of the Program Manager
- How to work with group windows
- How to use the Program Manager's Control menu
- Techniques for using the keyboard and the mouse
- How to use the basic commands provided with the Program Manager
- How to move applications from one group window to another
- How to create group windows
- How to use the Options, Window, and Help menus

The Program Manager—A Close Look

The Program Manager is the heart of the Windows environment. It always appears after you start Windows, and remains in control until you exit the program. The Program Manager allows you to run your applications and to group them. In fact, the Program Manager manages the other applications, such as the File Manager, the Control Panel, and the DOS Prompt. The Program Manager allows you to combine different applications into units called *groups*, so you can easily organize your applications.

Figure 4.1 illustrates how a typical Program Manager window looks. The title bar (Program Manager) lets you identify this window at a glance. The menu bar indicates that this is an application window. Notice that several icons appear in the window, and each of them corresponds to a category or a group of programs. To select a group of programs, double-click on the icon for that group. When you start Windows, you'll see icons for Main, Accessories, and Games. You may also see icons for Windows Applications and Non-Windows Applications, if these program categories were present on your disk when Windows was installed.

When you double-click on an icon in the Program Manager window, a new window appears in front of the Program Manager. This window, called a *group window*, contains the icons associated with the tasks available for that group. For example, if you double-click on the Accessories icon, a new group window called Accessories appears where you'll see icons for applications such as Write, Paintbrush, Terminal, Notepad, Recorder, Cardfile, Calendar, Calculator, Clock, and PIF Editor (Figure 4.2). To select one of these applications, double-click on its icon.

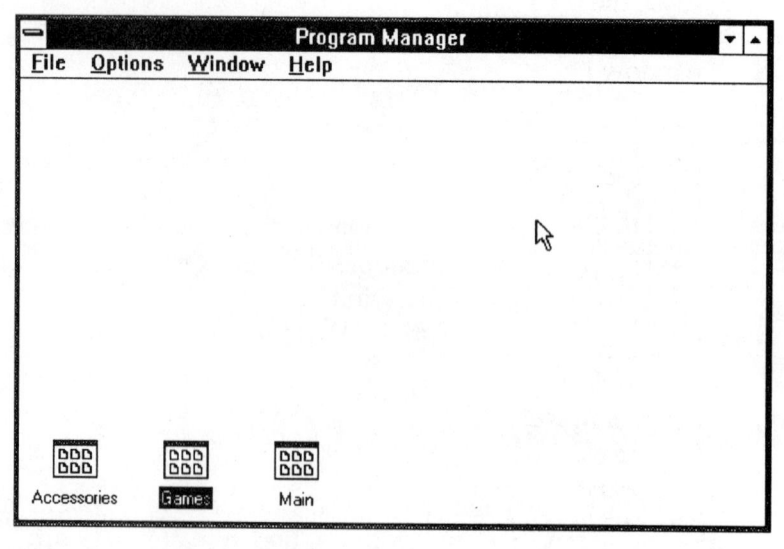

Figure 4.1. The Program Manager Window

Introducing the Program Manager

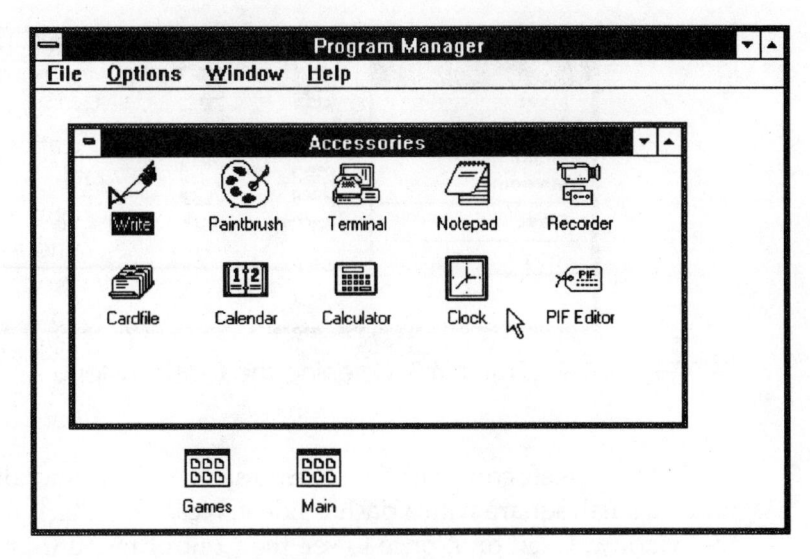

Figure 4.2. The Accessories Group Window

1. Open the Main group window (if it's not currently opened). What do you see?
2. Open the Control Panel application. What happens?
3. Minimize the Control Panel application.
4. Restore the Control Panel application. What happens?
5. Close the Control Panel. What happens?
6. How can you tell the difference between a program item icon and a group window icon?

---

1. *Double-click on the Main group window icon and a window appears with the title bar Main.*
2. *Double-click on the Control Panel icon. The application appears in its own window.*
3. *Click on the down arrow in the upper-right corner. An icon labeled Control Panel displays in the bottom-right corner of the desktop.*
4. *Double-click on the icon.*
5. *Double-click on the Control Panel's Control menu box. Control returns to the Program Manager.*
6. *Group icons are located at the lower edge of the Program Manager. They always look like a window with items inside. A program item icon resides inside a group window, and typically looks like the application it represents.*

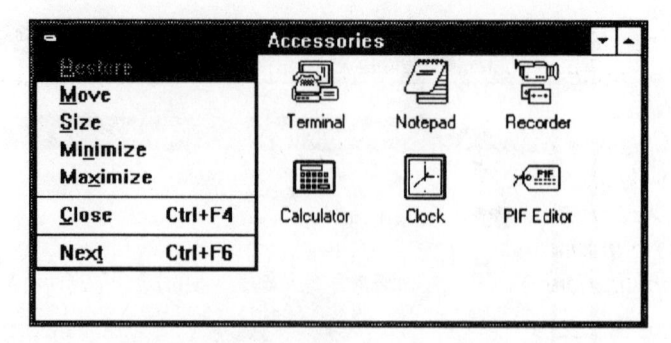

Figure 4.3. Opening the Control Menu

In the top-left corner of the Accessories window (and all other windows), notice a small square with a dash inside it; recall that this is the Control icon for the window. Click on it once to see the Control menu (Figure 4.3). Move the mouse cursor to the line that contains Close, and press the left mouse button once. The Accessories window disappears and you return to the Program Manager window.

Tip For a faster way to close any window that has a control icon, move the mouse cursor to the control icon and double-click on it.

Examine Figure 4.3 again—there are several important lessons to be learned here. The first is that all applications programs that adhere to the Windows presentation standard have a Control menu that provides a consistent way to exit from a window. Also, you can close the window for most applications by pressing Ctrl+F4. (This can be useful if your mouse is not working properly.) The other typical commands on the Control menu include Restore, Move, Size, Minimize, Maximize, and Next.

1. True or false? The Program Manager window is an application window.
2. Which window appears in the Program Manager when Windows first starts?
3. Select the Minimize command in the Program Manager's Control menu. What happens?
4. Which type of window is a group window: an application window or a document window?
5. How are group windows different from other windows?

1. True; however, keep in mind that the Program Manager serves as a shell to manage the group windows such as Main, Accessories, and Windows Applications.
2. Main.
3. Windows converts the application to an icon, and places it at the bottom of the desktop.
4. Document window.
5. Group windows organize application icons, instead of simply displaying data. The applications stored in group windows can be launched from the Program Manager.

A Closer Look at Group Windows

The more you work with the Program Manager, the more you'll appreciate the flexibility and usefulness of group windows. You can perform these and other operations with group windows:

- Move application icons from one group window to another.
- Shrink a group window to an icon.
- Create and delete group windows.
- Change the contents of a group window.
- Edit group window titles.
- Control how group windows are displayed.

Each group window contains a set of applications represented by icons. These icons are also called *program items*. When an icon from a group is selected by double-clicking on it or by highlighting it and pressing the Enter key, Windows immediately launches the application associated with that icon. Double-click on the Control Panel icon in the Main group window, and notice that the Control Panel starts up.

The three main menus provided with the Program Manager—File, Options, and Windows—are always available to help you control your group windows and the program items stored in the group windows. With a few commands, you can perform a variety of operations.

1. What is the difference between group windows and group icons?
2. True or false? Each group window has its own Control menu.
3. Open the Main group window (if it's not currently open). Try to move the window outside the Program Manager window. What happens?
4. True or false? A group icon can be moved outside the Program Manager.

5. Close the Main group window by selecting the Close command from its Control menu. What happens to the window?

---

1. *Group windows are document windows managed by the Program Manager, and contain icons that start up applications. Group icons are minimized group windows, and display at the bottom of the Program Manager window.*
2. *True.*
3. *Windows won't let you move a group window outside the Program Manager.*
4. *False.*
5. *The window closes, but it doesn't completely disappear like other document windows because Windows converts the closed group window to an icon.*

Working with the Keyboard and the Mouse

Windows allows you to perform all Program Manager-related commands, such as creating and deleting group windows, moving and copying icons between groups, and starting applications, from the keyboard. Let's say that when the Program Manager window appears, you decide to edit a letter using the Write program. To do so, you must activate the Accessories icon via the keyboard through the Window pull-down menu.

You can activate the Window pull-down menu from the keyboard in several ways. Press the Alt key on your keyboard, and notice that the File keyword on the Menu bar becomes highlighted. Now press the right arrow key once, and the highlight moves to the Options keyword. A second press of the right arrow key highlights the Window keyword; press the left arrow key to move the highlight in the opposite direction. When a keyword on the menu bar is highlighted, press the Enter key to display the pull-down menu for that keyword.

A second way to activate a pull-down menu is to press the Alt key and the Spacebar at the same time. The File menu expands, and you can use the left and right arrow keys to select other menus. (These menus automatically expand when their associated keyword is highlighted.)

A third method for selecting a pull-down menu is to press the Alt key and the key for the underlined letter in the keyword. For example, press the Alt key and the W key at the same time to select and expand the Window pull-down menu.

When a pull-down menu appears, you can select a command by scrolling the highlighted bar up and down, using the up and down arrow keys. When

Introducing the Program Manager

the desired option is highlighted, press the Enter key to activate it. A second way to select an option is to use the short-cut letter or number. The short-cut characters are underlined in each selection in the menu. For example, the Window menu in Figure 4.4 shows numbers in front of each option associated with an icon in the Program Manager window. In this case, press the number 1 to automatically highlight the Accessories option, and press the Enter key.

1. Which keys activate the Graphics window from the Program Manager's Window menu?
2. What happens if you press Shift+F4?
3. Press the Enter key inside the Program Manager Window. What happens?
4. True or false? Pressing Alt+A brings up information about the Program Manager.

1. *Alt+4.*
2. *Your windows display in a tile format.*
3. *The New Program Object dialog box displays.*
4. *True.*

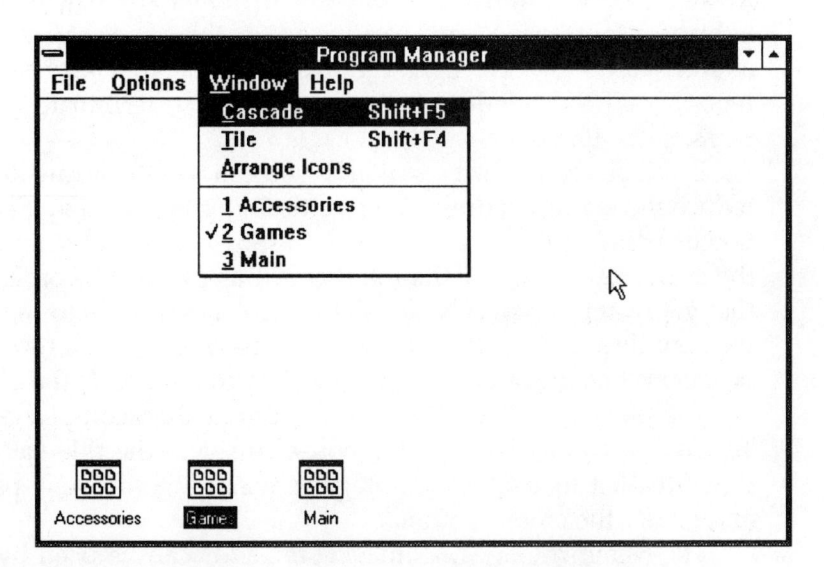

Figure 4.4. Using the Window Menu

If you decide at any time that you don't want to use a particular menu, you can make the pull-down window disappear by simply pressing the Alt key. (This is equivalent to moving the mouse cursor to a location away from the menu keywords and pressing the left mouse button.)

If you're using the mouse, you can activate a pull-down menu by moving the cursor on top of the desired keyword and clicking once. Select an option in the pull-down menu by moving the cursor over the desired option and clicking on it once.

Control Menu Options

Earlier in this chapter, we mentioned the commands in the Program Manager's Control menu: Restore, Move, Size, Minimize, Maximize, Close, and Next. Now we'll discuss these commands in more detail.

The Restore command is used by both keyboard and mouse users to resize a window to its normal size. If the window is an icon, the Restore command expands it into a full window. (The physical size of the window, and the visibility of icons in the window, depend upon the sizing information and other options that were in force when the window was reduced into an icon.) If the window had been expanded to take up the full screen, it's reduced to its normal size, so that other objects can be seen behind it.

The Move and Size commands are exclusively for keyboard users. If the Move option is confirmed by pressing the Enter key when the option is highlighted, a four-headed arrow appears on the screen. Move the window to another part of the screen via the arrow keys on your keyboard. When you've repositioned the window to the new location, terminate the command by pressing the Enter key.

If you select the Size command, you can use the arrow keys to expand or reduce the entire window either vertically or horizontally. Select the Size option by pressing the Enter key when the Size command is highlighted, and use the arrow keys to move the four-headed arrow to the border of the window that you want to move. Next use the same arrow keys to move the border in the new direction. (A low-intensity outline indicates the new location for the border.) When the outline reaches the desired size, press the Enter key.

The Move and Size operations are also easily accomplished with a mouse. To move a window, move the mouse cursor to the title bar, press and hold down the left mouse button, drag the window to the new part of the screen and release the mouse button.

The Minimize and Maximize commands can be used by both keyboard and mouse users to control window size. The Minimize command always reduces a window to an icon. Conversely, the Maximize command always expands a window to its maximum size.

The last two options in the Control menu are Close and Next. The Close command closes the window entirely. The Next command is used to move to other open applications and icons, and is only available when the current application is a document window.

1. Open the Control menu.
2. Activate the Move command.
3. Move the window to the right and down using the keyboard.
4. Anchor the window.

1. *Click on the Control menu icon, or press Alt+Spacebar.*
2. *Click on the Move option, or press Alt+M.*
3. *Press the right arrow key a few times, and then press the down arrow key.*
4. *Press the Enter key.*

Working with the Menu System

Earlier in this chapter, we introduced the basic commands for activating some of the pull-down menus on the menu line of the Program Manager. We'll look more closely now at the options available via the Menu bar.

The File Menu

The first keyword on the Menu bar is File. This pull-down menu provides access to the commands New, Open, Move, Copy, Delete, Properties, Run, and Exit Windows. All of these options (except the last one) are provided to help you manage group windows and program items. You can perform several major operations from this menu:

- Create and delete groups (New and Delete)
- Change the contents of a group (Copy and Move)
- Run an application (Run)
- Add a new application (program item) to a group window
- Select an icon for a group item (Properties)
- Associate a DOS filename with an icon.

The New Command

The New command performs two important operations: it creates a new program group or a new program item. (Recall that a program group is a collection of applications that you group together, and a program item is an application that resides inside a group window.) When you select New, a New Program Object dialog box opens (Figure 4.5). This dialog box contains two radio buttons: Program Group and Program Item.

If you select the Program Group option and then click the OK button, the New Program Object dialog box is replaced by the Program Group Properties box (Figure 4.6). Use the new dialog box to name and create your program group. After you create the group, you can add program items (icons) to it.

When you select the Program Item dialog box, the Program Item Properties dialog box appears (Figure 4.7). Use this dialog box to create and name a program item. When you create a program item, you effectively name the icon and specify the application's start-up command. Let's investigate the process of creating program groups and items in more detail.

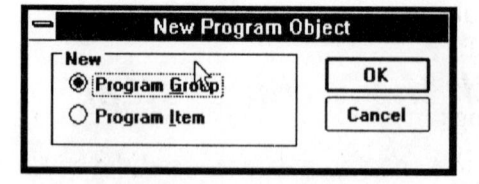

Figure 4.5. The New Program Object Dialog Box

Figure 4.6. The Program Group Properties Dialog Box

Figure 4.7. The Program Item Properties Dialog Box

☑︎ 1. What are some of the program groups provided with Windows?
2. What are some of the program items?
3. True or false? A program item is the same as an application icon.

1. *Main, Games, Windows Applications, and Non-Windows Applications.*
2. *File Manager, Control Panel, Clipboard, Notepad, and Write.*
3. *True.*

Creating a Program Group

When the Program Group Properties dialog box appears, enter a brief descriptive title in the box marked Description. Windows uses this title in the Title bar of the group window, and under the group icon in the Program Manager window. After you enter the description, click on the OK button to close the dialog box and create the new group. If you don't enter a group filename in the other box in the Program Group Properties dialog box, Windows defines one for you automatically. (The default file extension name for a program group file is .GRP.)

After you've created the group, you can transfer program item icons to it by opening the group window and selecting the New option from the File menu entry in that window. When the New Program Object dialog box appears, select the Program Item option and click the OK button. When the Program Item Properties dialog box appears (Figure 4.8), enter a brief description for the program icon on the line titled Description. Next, enter the filename (including the file extension) in the box titled Command Line. If the program isn't located in a directory that's automatically searched by DOS (via the DOS PATH command in the AUTOEXEC.BAT file), then you need to specify the full pathname. For example, if you were installing a program called BLINK.EXE, located in the directory C:\MYSTUFF, you would enter the following in the Command Line box:

C:\MYSTUFF\BLINK.EXE

Figure 4.8. Creating a Program Group

This information tells Windows exactly where to search for the desired program. If you don't know the exact pathname for the application, click on the Browse button to look through the directories. When the dialog box shown in Figure 4.9 displays, you can select a directory and a filename. After you've filled in both boxes in the Program Item Properties box, click on the OK key to complete the operation. The application is now available as an icon within the group icon.

---

1. Create a program group named Database.
2. What happens after you create the program group?
3. What happens if you leave the Group File text box blank when you create a program group?
4. True or false? If you include your own group filename, it should have the extension .GRP.

---

1. *Select the New command from the File menu. Select the Program Group radio button in the New Program Object dialog box and click OK. Type in the name Database in the Description text box. Click the OK button in the Program Group Properties dialog box.*
2. *The new group window appears in the lower-right corner of the Program Manager's window.*
3. *Windows automatically provides the necessary filename and assigns it the extension .GRP.*
4. *True.*

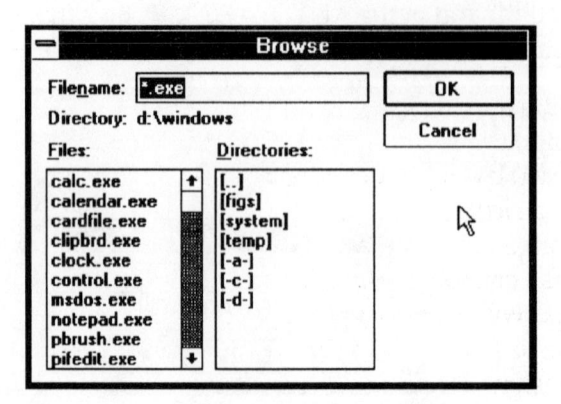

Figure 4.9. The Browse Dialog Box

Introducing the Program Manager

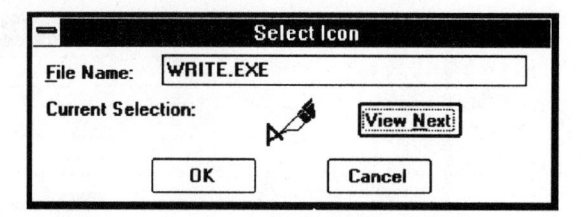

Figure 4.10. The Select Icon Dialog Box

Creating a Program Item

To create a new program item, follow these steps:

1. Select the New command from the Program Manager's File menu.
2. Select the Program Item radio button in the New Program Object dialog box.
3. Include a description for the program item in the Description text box.
4. Type the name of the DOS file to be associated with the program item in the Command Line text box. Remember that when you later double-click on the program item icon, the file associated with the icon is executed by the Program Manager.
5. Select the OK button to create the program item.

After you complete these steps, the Program Manager automatically selects an icon for your new program item and places the icon in the current group window. You can also choose an icon by selecting the Change Icon... button in the Program Item Properties dialog box which displays the Select Icon dialog box (Figure 4.10). Notice that the dialog box displays the icon currently associated with the program item. To select a different icon, keep pressing the View Next button until you get the icon that you want.

---

1. Create a new program item called Editor.
2. Assign the program item to the file WORD.EXE.
3. View the icon that is associated with the program item.
4. Which icon displays?
5. Change the icon to the Text icon.
6. Finish creating the icon.
7. What will happen if you now double-click on the new icon?
8. True or false? You can use the Browse button to locate a file and a directory to assign to a new program item.

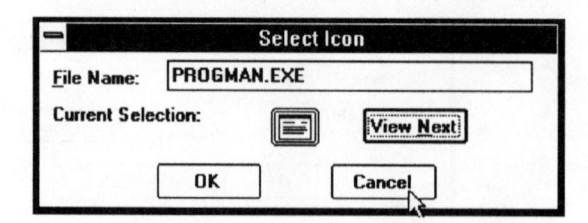

Figure 4.11. Selecting the Text Icon

1. *Type the name Editor in the Description text box in the Program Item Properties dialog box. (Follow the steps presented in this section to access this dialog box.)*
2. *Type WORD.EXE in the Command Line text box.*
3. *Select the Change Icon... button.*
4. *The DOS icon.*
5. *Keep selecting the View Next button until the Text Icon is displayed as shown in Figure 4.11.*
6. *Select the OK button in the Select Icon dialog box, and select OK in the Program Item Properties dialog box.*
7. *Windows tries to load the program WORD.EXE. If this file isn't in the current directory, or its path hasn't been previously defined by the PATH command, Windows won't find the file.*
8. *True.*

Including a Document with a Program Item

When you enter a DOS filename in the Command Line text box, keep in mind that you can also include a document name. If you use this technique, Windows automatically loads an application in a file when the application starts.

What steps do you take to create a program item named Text Editor that activates the program EDITOR.EXE and loads the text file NOTES.DOC?

First, access the Program Item Properties dialog box. Type Text Editor in the Description text box, and type EDITOR.EXE in the Command Line text box. Type NOTES.DOC in the Command Line text box after the filename EDITOR.EXE, leaving a space between the two files. Select the OK button.

Introducing the Program Manager

Figure 4.12. The Program Item Properties Dialog Box

Editing a Program Item

After you create a program item, you may find that it doesn't do exactly want you want. If you want it to load a different document file or have a different title, for example, select the Properties... command on the File menu. The trick to using this feature is to first select the program item icon you want to change, and then select Properties. As Figure 4.12 shows, this dialog box is the same as the dialog box displayed when you first create a program item. Again, notice that buttons are provided for locating a filename and a directory (Browse) and changing a program item's icon (Change Icon...).

Change the program item called Text Editor so that it loads the file DATA.DOC.

First, highlight the Text Editor icon. Select the Properties... command from the File menu, and change NOTES.DOC in the Command Line text box to DATA.DOC, and select the OK button.

The Open Command

Now that we've covered the basics of creating group windows and program items, let's return to the File menu commands. The Open command is designed mainly for use when a mouse isn't available. If the command is highlighted when you press the Enter key, the group icon with a highlighted description expands into a window. You can also select this command by clicking with the mouse, but, you'll find that it's much easier to open a group window by double-clicking on its icon.

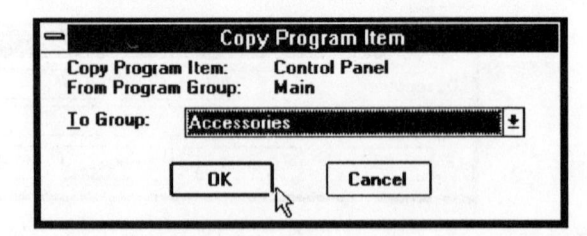

Figure 4.13. The Copy Program Item Dialog Box

The Copy and Move Commands

The Copy and Move commands are typically used to move a program item from one window to another when you're working without a mouse. The Copy command makes a duplicate of the application in the new window. The Move command transfers the copy to the new window without making a duplicate. These operations are extremely useful when you create special groups in the Program Manager.

To use these commands, first select and activate the group from which the application will be copied or moved. Next, use the arrow keys to highlight the object to be moved. Press Alt+F to activate the File pulldown menu. At this point, you can either move the highlight to the Move or Copy option (using the arrow keys) and use the Enter key or press the M key or the C key (for Move and Copy, respectively). These options invoke a dialog box (Figure 4.13) that lets you select the destination group using the up and down arrow keys.

1. Move the program item Clipboard in the Main program group to the Accessories program group.
2. Copy the moved Clipboard program item to the Main program group.
3. Delete the Clipboard program item from the Accessories program group.

1. *Highlight the Clipboard icon in the Main window by clicking on it or selecting it with the arrow keys. Select the Move... command from the File menu. Press Alt+Down arrow to display the list of groups available in the To Group menu (Figure 4.14). Select the Accessories group. (The top of the Move Program Item dialog box displays the program item name and the source group window.) Select the OK button.*
2. *Highlight the Clipboard icon in the Accessories window, and select the Copy... command from the File menu. Press Alt+Down arrow to display the list of groups available in the To Group menu (Figure 4.15). Select the Main group and select the OK button.*

Introducing the Program Manager

```
┌─────────────── Move Program Item ───────────────┐
│ Move Program Item:    Clipboard                 │
│ From Program Group:   Main                      │
│                                                 │
│ To Group:    │Accessories              │ ▼      │
│              │Accessories              │        │
│              │Games                    │        │
└─────────────────────────────────────────────────┘
```

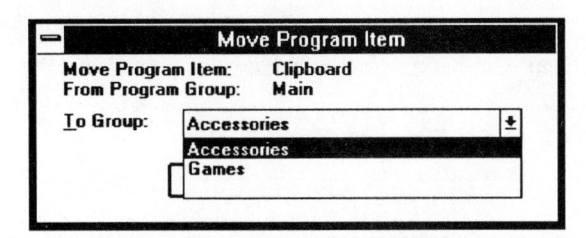

Figure 4.14. List of Group Windows in the To Group Menu Box

```
┌─────────────── Copy Program Item ───────────────┐
│ Copy Program Item:    Clipboard                 │
│ From Program Group:   Main                      │
│                                                 │
│ To Group:    │Accessories              │ ▼      │
│              │Accessories              │        │
│              │Games                    │        │
│              │Main                     │        │
└─────────────────────────────────────────────────┘
```

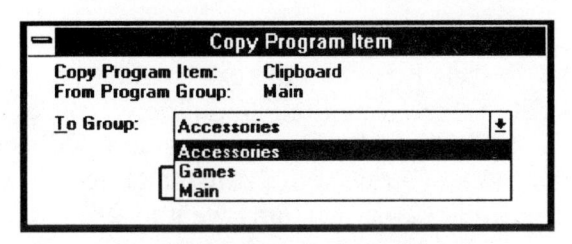

Figure 4.15. List of To Group Options in the Copy Program Item Dialog Box

3. Highlight the Clipboard icon in the Accessories window, and select the Delete command in the File menu.

Moving Program Items and Group Windows with the Mouse

The easiest way to move and copy program items and group windows is to use the mouse. To move a program item to a new group, click on the icon, drag it to the new group, and release the mouse button. If you try to move an icon to a location outside of a program group, the pointer changes to a small circle with a slash through it.

The process of copying an icon is similar to the process of moving one, but, you must hold down the Control key while you drag the icon. After you've copied an icon, you can edit it to create a custom version of the original.

1. Copy the Control Panel icon in the Main program group to the Windows Applications group.
2. What happens if you forget to hold the Control key down when you use the mouse to copy an icon from one group to another?

1. *First, open the Main window. Click on the Control Panel icon, hold the mouse button and the Control key down, and drag the icon to the Windows Applications group.*
2. *The icon is moved, instead of copied.*

Using the Delete Command

The Delete command is activated in a similar way to the Move or Copy options. First, select the item to be deleted by highlighting its description. Next, press Alt+F to activate the File pulldown menu, and use the arrow keys or press the D key to select the Delete option. A dialog box appears (Figure 4.16) to confirm that you want to delete the object. To confirm the delete operation, Press the Enter key. If you don't want to delete the program, press the Tab key to highlight the No button, and press the Enter key.

1. Delete the program item called Text Editor.
2. True or false? When you delete an application item, the application file is removed from the disk.

1. *Open the group window where the Text Editor icon is stored, and click on the Text Editor icon (or use the arrow keys to highlight it). Select the Delete command file from the File menu, and select Yes in the confirmation message box.*
2. *False.*

The Properties Command

As you know, you can select this command to edit a program item. Recall that when you select Properties..., a dialog box appears that lets you do the following:

- Change the name of a program item.
- Change the DOS executable file associated with a program item.
- Change the icon assigned to a program item.
- Include parameters, such as the name of a document file, that you want to load when an application starts.

Introducing the Program Manager

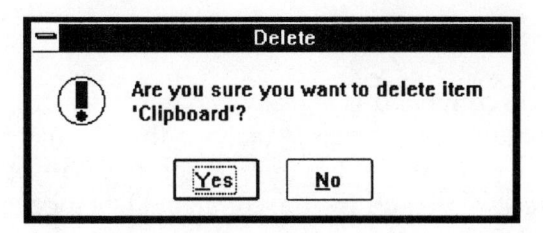

Figure 4.16. The Delete Warning Box

In addition to changing the properties associated with a program item, you can also change the properties of a group window. Highlight the group window icon and select the Properties... command to bring up the Program Group Properties dialog box shown in Figure 4.17. You can change the name of the group window (Description), and the name of the Group File.

Tip If you change the group filename, make sure your new file has the extension .GRP.

1. Highlight an application item and select the Properties... command. Next, select the Browse button to call up the Browse dialog box. What is this dialog box used for?
2. True or false? The text in the Command Line box is treated as a DOS command when an application icon is selected.
3. Which button do you select to change a program item's icon?

1. *It allows you to locate the filename and directory path for the Command Line text box.*
2. *True.*
3. *Change Icon...*

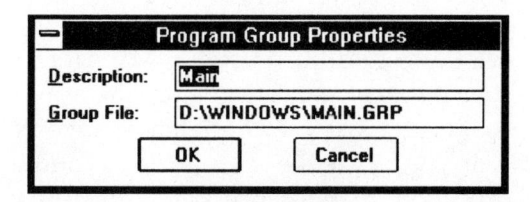

Figure 4.17. The Program Group Properties Dialog Box

The Run Command

The Run command is an easy way for keyboard users to activate a particular application. Press Alt+F to activate the File menu option, and use the arrow keys or press the R key to activate the Run option. A dialog box appears (Figure 4.18), requesting the command line for activating the program. Type in the path information and the full name of the application, and press the Enter key. (To abort this command, press the Tab key until the Cancel button is highlighted and press Enter.)

To use this command, you need to know where the application you want to run is stored on your hard disk. Type the full pathname for the file you want to execute into the Command Line text box. If the Program Manager can't find the file, it provides a warning message.

Activating an Application with the Mouse

The easiest way to start an application is to double-click on its icon. This step tells Windows to execute the command assigned to the application icon.

Tip — To view the command associated with an icon, highlight the icon and select the Properties... command from the File menu.

How can you find out which command is associated with the Cardfile application?

Open the Accessories group window, highlight the Cardfile icon, and select the Properties... command, and the CARDFILE.EXE command appears.

Exiting Windows

To exit windows from the Program Manager, select the Exit Windows... command from the File menu. A dialog box appears asking if you want to exit Windows. You can use the check box to save Windows-oriented changes. For example, if you want the Accessories window to be open when Windows begins execution, then set everything up in the way you want it to appear, select Exit, and set the check box to save changes (using the mouse or the Tab and Enter keys). Then select the OK (or Cancel) button.

Introducing the Program Manager

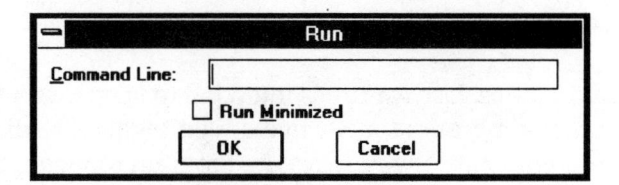

Figure 4.18. The Run Dialog Box

Using The Options Menu

Only two selections are available in the Options pulldown menu: Auto Arrange and Minimize on Use. You can toggle both options between their active and inactive states by clicking on them with the mouse, or using the arrow keys and the Return key. Let's take a closer look.

Auto Arrange

When the Auto Arrange option is active, Windows rearranges the icons within groups to fit in the window. For example, if you expand the Accessories icon into a window and resize it to be taller and narrower, Windows automatically rearranges the icons to fit (if possible), as shown in Figure 4.19.

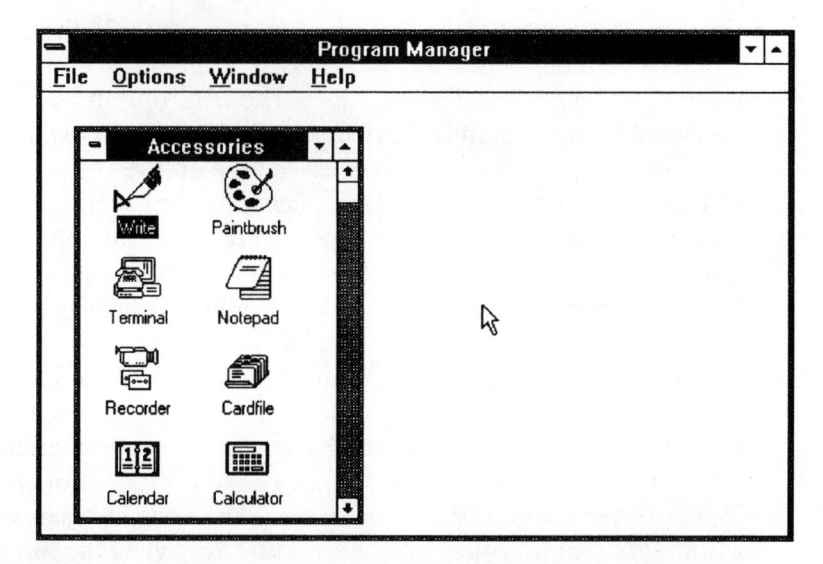

Figure 4.19. Using the Auto Arrange Option

Minimize on Use

The Minimize on Use feature is intended to keep the Program Manager visible when other applications are active. If you toggle this feature to the active state, Windows automatically reduces the Program Manager to an icon and places it along the bottom of the screen with the other minimized icons. To move back to the Program Manager, you can simply click on the minimized icon to expand the window. If this option is inactive and you want to return to the Program Manager, you need to either move your current application so that you can see enough of the Program Manager to activate it, or else minimize your current task to expose the underlying Program Manager window.

The Window Menu

The primary mission of the Window pulldown menu is to provide access to the various applications groups when a mouse isn't available. It's also used for activating certain operating characteristics of the Windows environment.

Cascade and Tile Options

These two options can be thought of as complements of each other. Whenever you activate the Cascade option via the pulldown menu or by pressing Shift+F5, the group windows currently open within the Program Manager are arranged so that the active window is in front and the title bars of the others are visible behind it (Figure 4.20). The Tile option (selected through the pulldown menu or Shift+F4) attempts to size the open windows so that they're positioned side by side (Figure 4.21). These options can't be toggled options, and they occur only when manually activated. For example, if you expand two icons in the Program Manager window and then press Shift+F4, the windows are placed side by side. If you now expand a third icon, it covers at least part of one of the previous windows. Pressing Shift+F4 again compels Windows to split the active area into three sections.

The Arrange Icons Command

This Arrange Icons command instructs Windows to arrange the group icons within Program Manager so that you can easily view as many as possible. This option comes in handy when you need to resize the Program Manager

Introducing the Program Manager

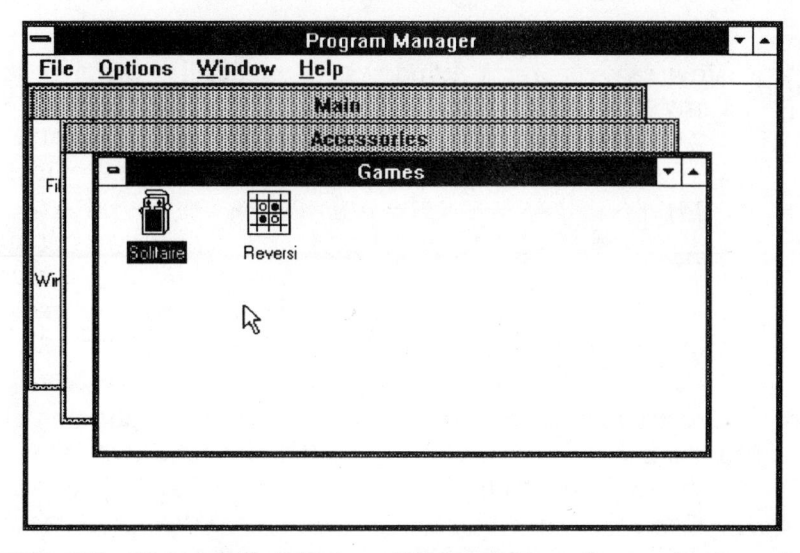

Figure 4.20. Windows Displayed in a Cascade Format

window so that it only occupies half of the screen. If the Program Manager window becomes tall and thin, the icons are rearranged one above the other; if the window is sized as wide but not tall, then the icons are rearranged in a horizontal orientation. If the window is too small to show all of the icons, it will show as many as possible.

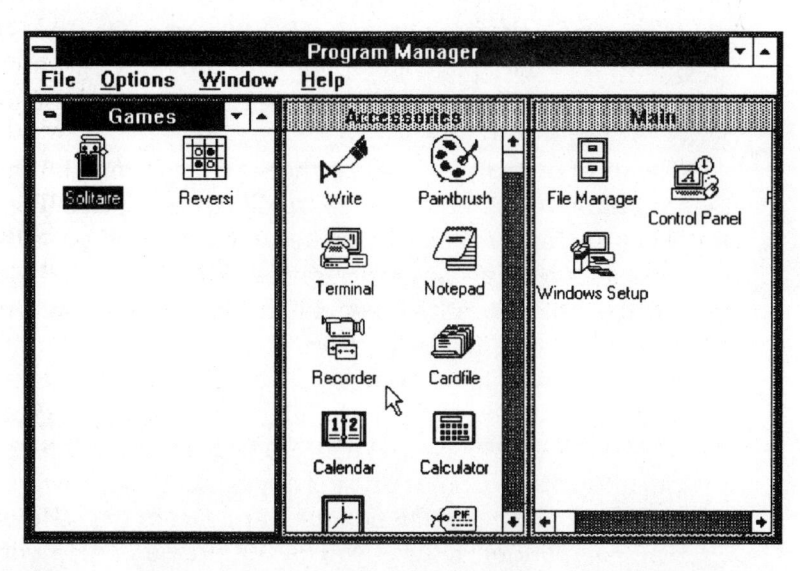

Figure 4.21. Windows Displayed in a Tile Format

> ☑ How can you make Windows automatically rearrange icons each time the Cascade or Tile commands are used to display windows?
>
> *Select the Auto Arrange option in the Options menu.*

Group Selection

Use the Group Selection option to select the application group to be opened. Look back at Figure 4.4 and note that the pulldown menu assigns numbers to each program group. To expand the icon for a given group, press Alt+W to activate the Window pulldown menu, and then press the appropriate number to activate the group. Alternatively, you can use the up and down arrow keys and the Enter key to make the selection.

The Help Menu

Windows provides an online Help system with many useful tips and hints. These can come in handy when you can't remember how to repeat an operation that you performed a few days before.

When the Help menu is expanded (Figure 4.22), it provides seven general categories for Help, plus one option that provides information about the Program Manager itself. All of the Help options support a group of buttons called Index, Back, Browse, and Search.

The most powerful of these is the Search command. When you click on the Search button, a window with two scroll boxes appears (Figure 4.23). Move the scroll bar to quickly highlight the desired topic, and press the Search button to initiate a search of the various Help files. When a list of the matches appears in the lower scroll box, move the highlight to the desired item and click on the Go To button to bring the help information for that topic into view. This is an extremely fast way to find out all of the information about a topic or keyword.

The Index button in the Help window brings up a general index that you can view via the scroll bars. When you find a topic of interest, move the mouse over that topic so that the cursor changes from an arrow to a hand. When you click on the topic, the discussion for it appears in the Help window.

The Back button returns you to the previous help window. The Browse buttons let you move forward and backward within a Help area.

Introducing the Program Manager

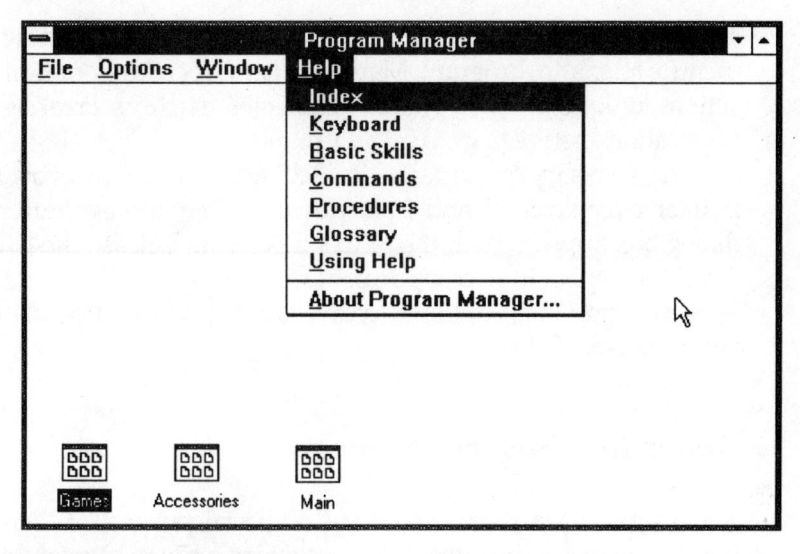

Figure 4.22. Using the Help Menu

Help Menu Options

The Index option in the Help menu opens a scroll box where you can select information about the Program Manager or Windows. The Keyboard option brings up an index of information about controlling Windows with the keyboard and the mouse. Basic Skills displays an index of topics on how to perform rudimentary operations (such as file transfers) in the Windows

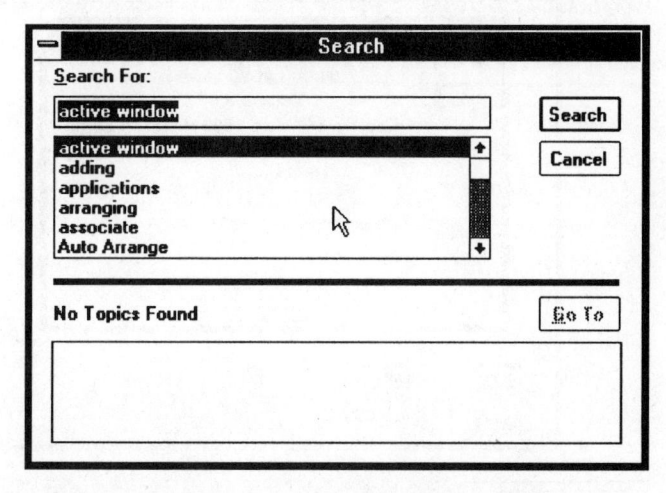

Figure 4.23. Using the Search Dialog Box

environment. The Commands option brings up a window listing all of the menu options in Program Manager. The Procedures option displays a list of actions unique to the Program Manager (such as creating groups, moving applications between groups, and so on).

The Glossary provides a limited list of terms. If you move the mouse pointer over an item and hold down the left mouse button, an explanatory dialog box appears with the term's definition. Release the left mouse button to make the explanation disappear.

The Using Help option displays general information about how to use the Help system.

About the Program Manager

The Program Manager option has a special purpose. When you activate this window, a dialog box opens and provides a range of useful information. First, it indicates which Windows mode is in operation (Real, 286, or 386 modes, see Figure 4.24). The next data item is the amount of disk space available in the dedicated caching file. The last item shows what percent of this dedicated file is available. If your system performance begins to degrade dramatically, bring up this window to ascertain if too many tasks are open for the amount of RAM available. If so, you may need to close some tasks to free up space.

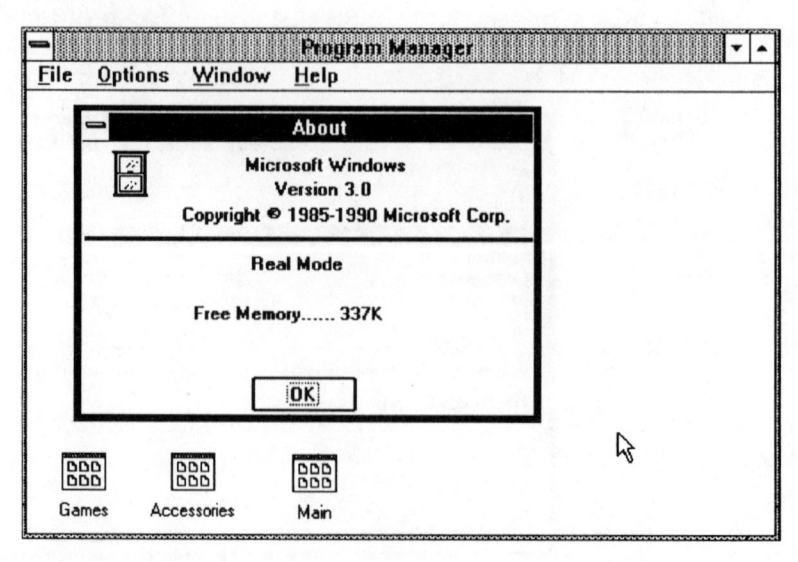

Figure 4.24. The About Windows Dialog Box

Summary

In this chapter you learned about the Program Manager, why it's a key feature in the Windows 3.0 design, and how to use each option available in the Program Manager's Menu bar.

Now that you understand how to open the various group windows, you are probably interested in trying out the applications. The next chapter will take you on a brief tour through some of the built-in applications provided by Windows, illustrating the power of the electronic desktop. The details of each application will be explained in later chapters of the book.

Exercises

The following set of exercises are provided to help you practice using the Program Manager.

What You Should Do	How the Computer Responds
1. Close all of the windows open in the Program Manager.	1. The only window you should see displayed is the Program Manager window.
2. Double-click on the Accessories icon to open the Accessories window.	2. The Accessories window displays, and you see icons such as Write, Paintbrush, Terminal, and so on.
3. Click on the Notepad icon, and try to drag it into the Program Manager's window.	3. Windows won't let you drag a program item into a window that isn't a group window.
4. Click on the Notepad icon.	4. The icon is highlighted.
5. Click on the File item in the menu bar.	5. The File menu opens and displays commands such as New..., Open, Move..., Copy..., and so on.
6. Click on the Move... command.	6. The Move Program Item dialog box displays.
7. Enter the text Main in the To Group text box and click the OK button.	7. The Notepad icon moves to the Main window.
8. Open the Main window, and drag the Notepad icon from this window to the Accessories window.	8. The Notepad icon returns to the Accessories window.

9. Click on the Control Panel icon in the Main window, and select the Properties... command from the File menu.

10. Select the Tile command from the Window menu.

11. Select the Main window as the active window, resize it using the mouse, and select the Arrange Icons command from the Window menu.

9. The Program Item Properties dialog box displays, and the filename CONTROL.EXE is listed in the Command Line text box. This command executes when the Control Panel icon is selected.

10. The displayed windows, Main and Accessories, are tiled.

11. The icons are rearranged in the window.

5

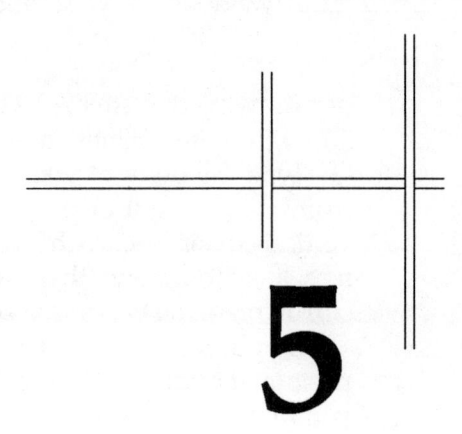

Putting Windows to Work

After seeing how easy it is to use Windows, you're probably eager to put Windows to work. To get you started, this chapter takes you on a brief tour of a few Windows applications. (This is only a small fraction of what Windows can do, but it will get you going.) In this chapter you'll learn how to:

- Create a document with the Write application
- Print a document with Write
- Save a document
- Create indexed cards using the Cardfile application
- Use the Calendar application
- Set an alarm

Writing a Document

Let's assume that you want to write a letter to your congressperson opposing a proposed federal tax on high-fiber cereals. Invoke Windows by typing WIN and pressing the Enter key. When the Program Manager window appears, expand the Accessories icon by double-clicking on it. If you don't have a mouse, press Alt+W to activate the Window menu and then select the Accessories option. When the Accessories window opens, double-click on the Write icon. (On higher-resolution displays, this icon looks like an old-style fountain pen drawing the letter A.) The desktop will look like the one shown in Figure 5.1, with Write – (Untitled) appearing in the highlighted title bar.

Type the body of your letter. Notice that the blinking vertical cursor remains to the right of the last character typed. If you keep typing when the vertical cursor reaches the right-hand edge, Write wraps the text to start on the next line. To remove the character immediately to the left of the vertical bar cursor, press the backspace key.

If you need to add or delete something in the text already on the screen, position the cursor at the desired location using the arrow keys or the mouse. If you locate the mouse cursor within the text area, the cursor changes from an arrow to a pointer that resembles a capital letter I. Move this pointer to the desired location and press the left mouse button once; the blinking vertical cursor will move immediately to that location.

After some typing, your window will look something like the one shown in Figure 5.2 Assume at this point that you need to go back to the top of the letter to add the name and address. Move the blinking cursor to the beginning of the word "Dear" and press the Enter key several times to create new lines ahead of the original text. Place the "I" cursor at the top line using the mouse or the arrow keys, and type the name and address.

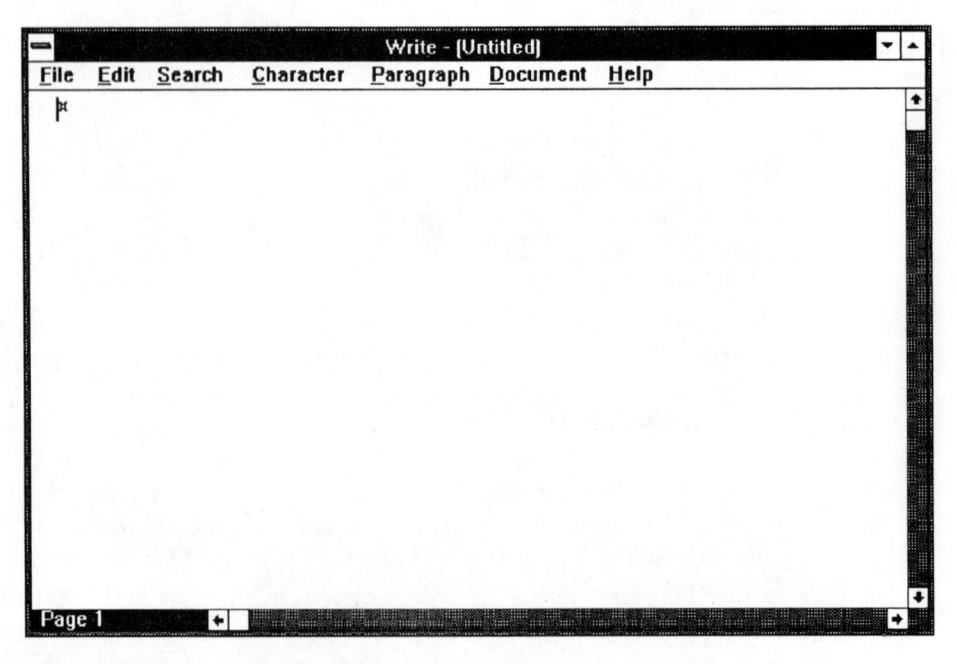

Figure 5.1. The Write Application

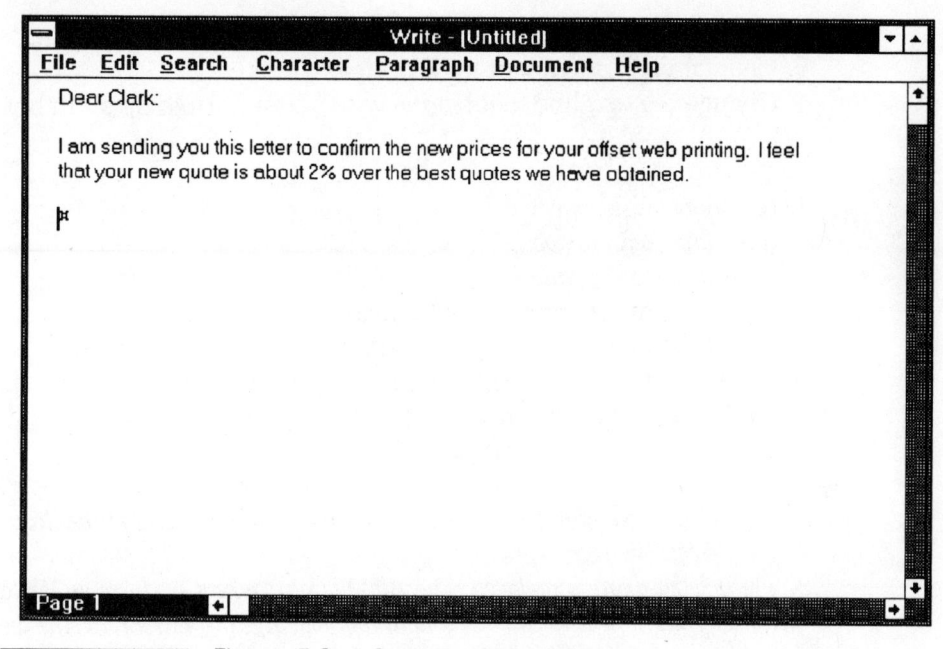

Figure 5.2. A Sample Write Window

1. Position the text cursor at the beginning of a line. What happens to the cursor when you press the following navigation keys?

    (a) Ctrl+Right arrow
    (b) Ctrl+Left arrow
    (c) End
    (d) Home
    (e) Ctrl+End
    (f) Ctrl+Home

2. Position the text cursor at the beginning of a line again. What happens to the cursor when you press the following text-selection keys?

    (a) Shift+Page Down
    (b) Shift+Page Up
    (c) Shift+End
    (d) Ctrl+Shift+End
    (e) Ctrl+Shift+Right arrow

3. Mark a word in your document and press the Delete key to delete the word. Then, press Alt+Backspace. What happens?

4. Change the font type of your document to Helvetica 12 point.
5. Change your document to be double-spaced.
6. Change the text line that begins with "Dear ..." to display in bold.

---

1. (a) *Moves right one word.*
   (b) *Moves left one word.*
   (c) *Moves to the end of the line.*
   (d) *Moves to the beginning of the line.*
   (e) *Moves to the end of the document.*
   (f) *Moves to the beginning of the document.*
2. (a) *Selects text down one window.*
   (b) *Selects text up one window*
   (c) *Selects text to the end of a line.*
   (d) *Selects text from the current cursor position to the end of the document.*
   (e) *Selects the next word.*
3. *The deleted word is replaced. The Alt+Backspace keys perform an undo operation.*
4. (a) *Highlight the entire document by placing the cursor at the beginning and pressing Ctrl+Shift+Home.*
   (b) *Open the Character menu by clicking on the Character item in the menu bar, or pressing Alt+C.*
   (c) *Select the Fonts... option.*
   (d) *In the Fonts dialog box shown in Figure 5.3, select the option Helv for the font style, and the number 12 for the point size.*
   (e) *Click the OK button.*
5. (a) *Highlight the entire document by placing the cursor at the beginning and pressing Ctrl+Shift+Home.*
   (b) *Open the Paragraph menu by clicking on the Paragraph item in the menu bar, or pressing Alt+P.*
   (c) *Select the Double Space option.*
6. (a) *Highlight this line with the mouse or keyboard.*
   (b) *Open the Character menu by clicking on the Character item in the menu bar or pressing Alt+C.*
   (c) *Select the Bold option. The shortcut for performing this operation is to press Ctrl+B.*

Editing Your Document

Imagine that you want to move the first sentence elsewhere in the letter. You can do so in several ways. The obvious way is to delete the text using the

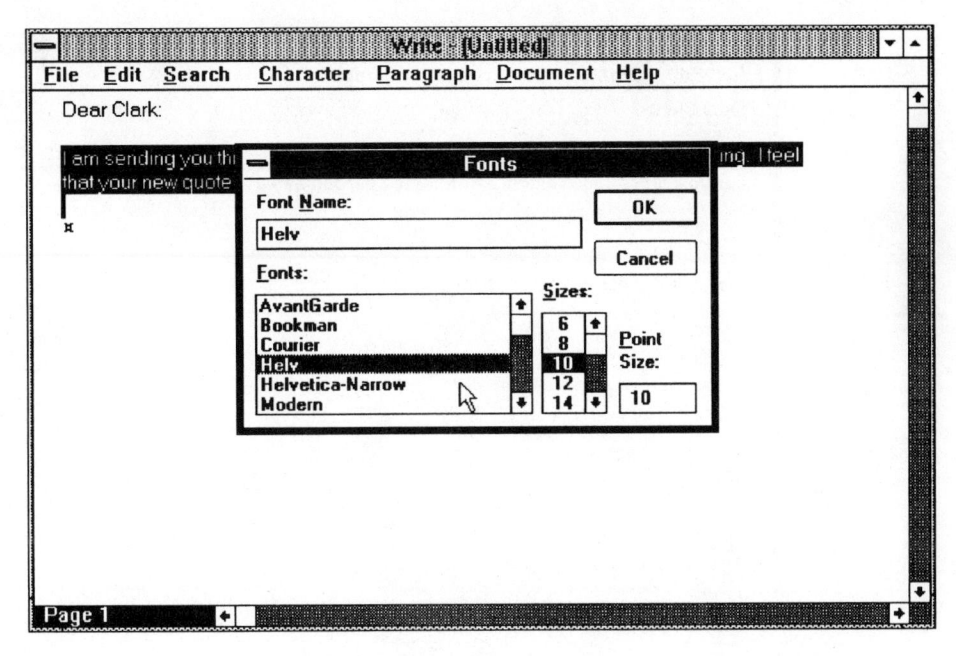

Figure 5.3. The Fonts Dialog Box

backspace key and retype it in the new location. The faster way is to mark the text to be moved, and then use the Cut and Paste Write commands to move it. To do this with the mouse, move the cursor to the beginning of the text to be moved, press down and hold the left mouse button, and drag the mouse across the screen until all of the text to be moved is highlighted. Next, release the mouse button (the text stays highlighted). Figure 5.4 shows a line of text that has been highlighted with the mouse.

After the text is highlighted, move the mouse cursor to the Edit keyword on the Menu bar. Click on the Edit item to activate the pull-down menu (Figure 5.5) and click on Cut to tell Write to cut out this text and place it into a buffer. Now move the mouse cursor to the location where you want to insert the text, and click the left mouse button to move the "I" cursor to that spot. Click on Edit in the Menu Bar again, and now click on the Paste option to paste the previously deleted text at the location of the "I" cursor.

If you don't have a mouse, you can perform the cut and paste operation using the following steps. Move the cursor to the first letter of the section of text that you want to move. Hold down the Shift key while you press the arrow keys to expand the highlighted text to include everything to be moved. Release the Shift key and press Alt+E to activate the Edit pull-down menu. Use the arrow keys to highlight the Cut command, and press the Enter key to activate the option. When the selected text disappears from the screen, move

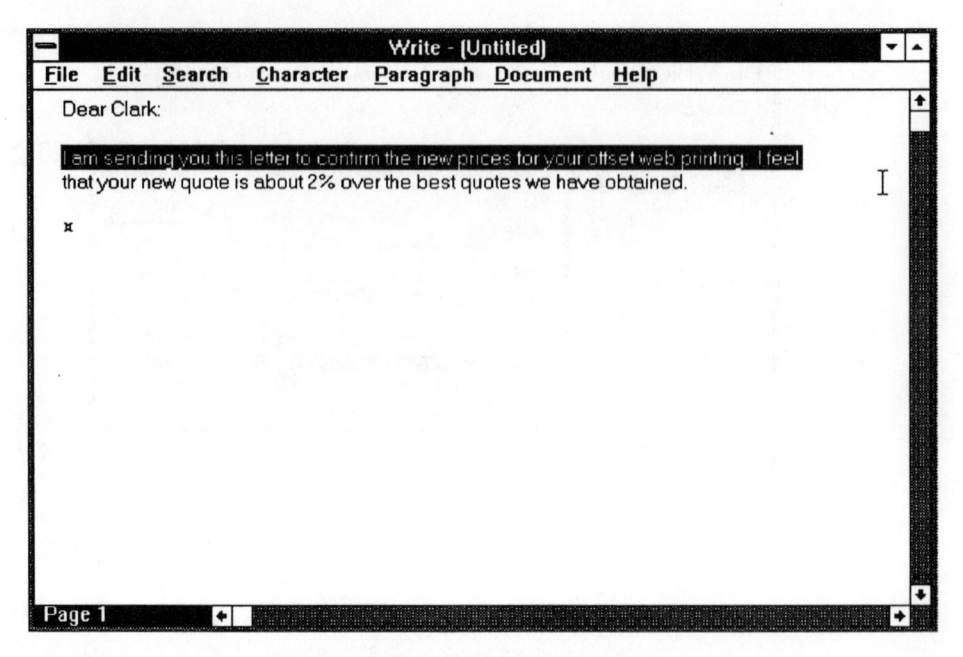

Figure 5.4. A Line of Text Highlighted

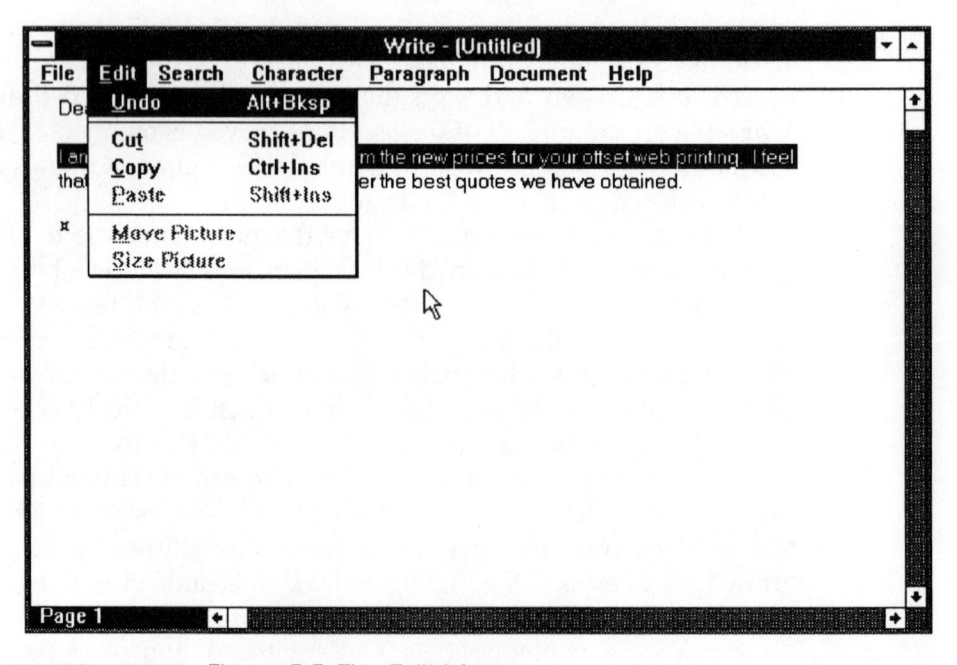

Figure 5.5. The Edit Menu

the cursor using the arrow keys to the spot where you want the text reinserted. Press Alt+E to activate the Edit menu again. This time, select Paste and press the Enter key to paste the deleted text at the new location.

Look closely at the Edit menu and notice the keyboard shortcuts at the right of the Cut and Paste commands. To use these shortcuts, highlight the text to be moved by using the mouse or the Shift and arrow keys. Next, press the Shift+Del keys together to perform the Cut. Move the cursor to the desired position and press Shift+Ins to paste the text.

1. Double-click the mouse on a line of text. What happens?
2. Click the mouse once. What happens?
3. Mark text, copy it by using the Copy command in the Edit menu, and then paste it with the Paste command. What happens?
4. Click the mouse at the beginning of your document, hold down the Shift key, move the mouse pointer down three lines, and press the mouse button. What happens?

1. *The current paragraph is selected.*
2. *The current line is selected.*
3. *The Copy command copies the selected text to the clipboard, and the Paste command pastes a second copy into your document starting at the position of the text cursor.*
4. *The first three lines are selected. The Shift key serves as an anchor so that you can select multiple lines using the mouse without having to drag the cursor.*

Saving Your Document

After you finish typing and editing your letter, you can save it by activating the File pull-down menu (using either the mouse or Alt+F) and selecting the Save As option. A dialog box asks you for the name of the file (Figure 5.6). To store the file in a different directory from the one shown in the dialog box, simply enter a full name (including the DOS path information) in the Filename text box. For example, assume you want to save your letter in the file FIBERTAX.WRI in the directory C:\MISC. (WRI is the extension for files created by the Write program.) First, type the string C:\MISC\FIBERTAX.WRI into the Filename text box so that the dialog box looks like Figure 5.7. When you're satisfied with the contents of the name field, select the OK button (using the mouse or the Tab and Enter keys).

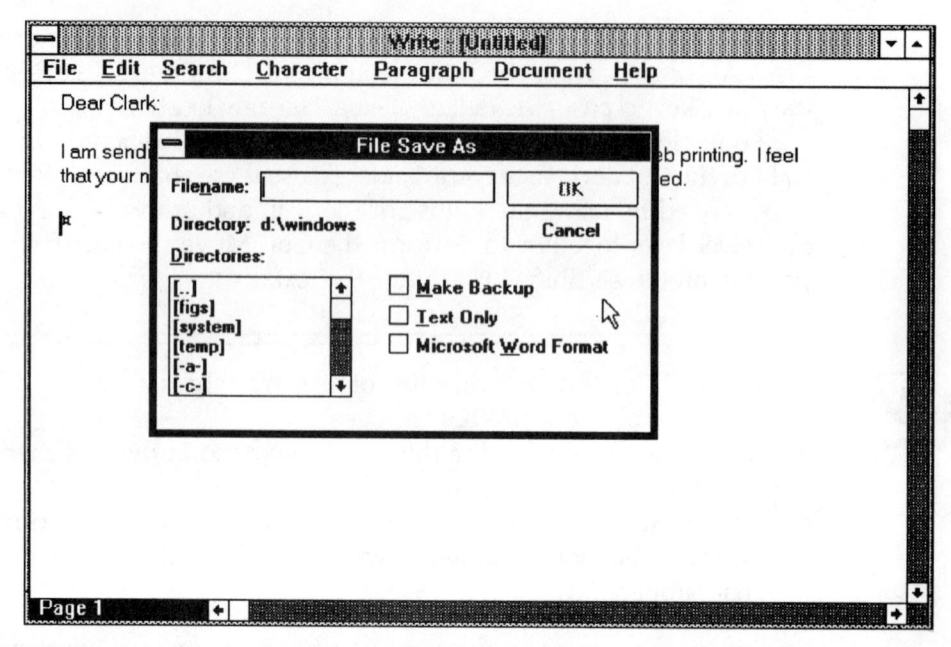

Figure 5.6. Saving a Document

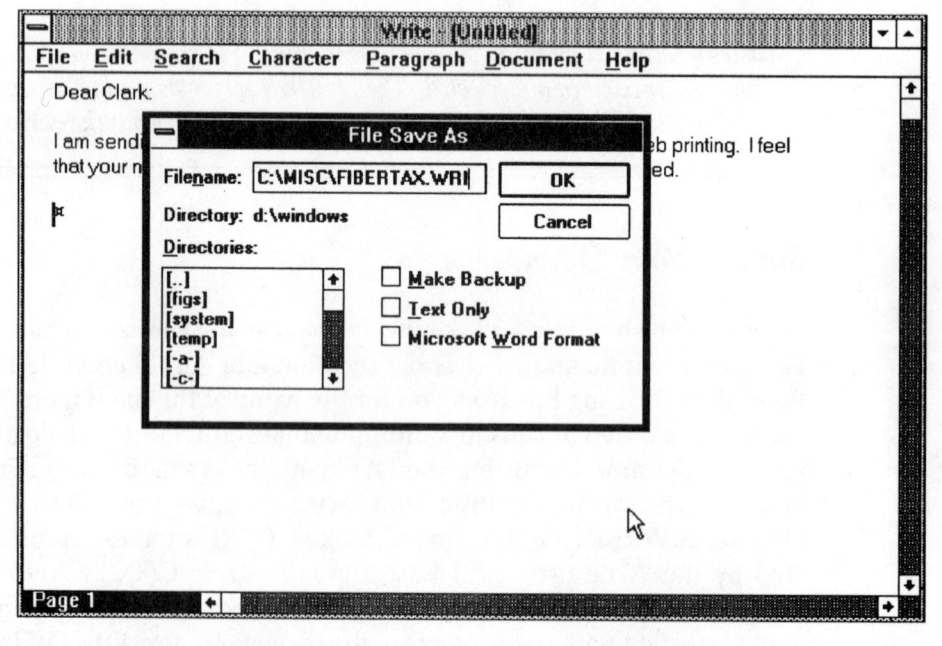

Figure 5.7. Saving the File FIBERTAX.WRI

Look closely at the File Save As dialog box in Figure 5.7 and notice that three check boxes are provided: Make Backup, Text Only, and Microsoft Word Format. Use these check boxes to select the format for saving your file, and to tell Write to make a backup copy of your file whenever you save it. If you select the first check box, Make Backup, Write makes two files for you whenever you save a file. The working file has the extension .WRI, and the backup file has the extension .BKP.

To save your file as a text file, select the Text Only check box before selecting the OK button in the File Save As dialog box. This option allows you to export your file so that it can be read by another word processor, such as WordPerfect or WordStar. If you want to use your file later with Microsoft Word, select the Microsoft Word Format check box.

1. While you're editing a document, open a second document by selecting the New command from the File menu. What happens?
2. What default file format does Write use to save your file?
3. Save the text file created by selecting the Make Backup check box. Which two files are created?

1. *Write displays the warning dialog box shown in Figure 5.8 to tell you that you must save the document you're editing.*

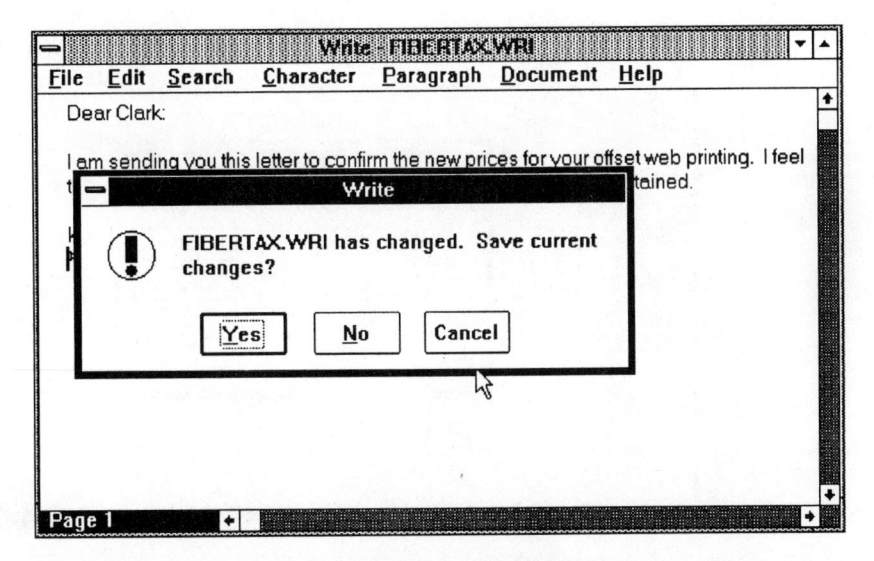

Figure 5.8. The Warning Dialog Box

2. *The Write format, with the file extension .WRI.*
3. *FIBERTAX.WRI and FIBERTAX.BKP.*

Printing Your Document

To print your letter, select the File option from the Menu Bar and then select the Print option to invoke another dialog box (Figure 5.9). In our particular example, use the Tab key until the dashed square surrounds the OK button, and then press the Enter key (with the mouse, simply click on the OK button).

If you want to print multiple copies of your document, enter a number other than 1 in the Copies text box. The Print dialog box also lets you specify a range of pages to print. To use this feature, select the From radio button and then type values into the From and To text boxes. For example, to print pages 2 through 7 of a document, type 2 into the From text box and type 7 into the To text box.

To use a printer different from the currently active printer, or to change the setup of your printer, select the Printer Setup... command from the File menu. The Printer Setup dialog box displays (Figure 5.10) with a list of the available printers. You can change the orientation of your paper, the paper size, the print resolution, and so on by selecting the Setup... button.

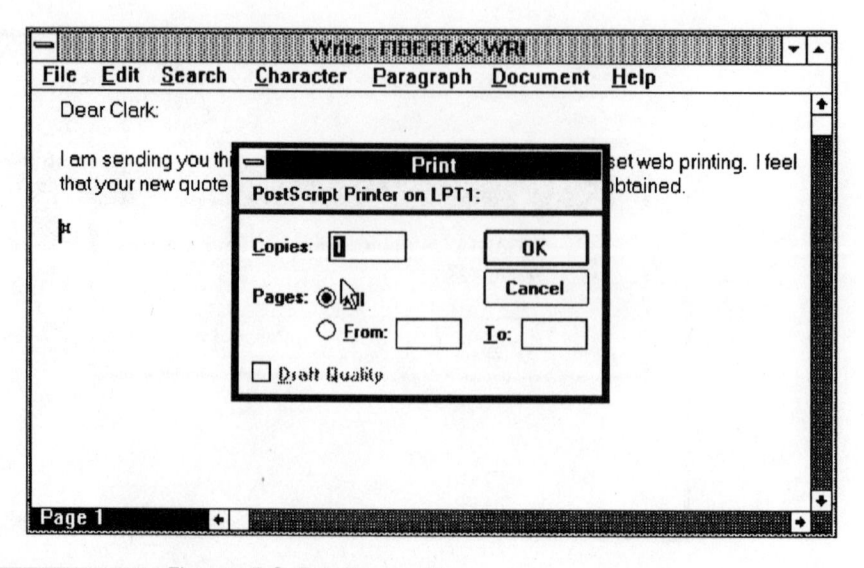

Figure 5.9. Printing a File

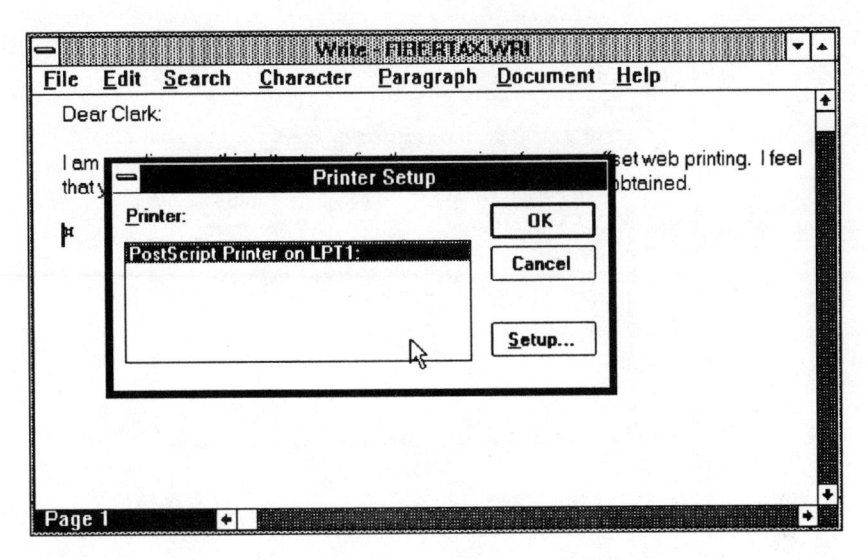

Figure 5.10. The Printer Setup Dialog Box

1. Turn off your printer and then use the Print command. What happens?
2. How can you can stop printing a document after Write starts printing?
3. Change the format of your document to print with 2" margins on the left, right, top, and bottom.

1. *The Print Manager displays a message box to indicate that the printer isn't connected.*
2. *When a document is being printed, a dialog box displays. To cancel your print job, select the Cancel button in this dialog box.*
3. *(a) Select the Page Layout... command from the Document menu to display the Page Layout dialog box (Figure 5.11).*
   (b) Type in the number 2 in the text boxes marked Left, Right, Top, and Bottom.
   (c) Select the OK button.
   (d) Select the Print... command to print your document.

Exiting Write

You can exit the Write program by selecting the File option Exit (by pressing Alt+F then X) or by double-clicking on the Control menu icon at the top-left corner of the Write window. If you've made changes to your document, a

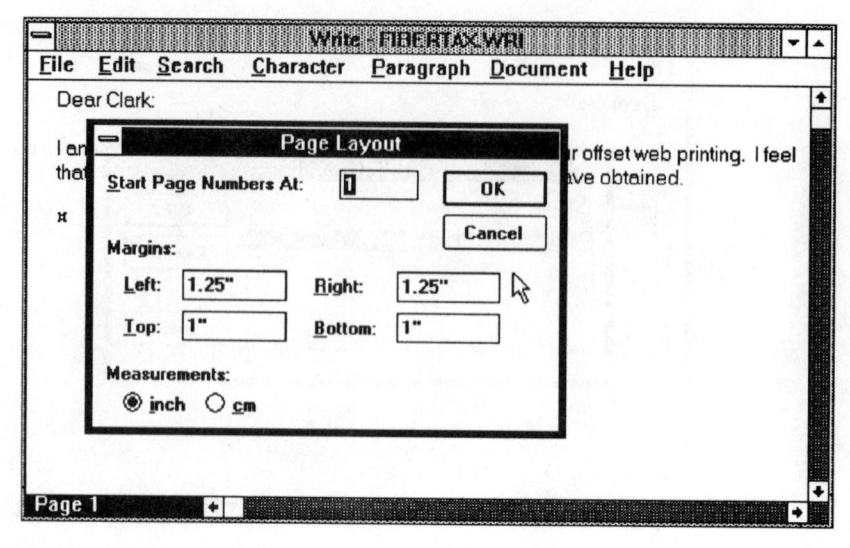

Figure 5.11. The Page Layout Dialog Box

dialog box displays to ask if you want to save your document before exiting. Select the OK button to save your most recent editing changes.

1. Make a few editing changes to your document and then select the Exit command. What happens if you select the Cancel button?
2. Which keyboard shortcut can be used to exit from Write?
3. True or false? After exiting Write, you'll be returned to the Control Panel.
4. True or false? Write allows you to edit multiple documents at the same time.

1. *Write returns you to your document.*
2. *Alt+X.*
3. *False. Windows returns you to the Program Manager.*
4. *False.*

Creating a Small Index File Using Cardfile

Another useful application you'll want to be familiar with is Cardfile. To invoke Cardfile, double-click on the Cardfile icon in the Accessories group (or

Putting Windows to Work

press Ctrl+Tab to select the Accessories group, and then use the arrow keys to highlight the Cardfile name before pressing the Enter key). When Cardfile starts (Figure 5.12), you can either begin a card collection or open an existing card file.

Cardfile opens with a blank card, ready to be filled in. At this point, simply fill in the index line with an appropriate title. The title serves the same function as a tab in a manual card-file system—it lets you quickly browse through a collection of cards.

To fill in the index information, select the Index... command of the Edit pull-down menu located on the Menu Bar (Figure 5.13). (The shortcut for this command is the F6 function key.) A dialog box appears (Figure 5.14) that allows you to enter the card title or index. After you've entered a title, activate the OK window button by clicking the mouse or pressing the Tab+Enter keys. When the dialog box disappears, the card displays with the Index line filled in and the text cursor located at line 1, column 1 of the data area (Figure 5.15).

The data area of a card contains 11 lines of forty characters each. If you type past the end of a line, Cardfile automatically word-wraps to the next line in the same way as the Write application. If you try to type past the 40th character of the last line, Cardfile beeps each time you enter another character. You can use the arrow keys to move the text cursor, and the backspace key to delete characters to the left of the cursor. You can also select text using the mouse or the Shift and arrow keys, and delete the selected text using the Delete key.

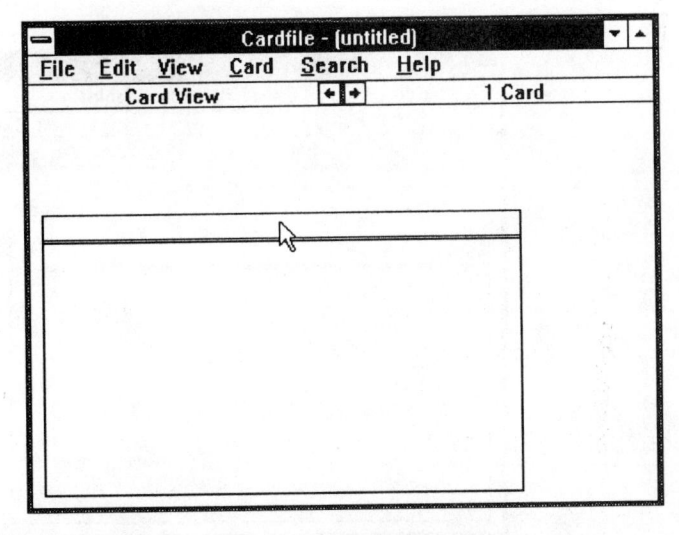

Figure 5.12. The Cardfile Application

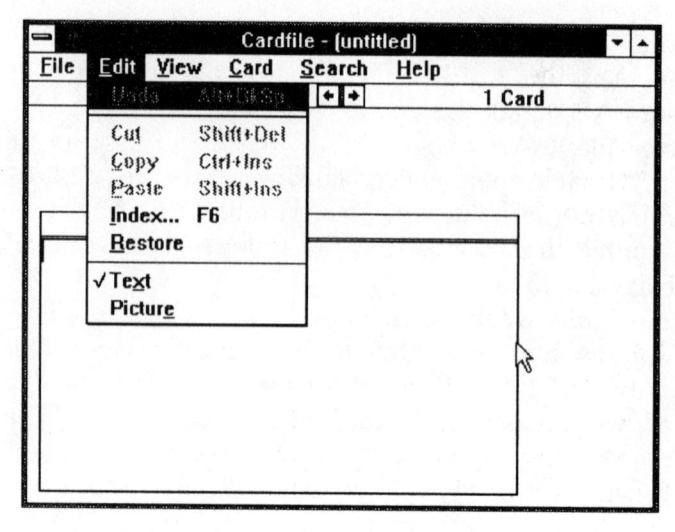

Figure 5.13. The Edit Pull-Down Menu

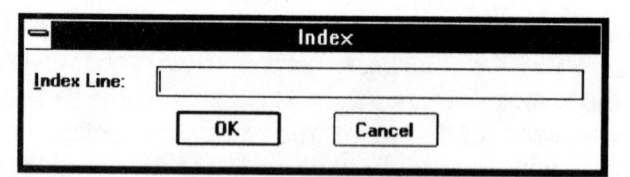

Figure 5.14. The Index Dialog Box

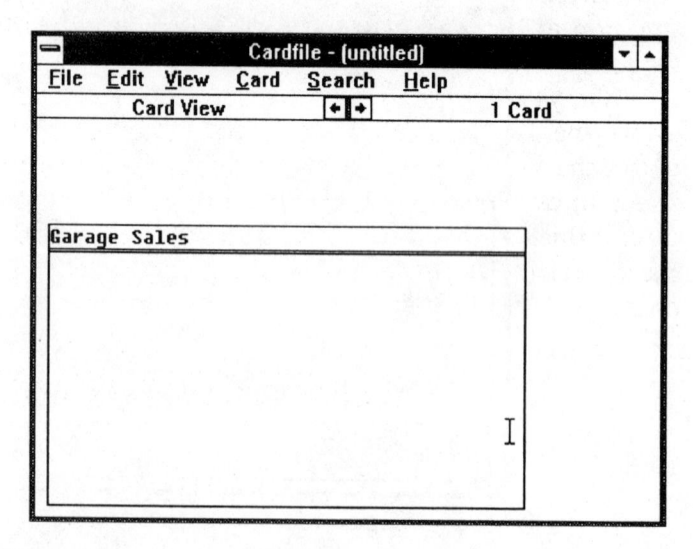

Figure 5.15. Card with Index Line

1. Open the Cardfile's File menu. Which commands are available?
2. What is the shortcut key for adding a card?
3. True or false? You can type in and edit text on a card just as if you were typing in and editing text in a window.
4. True or false? The maximum number of characters that will fit on a line is 40.
5. Open the Edit menu. Which text-editing commands are available?

1. Open, Save, Save As, Print, Print All, Page Setup, Printer Setup, Merge, and Exit
2. F7
3. True
4. True
5. Undo, Cut, Copy, and Paste

Starting a Cardfile

To begin a card file, select the Add... command from the Card pull-down menu on the menu bar. (The shortcut command for this application is the F7 function key.) A window appears, requesting the index label for the new card (Figure 5.16). After you fill in the index field, press the Enter key, or select the OK window button using the mouse. The dialog box disappears and a new blank card appears at the front of the stack. You can now add information to the new card.

After you've accumulated enough cards so that they're not all visible at the same time, you can use several methods to select the next card. One option is to use the View pull-down menu to select a List representation that lets you select the card (Figure 5.17). Another method is to click on the index field of the card. A third method is to click on the left and right buttons on the line below the menu bar. The last method allows you to browse through the entire deck in order.

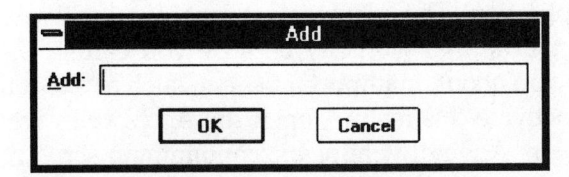

Figure 5.16. Adding a Card

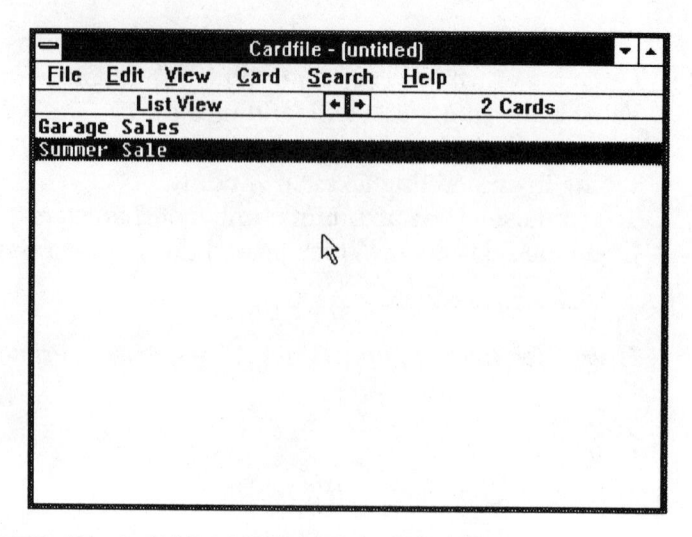

```
┌─────────────────────────────────────────────────┐
│ ═              Cardfile - (untitled)        ▼ ▲ │
│  File  Edit  View  Card  Search  Help           │
│            List View        ← →       2 Cards   │
│ Garage Sales                                    │
│ Summer Sale                                     │
│                                                 │
│                          ▷                      │
│                                                 │
└─────────────────────────────────────────────────┘
```

Figure 5.17. Viewing Multiple Cards

If you decide that a card is no longer useful to you, bring it to the front of the stack and select the Delete option of the Card menu. When a dialog box asks for confirmation, use the mouse or the Tab+Enter keys to select the OK box. The selected card will immediately disappear.

☑ Create a card using the Add... command. Select the card and activate the Duplicate command from the Card menu. What happens?

The card is duplicated.

Setting an Alarm Using Calendar

The third topic we'll explore in this chapter is the Alarm feature of the Calendar application. The Alarm is extremely valuable when you use a computer during the normal workday because you can set an alarm to go off later to remind you about an important event, such as a meeting.

To activate this feature, open the Accessories window and select the Calendar icon. A window appears, containing a scroll box and what looks like a page out of a standard desk calendar (Figure 5.18). The top of the scroll box shows the current time and date. You can add entries to this page in the same

Putting Windows to Work

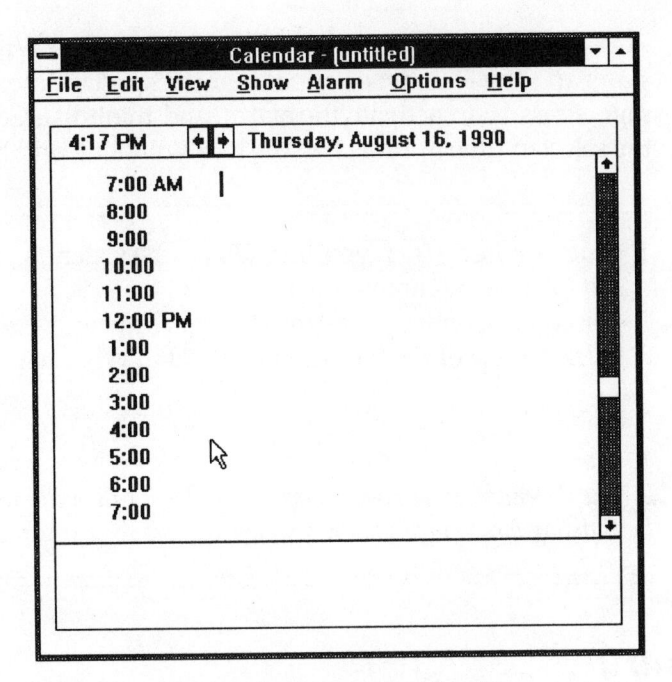

Figure 5.18. The Calendar Application

way you add entries to the cards in the Cardfile application. Just use the arrow keys or the mouse to move the vertical-bar text cursor to the desired location, and enter your appointments for the day. You can also use the left and right buttons at the top of the scroll box to select different days. You can even use the Month option in the View pull-down menu to select a different day or a different month.

For now, we want to set the alarm feature. First, make certain that the time shown in the Calendar window is correct. If it's not correct, exit Windows and use the DOS TIME command to set it to the proper value. (There's a much easier way to correct the time through the Control Panel application in the Main program group. We'll explain this method later.)

Once you're in the Calendar and the proper time is set, move the text cursor to the time of your meeting and type in a brief reminder message. When you're satisfied with the message, press the F5 key to set the alarm. A small icon appears to the left of the time to show that the alarm is set. You can also turn on the alarm by pressing Alt+A to activate the Alarm pull-down menu and then press S (for Set).

If you want to set an alarm for a special time, press the F7 function key to activate the Special Time option of the Options pull-down menu. Enter the desired time and select AM or PM using the A or P key (the default is AM).

Press the Enter key to install the particular time. When the dialog box disappears and the text cursor appears at the special time, enter the reminder message. Press F5 to activate the alarm, and minimize Calendar to an icon. When the selected time approaches, the icon will blink and beep.

1. True or false? When you first call up the Calendar, it's formatted like a page out of an appointment book.
2. Select the Month option from the View menu. What happens?
3. Click on one of the days in the calendar. What happens?

1. True.
2. The Calendar window displays a calendar for the full month.
3. A dialog box named Day Markings appears so that you can mark the selected day.

Summary

You've now been introduced to just a few of the useful applications provided with Windows to give you a glimpse at what is available, and to encourage you to explore.

The next chapter will take you through an in-depth look at the Windows Control Panel, which allows you to customize the appearance of your Windows environment.

Exercises

Use these exercises to practice using the applications explored in this chapter: Write, Cardfile, and Calendar.

What You Should Do	How the Computer Responds
1. Open Write by double-clicking on the Write icon.	1. The Write application starts up with a window that has the title bar Write—(Untitled).
2. Select the Open... command from the File menu.	2. The File Open dialog box appears.

3. Type in the filename FIBERTAX.WRI in the Filename text box. Press the OK button.

4. Change your document so that it starts on page 5. Select the Page Layout... command from the Document menu.

5. Type in the number 5 in the Start Page Numbers At text box. Click the OK button.

6. Scroll to the middle of the document, position the cursor on a line, and press Ctrl+Enter.

7. Highlight the inserted dotted line and press Delete.

8. Select the Ruler On command from the Document menu.

9. Mark your document by moving the cursor to the top and pressing Ctrl+Shift+End.

10. Click on the centered-alignment icon located above the ruler. This icon is the third one from the right.

11. Click on the double-space icon in the ruler bar. This icon is the fifth one from the right.

12. Select the Header command from the Document menu.

13. Type the text Memo #121 into the Header window and select the Return to Document button in the dialog box.

14. Minimize the Write application by selecting the Minimize button in the right corner of the window.

15. Open the Cardfile application by double-clicking on the Cardfile icon.

---

3. The File Open dialog box disappears, the file FIBERTAX.WRI displays in Write's window, and the title bar changes to Write - FIBERTAX.WRI.

4. The Page Layout dialog box displays.

5. The Page Layout dialog box disappears. The page number indicator in the left corner of the Write window changes to read "Page 5."

6. A dotted line is inserted above the cursor to indicate that a page break has been inserted.

7. The inserted page break is removed.

8. A ruler is added to the top of the document displayed in Write's window.

9. The entire document is highlighted.

10. The document is center aligned.

11. The document is double spaced.

12. The Page Header dialog box displays, along with a window containing the title bar HEADER.

13. The document now has a header.

14. Write is converted to an icon on the desktop.

15. The Cardfile application starts up with a window containing the title bar Cardfile - (Untitled).

16. Create a new card by selecting the Add... command from the Card menu.	16. Cardfile displays the Add dialog box.
17. Enter the text for the card's index line in the Add dialog box. Press the OK button.	17. The dialog box disappears and the new card displays.
18. Type in text for the card and highlight the text by selecting it with the mouse.	18. The text is highlighted.
19. Select the Copy command from the Edit menu to copy the selected text to the Clipboard.	19. The text is copied to the Clipboard.
20. Minimize the Cardfile application by clicking on its Minimize button.	20. The Cardfile application is converted to an icon.
21. Reactivate Write by clicking on the minimized icon.	21. The Write application starts up again.
22. Paste the text stored in the Clipboard by selecting the Paste command from the Edit menu.	22. The text copied from the Cardfile application displays in the document window.
23. Exit Write by selecting the Exit command from the File menu.	23. Control returns to the Program Manager.

What If It Doesn't Work?

1. Make sure you look for both the Write and Cardfile applications in the Accessories Group window.
2. If you don't have a mouse, remember that you can perform all of the necessary operations, such as launching applications and selecting commands from the menu bar, by using the keyboard. If you forget how to use the keyboard to perform an operation, review the basic skills presented in Chapter 3.

6

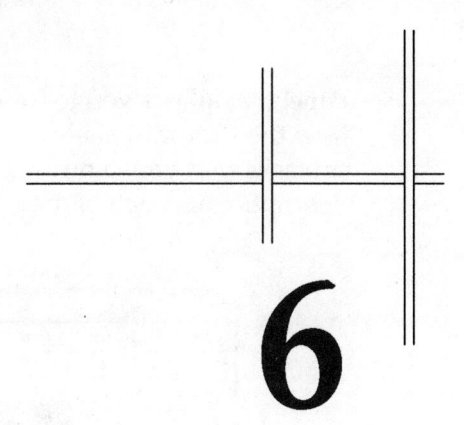

The Control Panel

If you've been wondering how you can customize the Windows environment to suit your own needs, then you've come to the right place. In this chapter, you'll learn how to use the Control Panel to perform setup operations such as:

- Selecting your own colors
- Creating custom colors
- Setting the system time and date
- Creating background screens
- Changing international settings
- Configuring the keyboard and the mouse
- Installing icons
- Selecting and configuring printers
- Configuring ports
- Configuring networks

Overview of the Control Panel

You've probably heard the old joke about three people in one room having four separate opinions; the same principle applies to software users! No matter what colors and basic configuration features a software product has, users will want more. Fortunately, Windows provides a powerful and flexible Control

Panel that allows you to easily customize your own desktop. Figure 6.1 shows how the Control Panel window looks when invoked, and Figure 6.2 lists the subtasks that you can run from the Control Panel. Table 6.1 provides a short description for each of these subtasks.

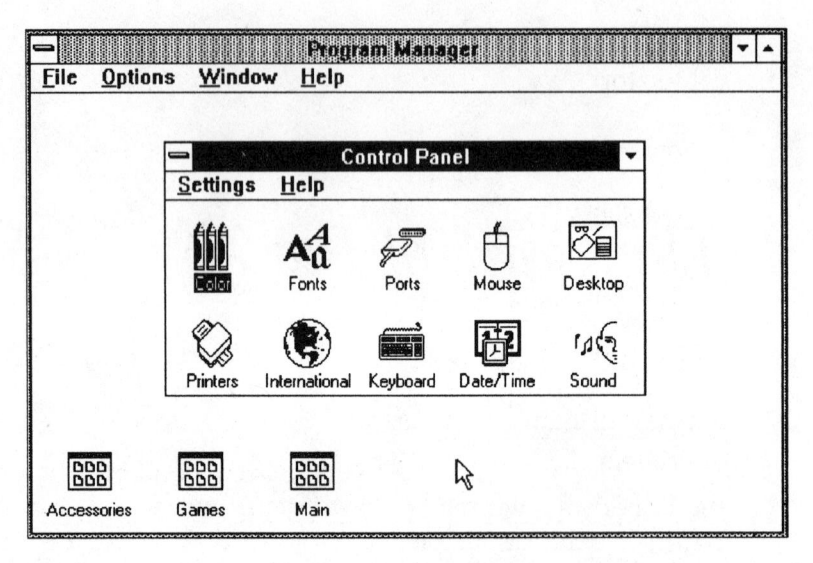

Figure 6.1. The Control Panel Application

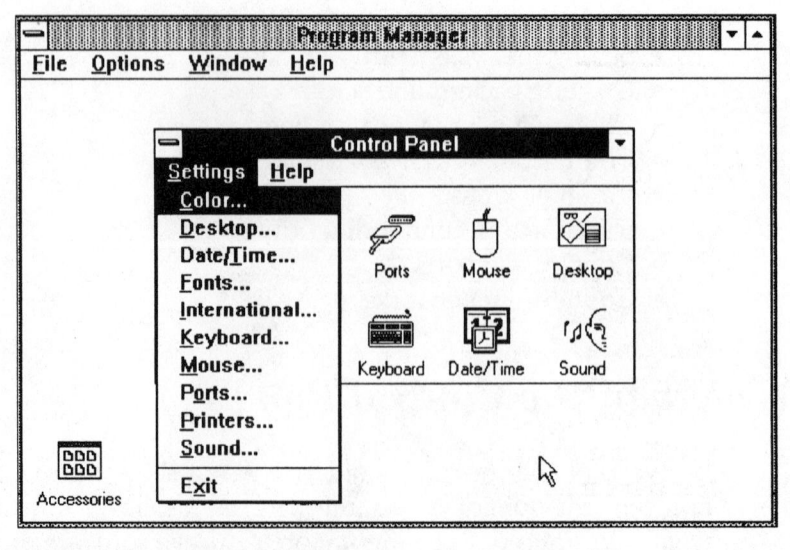

Figure 6.2. The Control Panel Options

Table 6.1. Control Panel Options

Option	Description
Colors	Customizes the colors of the parts of the Windows environment.
Date/Time	Updates the system date and time.
Desktop	Customizes the appearance and the operation of the desktop.
Fonts	Selects or deletes fonts to be used in the Windows environment or with your printer.
International	Customizes country-related parameters, such as currency symbol, date and time formats, and so on.
Keyboard	Adjusts the keyboard autorepeat rate.
Mouse	Adjusts the mouse parameters.
Network	Changes the parameters associated with a PC network (only works if you're connected to a network).
Ports	Sets the parameters associated with each I/O port.
Printers	Updates/adds/deletes the installation information associated with a printer.
Sound	Enables or disables the warning tone.
386 Enhanced	Adjusts the percentage of time devoted to foreground/background tasks, and controls how these tasks share peripheral devices (only available when running Windows in 386 enhanced mode).

Starting the Control Panel

Before you can customize your Windows environment, you need to learn how to start the Control Panel. Because this tool is a Windows application, you can start it by opening the Main window group and double-clicking the Control Panel icon. If you don't have a mouse installed, highlight the icon and press the Enter key.

When the Control Panel window appears, it displays a set of icons that you'll use to change Windows settings. If you're running Windows in 286 standard mode, you'll see 10 icons. If you're running the 386 Enhanced mode, 11 icons are provided. (The extra icon controls the 386 Enhanced settings.) You'll also see one extra icon if you're running Windows on a network. This extra icon, called Network, allows you to change network settings.

Tip | Keep in mind that the icons correspond to the commands provided in the Control Panel's Settings menu. You can easily set configuration options using the mouse or the keyboard.

Start up the Control Panel by double-clicking on the Control Panel icon.
1. Double-click on one of the configuration icons, such as Colors. What happens?
2. Get help information for the Control Panel.
3. Which command is used to exit the Control Panel?
4. True or false? The Control Panel is the only application available for changing hardware default settings.

---

1. *A dialog box displays with the name of the setting option, so that you can change the configuration options. For example, if you double-click on the Color icon, the Color dialog displays.*
2. *Click on the Help menu item or press Alt+H.*
3. *The Exit command in the Settings menu.*
4. *False. The Windows Setup application is provided to set up hardware such as the monitor, the keyboard, and so on.*

Selecting Colors

When you activate this task (the easiest way is to double-click on the crayons icon), a window appears (Figure 6.3) that contains several buttons. The top of the window contains a pull-down scroll box inside a box called Color Schemes. When you click on the scroll box containing the down-arrow (or press Alt and the down arrow), it expands into a scroll box that shows the color combinations provided by Windows (Figure 6.4). Use the scroll bar with the mouse to find the color scheme you want, and click on the name to see it demonstrated on the Windows minienvironment at the center of the window.

If you don't have a mouse, you may find it easier to view the options by simply pressing the down arrow key. Each time you press this key, the next available color scheme is demonstrated in the minienvironment, and the name of the option set appears in the one-line scroll box. When you've viewed the available options, you can work your way back up the list using the up arrow key until you return to the default scheme. If you prefer one of the other color

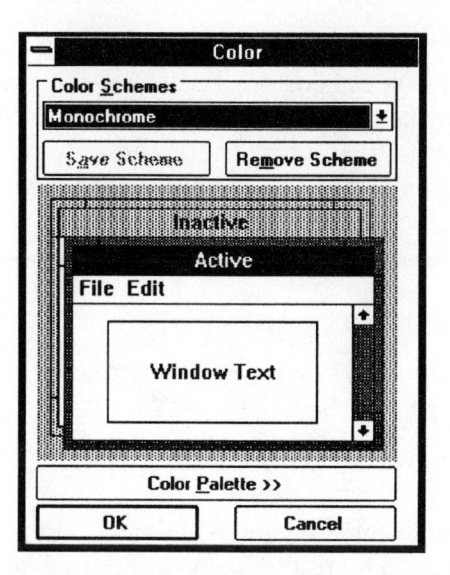

Figure 6.3. The Color Selection Window

schemes, leave it visible in the minienvironment and use the Tab key to select the OK button. Press the Enter key to activate the OK button and simultaneously drop back to the Control Panel.

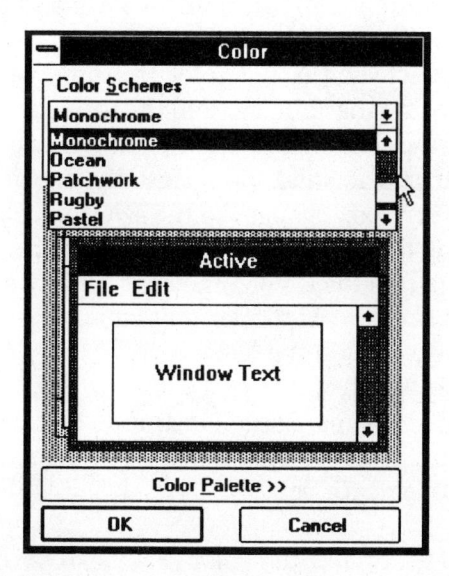

Figure 6.4. The Windows Color Schemes

> Start at the Color dialog box by double-clicking the Color icon.
> 1. Click on the Color Schemes pull-down box. What is the name of the color scheme provided for monochrome systems?
> 2. What is the name of the default color scheme?

1. *Monochrome.*
2. *Windows Default.*

Creating Your Own Color Scheme

If you want to create a completely new color scheme, activate the Color Palette window button by using the mouse, the Tab and the Enter keys, or by pressing Alt+P. The window expands to the right to show a group of multicolored boxes at the top right (Basic Colors), and a group of blank boxes below them (Custom Colors) (Figure 6.5). If you expand the Screen Element scroll box (using the mouse, ALT+E, or the Tab key and Alt+Down Arrow), a number of individual Windows items appear that you can assign unique colors. Select an item to be modified by clicking on the name with the mouse, or by moving the highlight using the up/down arrow keys and then pressing Alt+Up Arrow to close the scroll window with the selected item visible.

Next, select the desired color from the palette by clicking on it with the mouse, or using the Tab key until the top-left color is enclosed in a dotted box. If you're using the keyboard only, use the arrow keys to move the dotted box to the desired color and then press the space bar. The item viewable in the Screen Element box changes to the selected color. Repeat these steps until you finish setting the colors of the Windows environment. Next, move the cursor to the name field in the Color Schemes window and create a new name for your version. To save the new color scheme under the new name, click on the Save Scheme button. Select the OK window button to close this window.

You can also use this procedure to modify an existing color scheme. To delete a color scheme, select its name so that it appears in the single-line Color Schemes box. When you click on the Remove Scheme button, Windows deletes this color scheme for you.

Tip If you remove one of the color schemes that comes with Windows and you decide later that you want to use it, you'll need to either reinstall Windows or else create the color scheme using the Color dialog box.

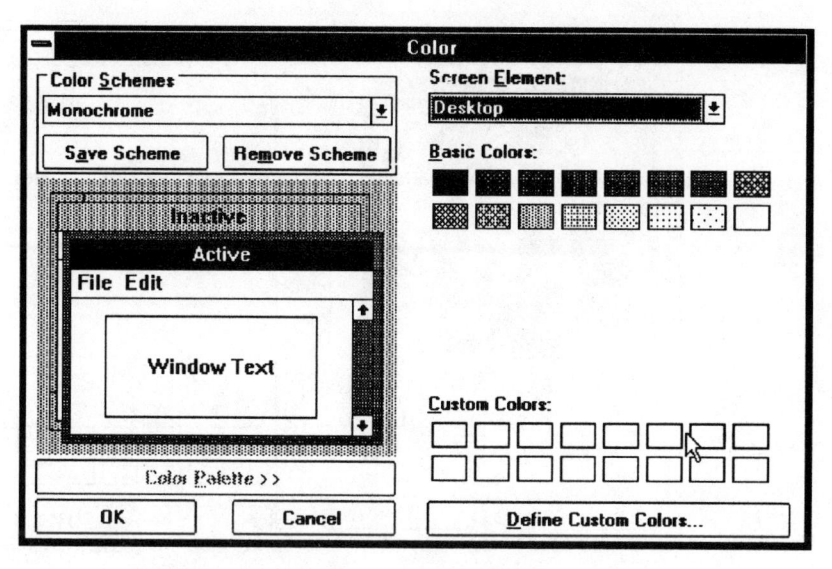

Figure 6.5. Selecting Colors

Creating Custom Colors

What if you don't like the set of colors in the default palette? If your PC has an EGA or better graphics display adapter, you can activate the Define Custom Colors button to create your own colors. When you select this option, the window shown in Figure 6.6 appears. Notice that a "bombsight" appears somewhere in the large multicolored square at the top-left of the window. You can move this indicator by locating the mouse cursor at a different spot within the rectangle and clicking the left mouse button. When this happens, the numbers in the boxes immediately below the multicolored box change to the values that represent the color you just selected.

You can also move the color mix indicator by activating the up and down scroll buttons with the mouse, or by tabbing over to the color attribute box and changing the number in the box. The numbers for Red, Green, and Blue range from 0 to 255, where 255 indicates maximum brightness. If all three colors are set to 255, you get bright white. If all three colors are set to 0, you get pure black. Intermediate mixes produce various colors. Notice that when you modify the numbers, the colors in a small box to the left of the controls change to show the new settings. The part on the left side marked "Color" shows the current adjustment, and the part on the right marked "Solid" indicates the closest pure color that your screen can display.

After you've selected a color combination, click on an empty box in the Custom Colors section of the window and click on the Add Color button to

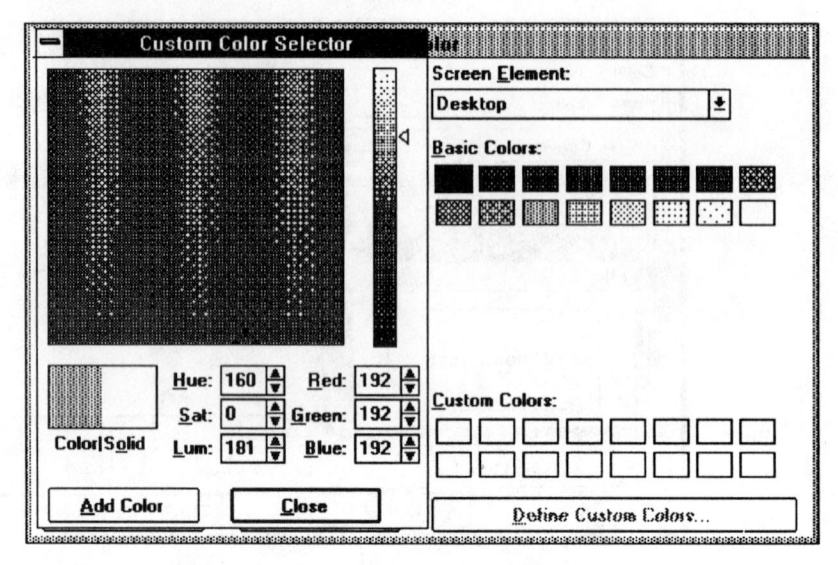

Figure 6.6. Creating Custom Colors

transfer this setting to the selected box. Click on the Close button to close this window and return to the previous Color Palette window. You can now set any of the Windows elements to be a particular custom color by repeating the process for selecting the default colors.

Bring up the Color dialog box.
1. Display the palette so that you can select your own colors.
2. How many basic colors are provided for creating a color scheme? How many custom colors can be created?
3. Create a new color scheme. What happens when you select the OK button in the Color dialog box?
4. Create a new custom color and then try to delete it. What happens?
5. What is the difference between a color scheme and a custom color?

---

1. *Select the Color Palette button.*
2. *48 basic colors and 16 custom colors.*
3. *First, choose the screen element whose color you want to change by using the Screen Element drop-down box. Select a color by clicking on one of the boxes in the Basic Colors group. Repeat this process for each screen element. After you select the OK*

button, you can view the selected colors without saving them or exiting the Color dialog box.
4. *Select the Define Custom Colors... button, and click on the square color grid to select a color. To change the brightness or intensity of the color, click and slide the triangular slider bar to the right of the color grid. When the color is correct, select the Add Color button. You can't remove a custom color; you can only replace it with another color. You can, however, set a custom color to white so that it appears to be blank.*
5. *A color scheme consists of the set of colors used to display the various Windows interface components. A custom color is an individual color that you can create using color mixes.*

Setting the Date and Time

When you double-click on the icon marked Date/Time, a window similar to the one shown in Figure 6.7 appears. This window allows you to modify the system time and date (the time and date kept by your PC). The first step is to select the field to be updated.

Imagine that your minutes display is a couple of minutes slow. Use the Tab key or the mouse cursor to move the highlight to the Minutes field on the display. Type in the correct value for this field, or use the up and down buttons next to the time display to increase or decrease the number in the field. Repeat the same technique with the other numeric fields in the window until the time and the date are correct. Next, use the Tab+Enter keys or the mouse to activate either the OK or the Cancel button. Either action returns you to the Control Panel window.

Tip — You can also change the display format for the date and time by using the International dialog box. To open this dialog box, double-click on the International icon.

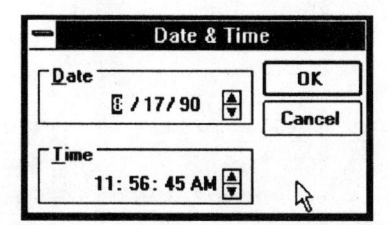

Figure 6.7. Setting the Date and Time

1. True or false? Any changes you make to the date and time affect your computer's clock.
2. True or false? You can use The Date & Time dialog box to set an alarm.
3. Change only the month portion of the date.

---

1. *True.*
2. *False. The Calendar application is used to set an alarm.*
3. *Highlight the month component by double-clicking on it with the mouse, and then click on the up or down arrows to change the month number.*

Setting the Desktop

The Desktop icon allows you to customize the appearance of Windows to a great extent. As you can see from Figure 6.8, the first option (starting from the top-left corner of the window) is called Pattern. Use this option to select a background pattern for the desktop; you can either select an existing pattern, or you can create one of your own. Select the option using the Tab key or the mouse cursor. If you use the keyboard, press Alt+Down Arrow to expand the scroll box. Use the up and down arrow keys to scroll through the various options, and then press Alt+Up Arrow to keep the selection.

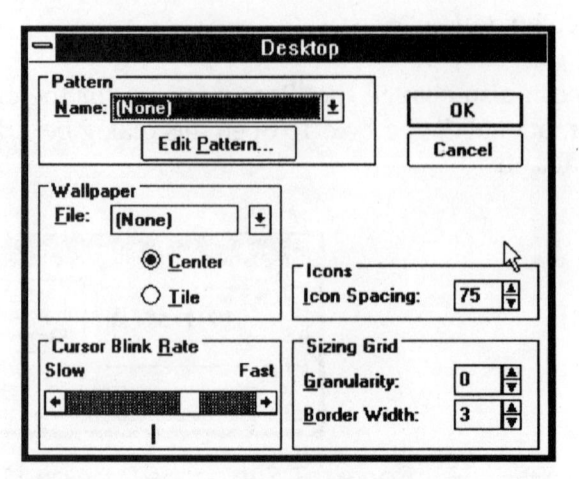

Figure 6.8. The Desktop Dialog Box

The Control Panel

If you use the mouse, simply scroll up or down using the scroll bar and then click an item to select it. Next, use the Tab+Enter keys or the mouse to select and activate the OK button for the Desktop window. Notice that the rearmost window (which typically is the Windows Desktop) changes from a simple monochrome to the pattern you selected.

Creating Your Own Desktop Pattern

If you're not happy with the patterns provided with Windows and you have a mouse, you can easily create your own patterns by selecting the Edit Pattern... button. When you activate this button, another window appears over the Desktop window (Figure 6.9). If you didn't select a pattern to edit (the name field showed None), Windows will beep and expect you to enter a name for the pattern. (Make one up if you're creating a new pattern rather than modifying an existing one).

Next, click on the large blank square in the middle of the window and watch it change from gray to black. This box represents a grid of 8 by 8 squares that can each be changed from gray to black, and back to gray again, by clicking on the particular square. The elongated box on the left, marked Sample, shows how the pattern looks when it's replicated many times on the desktop. Try playing around with various patterns until you get the hang of how this feature works. You can save the pattern by activating the Add window button. If you want to quit without saving your work, select Cancel. Activate the OK button to exit from this window.

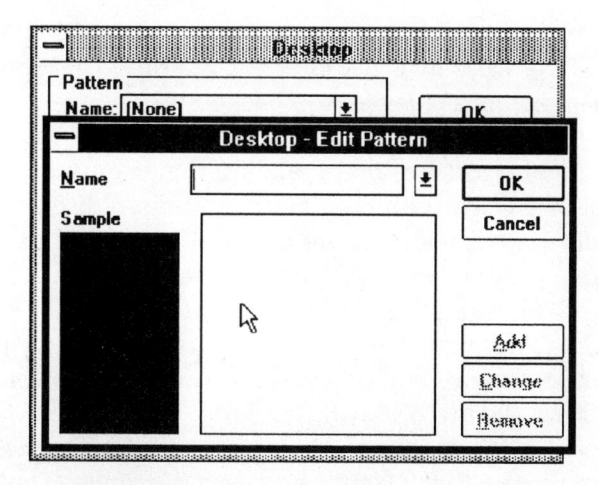

Figure 6.9. Creating a Desktop Pattern

1. Select the Name drop-down box in the Edit Pattern dialog box. Which patterns are provided with Windows?
2. True or false? If you create a new pattern and select it, the pattern will be used by Windows even after you exit and start Windows again.
3. After you create a pattern and select it, select the Remove button in the Edit Pattern dialog box. What happens?

1. *The patterns are 50% Gray, Boxes, Critters, Diamonds, Paisley, Quilt, Scottie, Spinner, Thatches, Tulip, Waffle, and Weave.*
2. *True.*
3. *A message box displays to ask you to verify the deletion of the pattern.*

The main disadvantage of selecting a pattern for the desktop is that the new pattern may make your icons or other screen objects hard to read. As an example of this problem, activate the Cardfile application from the Accessories group, and then reduce it to an icon by clicking on the Minimize box at the top-right corner of the screen. If you have selected a pattern for the Desktop, note that it's virtually impossible to read the legend under the Cardfile icon. For this reason, test out your patterns to make sure that they're not too busy.

Using Wallpaper

Returning to the Desktop window, the next option available on the left-hand side of the window is the Wallpaper option. This option allows you to select a bitmap picture as the desktop background.

Bitmaps tend to be large files that contain color information about each individual *pixel* (dots that make up the picture) on the screen. These files are typically created with the Paint application (discussed in greater detail in the chapter on Accessories), but can also be created using special programs that bring in pictures from scanners or video cameras.

Unlike the pattern option that limits you to an 8 by 8 grid, the Wallpaper option allows you to fill the entire screen with only one image. Open the File scroll box in the Wallpaper section to see a list of .BMP files provided by Windows (Figure 6.10). If you select one of these files and activate the OK button for the Desktop window, the pattern appears as the desktop background screen the next time you start Windows. (The pattern may appear right away if Windows isn't operating in real mode with extended memory.)

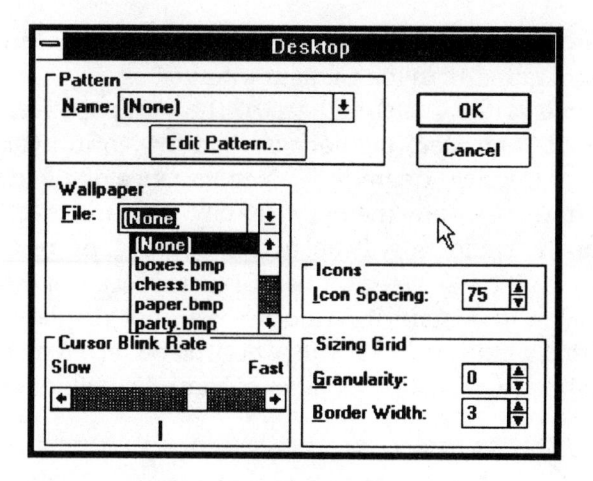

Figure 6.10. Viewing .BMP Files

All of the bitmap files provided by Windows are fairly large in size, so leave the options in the Wallpaper area set to Center. Figure 6.11 presents a sample of some of the wallpaper images. If you decide to create a picture later using Windows Paint, you can display it on the desktop by following these steps:

1. Move the file to the same directory where the Windows files are located.
2. Select the filename in the Wallpaper scroll box.
3. Activate the OK button.

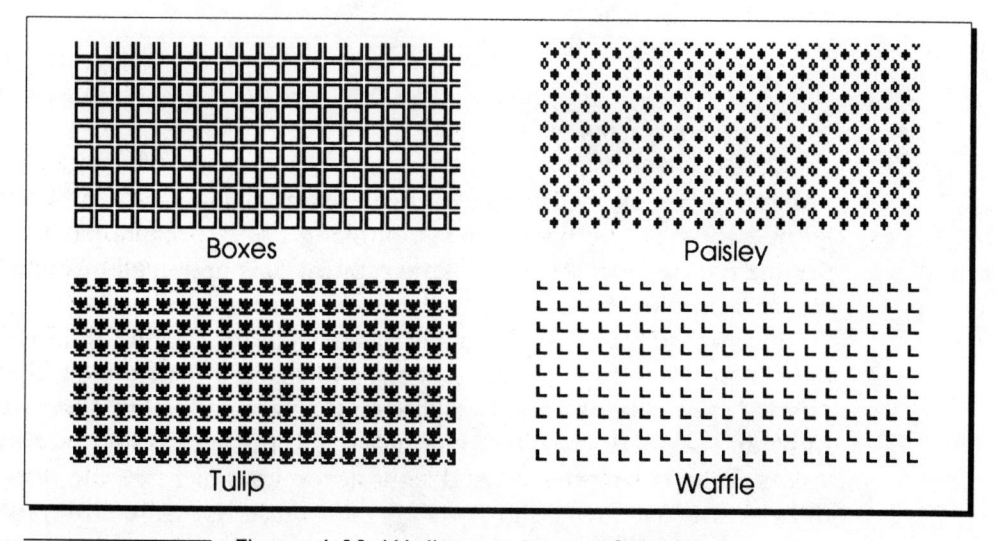

Figure 6.11. Wallpaper Image Samples

If your bitmap file is small, display it several times by activating the Tile option, rather than the Center option.

One of the disadvantages of the Wallpaper feature is that some of your computer's system memory is used for storing your wallpaper pattern. This may perceptibly degrade the performance of Windows if you have a modest amount of system memory. It may also make Windows slower at startup because Windows will need to move a copy of the file from the disk into memory. If the selected bitmap file is too large, or if there isn't enough memory available to contain it, Windows will not display the file at all. If you have selected a pattern and a wallpaper, the pattern may be visible around the edges of the desktop if the wallpaper bitmap is smaller than the entire desktop.

1. True or false? Files created by Paint to be used as wallpaper screens must be saved with the extension .BMP.
2. Select (None) for the File name in the Desktop dialog box. What happens?
3. Select the Chess wallpaper pattern. Does it fill the entire screen when the Center option is selected?
4. Try to use both a wallpaper pattern and a basic pattern? What happens?

1. *True.*
2. *The wallpaper pattern is removed.*
3. *Yes.*
4. *The wallpaper covers up the pattern.*

Setting the Cursor

The last option on the left side of the Desktop dialog box is Cursor Blink Rate. Some people are bothered by fast-blinking objects; others have a hard time finding the cursor if it isn't blinking rapidly. This option allows you to select a comfortable blink rate.

Pay careful attention if you use the keyboard to set this option because the only change in appearance is that the slide square blinks when this option is selected. The rate of blinking speeds up when you move the square to the right, and slows down when you move it to the left. Block movement can be accomplished using the left and right arrow keys or by clicking on the left or right arrow window buttons using the mouse. Observe the screen closely:

Immediately below the speed slide bar is a vertical cursor that blinks at the selected rate. If you change the blink rate, the square continues to reflect the selected blink rate, but the cursor may blink at some other rate or may disappear completely! If you tab over to another option, the cursor reappears and blinks at the correct rate.

True or false? You don't need to select the OK button after changing the cursor blink rate to make Windows change the blink rate.

False.

Controlling Icon Spacing

At the top-right of the Desktop dialog box, notice a section for controlling Icon spacing. Windows defaults this setting to a value that adequately spaces icons with typical descriptions. Unfortunately, some icons need more space than others. A good example of the need for this option is the Non-Windows Applications.

If your PC contains non-Windows applications that were recognized during installation, these applications were placed in a special group called Non-Windows Applications. Unfortunately, this description is so long that it interferes with the descriptions of adjacent icons. By increasing the number for icon spacing, you can tell Windows to move the icons farther apart when it builds a window. The number in the box refers to pixels, which are the smallest units (dots) on the screen. For example, a typical VGA display is 640 pixels wide and 480 pixels high.

Setting Border Widths

The last section, Sizing Grid, allows you to change the way that windows are placed on the screen, and to adjust the thickness of the window borders. When Windows first comes up, it sets the grid size to zero, which means that you can leave a window or an icon in any location on the screen. If you set the number in the Granularity box to a nonzero value, Windows defines a grid on which to align all windows and icons. The larger the number, the coarser the grid.

These grid lines are invisible; you only see the effect of the granularity setting. For example, set the value in the Granularity box to the maximum of 49, and activate the OK button to keep the value. Try moving the Main window by a small amount. Notice that the window seems to "jump" to a new location when you release the mouse button. Many users find this option somewhat disturbing and simply keep the Granularity set to zero so that the grid is turned off.

The Border Width box allows you to define the thickness of the window border that you use to resize a window. Allowable values range from 1 to 49, but you will probably find anything larger than 10 to be rather extravagant. To experiment with this setting, use the Tab key to select the box and type in a desired value (or use the mouse cursor and the up/down boxes). When you've set a value, activate the OK button to keep the setting.

1. What is the default setting for the Border Width option?
2. Can you see the frame of a window with Border Width set to 1?
3. What is the largest value that can be used to set the Granularity?

1. 3.
2. Yes.
3. 49.

Selecting Fonts

If you have a high-resolution display such as an EGA or VGA, Windows can display various character styles (fonts) on the screen at the same time. You can easily add new font files by double-clicking on the Fonts icon, or selecting the Fonts option from the Settings menu. The upper part of the Fonts dialog box (Figure 6.12) contains a scroll box listing the fonts provided by Windows. Move through the list using the mouse (or the up and down arrow keys) and notice that the contents of the lower box (labeled Sample of Font) changes to show how the particular character style looks. Notice also that two buttons, Remove and Add..., are provided for removing and adding font files, respectively.

These different fonts may not mean a great deal to you if you own a daisy-wheel printer or a simple dot-matrix printer, but they are quite useful if you own a high-capability device, such as a laser or ink-jet printer.

The Control Panel

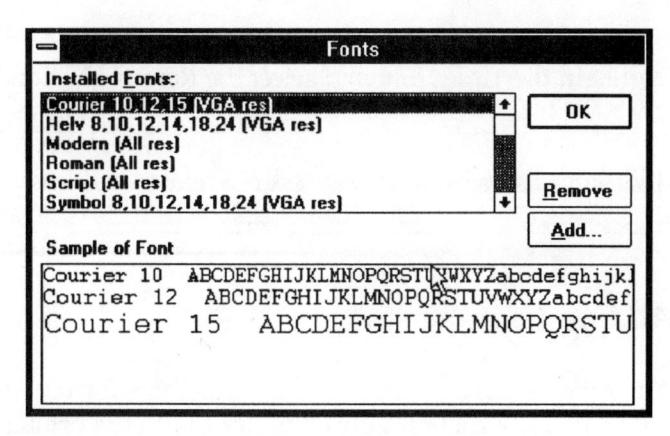

```
┌─────────────── Fonts ───────────────┐
│ Installed Fonts:                    │
│ Courier 10,12,15 (VGA res)    ▲  ┌──────┐│
│ Helv 8,10,12,14,18,24 (VGA res)  │  OK  ││
│ Modern (All res)                  └──────┘│
│ Roman (All res)                          │
│ Script (All res)                  ┌──────┐│
│ Symbol 8,10,12,14,18,24 (VGA res) │Remove││
│                               ▼   └──────┘│
│ Sample of Font                    ┌──────┐│
│                                   │ Add..││
│ Courier 10   ABCDEFGHIJKLMNOPQRSTUVWXYZabcdefghijk│
│ Courier 12   ABCDEFGHIJKLMNOPQRSTUVWXYZabcdef     │
│ Courier 15   ABCDEFGHIJKLMNOPQRSTU                │
│                                                   │
└───────────────────────────────────────────────────┘
```

Figure 6.12. The Fonts Dialog Box

✓ Bring up the Fonts dialog box. What fonts are shown in the Installed Fonts list?

Some of the fonts include Courier, Helv, Modern, Roman, and Script.

Removing Font Files

If you think you might not need some of the fonts listed in the Installed Fonts list, you can remove them by highlighting them and selecting the Remove button.

For example, imagine that your Windows files are in the directory C:\WINDOWS and that Windows installed your font files in a subdirectory that it created called SYSTEM. (You can check that the font files are in that subdirectory before starting Windows by entering

   CD C:\WINDOWS\SYSTEM

and then typing DIR *.FON. You'll see a list of the Windows font files, which have the extension .FON.)

To remove a font file, select one of the less-useful fonts for deletion, and write its name on a piece of paper. (The Helvetica font is used by many Windows applications, so don't delete it or you may encounter some unusual problems.) Activate the Font Remove button. When the dialog box pops up, confirm that you want to remove the font.

> Highlight the Times font and select the Remove button. What happens?

A warning dialog box displays to ask if you want to delete the selected font file.

Adding Fonts

A number of companies create and sell fonts for use with Windows and various printers. Sometimes the fonts come with the printer or can be purchased as font cartridges that are plugged into the printer. If you need to install additional fonts, select the Fonts application and then activate the Add... button. The Add Font Files dialog box (Figure 6.13) appears.

To see how this feature works, let's add the font file we just deleted. Activate the Font Add windows button, enter C:\WINDOWS\SYSTEM*.* in the top box, and then press the Enter key. When a group of files appears in the lower scroll box, try to select the font file that you previously deleted. Once you've found it and the filename is highlighted, activate the OK window button to install the font file again.

Tip — Here's a keyboard shortcut for marking multiple font files so that they can be added: Hold down the Control key and click the mouse on each font file that you want to add. After you've highlighted the desired font files, select the OK button.

You can also use the Add Font Files dialog box to install font files stored on a diskette. Place the diskette with your fonts in drive A, and select the [-a-] item in the Directories list box. The dialog box lists all of the available font files.

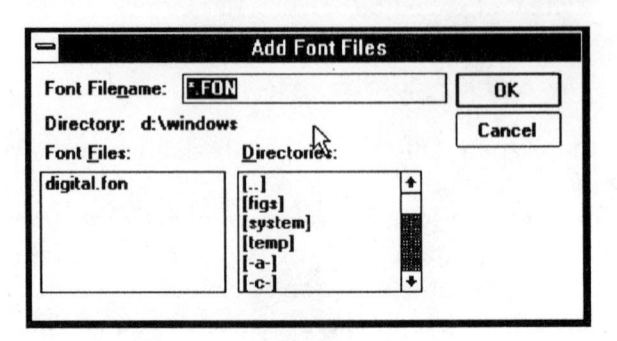

Figure 6.13. Adding a Font File

1. Verify that a font has been properly installed.
2. True or false? Only font files with the extension .FON can be installed.

---

1. *Return to the Fonts dialog box, select the font in the Installed Fonts list box, and make sure the font displays correctly in the sample text that is provided.*
2. *True.*

International Settings

You can use this configuration option to customize certain display defaults that tend to be language/culture dependent. Figure 6.14 illustrates how the default International dialog box looks. The first four boxes—Country, Language, Keyboard Layout, and Measurement—allow you to specify the default country, language, keyboard layout, and basis of measurements. You won't need these four settings unless you plan to use Windows in a foreign country. If you select a different country and language, Windows requests that you insert a particular diskette in the A: drive so that it can read the information associated with that installation option.

The fifth box in the International dialog box allows you to select a different list separator. The default value is the comma, but this can easily be replaced with any other character (for example, the hyphen or the vertical bar). Unless

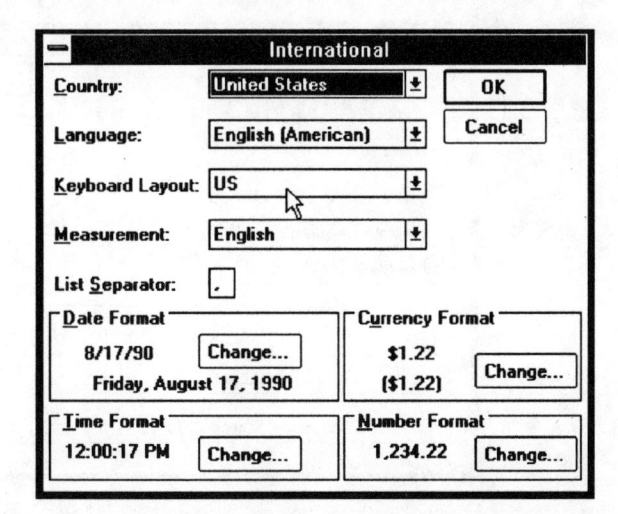

Figure 6.14. The International Settings Dialog Box

you need to change this to get around an unusual problem, leave this option unchanged. The important thing is that the option is available should you need to use it.

Setting the Date Format

When you activate the Change window button in the Date Format box, the dialog box shown in Figure 6.15 appears. Use the three options along the top of the dialog box to specify month/day/year, day/month/year, or year/month/day as the template for the short date format. The Separator box allows you to replace the slash character, which is normally used to separate the date fields, with any other valid character. (Some practical alternatives are the hyphen and the underscore.)

You can use the three other options in the Short Date Format group to select leading zeros for the day and month numbers when they are each single digits, and to identify whether only the two last digits should be displayed for the year. If either the Day or Month boxes contain an X, the leading zero appears for single-digit days or months. If the X is present for the Century option, all four digits displayed for the year field of the Short Date Format.

The other group provided with the International Date dialog box is called Long Date Format. Its three option buttons, MDY, DMY, and YMD, allow you to select the displayed order for the date in the same way you selected the Short Date Format.

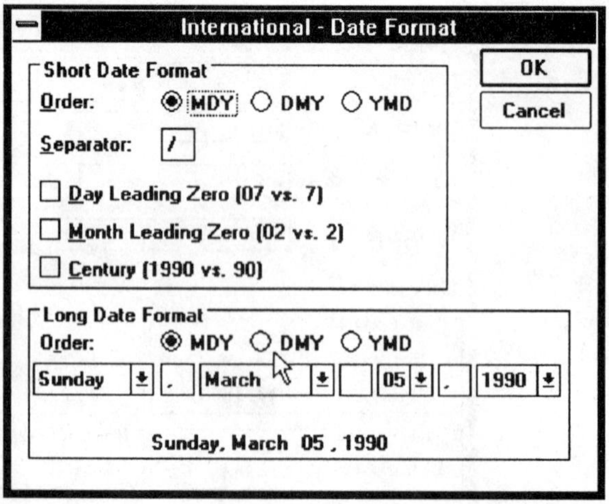

Figure 6.15. Setting the International Date Format

You can use the drop-down scroll boxes to select abbreviations for the day of the week and the date. To make a selection, expand the scroll box by clicking on it with the mouse or using the Tab key and Alt+Down Arrow.

Once you've made your selection, close the menu by clicking on the arrow box immediately above the up scroll arrow box or by pressing Alt+Up Arrow. The small square data boxes between drop-down menus allow you to define custom separators between each field in the Long Date Format. The first and last boxes contain commas because this is the standard separator used in the United States.

Experiment with various symbols such as slashes and asterisks for unusual effects. To move from one data field to another, either click on the field that you want to change or use the Tab key to move the highlighting there. The changes that you make to the Long Date Format are immediately reflected in the sample date at the bottom of the box. When you're satisfied with your changes, activate the OK window button to save them.

---

1. Display a short date in the format 11-02-59.
2. Display the date as 11-02-1959.
3. What is the main difference between the Short Date Format and the Long Date Format?

---

1. *Select Order: MDY and Separator: -.*
2. *Select Century (1990 vs. 90).*
3. *The Short Date Format represents a date numerically, and the Long Date Format represents a date in a completely spelled-out format.*

Setting the Time Format

The next application in the International menu allows you to customize the time format. When you activate the application, the dialog box shown in Figure 6.16 appears. You can select a 12-hour format or a 24-hour format. If you select the 12-hour format, an additional data box appears to the right of the time field, containing the letters AM. You can change the contents of these boxes to a new description of up to 8 characters in length.

For example, if you set your PC clock to Greenwich Mean Time (the international reference), you could change the AM field to AM ZULU. (The term for

Figure 6.16. Setting the International Time Format

the international time reference is UCT, Universal Coordinated Time, but most people still call it by the older name, ZULU.)

The box labeled Separator allows you to change the character that separates the various time fields. If you locate the cursor to the right of the colon and press the backspace key, you eliminate the separator altogether and get military time. Unfortunately, when you remove the colon between the hours and the minutes, you also remove the separator between the minutes and the seconds, so you end up with a five- or six-digit display for the time.

The last option allows you to select or delete a leading zero on the Hours field. When you've made your selections, activate the OK button to keep the changes.

Setting the Currency and Number Format

The final two applications of the International window are of limited value to most users. The International Currency Format (Figure 6.17) lets you define how to show information associated with money fields. You can place the currency symbol in several different places, and show negative numbers by various permutations of the currency symbol and either a hyphen or a parentheses.

The other application, International Number Format (Figure 6.18), allows you to customize the separator between the hundreds and thousands digits, the decimal separator and the number of digits displayed to the right of the

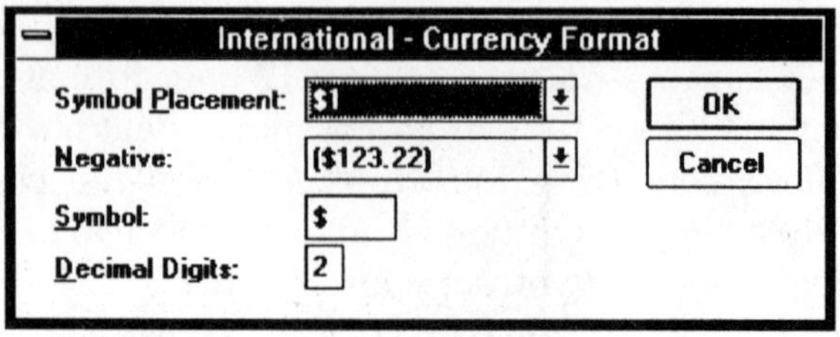

Figure 6.17. Setting the International Currency Format

The Control Panel

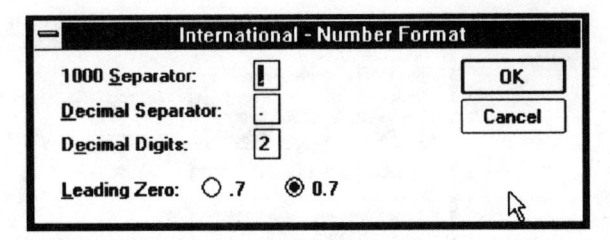

Figure 6.18. Setting the International Number Format

units digit. (In Europe, many countries use a comma to separate the whole units from the fractional part.) The main intent of these applications is to provide standard information for future applications (such as accounting packages) that will run under Windows 3.0 and future releases. When you complete changes to each window, remember to activate the OK button to keep your changes.

Setting the Keyboard

The Keyboard option brings up a simple dialog box (Figure 6.19) that allows you to speed up or slow down the rate at which a key repeats when it's held down (the *autorepeat* rate). Use the mouse or the Tab and keyboard arrow keys to move the slide box to a desired speed setting. Then Tab (or click, or press Alt+T) down to the test area and hold down a letter key to see how fast it repeats. When you're comfortable with the speed setting, activate the OK button to save your changes.

Setting the Mouse

You can select the Mouse option (Figure 6.20) to customize the speed at which the mouse cursor moves across the screen, and the speed with which you have to click the left button to count as a double-click. When you move the slide box

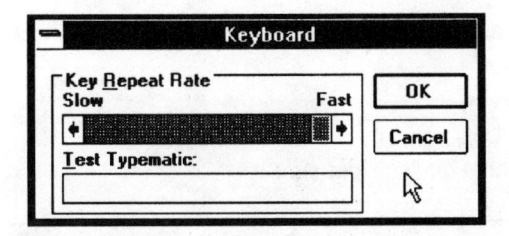

Figure 6.19. The Keyboard Dialog Box

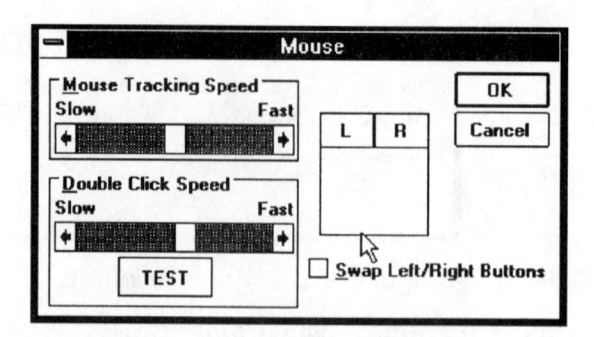

Figure 6.20. The Mouse Dialog Box

for the Mouse Tracking Speed to the right, notice that the mouse appears "twitchier." When you move the box to the left, mouse travel appears slower and smoother.

If you move the Double Click Speed slide box to the right, you need to click the button faster for Windows to recognize it as a double-click. Moving the slide-box to the left allows you to take your time between clicks. To allow you to experiment with the click speed, Windows provides a Test box immediately below the speed selector. If you move the cursor to the test area and double-click fast enough, the box changes from white to black. Double-clicking again at the proper speed changes the color back. This adjustment is rather personal and important because some users are speed demons and other like to do things at a slower pace.

The last option available in this window is the button swap box. If you activate this option, the functions of the left and right mouse buttons are switched. This feature enables left-handed users to use the physical right button on the mouse to click or double-click on objects. If you activate this option, it goes into effect immediately, so you have to use the physical right button to click on the OK to save the changes. Of course, if you change your mind at a later date, you can always activate the Mouse application again and use the Swap option to change back to the default button operation.

Select the Swap Left/Right Buttons option. What happens in the box above the check box?

The L is now on the right side.

Setting Network Options

The icon for this option appears only if you told Windows during installation that your PC is connected to a network. When you activate the Network application, a dialog box provides the necessary information for your particular network. You can use this window to specify information about logging on and off the network (including passwords) and the protocol for sending messages to other users on the network.

Setting Ports

The Ports option allows you adjust the settings for a particular serial communications port. *Serial ports* are information paths between computers where only one wire carries the information in each direction (as compared to a parallel port, where data is usually transmitted over 8 data lines at the same time). Serial ports are typically used for hooking up modems, mice, and printers. You will often hear the term *RS-232 port* used to refer to a serial port because this is the name of the standard that specifies the voltage and wiring characteristics of these ports.

When you select the Ports option, several icons identify the possible output ports (Figure 6.21). When you select the port to be updated, the Ports Settings dialog box appears (Figure 6.22). The drop-down scroll box called Baud Rate indicates the speed at which your data is sent and received by this particular port.

The standards for serial ports define certain fixed speeds for these transfers (such as 300 baud, 1200 baud, and 2400 baud). You must find out what baud rate is expected by the device on the other end of the wire. The communications speed for most printers and modems is specified in the owner's manual.

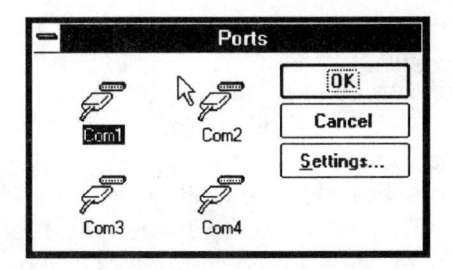

Figure 6.21. The Ports Dialog Box

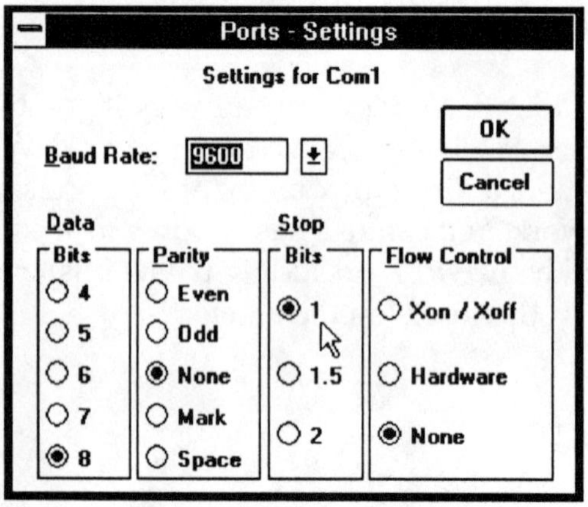

Figure 6.22. The Ports-Settings Dialog Box

The common settings for baud rates are 9600 for printers and 300, 1200, and 2400 for modems.

The left-most column along the bottom of the dialog box allows you to identify the number of bits of data sent out in one group. (The sender has to pause between groups in order to give the receiving equipment a chance to look at the incoming data and to do something with it.) Most equipment today expects either 7 or 8 bits of data at a time, but this can be verified from the owner's manual.

The Parity column allows you to select the error-detection method used by the devices. When each group of data bits is sent, the serial port can send another bit to indicate the parity of the sum of the data bits. In other words, the serial port hardware can add the 1s and 0s for a group, and then insert a 1 or a 0 at the end to make the sum of all of the bits in the group either odd or even. If you select the None option, no parity bit is calculated. The Mark option forces the parity bit to a 1, and the Space option forces it to a 0. The use of parity can be very important when your computer is operating in an electrically noisy environment (such as a manufacturing area with many induction motors or fluorescent lights).

The Stop Bits column allows you to specify the minimum pause between data groups. This is typically either 1 or 1.5 bits. (Again, check the manual of the other machine for this information.)

The Flow Control column allows you to select data metering between the hardware units. The serial hardware specification identifies additional wires that can be run between the computers to request that the sender pause for a while. The receiving unit can also send a software code on the data wire back

The Control Panel

to the sender to instruct the sender to pause. This software code is typically used with modems (because the communications between modems consists of unique tones that signify 1s and 0s for the sender and the receiver), and is known as Xon/Xoff. Of course, if you are using a serial protocol to send information between two PCs in the same area, use the hardware flow control (rather than the software code) to allow the PCs to send pure data without wasting time checking the data stream for the Xon/Xoff codes.

1. True or false? The standard Microsoft Mouse hooks up to a serial port.
2. Open the Ports Settings dialog box for Com1. Which default settings are listed?
3. If you have a mouse, drag one port icon on top of another. What happens?

1. *True.*
2. *Baud Rate—9600; Data Bits—8; Parity—None; Stop Bits—1; Flow Control—None.*
3. *By dragging a port icon on top of another, you are effectively copying the port settings from one port to another port. This action produces a dialog box such as the one shown in Figure 6.23.*

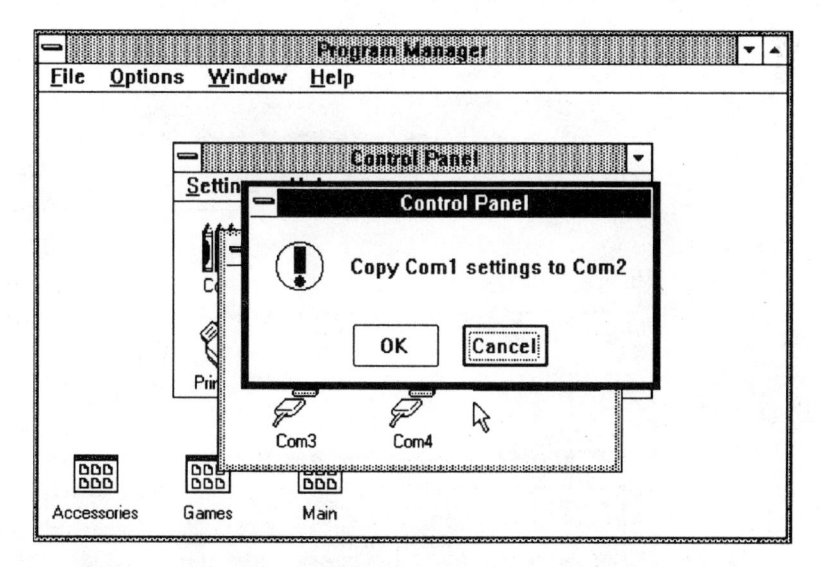

Figure 6.23. Copy Port Settings

Installing Printers

When you select the Printers option, you see the same dialog box that was presented for printer installation when you installed Windows. (The Windows Installation invoked the Control Panel Printers application so that you could tell Windows which printers were available.)

When you activate the Printers configuration icon, a rather complicated window appears (Figure 6.24). Use the Add Printers button to select additional printers that you may have added to the system. After you select a printer, activate the Install window button (Figure 6.25). A dialog box asks you to insert a specific Windows diskette in the A: drive so that Windows can obtain the printer driver file.

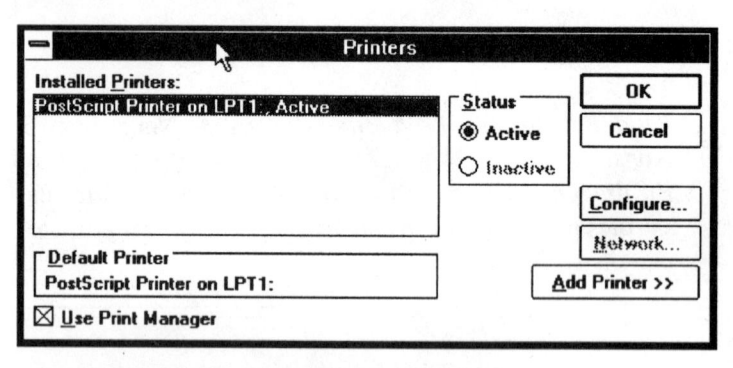

Figure 6.24. The Printers Dialog Box

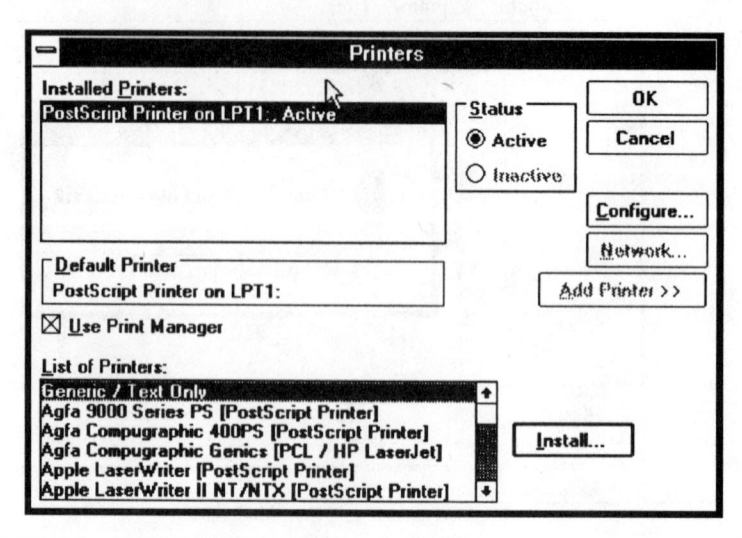

Figure 6.25. Installing a Printer

The Control Panel

Insert the diskette and activate the OK button. When the dialog box disappears, activate the Configure button to select the output port for the new printer (Figure 6.26). Use the scroll box to select the output port. (One of the options even allows you to send the data to a file, instead of a port.) Next activate the Setup button to move on to selecting printer details (Figure 6.27).

Use the Setup dialog box to select between various printers that share the same print driver, and to define the paper size, graphics resolution, and so on

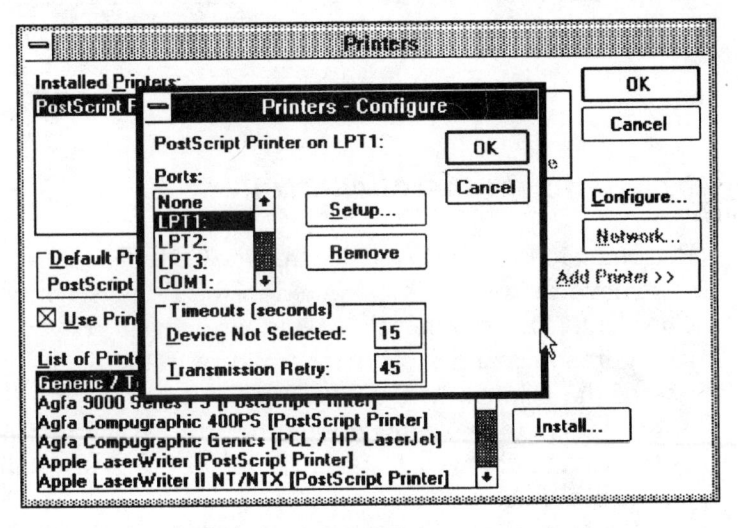

Figure 6.26. Configuring an Output Port

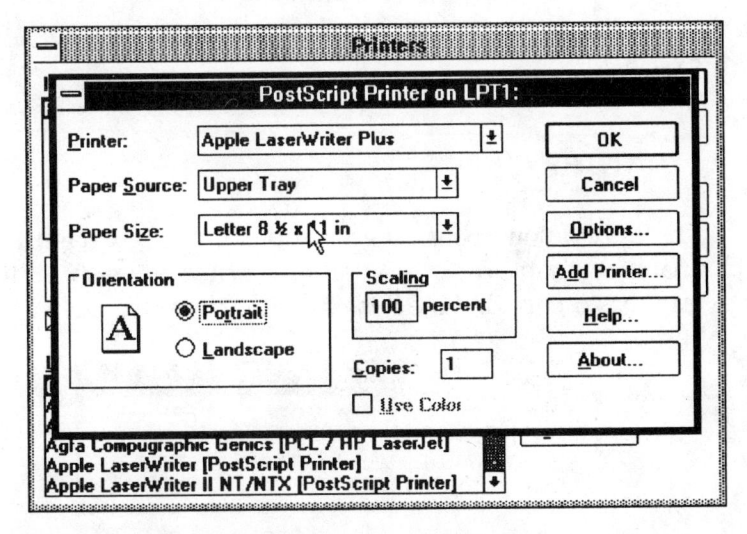

Figure 6.27. Setting Up a Printer

for the particular printer. (The information in the Setup window varies depending upon the type of printer selected.) After you've made the desired changes, activate the OK button to save them.

> True or false? When the Printers dialog box displays, the active printer is highlighted.

True.

Removing an Installed Printer

Returning to Figure 6.27, notice that the Configure dialog box can also be used to remove the printer highlighted in the Printers window. When you're finished with the configuration window, activate the OK button to save your configuration changes. When you return to the main Printers window, select one of the printers in the Installed Printers list, and then select the Active option button to make this printer the active system printer. The other printers in the list are changed to inactive because Windows allows only one active printer at a time.

Windows also allows users with Network printers to install them by activating the Network window button in the main Printers window. If you're not connected to a network, this window button displays at half-intensity (it's not available).

Setting Sound

This application opens a very simple dialog box (Figure 6.28) where you can enable or disable the computer beep that Windows uses to tell the user that an error has occurred. If the X is present in the Warning Beep check box, Windows

Figure 6.28. The Sound Dialog Box

beeps when you do something wrong. If the box is empty, the sound is turned off. Activate the OK window button to save any change.

> Open up the Sound dialog. What is the default setting for the Warning Beep option?

The Warning Beep is on.

Setting 386 Enhanced Mode Options

This icon appear only when Windows is running in 386 mode. When it's activated, the first option allows you to define how Windows should react if several programs try to access the same I/O hardware at the same time. (This will usually happen only if non-Windows applications access a port at the same time when Windows tries to access it.) The three options for each port are: Always Warn, Never Warn, and Idle.

Always Warn means that whenever Windows detects a conflict, a warning dialog box appears to allow you to decide what to do. Never Warn is the "What, me worry?" option; you know that a conflict will never arise because you only use 100% Windows 3.0-compatible applications. The Idle option tells Windows to wait for the number of seconds specified in the box to the right of the option, before trying to use that particular port again. No warning will be issued if you select the Idle option because it will just keep trying until it succeeds.

The Scheduling options allow you to identify what percentage of the total execution time should be consumed by Windows when it runs in foreground and in background. Unless you plan to run a non-Windows task in the background (such as your own custom serial port program), leave the Windows in Foreground option at 100%. If you want Windows to be suspended while you run a non-Windows program, you may want to reduce the Windows in Background percentage to something very small. The Exclusive in Foreground option indicates that only Windows tasks should run when Windows is in the foreground.

The Minimum Timeslice option identifies how long a span of time will be allowed for either a non-Windows task or for all active Windows tasks. The larger the number, the higher the apparent system throughput (less interruptions), but the response time to your actions (as the user) might become slower (the interface may appear "jerky"). The default value of 20 milliseconds is probably a good compromise, but you may wish to experiment with different values to optimize system operation for your typical mix of programs. As always, activate the OK button to save the changes when you're finished.

Summary

In this chapter, you've been exposed to the configuration applications available under the Control Panel. As you can see, Windows is a complex and flexible package that needs to know a great deal about the available hardware and software in order to run at peak efficiency. The positive side to this complexity is that Windows allows you to customize the environment to suit your own individual needs.

The next chapter will cover a much simpler topic: How to use the file-management capabilities of Windows to organize the information on your disks.

Exercises

Use these exercises to learn more about how to use the Control Panel to customize Windows.

What You Should Do	How the Computer Responds
1. Start the Control Panel by double-clicking on the Control Panel icon in the Main group window.	1. The Control Panel window displays with its associated icons. Some of these icons include Color, Fonts, Ports, Mouse, and Desktop.
2. Double-click on the Desktop icon.	2. The Desktop dialog box displays.
3. Click on the Name pull-down box, and select the Diamonds pattern.	3. The text in the Name box changes from (None) to Diamonds.
4. Click on the Edit Pattern... button.	4. The Desktop - Edit Pattern dialog box displays. This dialog presents an example of the Diamonds pattern.
5. Click the OK button.	5. Control returns to the Desktop dialog box.

6. Click the OK button in the Desktop dialog box.

7. Click the Mouse icon in the Control Panel menu.

8. Slide the scroll box in the Mouse Tracking Speed option toward the Fast indicator (to the right).

9. Click the OK button.

10. Slide the mouse around on your desktop.

11. Double-click on the Ports icon.

12. Double-click on the Com1 icon.

13. Click on the Baud Rate pull-down box.

14. Leave the baud rate unchanged, and click the Cancel button.

15. Exit the Control Panel by selecting the Exit command from the Settings menu.

6. The background screen changes from the default pattern to the Diamonds pattern.

7. The Mouse dialog box appears.

8. The scroll box moves to the right.

9. The dialog box disappears.

10. The response time for the mouse is faster.

11. The Ports dialog box displays.

12. The Ports–Settings dialog box displays.

13. The list of available baud rates displays.

14. The Ports–Settings dialog box disappears.

15. Control returns to the Program Manager.

What If It Doesn't Work?

1. If you didn't install a mouse, setting the mouse tracking rate won't have any effect.

2. If your computer doesn't have any ports, you won't see any of the port icons, such as Com1.

7

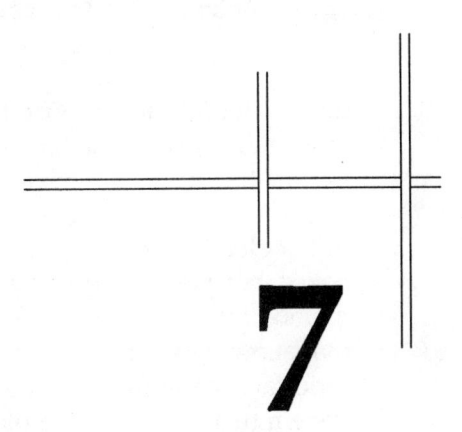

The File Manager

The most difficult part of using the PC is learning the commands for performing basic file management operations, such as creating directories and copying files. Fortunately, Windows removes most of the difficulty by providing an interactive tool called the File Manager. From this environment, you can perform all of the file management operations.

Our goal in this chapter is twofold: to explain the basics of DOS file management, and to show you how to use the Window's File Manager. We'll begin by taking a brief look at DOS directories, and then we'll move on to explore the powerful File Manager features. In this chapter, you'll learn:

- How files and directories are stored and accessed under DOS
- What a tree-structured directory is
- How to start up the File Manager
- How to use the File Manager to copy and delete files
- How to use the File Manager to create and delete directories
- How to use the File Manager to print files

DOS Directory Basics

If you're an experienced DOS user and you know how to create and use directories, skip this section and move directly to the next section, where we'll cover the File Manager. If you're a relatively new DOS user, you'll want to read this section. In order to understand why DOS does certain things, you must first understand some basics about your computer. We'll start with a simple explanation about how disk drives work.

You can think of a blank disk (especially a hard disk) as a huge warehouse full of identical shoe boxes. You can store all kinds of information in these shoe boxes, but you will quickly lose track of the information unless you have a method for organizing it. DOS provides special disk partitions called *directories* that allow you to group related files. You can issue commands to create directories and copy files into the new directories. DOS is a hierarchical directory system that allows you to place one directory (subdirectory) inside of another, creating a directory system called a *tree directory*.

Figure 7.1 presents an example of a tree directory system. The *root directory* is the very top of the tree. This directory is usually the only directory present when a disk is first formatted.

You can use DOS commands (such as MKDIR) to create subdirectories. (Later in this chapter, we'll show how to create and delete subdirectories using the Windows File Manager). For example, Figure 7.1 shows a subdirectory called WINDOWS immediately below the root directory (\), and a directory called SYSTEM that is connected to the WINDOWS subdirectory. Thus, the root directory (\) is considered to be the *parent* of the WINDOWS directory, and the WINDOWS directory is the parent of the SYSTEM directory.

Notice that the root directory is also the parent of another directory called DOS (a good place to keep most of the DOS files). Within practical limits (which keep growing with subsequent versions of DOS), you can have as many subdirectories as you wish, and can connect as many subdirectories as you want to a single directory. The obvious limitation is that you can't define

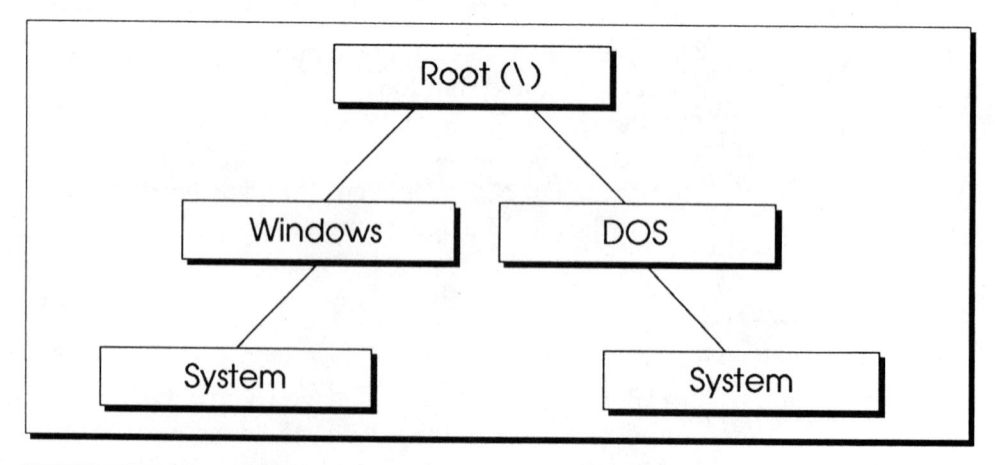

Figure 7.1. A Sample Tree Directory

directory dependencies in such a way that a grandchild directory becomes the parent to one of its predecessors.

For this self-check, exit Windows and use the DOS command prompt.
1. Move to the root directory.
2. Display the contents of the root directory.
3. What symbol represents the root directory?
4. What is the difference between a root directory and a subdirectory?
5. Can a subdirectory itself be a parent for another subdirectory?

---

1. *Issue the command CD \.*
2. *Issue the command DIR.*
3. *The backward slash (\).*
4. *A root directory serves as the parent for subdirectories, and a root directory cannot be a subdirectory.*
5. *Yes*

Directory Requirements

Let's return to our simple directory model in Figure 7.1. The root directory in this example would be referred to as C:\. The WINDOWS subdirectory would usually be identified as C:\WINDOWS, and the system directory under it as C:\WINDOWS\SYSTEM. Notice that the separator character between the subdirectory names is the backslash. (If you use a normal slash, which leans in the opposite direction, DOS gets very confused.)

Another limitation placed by DOS is that each directory can only have one parent. Thus, in our previous example, it would be possible to create a subdirectory from the DOS directory called SYSTEM. This directory would be identified as C:\DOS\SYSTEM, and would be completely independent of the subdirectory under WINDOWS, which would be identified as C:\ WINDOWS \SYSTEM.

When you create directories and place files in them, try to limit the number of files you put into any one directory. A large directory slows DOS down because DOS must search through more files. If you think your directories are becoming too large, reorganize them by using more subdirectories.

Here's one last detail about DOS operations: Due to a design limitation that dates back to single-sided floppies, DOS does not allow you to put multiple versions of a file in the same directory. For example, say that you have a file named JALAPENO.DOC that contains a killer recipe for hot sauce and you edit the file using a word processor. When you complete the editing task, you'll find a recently created file in your directory called JALAPENO.DOC. The older, original recipe file will either be written over or renamed JALAPENO.BAK (where BAK stands for backup). (The actual result depends on your word processor.) If you edit the recipe again, the JALAPENO.DOC file might be renamed JALAPENO.BAK and the original recipe file might be deleted because of the DOS limitation. This is mentioned here because it is probably the single most objectionable limitation of DOS file handling, and may become important to you later when you begin to create and modify data files.

1. Refer to Figure 7.2 to answer the following questions:
   (a) How many subdirectories are present?
   (b) How many parent directories contain subdirectories?
   (c) Specify the path to access a file in the subdirectory INVOICES.
   (d) Specify the path to access a file in the subdirectory BILLS.
2. Go to the DOS prompt and execute the TREE command. What happens?

1. (a) 7
   (b) 4
   (c) \RUTH\INVOICES
   (d) \JEFF\BILLS
2. DOS lists all of the subdirectories available in your system.

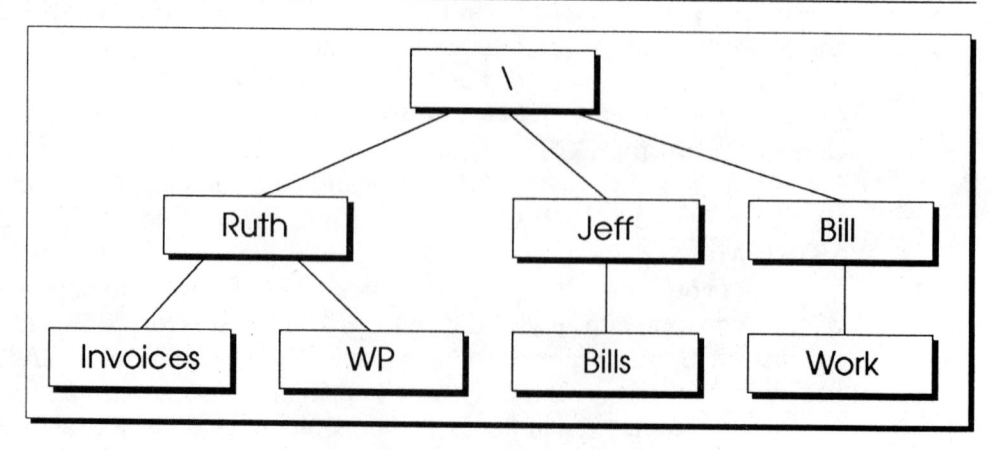

Figure 7.2. A Directory Tree Example

Introducing the File Manager

Now that you've had an opportunity to review the basics of disk organization under DOS, let's explore the File Manager—the tool Windows provides for accessing files and directories. The File Manager performs all of the major file and directory management operations that can be performed by DOS, including:

- Copying, moving, and deleting files
- Renaming files
- Viewing files in selected directories
- Viewing directories
- Selecting directories
- Creating and deleting directories
- Searching for files
- Running programs
- Formatting diskettes
- Selecting drives

In fact, the more you work with the File Manager, the more you'll be surprised at how easy it is to use.

Starting the File Manager

The easiest way to start the File Manager is to double-click on the File Manager icon, located in the Main group window.

If you don't have a mouse, open the Window menu in the Program Manager by pressing Alt+W and select the number for the Main window. After this window appears, use the arrow keys to highlight the File Manager icon and press the Enter key.

A Quick Look at the File Manager

Figure 7.3 shows how the File Manager window looks when it starts up. The File Manager actually has two separate parts: the File Manager window (containing the typical Windows menu bar), and the Directory Tree window (which illustrates the top level of directories on the default drive).

The File Manager Window provides the set of file-management commands. To access these commands, select the menu items, such as File, Disk, Tree, View, and so on. The main file and directory maintenance commands are located in the File menu.

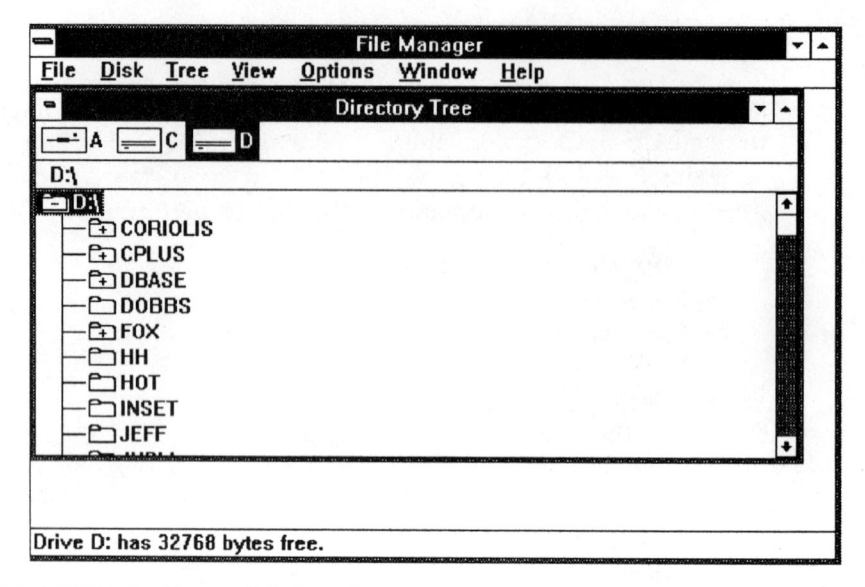

```
┌─────────────────────────────────────────────────────┐
│ ▬                      File Manager            ▼ ▲  │
│ File  Disk  Tree  View  Options  Window  Help       │
│ ┌─────────────────────────────────────────────┐ ▼▲ │
│ │               Directory Tree                │    │
│ │ ▭A  ▭C  ▭D                                  │    │
│ │ D:\                                         │    │
│ │ ▭ D:\                                    ↑  │    │
│ │   ├─ ⊞ CORIOLIS                             │    │
│ │   ├─ ⊞ CPLUS                                │    │
│ │   ├─ ⊞ DBASE                                │    │
│ │   ├─ ▭ DOBBS                                │    │
│ │   ├─ ⊞ FOX                                  │    │
│ │   ├─ ▭ HH                                   │    │
│ │   ├─ ▭ HOT                                  │    │
│ │   ├─ ▭ INSET                                │    │
│ │   ├─ ▭ JEFF                              ↓  │    │
│ └─────────────────────────────────────────────┘    │
│                                                     │
│ Drive D: has 32768 bytes free.                      │
└─────────────────────────────────────────────────────┘
```

Figure 7.3. The File Manager

The Directory Tree window provides a great deal of information at a glance. A set of icons appears on the line immediately below the title bar. The leftmost icon indicates that drive A is a floppy disk drive, and the second icon looks like the front of a hard disk. (In this example, drive D is a hard disk.) The background area around the icon for drive D appears dark because this icon is highlighted to indicate that drive D is the currently selected drive. These icons represent all of the installed drives that DOS detects for your system.

To select a different drive as the active one, click on the drive's icon. From the keyboard, use the Tab key to place the selection frame around the desired drive and then press the Enter key. The Directory Tree window changes to display the new directory information, starting with the root directory of the current drive.

☑ Start at the File Manager by double-clicking on the File Manager icon.
1. How many disk drives does your system have?
2. What's the difference between a floppy drive icon and a hard disk icon?
3. Open the File menu. What are the available commands?
4. Open the menus in the File Manager. Where is the Format Diskette... command located?
5. What information displays in the status bar at the bottom of the File Manager window?

1. Count the icons that appear under the Directory Tree title bar.
2. A floppy disk icon has a door that looks like a floppy disk faceplate.
3. Click on the File menu item, or press Alt+F. The commands are, Open, Run, Print, Associate, Search, Move, Copy, Delete, Rename, Change Attributes, Create Directory, Select All, and Delete All.
4. In the Disk menu.
5. The letter of the current drive and the amount of free disk space available.

The area directly below the drive icons provides useful file-status information. The text inside the square brackets identifies the volume label for the selected drive. This information can be very useful when working with removable media drives, such as floppy disks and removable hard disks. The second item on this line identifies the full pathname to get to the highlighted directory in the window area.

Using the Directory Tree Window

The Directory Tree window in Figure 7.4 shows a directory structure with the root directory D: and numerous subdirectories. Each subdirectory is represented with a file folder icon. Notice that the subdirectory icons for the WINDOWS and TEMP subdirectories contain a plus sign (+). This symbol indicates

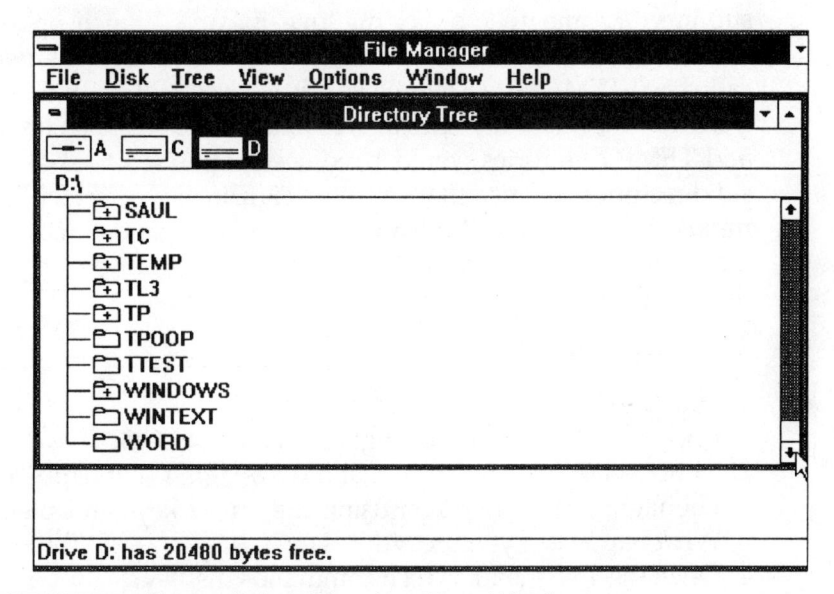

Figure 7.4. A Directory Tree Window

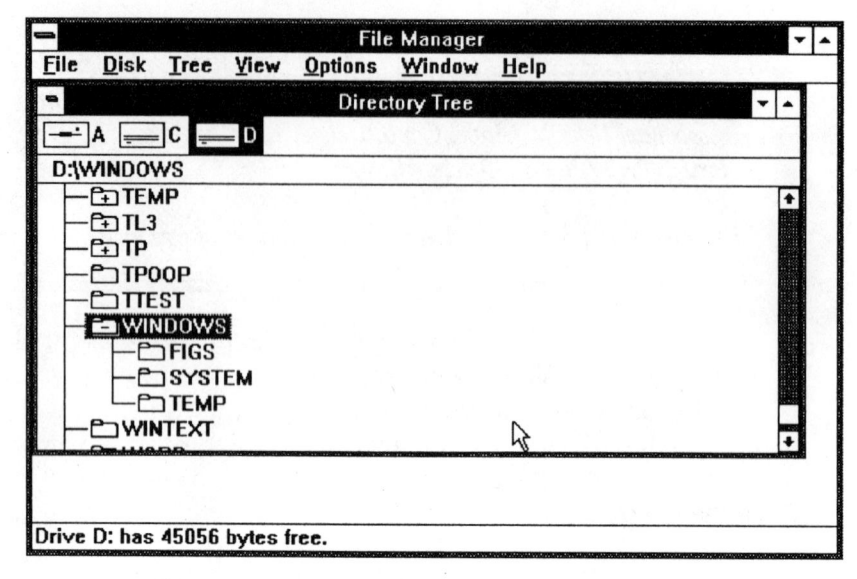

Figure 7.5. The WINDOWS Subdirectory

that these two directories contain other subdirectories. You'll also find a minus sign (-) on some directory icons. This symbol indicates that a directory has been expanded. If you click on the icon, the subdirectory branches extended from that icon are collapsed.

Figure 7.5 shows what happens if you click on the WINDOWS subdirectory and then select the Tree Expand Branch option from the Tree menu. As you can see, the WINDOWS subdirectory has two subdirectories, called SYSTEM and TEMP. (If you had selected the Tree Expand All option from the Tree menu rather than Tree Expand Branch, then both the WINDOWS and TEMP directories would have been expanded to show the next level of subdirectories.) Notice that the plus sign in the directory icon changes to a minus sign when the WINDOWS directory expands. Recall that this symbol indicates that you can make the subdirectories disappear again by clicking on the icon containing the minus sign.

Start at the Directory Tree window.
1. Click on a directory to highlight it. What happens?
2. Double-click on a directory that has a + sign. What happens?
3. Highlight a directory icon using the arrow keys and then press the * key. What happens if you press the - key?
4. Open the Tree menu. Which commands display?

1. *A directory displays as a file folder icon.*
2. *The selected directory expands in the Directory Tree window.*
3. *The highlighted directory expands. Pressing the * is the same as selecting the Expand Branch command. When you press -, the tree branch collapses.*
4. *Expand One Level, Expand Branch, Expand All, Collapse Branch.*

Viewing a Directory

Now that you've seen the basic features of the File Manager, let's examine how the contents of directories are displayed. You can open a window containing a list of the files in a directory by double-clicking on the directory icon. For example, Figure 7.6 illustrates what you see if you open the WINDOWS directory just described. Notice that the first two entries are the .. and FIGS subdirectories. Windows provides a consistent location for subdirectories by placing the subdirectory icons at the beginning of the listing, so you don't have to search through a directory to find a particular subdirectory.

To use the keyboard to open a directory, first highlight the directory and then press the Enter key or select the Open command from the File menu.

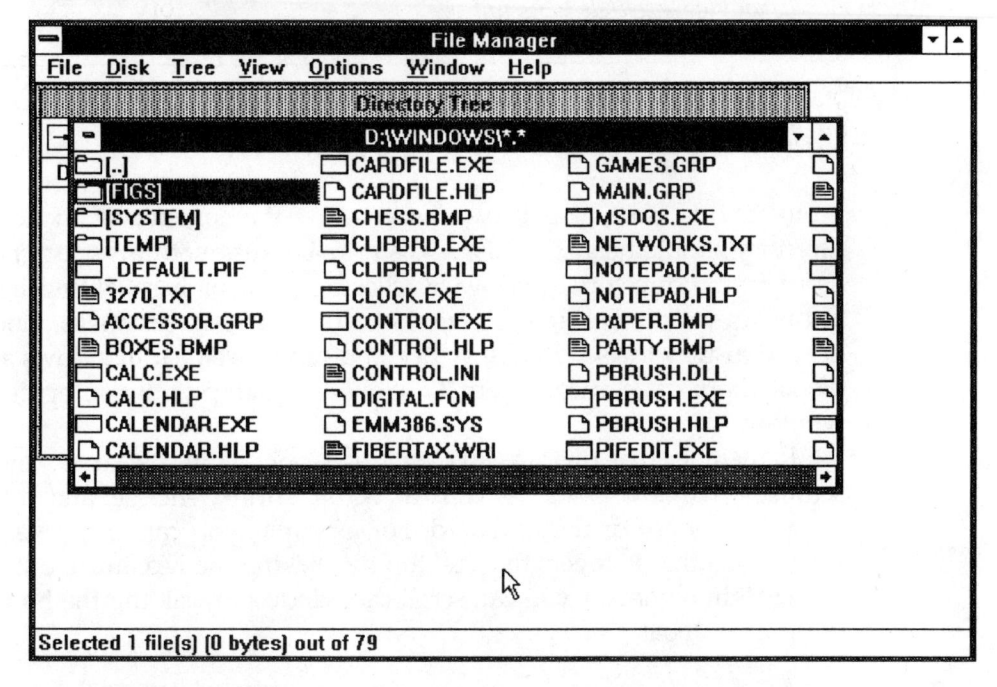

Figure 7.6. Opening the WINDOWS Subdirectory

When you open a directory, its contents always display in a window. As Figure 7.6 shows, the title of the window represents the full pathname for the selected directory. A filename pattern after the directory name indicates the types of files that appear in the directory window.

---

1. What is the full directory path for the directory window shown in Figure 7.6?
2. What is the file pattern shown in Figure 7.6?
3. What information displays in the status bar at the bottom of the window?
4. True or false? The Directory Tree allows you to display the directory structure of one drive at a time.
5. Double-click on the title bar of a directory window. What happens?

---

1. *D:\WINDOWS.*
2. **.* (All files).*
3. *The number of files selected, the number of bytes in the selected files, and the total number of files listed in the window.*
4. *True.*
5. *The window expands to its full size.*

Opening Multiple Directory Windows

From time to time, you may need to view the contents of more than one directory simultaneously. This task is easy because you can select a directory listed in the directory window by clicking on it or highlighting it with the arrow keys and pressing the Enter key. The File Manager opens another window to display the selected directory. You can move these windows around to display both directories. Figure 7.7 shows a desktop with two open directory windows.

Remember that the directory windows operate in the same way as other scrollable windows. That is, you can scroll, shrink, enlarge, and move them using the mouse or the keyboard. For example, you can enlarge a directory window so that it covers the desktop by clicking the Maximize button in the upper-right corner, or you can scroll the window by sliding the horizontal or vertical scroll bar.

The File Manager

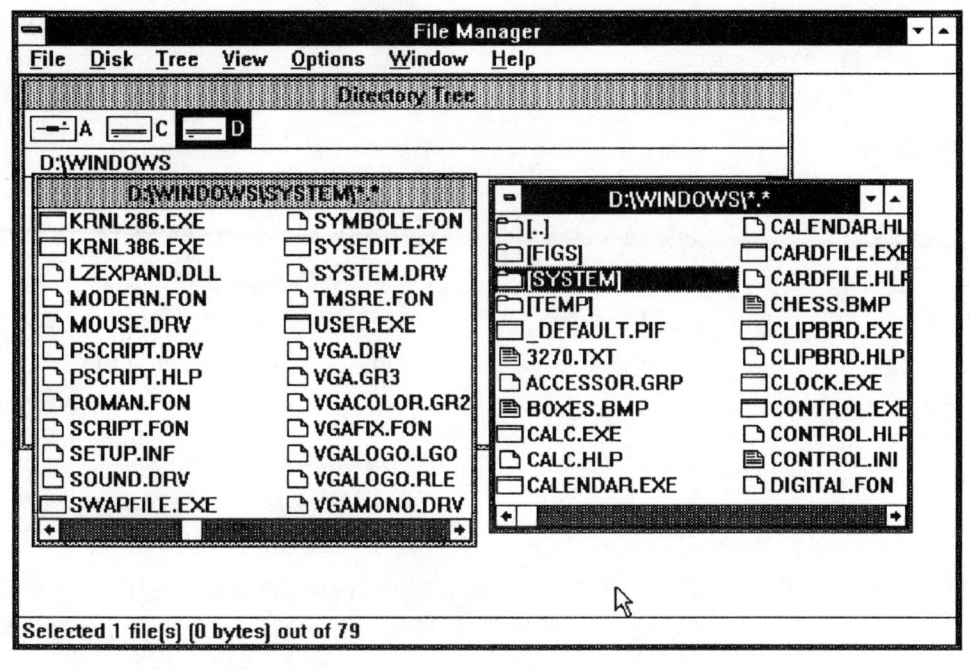

![File Manager window showing Directory Tree with D:\WINDOWS selected, and two open directory windows: D:\WINDOWS\SYSTEM*.* containing files like KRNL286.EXE, KRNL386.EXE, LZEXPAND.DLL, MODERN.FON, MOUSE.DRV, PSCRIPT.DRV, PSCRIPT.HLP, ROMAN.FON, SCRIPT.FON, SETUP.INF, SOUND.DRV, SWAPFILE.EXE, SYMBOLE.FON, SYSEDIT.EXE, SYSTEM.DRV, TMSRE.FON, USER.EXE, VGA.DRV, VGA.GR3, VGACOLOR.GR2, VGAFIX.FON, VGALOGO.LGO, VGALOGO.RLE, VGAMONO.DRV; and D:\WINDOWS*.* containing [..], [FIGS], [SYSTEM], [TEMP], _DEFAULT.PIF, 3270.TXT, ACCESSOR.GRP, BOXES.BMP, CALC.EXE, CALC.HLP, CALENDAR.EXE, CALENDAR.HL, CARDFILE.EXE, CARDFILE.HLP, CHESS.BMP, CLIPBRD.EXE, CLIPBRD.HLP, CLOCK.EXE, CONTROL.EXE, CONTROL.HLP, CONTROL.INI, DIGITAL.FON. Status bar reads "Selected 1 file(s) (0 bytes) out of 79".]

Figure 7.7. Two Open Directories

If you plan to use multiple directories but you don't want to see them all open simultaneously, select the Replace on Open option from the File Manager's View menu. This option tells the File Manager to remove the current directory window when you select a new directory to be opened. If this option is not active, new directory windows appear in a tiled format over the previously displayed directory window. This tiling can get quite cluttered after a few directories have been opened.

Tip || To display directory windows in a cascade format, press Shift+F5 at any time.

Navigation Shortcuts

You can use the mouse to easily access all of the File Manager commands and perform navigation-related tasks in the Directory Tree and directory windows. If you use the keyboard, a number of shortcuts will help you navigate and perform basic commands. Table 7.1 lists the keyboard shortcuts for each of the three main windows provided with the File Manager.

Table 7.1. Shortcut Keys for Navigating in the File Manager

Key	Area	Description
Shift+F4	File Manager	Tile document windows
F5	File Manager	Issue the Refresh command
Shift+F5	File Manager	Cascade document windows
F7	File Manager	Issue the Move... command
F8	File Manager	Issue the Copy... command
Delete	File manager	Issue the Delete... command
-	Directory Tree	Collapse a directory
+	Directory Tree	Expand a directory
*	Directory Tree	Expand entire branch of directory
Ctrl+*	Directory Tree	Expand all directories
X	Directory Tree	Move to directory with first letter X
Ctrl+X	Directory Tree	Select and activate disk drive with first letter X.
Right arrow	Directory Tree	Move to first subdirectory of selected directory
Left arrow	Directory Tree	Move to directory in previous directory level
Ctrl+Up arrow	Directory Tree	Move to previous directory in same level
Ctrl+Down arrow	Directory Tree	Move to next directory in same level
Page Up	Directory Tree	Move up one directory
Page Down	Directory Tree	Move down one directory
Home	Directory Tree	Move to root directory
End	Directory Tree	Move to the last directory
Up Arrow	Directory windows	Move to file or directory above selected one
Down Arrow	Directory windows	Move to file or directory below the selected one
Page Up	Directory windows	Move to first file/directory in previous window
Page Down	Directory windows	Move to first file/directory in next window
Home	Directory windows	Move to first file/directory in window
End	Directory windows	Move to the last file/directory in window
Ctrl+/	Directory windows	Select all files in window
Ctrl+\	Directory windows	Deselect all files in window

1. Open a directory so that its contents display in a directory window. Press Ctrl+/. What information displays in the bottom status bar?
2. Highlight a directory and press the Enter key. What happens?
3. If multiple directory windows are displayed, which keys are available for switching between the windows?
4. True or false? You can move to a directory listed in a directory window by typing the first letter of the directory's name.

1. *The number of bytes required to store all of the files, and the number of files in the selected directory.*
2. *A new directory window displays, listing the contents of the selected directory.*
3. *Page Up and Page Dn.*
4. *True.*

Determining File and Directory Information

Returning to Figure 7.7, notice that the nondirectory files are sorted alphabetically by name. In addition, directories are listed before files. This is fine if you just want to find a specific file, but what if you want to know how big a file is, determine the attributes of a file, or view all files having the same extension in one group? Fortunately, the File Manager provides a number of options to help you view files and directories. You can perform these major tasks:

- List files and directories in alphabetical order.
- List files categorized by their extensions.
- Sort files by their size or their last modification date.
- List files and directories with all of their attributes displayed.
- List hidden and system files and directories.
- List only selected file types.

Finding the Size of a File

As we've seen, you can find a file's size by looking at the status bar at the bottom of the Directory Tree window. When you scroll down the file list using the Up and Down Arrow keys, the highlighted bar moves to the next file on the list. When each new file is highlighted, the Status Bar indicates that file's size. You can also highlight a file with the mouse by using the scroll bar to position the window in the directory list and clicking on a filename.

Viewing File Information

Another way to get more information about files is to select the File Details option from the View menu. Notice that the previous default was View Name (a checkmark appeared next to the option). Figure 7.8 shows how the directory window looks when the File Details option is active. The files are still sorted in alphabetical order by name, but now you can see the size of each file, the date and time when the file was last modified, and file flags that indicate whether the file is a Hidden file, a System file, a Read only file, and an Archived file.

If you only want to view some of the file status information, select the Other... option from the View menu to bring up the dialog box shown in Figure 7.9. Select the attributes you want to see by selecting the corresponding check

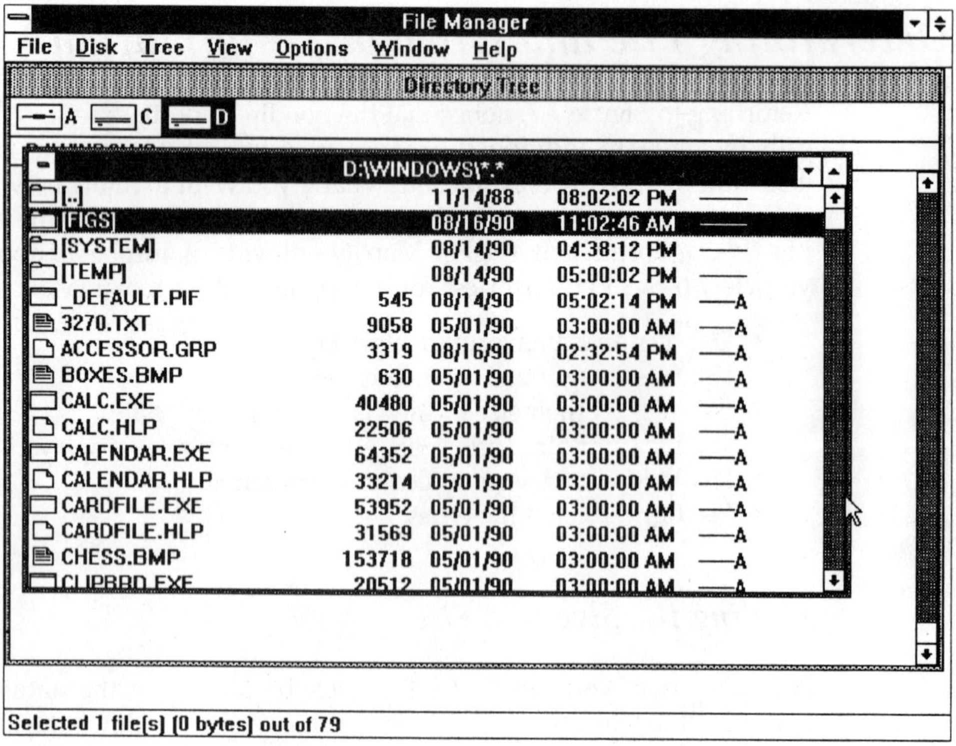

Figure 7.8. Viewing with the File Details Option

The File Manager

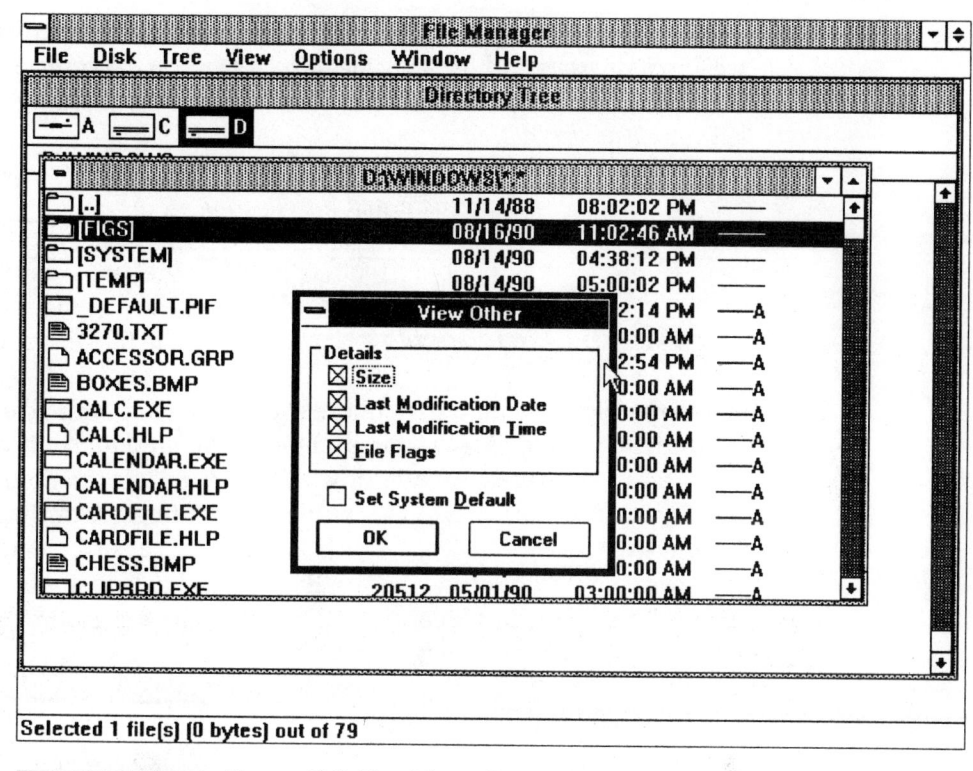

Figure 7.9. The View Other Dialog Box

box. This option provides a great deal of control over your directory display. Notice that below the file attribute options, an additional box marked Set System Defaults appears. If you select this check box before activating the OK window button, the File Manager applies this set of defaults to all directory windows. If this option is not activated, only the current directory window is affected.

Start at the Directory Tree window. Make sure that one of your hard disk drives is selected by clicking on a drive icon.
1. Open one of the directories listed in the directory tree. What happens?
2. Configure the directory window so that all of the file attributes display.
3. Select the Other... command from the View menu. What happens?
4. Click on the File Flags check box (or press Alt+F) to deselect this option. Then, select the OK button. Which attributes display?

1. *Double-click on a directory icon. A directory window with the same name as the selected directory opens, and the set of files displays for that directory.*
2. *Select the File Details option from the View menu. Each file is listed with its attributes, such as size, date, and time.*
3. *The View Other dialog box displays, and all of the check boxes are selected.*
4. *Only the attributes for file size, date, and time display.*

Viewing Files by Categories

Returning to the View menu, we'll explore several more options. The first three items in the menu (Name, File Details, and Other) identify the level of information displayed in the directory window. The second group of options (By Name, By Type, and Sort by...) identify how your files are arranged in the directory window.

The first option in the second group, By Name, displays the files in alphabetical order based on the filename to the left of the extension. The second option, By Type, arranges the files in alphabetical order based on the file extension, such as .DOC or .EXE. As we'll see next, the third option allows you to view your files in a sorted order.

Sorting and Excluding Files

The Sort by... command brings up the dialog box shown in Figure 7.10. The first two options, Name and Type, perform the same sorting operation as the By Name and By Type options in the View menu. The third option, Size, displays files in order of decreasing size. The fourth option, Last Modification Date, sorts files for display using the date when the files were last written; the most recently modified files display first.

The Sort By dialog box also contains a Set System Default check box so that you can select a sorting arrangement to be used for all of your directory displays. If you select this check box while you're setting the sorting options, each new directory window displayed later will use the same sorting options.

In addition to displaying directories in sorted order, you can tell the File Manager which files you want to view by using the Include... command in the View menu. The main advantage of using this feature is that you can limit the number of files displayed in a window. For example, you can use this option to list only the directories or files with the extension .EXE .

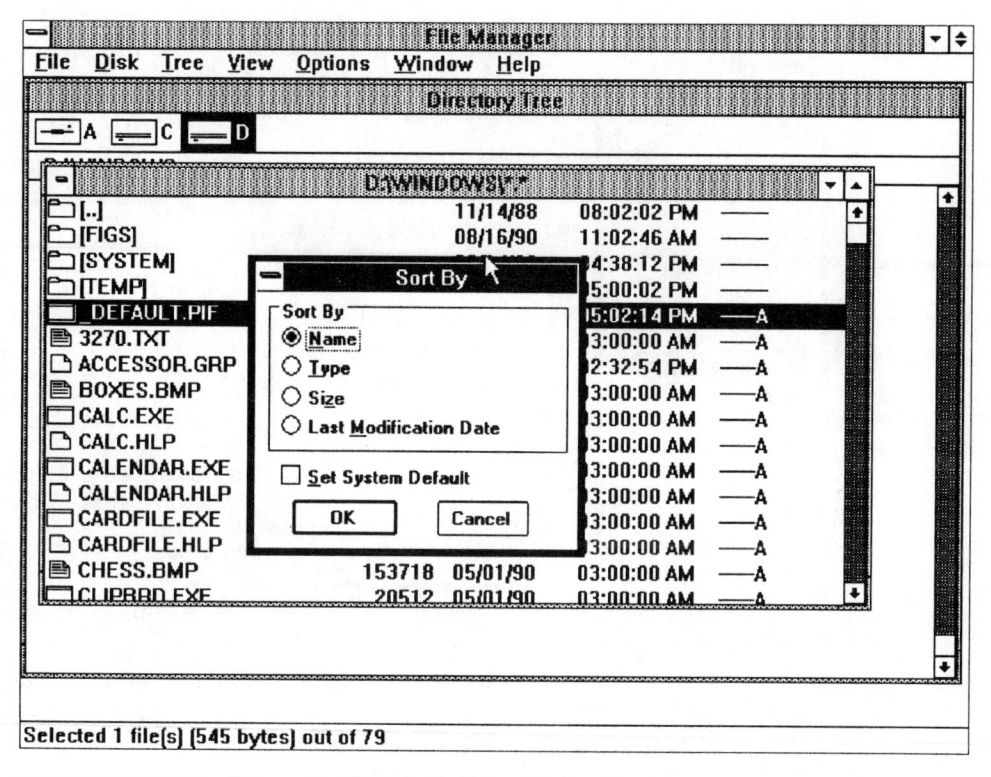

Figure 7.10. The Sort By Dialog Box

The Include... command opens the dialog box shown in Figure 7.11. Notice that you can select categories of files such as directories, programs, and documents.

To view only directories, deselect all of the check boxes in the File Type group except the Directories option. To view files that have a program icon select only the Programs option. You can select the Documents option, on the other hand, to view all files that serve as document files for applications. (A Word for Windows or Write document file would fit in this category.) To view all files that don't belong to the other categories directories, programs, and documents, select the Other Files category.

Using a Filter

You can also specify that only a particular group of files should display by filling in the filter information in the Name text box at the top of the Include

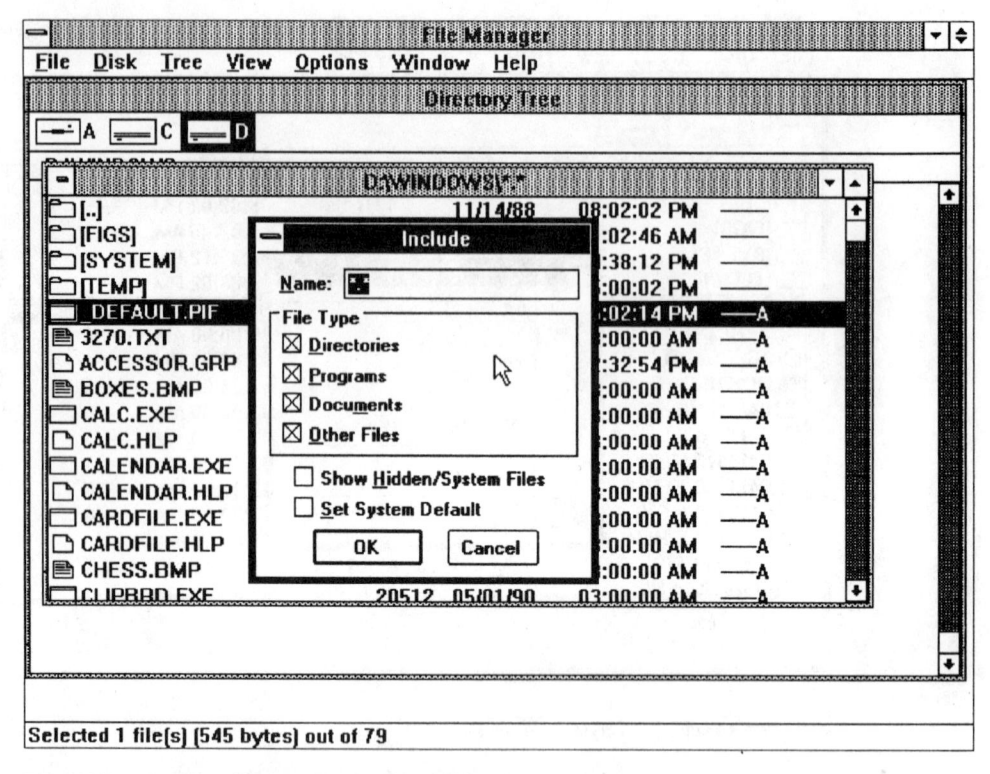

Figure 7.11. The Include Dialog Box

dialog box. To specify a filter, use the two standard DOS wildcards: ? and *. The ? wildcard represents a single character, and the * wildcard represents a series of characters. For example, if you want to display all files with the .BMP extension (recall that .BMP files are created by Windows Paint and can be used as the Desktop Wallpaper), type the five characters *.BMP in the text box. To view .BMP files whose name fields start with the letter "C," type the six characters C*.BMP into the box at the top of the View Include window.

The Include dialog box contains two additional check boxes: the familiar Set System Default option (which operates the same as in the other windows), and the Show Hidden/System Files option. The second option allows you to view the names, sizes and other information associated with files that are normally hidden from the user.

Bring up a directory window by double-clicking on a folder icon in the Directory Tree window.
1. Set up the directory window to list the files in the directory by type.

2. Sort your files by their size.
3. Sort your files by their last modification date.
4. Have the directory window list only directories.
5. Have the directory window list hidden files and programs.

---

1. *Select the By Type option from the View menu.*
2. *Open the Sort By dialog box by selecting the Sort by... command from the View menu and select only the Size option.*
3. *Select the Last Modification Date option.*
4. *Open the Include dialog box by selecting the Include... command from the View menu, and select only the Directories check box.*
5. *Select the Show Hidden/System Files and the Programs check boxes.*

Selecting Files and Directories

Before you can use the File Manager to perform file and directory operations such as copying, deleting, and renaming, you need to know how to select them. We've already seen how to click on a single directory to select it from the Directory Tree window, and how to click on a file or a directory to select it from a directory window. With the keyboard, you can use the arrow keys and the other direction keys (Page Up, Page Dn, Home, and End) to highlight a file or a directory.

To perform some file management operations such as copying files or deleting directories, you need to select multiple files or directories. If the files or directories are listed together, click on the first file or directory, press the Shift key, and then click the last file in the group. The File Manager highlights the group of files for you. You can use the keyboard to highlight the first item, press and hold down the Shift key, and then press the up or down arrow to select the rest of the files in the group.

How can you select files that aren't listed together? Using the mouse, click on the first item, and then press the Ctrl key and click on each additional item. Each time you click on an item, it becomes highlighted. If you select an item that you don't want, simply click on it again. To select nongrouped files with the keyboard, press Shift+F8 to activate the selection frame (Figure 7.12). Move the selection frame around with the arrow keys, and press the spacebar to select an item. When you're done selecting files or directories, press Shift+F8 again.

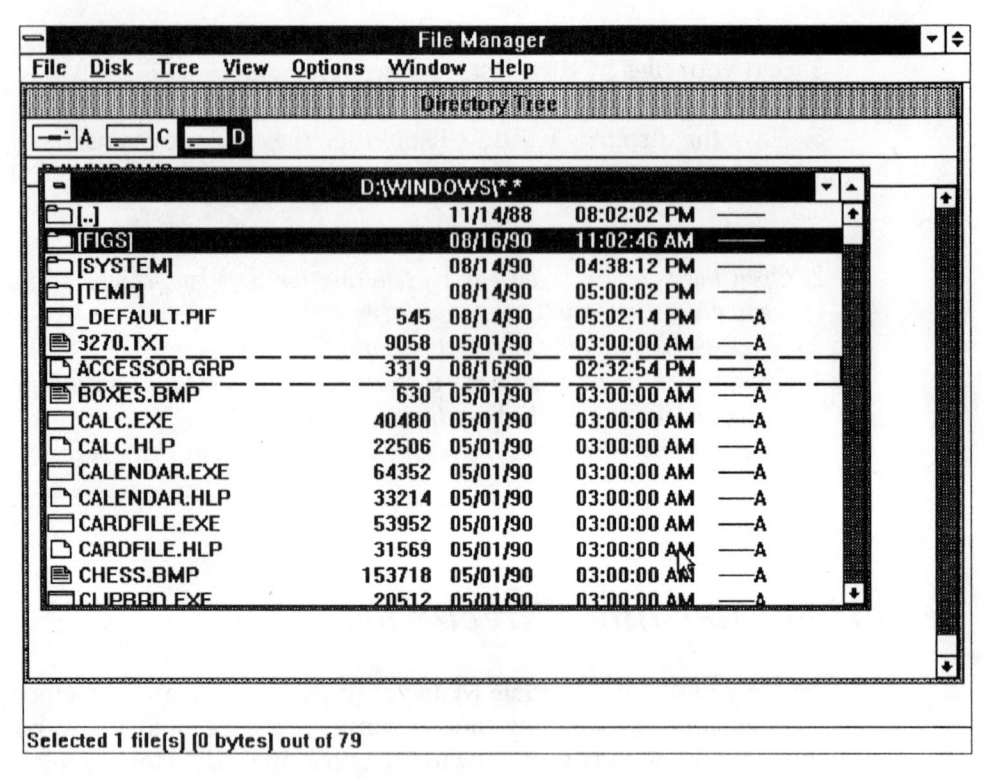

```
                          File Manager
File  Disk  Tree  View  Options  Window  Help
                          Directory Tree
 ▭A  ▭C  ▭D

                       D:\WINDOWS\*.*
  [..]                          11/14/88   08:02:02 PM   ——
  [FIGS]                        08/16/90   11:02:46 AM   ——
  [SYSTEM]                      08/14/90   04:38:12 PM   ——
  [TEMP]                        08/14/90   05:00:02 PM   ——
  _DEFAULT.PIF            545   08/14/90   05:02:14 PM   ——A
  3270.TXT               9058   05/01/90   03:00:00 AM   ——A
  ACCESSOR.GRP           3319   08/16/90   02:32:54 PM   ——A
  BOXES.BMP               630   05/01/90   03:00:00 AM   ——A
  CALC.EXE              40480   05/01/90   03:00:00 AM   ——A
  CALC.HLP              22506   05/01/90   03:00:00 AM   ——A
  CALENDAR.EXE          64352   05/01/90   03:00:00 AM   ——A
  CALENDAR.HLP          33214   05/01/90   03:00:00 AM   ——A
  CARDFILE.EXE          53952   05/01/90   03:00:00 AM   ——A
  CARDFILE.HLP          31569   05/01/90   03:00:00 AM   ——A
  CHESS.BMP            153718   05/01/90   03:00:00 AM   ——A
  CLIPBRD.EXE           20512   05/01/90   03:00:00 AM   ——A

Selected 1 file(s) (0 bytes) out of 79
```

Figure 7.12. Selecting Nongrouped Files

Tip Here's a shortcut for selecting all of the files in a directory window: press Ctrl+/, or click on the Select All command from the File menu.

Moving Files and Directories

One of the advantages of working with multiple directories is that you can maintain temporary or extra copies of files in different directories. For example, if you're using a word processor (such as Word for Windows) to create document files that you're storing in a directory named \WORD\DOCS, you can keep extra copies of the files in another directory named \WORD\DOCS\BACKUP.

The process of moving and copying files or directories from one directory to another is quite easy with the File Manager, especially because you don't have to memorize any cryptic DOS commands. Let's examine the move operation first, and then we'll show you how to copy files and directories.

The File Manager

When you move a file from one directory to another on the same disk drive, an image of the file is moved to the destination directory, while the original image is deleted from the source directory. When you move a directory, on the other hand, the File Manager physically places that directory into the destination directory, so all of the files and subdirectories associated with that directory are also moved.

To move one or more files or directories using the mouse, open the directory where the item you want to move is stored. You must also know where you want to move the item, and make sure that this destination directory is visible on the desktop. (If you've opened many directory windows, remember that you can minimize a directory window and represent it as an icon.) When both the source and the destination directories are in plain view, click on the item you want to move and drag it to the destination directory. This action brings up the Confirm Mouse Operation dialog box (Figure 7.13). Click the Yes button to complete the operation.

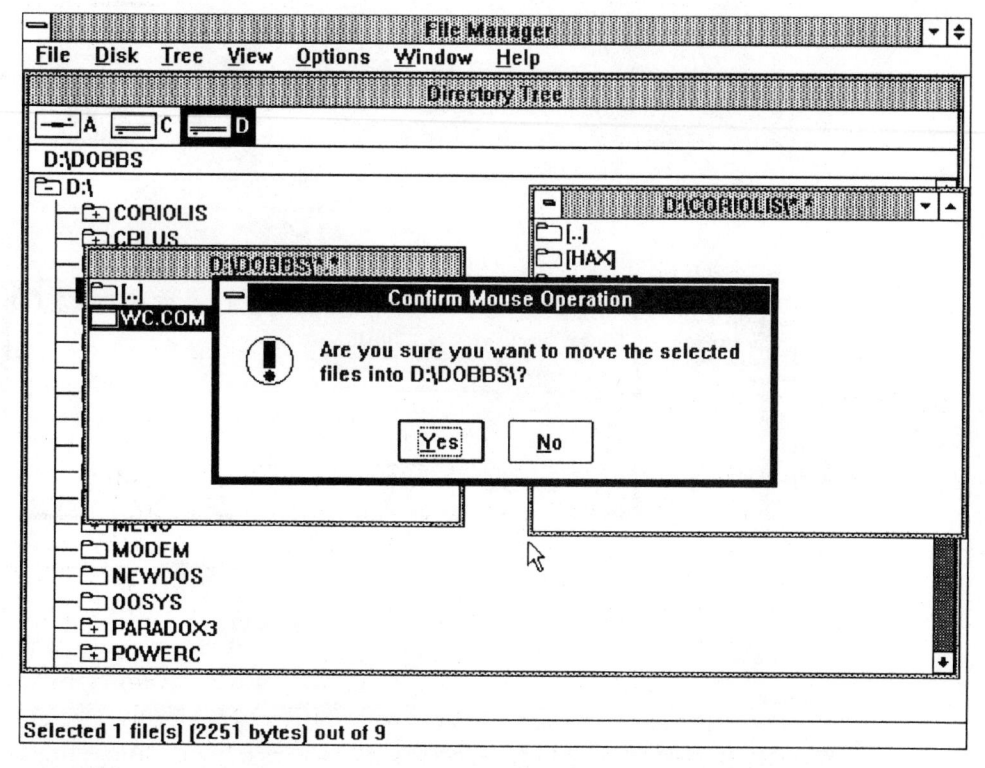

Figure 7.13. The Confirm Mouse Operation Dialog Box

When moving files or directories, keep in mind that you can also move multiple files or directories at the same time. Hold the Ctrl key down and click on each item you want to move until they're all highlighted. Next, release the Ctrl key and drag the group of selected items to the destination directory.

Tip When dragging files to a new directory window, make sure the files are placed in an open area of the window and not on top of a file folder icon. If you drag the highlighted items on top of a file folder, the files are placed into the directory represented by the icon, and not into the directory represented by the directory window.

As an alternative to using the mouse to move a file or directory, the File manager provides the Move... command in the File menu. To use this feature, select the items you want to move and activate the Move... command. The dialog box shown in Figure 7.14 asks you to specify a destination directory. The From text box lists the files or directories that you have selected to be moved. Type the name of the destination directory, including a complete pathname

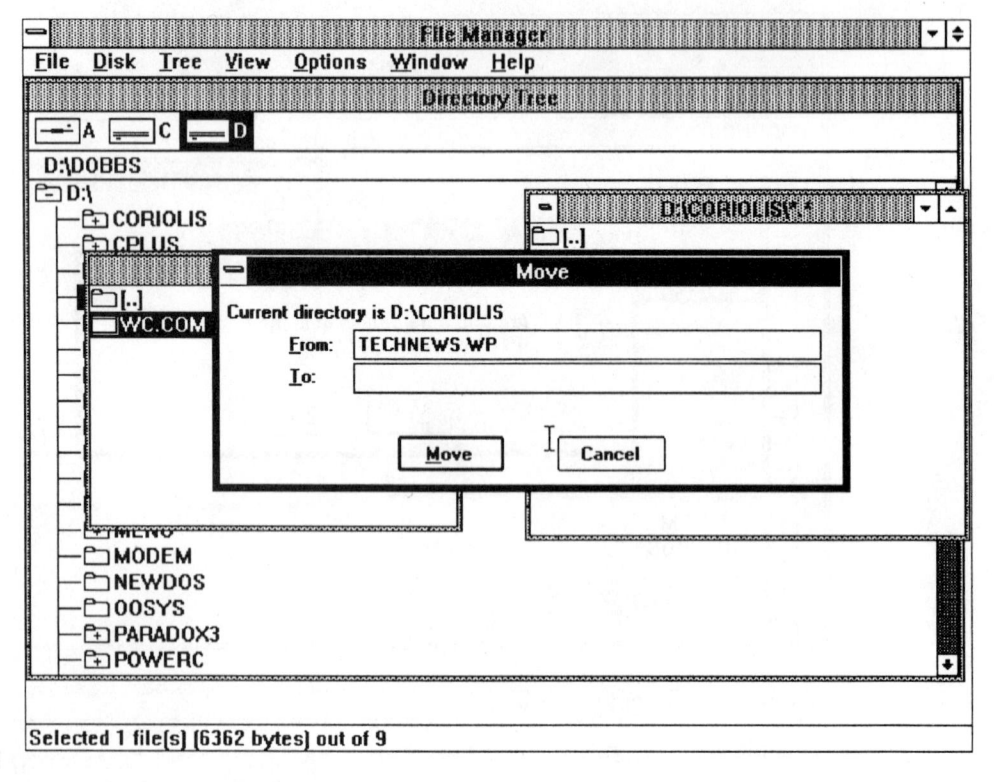

Figure 7.14. The Move Dialog Box

into the To text box. For example, if you want to move files to the directory C:\WORD\DOCS\BACKUP, type C:\WORD\DOCS\BACKUP in the To box. Select the Move button to finish the operation.

Up until this point, we've explained how you can move files and directories between directories on the same drive. In some cases, you'll also want to move them between drives. For example, you might want to move a document file on drive C to a diskette in drive A to make a backup copy. Moving items between drives with the mouse is essentially the same as moving items on the same drive. The only difference is that you must hold down the Alt key when dragging the item.

Start at a directory window for one of the hard disks installed on your system.
1. Move a file in one directory to a new directory.
2. Move a file in one directory to a new directory so that the file has a new name in the destination directory.

---

1. (a) *Make sure that the window or icon for the destination directory is in view.*
   (b) *Select the file to be moved by clicking on it.*
   (c) *Drag the file to the destination directory window or icon.*
   (d) *Click the Yes button in the Confirm Mouse Operation dialog box.*
   (e) *Examine the source directory to make sure the file has been moved.*
2. (a) *Select the file to be moved by clicking on it.*
   (b) *Press Alt+F to open the File menu, and then select the Move... command.*
   (c) *Enter the destination directory and the new filename for the file.*
   (d) *Select the Move button.*

Copying Files and Directories

The process of copying a file or directory is different from moving one because the File Manager makes a duplicate of the selected file or directory in the destination directory without affecting the original version. To copy a file on the same drive, first open the source directory so that the file is visible. Drag the directory to another part of the screen so that you can see both the filename and the destination directory icon in the File Manager window at the same time. Move the mouse cursor to the file to be copied, hold down the Ctrl key, press down the left mouse button, and drag the resulting icon to the directory tree area so that it overlays the destination directory. Release the left mouse button and then the Ctrl key. When the Confirm Mouse Operation dialog box appears (Figure 7.15), click on the Yes button.

The File Manager allows you to copy multiple files or directories at once. Again, you must first select all of the files or directories to be copied. Recall that to select a group of files that appear together in the directory listing, click on the first one and then press the Shift key while clicking on the last file in the group. (You can also click on the last file and Shift+click on the first file.) To select several files that don't appear together in the directory window, click on the first one and hold down the Ctrl key while you click on the other files.

Another useful operation is copying a file from one drive to another. To do this, simply drag the selected items to the destination directory without holding down the Ctrl key.

If you are using the keyboard, you can copy files by following the basic procedure we described for moving files. First, highlight the files or directories to be copied, and then select the Copy... command from the File menu. When you see the dialog box shown in Figure 7.16, type the complete pathname of the destination directory into the To text box, and select the Copy button.

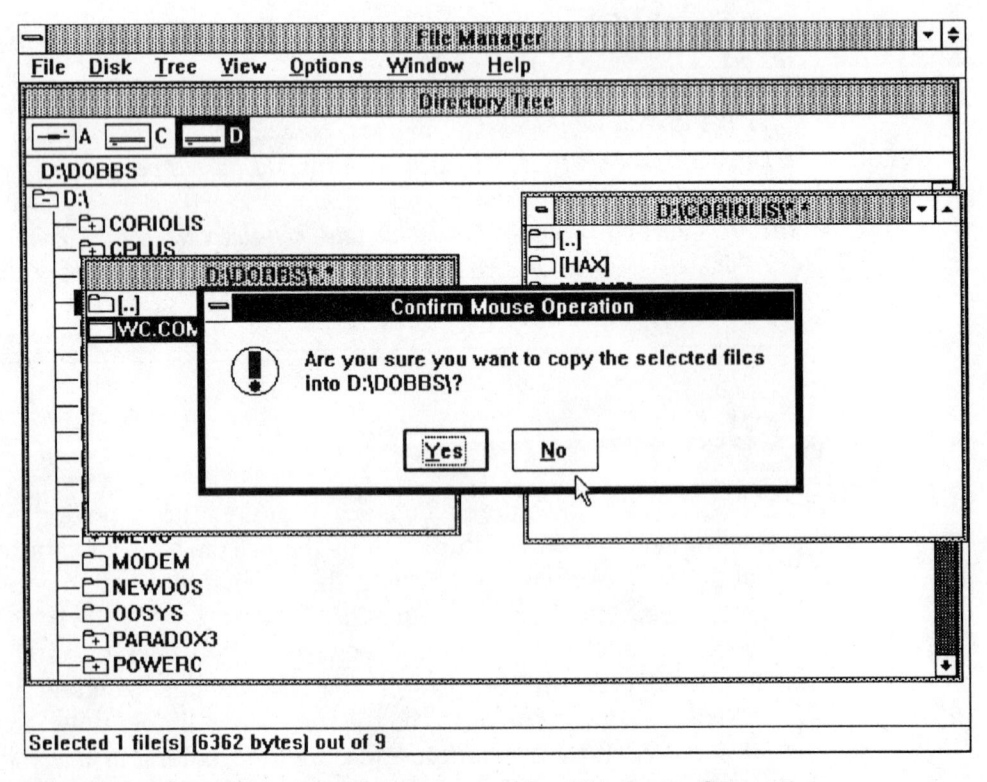

Figure 7.15. Confirming the File Copy Operation

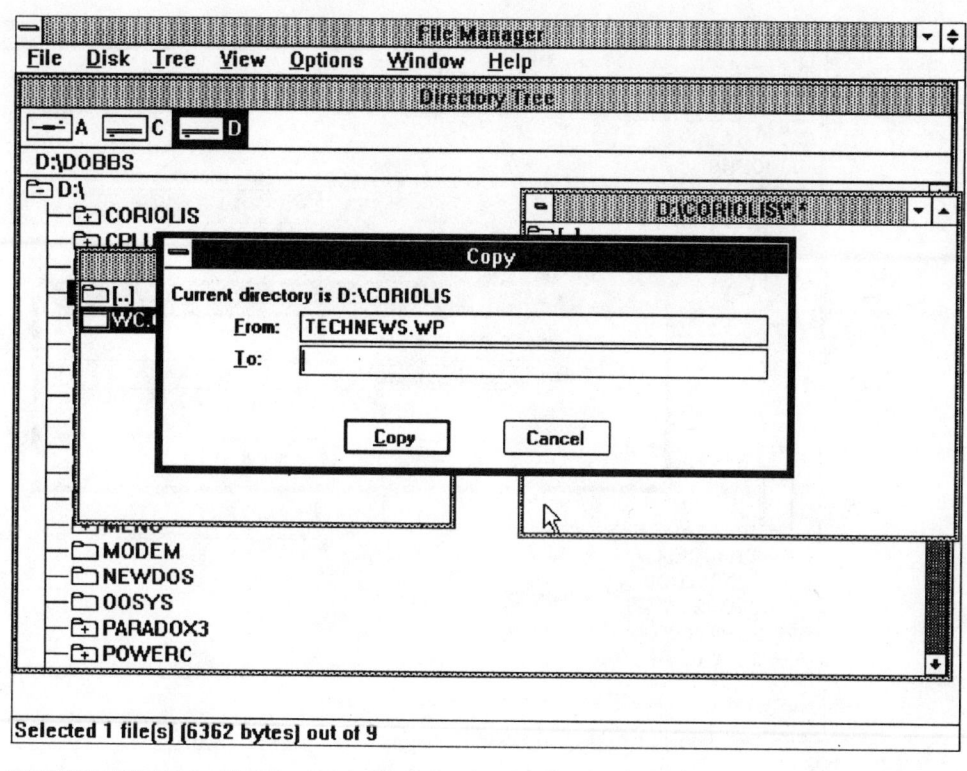

Figure 7.16. The Copy Dialog Box

Tip To copy a file to a directory and change the file's name, simply enter a destination path and new filename in the To text box. For example, to copy the file BUDGET.DOC in the directory \WORD to the directory \WORD\DOCS and give it the new name OLDBDG1.DOC, type the text \WORD\DOCS\OLDBDG1.DOC into the To box.

Deleting Files and Directories

Deleting a file is quite easy—but remember, once you delete a file it will be unaccessible unless you use a separate file undelete utility (not included in Windows) to recover it. To delete a file, click on the filename to highlight it, and press the Del (or Delete) key on the keyboard. The File Manager displays the Delete dialog box (Figure 7.17), asking you to confirm the delete operation. When you click the Yes button, the file is deleted. If you marked multiple files for deletion, a warning dialog box displays for each file.

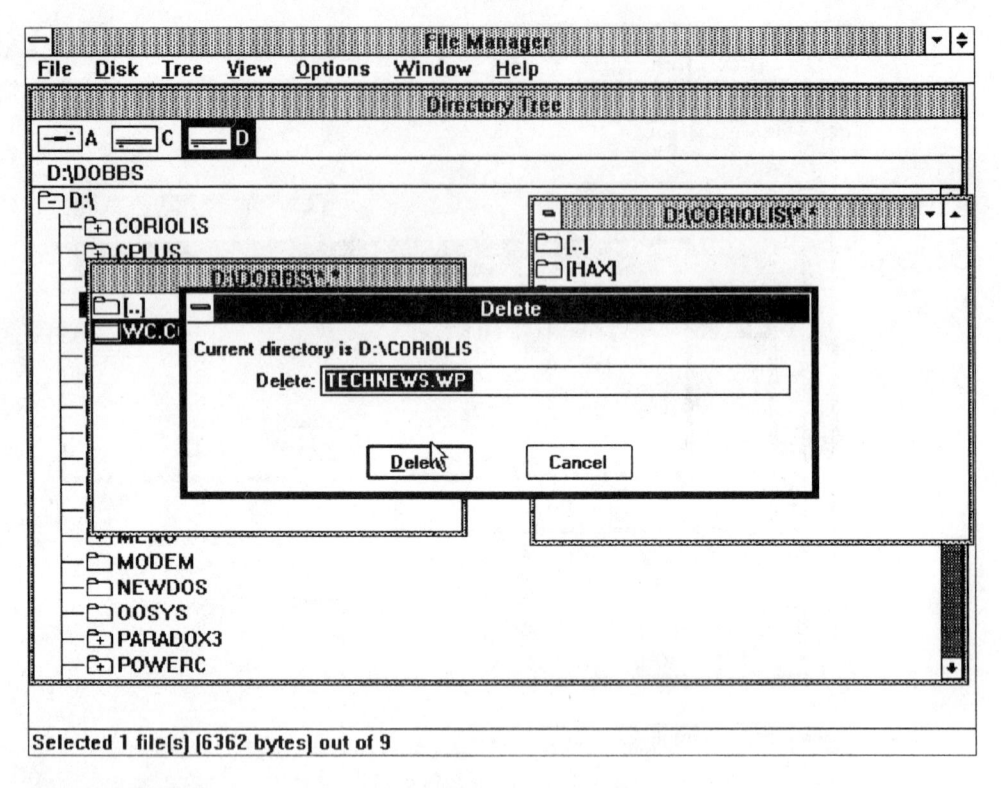

Figure 7.17. The Delete Dialog Box

> Start at a directory window for one of the hard disks installed on your system.
> 1. Copy a file in one directory to a new directory on the same hard drive.
> 2. Copy a file in one directory to a new directory on a different hard drive, so that the file has a new name in the destination directory.
> 3. Delete the file just copied.

1. *(a) Make sure that the window or icon for the destination directory is in view.*
   (b) Select the file to be copied by clicking on it.
   (c) Hold down the Ctrl key.
   (c) Drag the file to the destination directory window or icon.
   (d) Click the Yes button in the Confirm Mouse Operation dialog box.
2. *(a) Select the file to be copied by clicking on it.*
   (b) Press Alt+F to open the File menu, and then select the Copy... command.
   (c) Enter the destination directory and new filename for the file.
   (d) Select the Copy button.

3. (a) *Select the file to be deleted.*
   (b) *Open the File menu and select the Delete command.*
   (c) *Click the Yes button in the warning dialog box.*

Searching for Files and Directories

If you have a typical hard disk that contains numerous files and subdirectories, you already know how difficult it can be to locate a file or directory. Fortunately, if you know the name of the file or the directory, you can easily locate it using the File Manager. The File Manager simplifies the work of searching for "misplaced" files through the Search... command of the File menu.

Before invoking this command, you must decide where you want Windows to begin the search. Searching always begins in the directory highlighted in the Directory Tree window. If the selected directory contains subdirectories, those subdirectories are also searched. Figure 7.18 shows the dialog box that

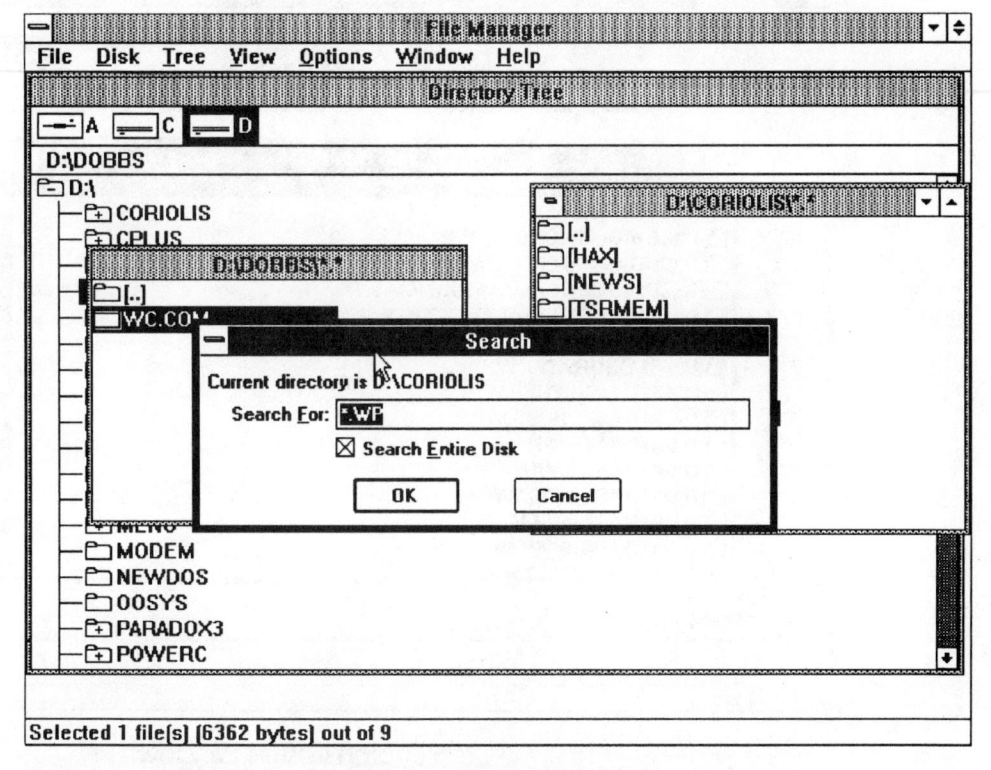

Figure 7.18. The Search Dialog Box

appears when Search... is invoked. Enter the desired filename in the Search For text box at the top of the dialog box, and click the OK button to start the search. For example, imagine that you created a Windows Write file that started with the three letters JOE, but you can't remember the rest of the filename. Write files have the .WRI extension, so you can type the eight characters JOE*.WRI in the box, and then click on the OK window button.

If you don't remember where a file is located, select the Search Entire Disk check box. Be prepared to wait for a while because a complete disk search takes time.

The results of a search are shown as icons in a Search Results document window (Figure 7.19). Each icon provides the full path of the filename. You can access these icons just as you would access the file icons in a directory window. That is, you can open, delete, rename, move, or copy any of them. When you're done using this window, double-click on its Control menu icon to close it, or press Alt+F4.

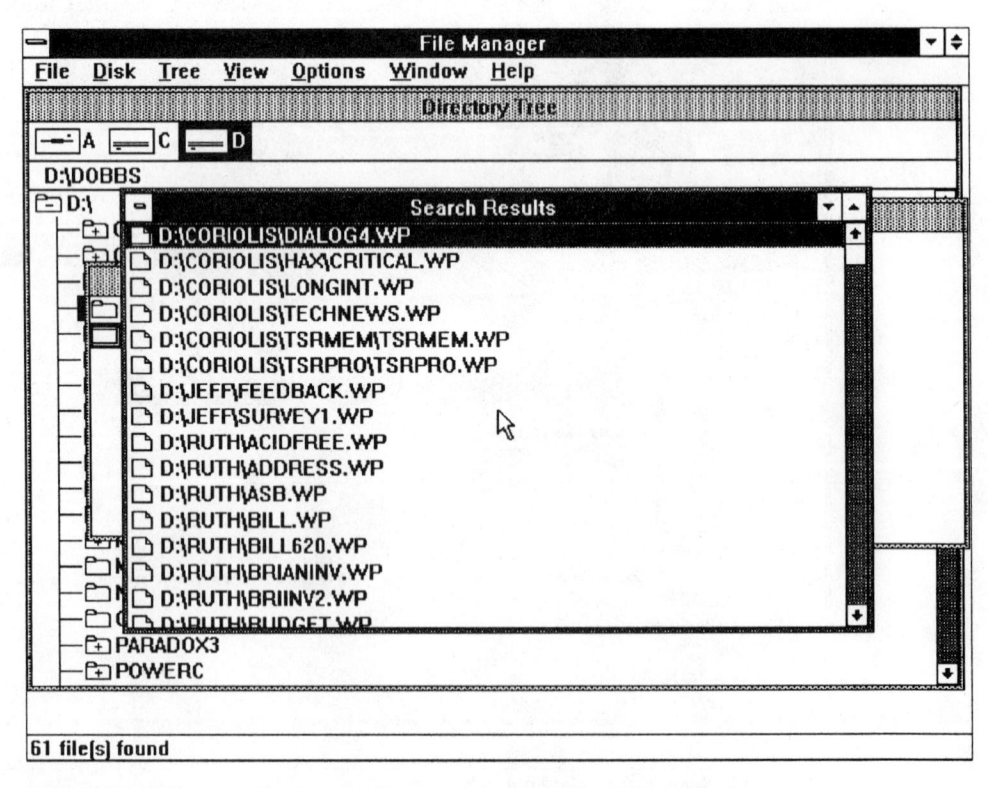

Figure 7.19. The Search Results Window

The File Manager

> ✓ Start at a directory window for one of the hard disks installed on your system. Search for all of the program files (.EXE) in all of the directories of your hard disk.

Select the Search... command from the File menu, and type the search text *.EXE in the Search For text box. Select the Search Entire Disk check box so that it contains an X, and click the OK button.

Creating and Deleting Directories

The File Manager makes it extremely easy to create and delete directories. To create a directory, move to the Directory Tree window and select the directory that will be the parent (be located immediately above) the new directory. When the parent directory is highlighted, select the Create Directory... command from the File menu. A dialog box appears (Figure 7.20) to show the current directory name and to ask you for the name of the new subdirectory. Type the new name (no more than 8 characters long) into the Name text box and select the OK button. The new directory is now created and ready to accept files.

If you're unfamiliar with the rules for naming DOS files and directories, keep in mind that you can use only eight characters in a name. You may use any characters you want, except a period, comma, forward slash (/), backslash (\), vertical bar (|), semicolon, colon, quotation marks, or brackets ([]).

You can delete a directory almost as easily as you can create one. First, delete the files within the subdirectory. Make certain first that you aren't deleting files you'll need later. Close the directory window and verify that the directory to be removed is highlighted in the Directory Tree window. Select the Delete command from the File menu, or press the Del key. A dialog box (Figure 7.21) identifies the current directory and asks if you want to delete it. When you select the Delete key on the window, a second dialog box asks if you want to delete the path to that directory. When you answer in the affirmative, the directory is deleted.

Renaming Files and Directories

The more files and directories you add to your system, the more you'll have the need to rename older files and directories. The Program Manager allows

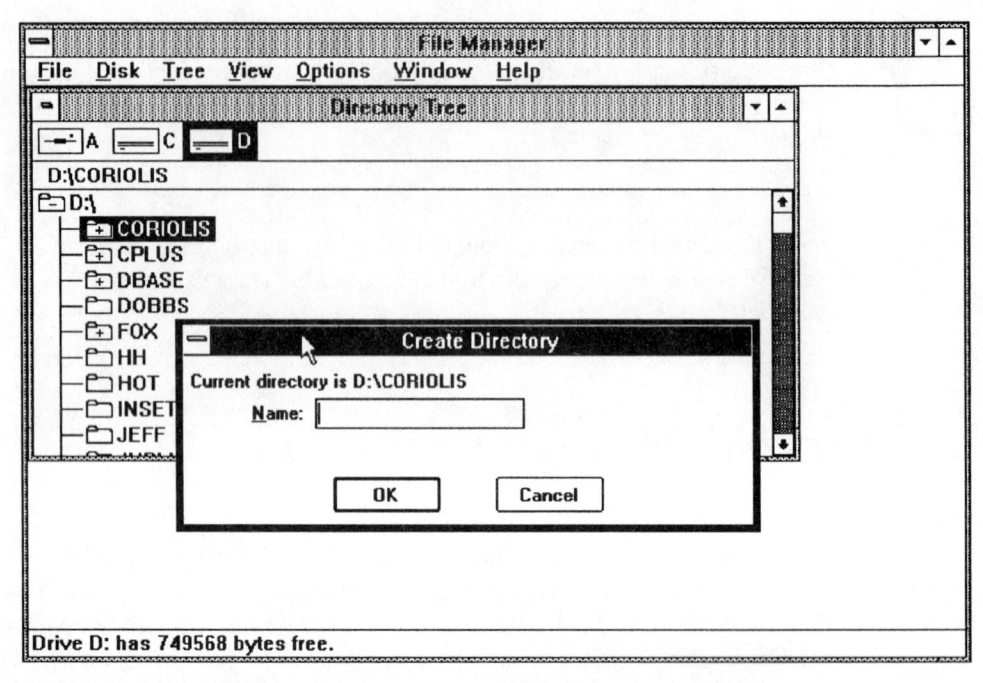

Figure 7.20. The Create Directory Dialog Box

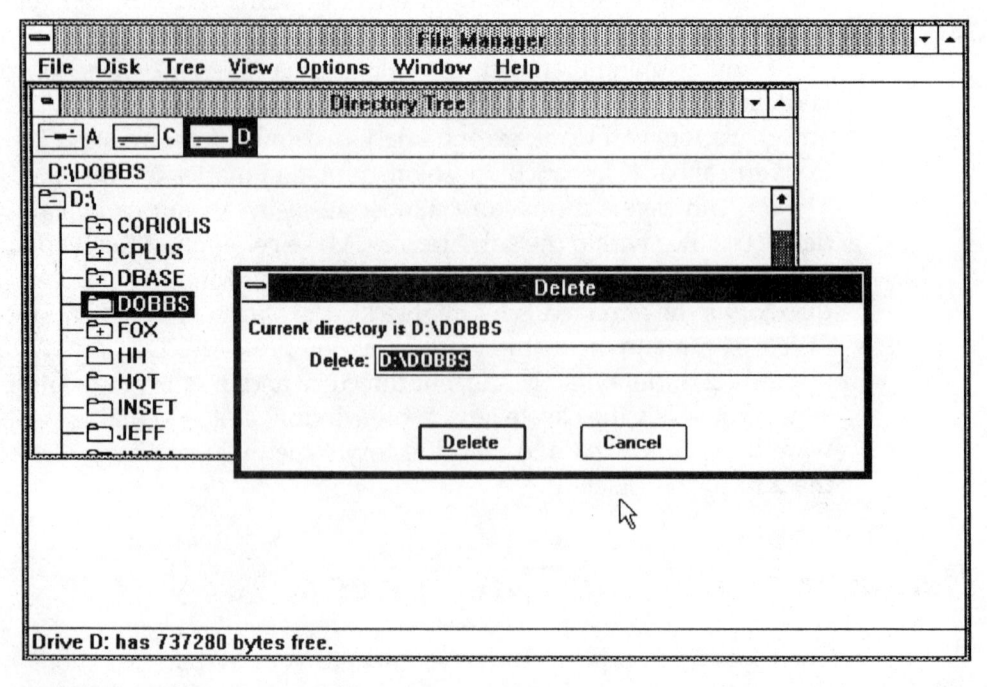

Figure 7.21. Deleting a File

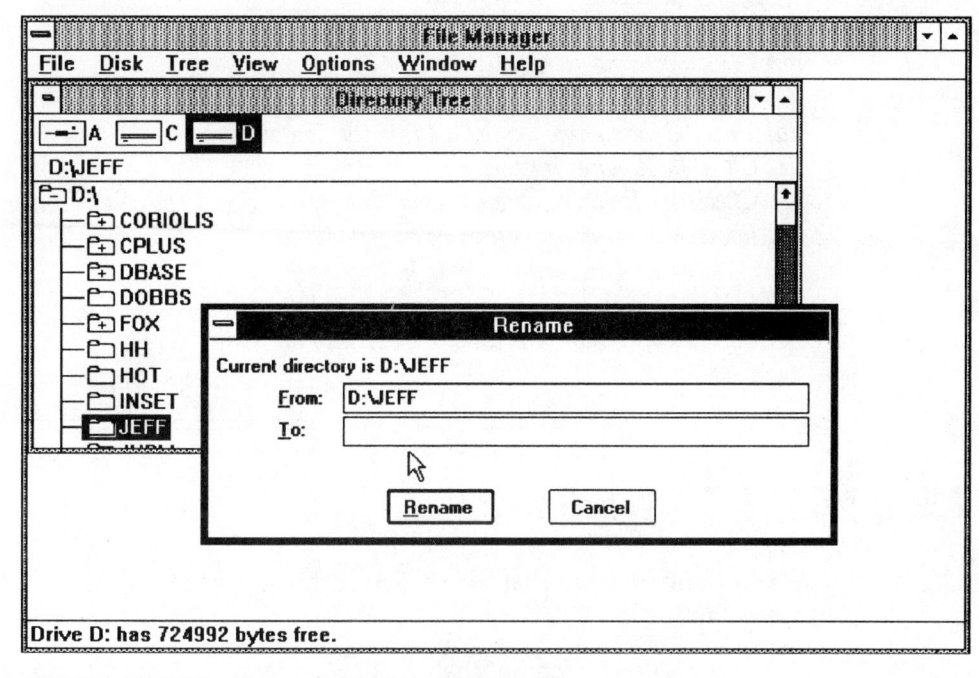

Figure 7.22. Renaming a File

you to rename a file or directory at any time by using the Rename... command in the File menu. To rename a directory, click on the old directory name and select the Rename... command. The dialog box shown in Figure 7.22 shows you the current directory name and asks you to provide the new name. Enter the new name (no more than 8 characters long) and click on the Rename button. One word of caution: If you rename a directory, the path command in your AUTOEXEC.BAT file may need to be updated to reflect the new name. Also, any batch files or programs that try to access the directory by its old name will fail, so they need to changed also.

To rename a file, click on the filename in a directory window and activate the Rename command. The rest of the procedure is the same as the procedure for renaming a directory.

Start at a directory window for one of the hard disks installed on your system.
1. Rename a file.
2. Rename a directory.

1. (a) *Open a directory to locate the file you want to rename.*
   (b) *Click on the file to highlight it.*
   (c) *Select the Rename... command from the File menu.*
   (d) *Type the new name for the file into the To text box.*
   (e) *Click the Rename button.*
   (f) *Check the directory where the file was stored to make sure it's been renamed.*
2. (a) *Locate the directory you want to rename using the Directory Tree window, and click on the directory to highlight it.*
   (b) *Select the Rename... command from the File menu.*
   (c) *Type the new name for the directory into the To text box.*
   (d) *Click the Rename button.*

Changing File Attributes

We mentioned earlier that all DOS files have special attributes. The four attributes are:

- Read Only, indicating that the file can only be viewed and not modified.
- Archive, indicating that changes have been made to the file.
- Hidden, indicating that the file is not displayed in normal directory listings.
- System, indicating that the file is a special DOS system file.

Each file stored in a directory can be assigned any combination of these attributes. For example, a file can be read-only and hidden. The File Manager allows you to change a file's attribute by selecting the Change Attributes... command from the File menu. To use this feature, highlight a file and select Change Attributes... When the dialog box shown in Figure 7.23 appears, notice that check boxes are provided for each of the four attribute types. Select the attribute options you want, and click on the OK button.

Launching Applications

The File Manager allows you to launch applications from its environment. This means that you can use the directory windows to locate an application and then start up the application. (You don't need to exit the File Manager and use the Program Manager to run the application.) The easiest way to start an application is to double-click on an icon displayed as a rectangle with a blue stripe. If the icon represents a Windows application, such as Write or Notepad,

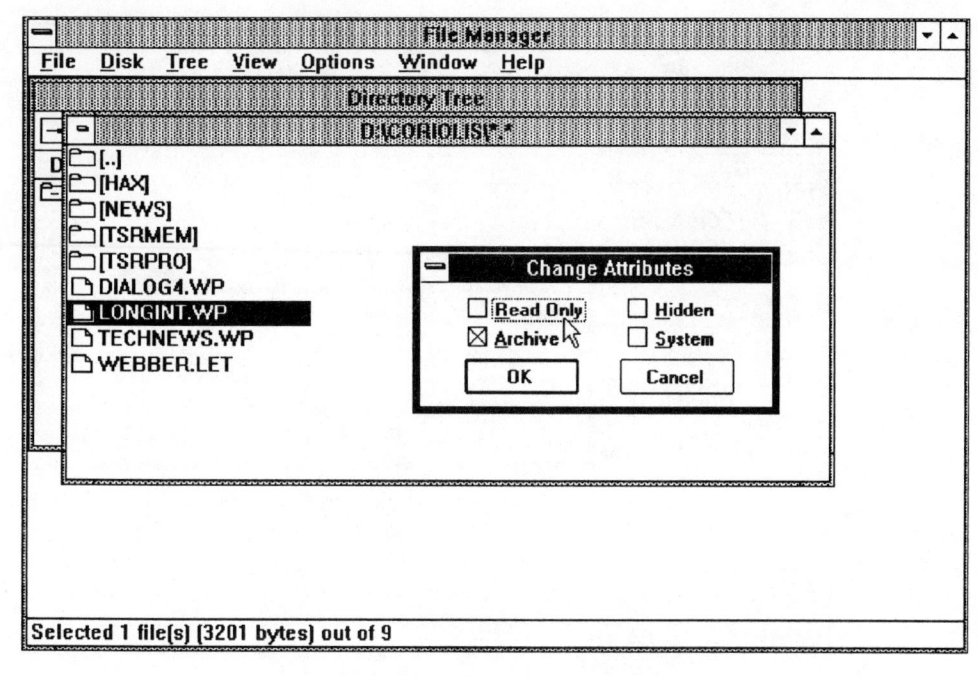

Figure 7.23. Changing File Attributes

the application is launched in its own window. If the application is a DOS program, on the other hand, it's executed in the DOS full-screen area.

If you're using the keyboard, launch an application by selecting the Run... command from the File menu. As Figure 7.24 shows, this command brings up a dialog box where you enter the application's name. If the application is not in the directory currently selected, include the full directory path for the application so that the File Manager can locate it.

Printing Files

The File manager provides a Print... command in the File menu so that you can print ASCII text files. If you have other types of files, such as Word document files, use the application that created the files to print them.

To print a text file, highlight the file and select the Print... command from the File menu. The Print dialog box (Figure 7.25) appears, displaying the name of the file you selected in the Print text box. If the filename is correct, select the OK button to start printing the file. The File Manager uses the currently selected printer to print the file.

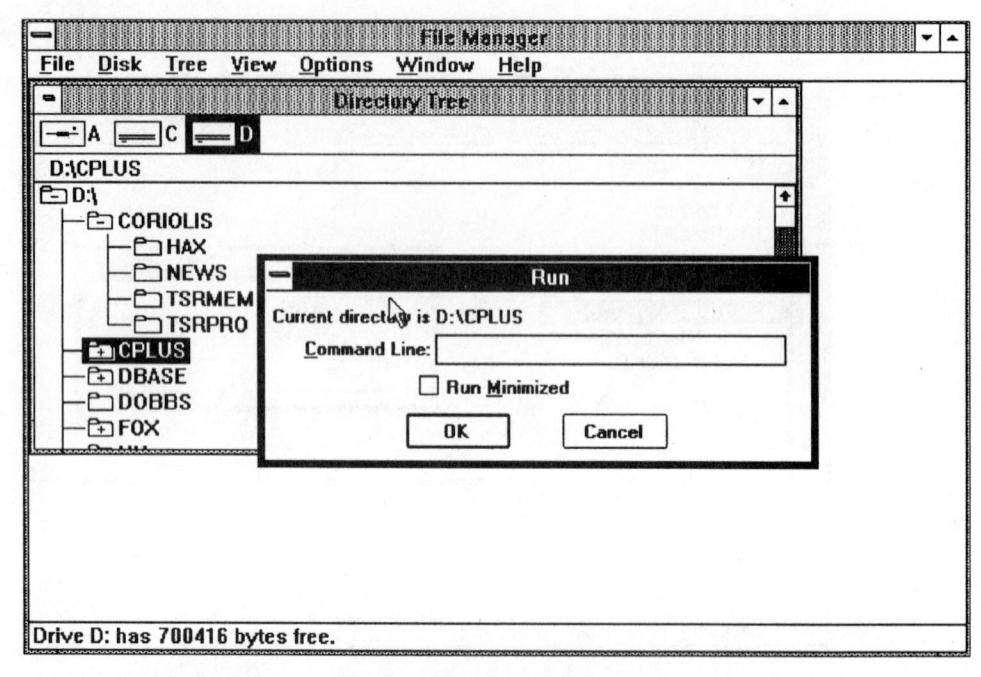

Figure 7.24. Running an Application

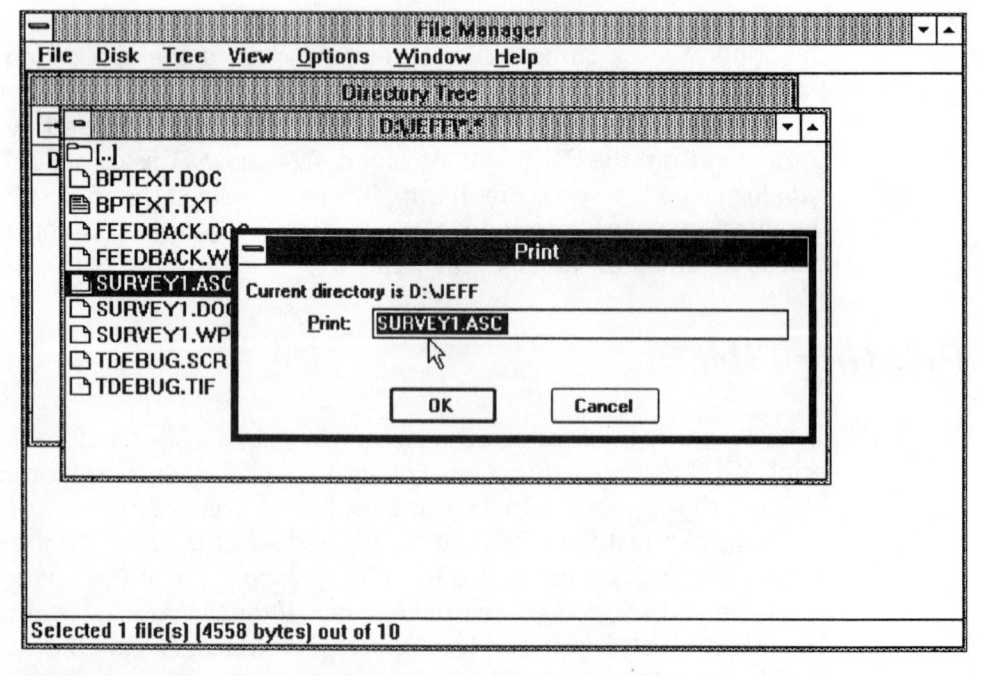

Figure 7.25. Printing an ASCII Text File

The File Manager

Performing Disk Maintenance

So far, we've discussed all of the basic file and directory-related operations that the Program Manager performs. Before we leave the File Manager, let's look at two important disk-related operations—copying and formatting disks. To start these operations, use the Disk menu.

Copying Disks

Follow these steps to copy a disk:

1. Place the disk you want to copy into one of your floppy disk drives. This disk is called the *source diskette*.
2. Click on the drive icon for the source disk. Recall that the drive icons display in the Directory Tree window. If a disk is not in the drive represented by the selected icon, you'll receive a warning dialog box.
3. Select the Copy Diskette... command from the Disk menu to display the dialog box shown in Figure 7.26.
4. Select the Copy... button. When the Copy Diskette dialog box (Figure 7.27) appears, verify that your source diskette is in the selected drive.

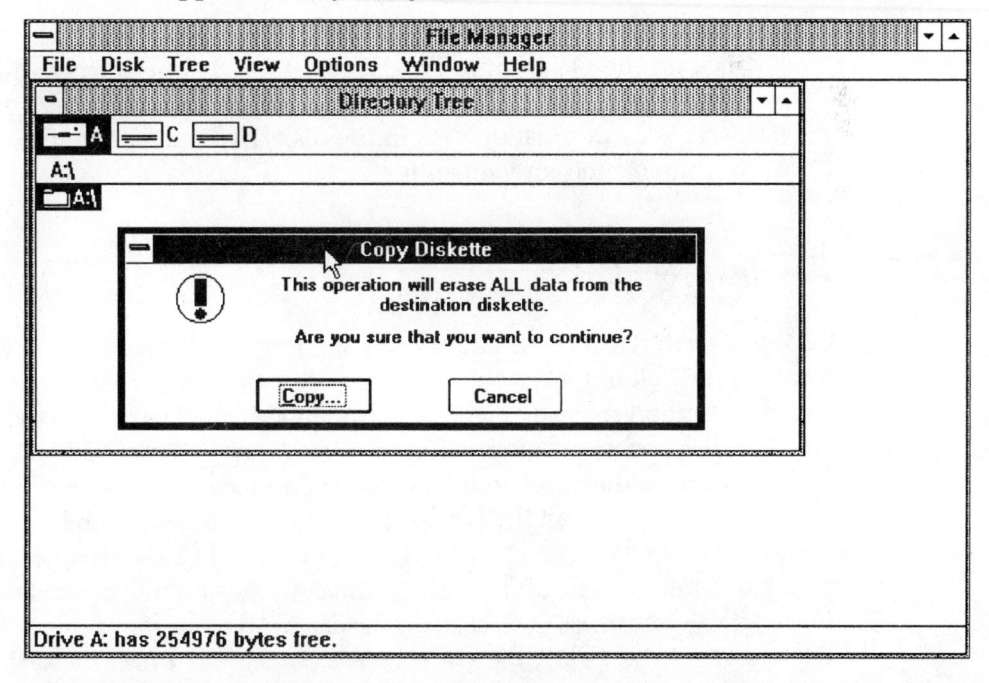

Figure 7.26. The Copy Diskette Warning Box

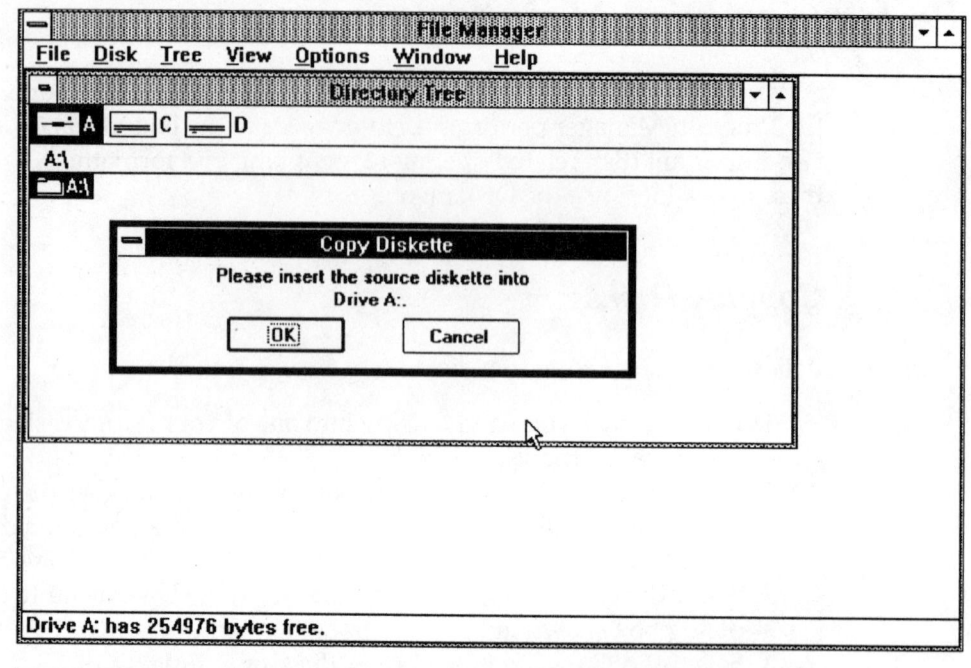

Figure 7.27. The Copy Diskette Dialog Box

5. Click on the OK button. The File Manager begins to copy the diskette. When the disk's data has been read, you see the Copy dialog box.
6. Insert your destination disk in the disk drive, and select the OK button to complete the copy operation.

Formatting Disks

As you know, disks must be formatted before they can be used. When you format a disk, all of the data stored on the disk (if there is any) is removed. The format operation maps a disk into components, called *sectors*, so that DOS can read the disk and store information on it.

To format a disk with the File Manager, place the disk into one of your floppy drives, and select the Format Diskette... command from the Disk menu. When the Format Diskette dialog box appears, select the drive name for the disk you want to format. The Disk option consists of a pull-down box that lists the available floppy drives. Click on the arrow to the right of this box, or press Alt+Down arrow. Select the correct disk name, and press the OK button to start the formatting process.

The File Manager

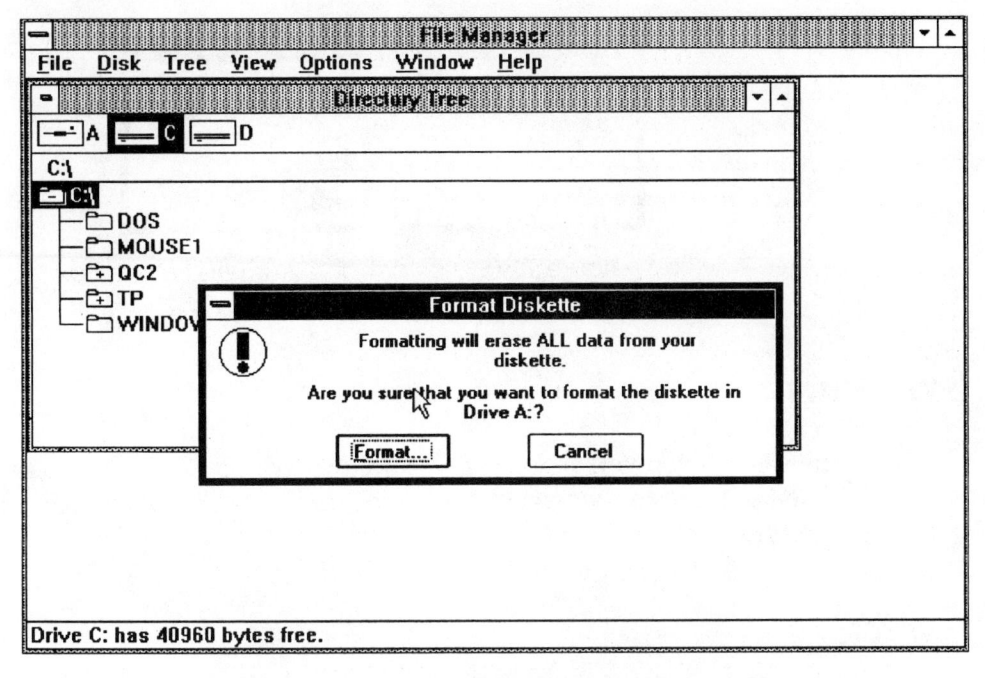

Figure 7.28. The Format Diskette Warning Box

Before the format operation starts, Windows displays the Format Diskette warning box (Figure 7.28) to remind you that the data on the disk you plan to format will be lost. To proceed, click the Format... button, and then specify the type of disk you are formatting: high or low capacity. As Figure 7.29 indicates, you can also choose to copy the DOS boot information to your diskette.

While the format operation is underway, a status box shows you its progress. When your disk is formatted, the dialog box shown in Figure 7.30 asks if you want to format another diskette.

Figure 7.29. The Format Diskette Dialog Box

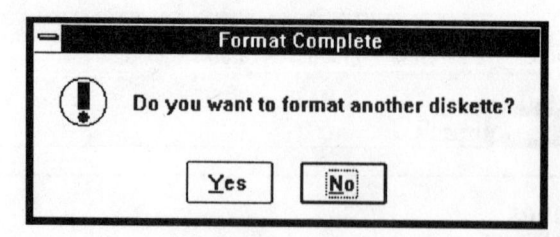

Figure 7.30. The Format Complete Dialog Box

Summary

In this chapter, you've been introduced to Windows file manipulation using File Manager. In the next chapter, we'll cover the Print Manager to help you print files from Windows.

Exercises

Use these exercises to gain more experience using the File Manager.

What You Should Do	How the Computer Responds
1. Start the File Manager and select one of the hard disks listed in the Directory Tree window.	1. The window displays the main directory paths for the selected hard disk.
2. Select a floppy disk drive.	2. The directory paths for the selected floppy disk drive display. If the selected drive is empty, File Manager asks you to insert a diskette.
3. Click on a file folder that has a + symbol.	3. The subdirectories for that directory display.
4. Double-click on a file folder.	4. A directory window opens for the selected directory so that you can view its subdirectories and files.
5. Select the Run... command from the File menu.	5. A dialog box displays so that you can type in the name of a program to run.
6. Rename a file using the Rename... command in the File menu.	6. The file's name changes, and the directory window lists the new filename.

7. Delete a file.

7. The file disappears and its name is no longer listed in the directory window.

8. Search for a group of files, such as *.EXE, using the Search command.

8. The located files display in a special Search Results window. You can select a file and open, rename, or delete it.

9. Change the attributes of a file.

9. The file is listed in a directory window with its new attributes. To view the attributes, select the File Details option from the View menu.

10. Format a diskette using the Format Diskette... command from the Disk menu.

10. You're asked to place a diskette in a floppy drive. A dialog box warns you that this operation will erase the data on your diskette.

What If It Doesn't Work?

1. If a drive can't be selected, the disk drive might be defective.
2. If you don't have any subdirectories, none of the file folders listed in the Directory Tree window will have a + symbol.
3. If no files match your search specification, a Search Results window won't display.

8

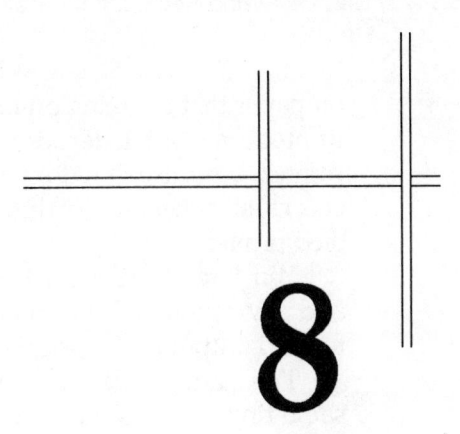

The Print Manager

By now you probably realize that you can be very productive with Windows because you can access different applications without exiting one to start another. If you own an 80386-compatible PC, you can even run non-Windows applications in the background while a different application runs in the foreground. Print Manager, the Windows application for spooling your printer, is one such application that can help you be more productive. This background application allows you to control multiple print jobs when your PC can create the output much faster than the output device can put ink to paper.

This chapter will show you how to use the Print Manager to control your printer. After you complete the chapter, you'll know how to:

- Start the Print Manager
- Use the print queue
- Use multiple printers
- Print to a file

The Problem with Printing

Imagine that you're a consultant who performs studies for multiple customers. Your job requires you to prepare reports (including graphs, pie charts, and other illustrations) as well as memos and proposals. Your reports are printed on paper that contains preprinted information. The memos and proposals are printed on your letterhead; both of these are processed through your laser printer. You also have an accounting program that prints continuous-form checks, and checks are printed on tractor-feed continuous forms using a tractor-feed printer.

You have to finish a large report (including several Paintbrush pictures) and pay a group of bills today. You instruct each of your Windows applications to send output to the printer. And then you wait....

The main problem is that each of your applications wants the printer at the same time—this is where Print Manager comes in. Print Manager is an electronic traffic cop; it controls which job goes out to which resource. Print Manager allows you to adjust the priority of print jobs and control the order in which they'll be printed. You can also pause and restart print queues, and activate and deactivate each of the printers on your system.

How Print Manager Works

If you've ever used a basic word processor, you know that you can't edit a file or exit the program while it's printing. Fortunately, Windows applications are much more flexible. When you activate a print command from an application, a temporary file is created on your disk and the information created by the application is sent to this file. The file is then closed, and the Print Manager takes over and prints it. This process is illustrated in Figure 8.1. If several files are created, Print Manager sends the first file to the printer while holding the other temporary files in reserve. When the first file is finished, Print Manager deletes it and begins to print the next file in the print queue.

A queue is an ordered list of items, such as a line of customers at a grocery store who will be serviced according to their order in the line. This First-In First-Out queue (called a FIFO) is not necessarily the best. Queues should be flexible—a small job should be able to go in front of a larger one that requires more time. Size, however, should not be the only criteria for promoting a job within a queue—the job's priority is also a factor. You can use the Print Manager to change the priorities of all pending jobs. (Once the Print Manager begins to print a job, that job has the highest priority in the queue.)

Selecting Print Manager

You can turn the Print Manager on or off from the Control Panel. To select it, start the Control Panel and double-click on the Printers icon. When the Printers

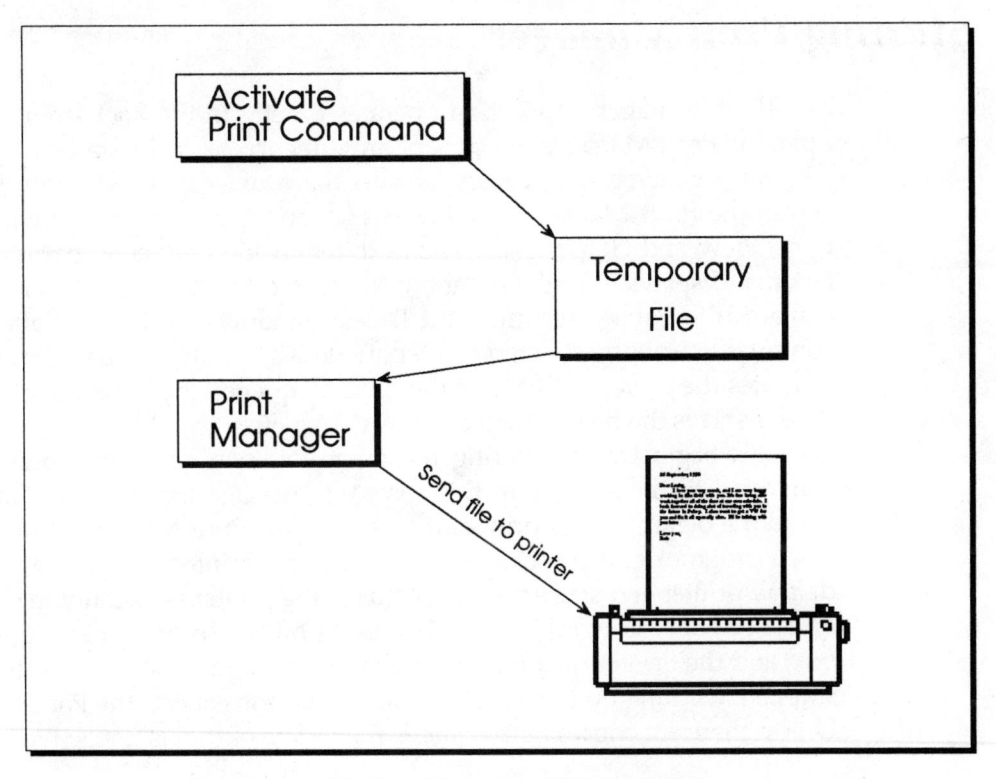

Figure 8.1. The Process of Printing a File

dialog box (Figure 8.2) appears, click on the check box at the bottom of the dialog box, called Use Print Manager. After you select the Print Manager, it automatically manages your print jobs. You can choose a number of options that control how the Print Manager operates. To access these features, you need to run the Print Manager application.

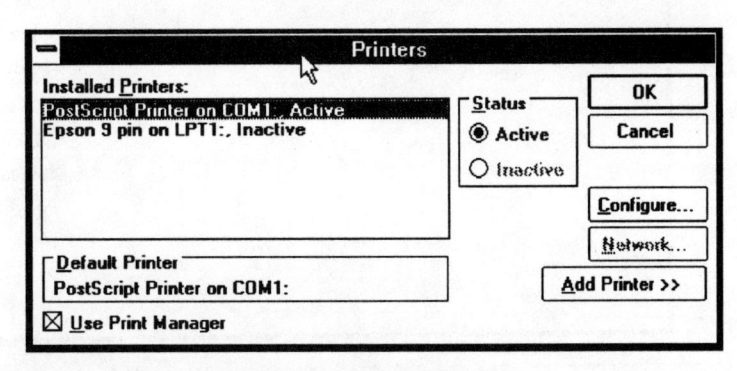

Figure 8.2. The Printers Dialog Box

Starting Print Manager

The Print Manager application operates quietly in the background. You can open the Print Manager window at any time to check the status of your print jobs by double-clicking on its icon in the Main group window. Figure 8.3 shows the Print Manager window, which contains a menu bar with the Options, View, and Help menus. The next item below the menu bar is a message box that displays information about the currently active printer. This area also contains the Pause, Resume, and Delete window buttons that allow you to control the currently selected printer queue. The printer queue information line indicates the current activity of the selected queue. The remainder of the window displays the files in each of the active queues.

Let's begin by considering the most common case: only one printer is connected to the system. In this case, the message box contains information about the default (only) printer. If you open the Print Manager window in the Main program group when no files are being printed, the box identifies the default printer and states that the status of the printer is idle. If you click on the Pause button, the word "Paused" appears on the second line of the message box, and the printer queue information line changes to show that the queue is stopped. Clicking on the Resume window button cancels the Pause operation. Unless there are entries in the queue, the Delete button is not active.

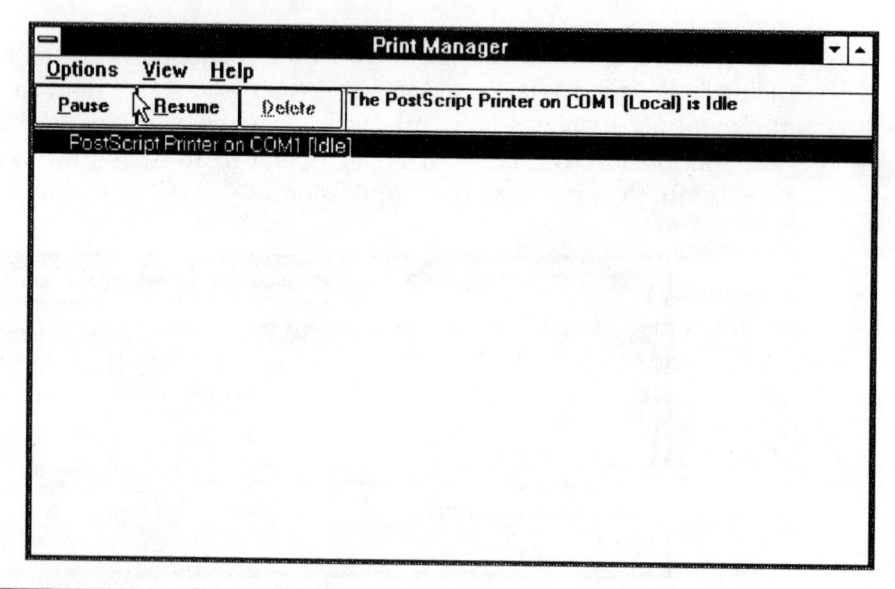

Figure 8.3. The Print Manager Window

The Print Manager

1. Make sure that the Print Manager is selected.
2. Print a file from an application, such as Notepad.
3. Start the Print Manager to view the status of the print jobs in the queue. What happens?
4. Pause your print job.
5. Continue printing.

---

1. *Start the Control Panel and double-click on the Printers icon. Select the Use Print manager check box in the Printers dialog box. Click the OK button and exit the Control Panel.*
2. *Open the application by double-clicking on its icon, load in a file, and select the Print... command from the file menu.*
3. *You see the name of the installed printer and the file you have just started printing from your application. If multiple files were being printed, you would also see a list of each file and the time and date when it was being processed by the Print Manager.*
4. *Click on the Pause button.*
5. *Click the Resume button.*

Working with the Queue

If the queue has several entries and you want to delete an entry, move the mouse cursor to the item to be removed and click on it once to highlight it. Next, click on the Delete button to remove the entry from the queue.

If you want to move a print job to the rear of the queue, click on the item to be moved, drag it to the bottom of the queue list, and release the mouse button. You can use the same principle to move a print job ahead of other print jobs: Click on the item to be advanced, drag it toward the front of the queue, and release the mouse button. Notice that you can only rearrange the order of items waiting to be printed. The topmost item in a queue is currently being printed, and other print jobs can't be moved in front of it.

Using Multiple Printers

If you have multiple printers, things get a bit more complicated. Imagine that you've already queued up several jobs to the laser printer on LPT1:, but you want to send a quick Notepad memo to a dot-matrix printer connected to

COM2:. Assuming that you've installed the printers correctly (see the chapter about the Control Panel for details), take the following steps:

1. Select the Printer Setup option from the File menu in the Notepad.
2. Click on the line containing the information for the dot-matrix printer.
3. Activate the OK window button to confirm your selection.
4. Activate the Print option from the File menu.

The memo in Notepad is sent to the alternate printer that you selected (rather than the primary laser printer). Open the Print Manager window and notice that an additional entry has been created to show the status of the other printer. If you want to stop or resume this new queue, click on the file in the queue. The information in the message box, and in the printer queue information line, changes to display information about the dot-matrix printer. The Pause and Resume window buttons now affect the operation of the newly selected queue.

The Options Menu

The Options menu allows you to control certain attributes of the Print Manager. You can use the first three entries in the menu to define the priority for the Print Manager as Low, Medium, or High.

As we mentioned in previous chapters, many microprocessors in PCs (especially the 80386 and 80486 chips) are capable of sharing the available execution time with several tasks. The first three entries in the Options menu tell Windows about the relative importance of the print operation. For example, if your printer is slow, you prefer to use most of the computer's processing time for the current foreground task, and you're in no hurry to get the printout, you can select Low Priority. If you want to bias computer time usage toward the foreground task, but you're willing to sacrifice some execution time for increased printing speed, select the Medium Priority setting. If you need the printout above all else, select High Priority to make certain that the printer is never waiting for information from the PC.

---

1. Use an application (such as Write) and start printing two files.
2. What is the default printing speed?
3. Set the printing speed so that the files are printed as slowly as possible.
4. What is the advantage of using the priority options?

---

1. (a) Start the application.
   (b) Open a file and print it using the Print... command.
   (c) Open another file and send it to the print queue using Print...
2. Start the Print manager and select the Options menu. A checkmark appears next to the Medium Priority option to indicate that this setting is the default.
3. Select the Low Priority option.
4. You can allocate more or less time to the printer so that your computer can perform other tasks.

Print Manager Messages

The next set of options, Alert Always, Flash if Inactive, and Ignore if Inactive, control how the Print Manager reacts when certain unusual events occur. For example, if your printer runs out of paper or the ink ribbon runs out, your PC receives a message from the printer that identifies the problem. Windows processes the information and takes one of three actions. If you select the Alert Always option, Windows displays a message box on the screen when the event is detected. (The message box won't display with a non-Windows application.)

When you select the second option, Flash if Inactive, your computer beeps once, and then flashes either the Print Manager icon or the title bar of the Print Manager window until the Print Manager becomes the active task. This option is handy when you're printing while performing another operation (such as editing a different file). When you hear the beep and see the icon blink, you know that the printer needs attention, and when you reach a convenient stopping point, you can enlarge the icon or bring the window forward to read the message. The Flash if Inactive option is the default when Windows is installed.

The third option is Ignore if Inactive. If you select this option and a problem arises while printing, and the Print Manager window is either an icon or not the active window, Windows won't make an attempt to get your attention. It's not a good idea to select this mode unless your activity is time-critical. For example, if you're using your modem to communicate with a computer network and the printer runs out of paper, you may want to ignore the messages from Print Manager until you're done with your Terminal session.

Using a Network

The Options menu also provides a feature for controlling a network. This option is only available if you've properly installed a network driver. If you select this option, an additional menu opens to allow you to inhibit automatic update of the network status, and to enable the printing of network jobs directly to the network. The first option minimizes the amount of useless network traffic. Print Manager requests the current status of the selected print queue whenever you expand the Print Manager icon to a window. It also requests updates at periodic intervals when the window remains expanded.

If you've connected a large number of PCs using Windows to the same network, you may discover that a measurable percentage of the network throughput is being consumed by this needless polling. By clearing the check box on the Update Network Display and clicking the OK button, you instruct Print Manager not to perform periodic polling. Unfortunately, the network queue status won't be updated again until this option is reenabled.

In many cases, the network server has the resources to schedule and control print jobs independently of your PC. In such cases, it's a waste of time and resources to get Print Manager involved. There is no simple answer for whether to bypass Print Manager; you will simply have to experiment and select the option that works best for you. To bypass Print Manager, activate the Options Network line, select the Print Net Jobs Direct check box, and click on the OK window button.

The View Menu

The first two options in the View menu are automatically enabled when Windows is installed, and allow you to control the information displayed for each file in the queues. You can activate or deactivate each option by clicking on it. The option is active when a check mark appears next to the entry. The Time/Date Sent option controls whether the time and the date when a print file was created appears in the queue. If you usually have a couple of files in the queue and you want to minimize onscreen clutter, disable this feature.

The second option is Print File Size. If the total size of the print job is unimportant, you can disable this option to minimize clutter.

The next three options in the View menu are provided for network users. Use the Update Net Queues option to retrieve fresh information from the network controller. To view the entire queue for a particular printer (some networks have more than one printer), activate the Selected Net Queue option. You can select the last option, Other Net Queue, to view network queues that you're not connected to. When you activate Other Net Queue, a dialog box requests the name and the location of the network queue to be viewed. Remember that viewing the status of a queue via the Other Net Queue option doesn't give you access to that queue for printing. If you wish to send a file to a queue other than the currently selected queue, first change the queue selection in the network section of the Control Panel.

Intercepting Print Jobs

An earlier chapter about techniques for printer installation with the Control Panel discussed how you can select a file as an output device. The Print Manager provides the other half of the control structure to make this option work.

Imagine that you have a Windows-compatible application that prints files, and you want to modify your output before it goes to the printer. Follow these steps to set up your system to operate in this manner:

1. Start the Control Panel by double-clicking on the Control Panel icon in the Main group window.
2. Double-click on the Printers icon to bring up the Printers dialog box.
3. Select the printer you want to use.
4. Click the Configure... button to bring up the dialog box shown in Figure 8.4.
5. Select the File option from the Ports list box.
6. Confirm the changes by clicking the OK button.

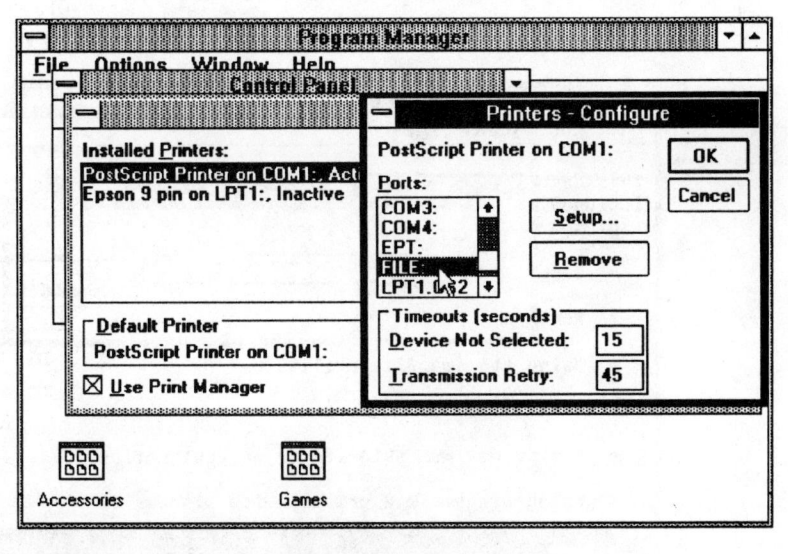

Figure 8.4. Configuring a Printer

If you've installed multiple printers, make certain to set the printer connected to FILE as the default printer. The easiest way to do this is to press Alt+D, while in the Configure dialog box. Click on the OK button to confirm your changes and return to the Control Panel window. Close the window and minimize the Main applications group back to an icon.

Activate the application whose output you wish to intercept and initiate a print session. If you didn't designate the printer connected to FILE as the default printer, select the printer using the Print Setup option of the File menu for your application. When Print Manager receives the print job, it detects that the job is destined to go to a file, and a dialog box (Figure 8.5) asks for the destination filename. You can specify destination disk and path information, as well as the filename.

Depending upon the attributes of the installed printer, you may need to use a text editor (such as Notepad) to modify the file. Of course, you can merge several of these files together into one large file by using the DOS COPY command, as in this example:

COPY MYFILE1.PRN+MYFILE2.PRN ALLMYFIL.ZZZ

where the plus sign shows that the files are to be added in the order indicated, and then saved as the target file ALLMYFIL.ZZZ. This technique comes in handy when the network printer is located at a substantial distance away from your PC. By combining several printouts together, you can minimize the likelihood that a listing will be picked up accidentally by another user.

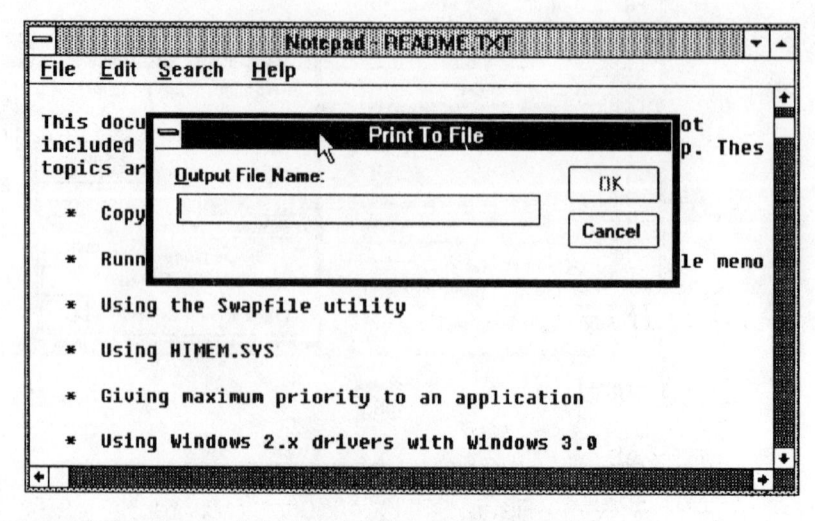

Figure 8.5. The Print To File Dialog Box

Summary

In this chapter you've learned the basics of using the Print Manager. We've covered the techniques for using queues, configuring the Print Manager, and using the Print Manager with the Installed Printers application of the Control Panel to divert printer output to a file for subsequent modification.

The next chapter will take a new direction and discuss how to run non-Windows applications.

Exercises

Use these exercises to learn how to use the Print Manager.

What You Should Do	How the Computer Responds
1. Make sure the Print Manager is active by selecting the Use Print Manager check box in the Printers dialog box.	1. The Print Manager will be used by each Windows application when a file prints.
2. Start printing a file from the Notepad application.	2. The file is managed by the Print Manager.
3. Start the Print Manager, and disable the Time/Date Sent option from the View menu.	3. The print queue doesn't display the time or the date when the file is sent to the printer.
4. Pause the print job.	4. Your file stops printing until you select the Resume button.
5. Print the file again, but this time send it to a file named SAMPLE.TXT.	5. The Print manager doesn't send your file to the active printer. Instead, your file is saved in the print file SAMPLE.TXT.

What If It Doesn't Work?

1. The Print Manager won't work if you haven't installed a printer. To install a printer, use the Control Panel. Make sure that you have the installation disks for installing a printer.
2. Make sure that your printer has paper and that the printer is selected to be on-line.

9

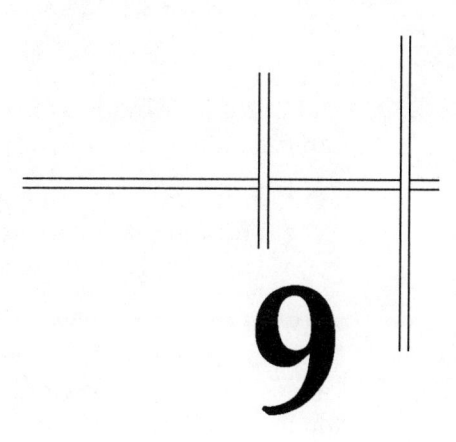

Working with Non-Windows Applications

So far, we've focused on the basics of Windows and the built-in applications provided with it. If you're like many PC users, you've probably been running programs under DOS. Perhaps you have a large database that would be hard to convert to a format that could be used by a Windows application.

In this chapter, we'll show you how to use the DOS Prompt application to run non-Windows applications. Along the way, we'll discuss a number of technical issues about working with DOS and Windows. After you finish this chapter, you'll know:

- The limitations of running non-Windows applications
- How to use Program Information Files (PIF)
- How to access the DOS Prompt application
- How to use the PIF editor
- How to use some basic DOS commands

Running Non-Windows Applications

Throughout this book, we've seen how Windows provides powerful features to make it easy for you to run Windows applications, such as Write, Notepad, and Cardfile. Windows also allows you to run non-Windows applications. You can run a non-Windows application in these ways:

- From the Program Manager
- From the File Manager
- From the DOS Prompt application

As we'll see later in this chapter, you can also use special files called Program Information Files (PIFs) to customize how Windows runs non-Windows applications. When a DOS application is started under Windows, Windows looks for the application's PIF file to determine which default settings should be used to run the application.

After we cover the basics of running non-Windows applications with the DOS Prompt, we'll show you how to create and modify PIFs with the PIF editor. We'll also show you how to install them.

Options and Limitations

Windows can't compensate for the limitations of your hardware. If you run Windows on an 8088-, 8086- or 80286-based system, you'll find that Windows can only run one non-Windows application at a time. These computers can't support the memory-management techniques offered by the 80386 and 80486 processors.

For example, if your computer runs Windows in the 386 Enhanced mode, program execution time is split between the non-Windows active task and the background tasks, as specified in the Control Panel 386 Enhanced window (see Chapter 6). Thus, you can arrange for Windows to give 80% of the available execution time to your DOS word processor or database management program and to give only 20% to the background tasks. If your computer has an 80286, 8086 or 8088 microprocessor, Windows must run the non-Windows foreground task 100% of the time.

You also have to be mindful of memory requirements. Although Windows can run in as little as 640K, you'll discover that 1 to 2Mb of system memory provide much better results when you run Windows in the 386 Enhanced mode. With the relatively inexpensive RAM prices available today, this seems a reasonable requirement. Windows even provides a special program for those of you who may be running older PCs with memory expansion boards that take the machine beyond 640K.

For now, let's step away from the technical details of operating Windows, and look at the general aspects of running DOS programs from Windows.

Working with Non-Windows Applications

1. True or false? Non-Windows applications can be run on 80286-based machines.
2. True or false? Non-Windows applications can run as background tasks on 80386-based machines.
3. What is a PIF?

1. *True.*
2. *True.*
3. *A Program Information File. These files tell Windows how to run a non-Windows application.*

The DOS Prompt Application

When you open the Main program group window, you'll see an icon named DOS that looks similar to a screen. Double-click on this icon and the DOS window appears. As Figure 9.1 shows, this window looks remarkably like the

```
Volume in drive D has no label
Directory of  D:\WINDOWS

.                  ..                SETUP    EXE    SYSTEM              SETUP    HLP
WIN      INI       SYSTEM   INI      WINHELP  EXE    WINHELP  HLP        WIN      COM
CONTROL  INI       SMARTDRV SYS      RAMDRIVE SYS    EMM386   SYS        WINVER   EXE
PROGMAN  EXE       TASKMAN  EXE      WINFILE  EXE    CALC     EXE        CALENDAR EXE
CARDFILE EXE       CLIPBRD  EXE      CLOCK    EXE    DIGITAL  FON        CONTROL  EXE
NOTEPAD  EXE       PBRUSH   EXE      PBRUSH   DLL    PIFEDIT  EXE        RECORDER EXE
RECORDER DLL       REVERSI  EXE      PRINTMAN EXE    SOL      EXE        TERMINAL EXE
WRITE    EXE       MSDOS    EXE      CALC     HLP    CALENDAR HLP        CARDFILE HLP
CLIPBRD  HLP       CONTROL  HLP      NOTEPAD  HLP    PBRUSH   HLP        PIFEDIT  HLP
PRINTMAN HLP       PROGMAN  HLP      RECORDER HLP    REVERSI  HLP        SOL      HLP
TERMINAL HLP       WINFILE  HLP      WRITE    HLP    PYRAMID  BMP        CHESS    BMP
WEAVE    BMP       BOXES    BMP      PAPER    BMP    PARTY    BMP        RIBBONS  BMP
README   TXT       NETWORKS TXT      WININI   TXT    WININIZ  TXT        SYSINI   TXT
SYSINIZ  TXT       SYSINI3  TXT      PRINTERS TXT    3270     TXT        MOUSE    SYS
PROGMAN  INI       MAIN     GRP      ACCESSOR GRP    GAMES    GRP        _DEFAULT PIF
WINGRAB  EXE       WGLIB    EXE      WINHELP  BMK    FIGS                WINFILE  INI
PRONOTE  CRD       TEST     CAL      MTDECK   CRD    100KML   CRD        ADACNTS  CRD
        85 File(s)    1376256 bytes free

15:25:38 ··· Wed 10-17-1990 ··· D:\WINDOWS
D>
```

Figure 9.1. The DOS Prompt Application

standard DOS prompt. Notice that the screen is blank except for the standard message that identifies the version of MS-DOS you're running. (You will also see the usual DOS prompt (usually C:\> if you run Windows from a hard disk installed as the C drive). The command to return to the Windows environment is EXIT. Type this command at the DOS prompt, press Enter, and return to Windows.

---

1. Double-click on the DOS icon to start the DOS application, and then use the mouse. What happens?
2. Type in the command DIR and press the Enter key. What happens?

---

1. *The mouse is disabled.*
2. *You see a listing of the files for the current directory.*

You can perform most non-Windows operations in the DOS area. For example, assume you have a small program named BLACK.EXE, which is stored in the directory C:\DOS. This program simply blanks out the entire screen except for an asterisk, which moves slowly at a diagonal. When it reaches the edge of the screen, the asterisk appears to bounce off the edge and keep going in a new direction. When it reaches the next screen edge, the process repeats. If you press any key on the keyboard, the program exits and returns you to the DOS prompt.

This program serves as a screen saver; if you leave a fixed image on a screen for too long, you could damage your display.

This program is even more useful under Windows because it can be used to blank the screen without having to exit any of the applications. To start the program in the DOS window, you would type:

C:\>C:\DOS\BLACK.EXE

and press the Enter key. Another way to execute the same program is to change the default directory and then invoke the program using these two commands:

C:\>CD C:\DOS
C:\>BLACK

The first line performs a DOS Change Directory command and sets the default directory to C:\DOS. The second line tells DOS to find and execute the program called BLACK. Keep in mind that DOS doesn't care whether the

Working with Non-Windows Applications

commands are in uppercase or lowercase. In fact, you can mix uppercase and lowercase letters on the same command line. Notice also that the second command doesn't specify the directory path or file extension for BLACK. If you don't tell DOS the file type, it looks for a file called BLACK.COM, BLACK.EXE, or BLACK.BAT. The first two files are machine-code files that can only be read by the computer. The third file is a batch file that you can edit and read.

The only drawback to running BLACK.EXE in the DOS windows is that you have to invoke the DOS window first and then type in sufficient information to run the program. An easier way is to set up an icon in one of the windows so that Windows does all of the work. You can do this can easily through the Program Manager.

---

1. Use the CD (Change Directory) command to select the root directory of the hard disk your computer boots up from.
2. Type out the contents of a .BAT file, such as AUTOEXEC.BAT. What happens?

---

1. *Type in CD \ and press the Enter key.*
2. *Issue the command:*

   TYPE AUTOEXEC.BAT

You see a list of batch commands.

Creating Your Own Built-In Applications

Let's assume that you want to install BLACK.EXE so that you can start it by simply double-clicking on the icon. First, decide which program group you want the icon to appear in, and activate the group by double-clicking on the icon (so that the group window expands and the title bar is highlighted). Click on the File option of the Program Manager and select the New command. A dialog box (Figure 9.2) allows you to select between Program Group and Program Item. Select the Program Item option and click on the OK button. The dialog box called Program Item Properties (Figure 9.3) appears.

Type the description information that appears immediately below the new icon into the text box called Description. We recommend that you keep this text brief. (For this example, we'll call the program icon BLACKOUT.) The next

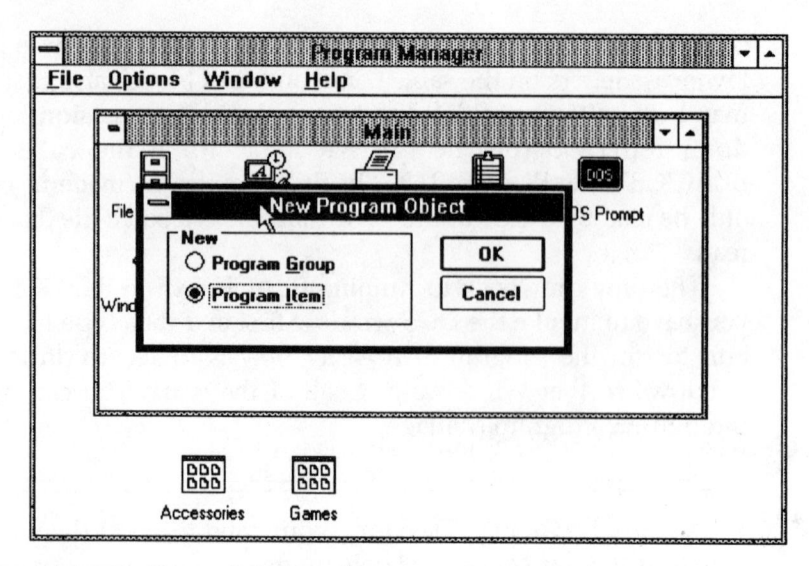

Figure 9.2. New Program Object Dialog Box

text box holds the command line that invokes the program. For consistency, this box should contain the complete directory path information. For our example program, we should type the following into this box:

C:\DOS\BLACK.EXE

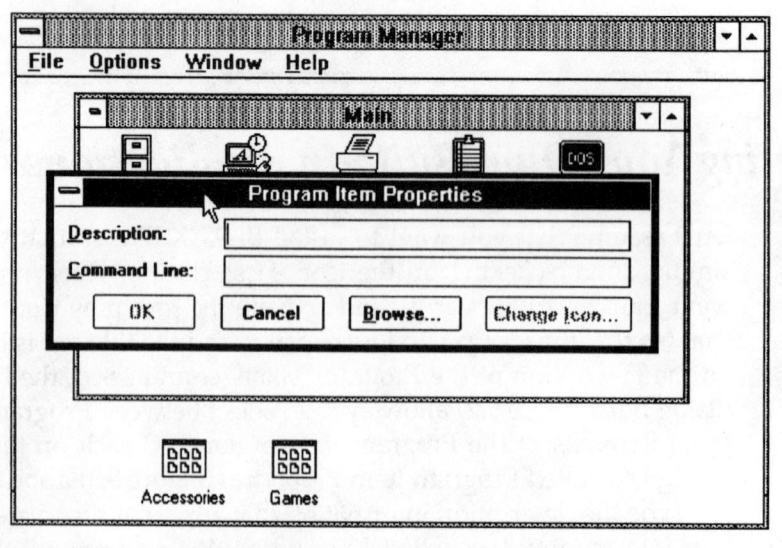

Figure 9.3. Program Item Properties Dialog Box

Working with Non-Windows Applications

Next, select one of the standard icons for your application by activating the Change Icon... button at the lower-right corner of the dialog box. This brings up the dialog box containing a button labeled View Next in the middle of the window. To the left of the button appears a Windows icon (Figure 9.4). Click on the button to request a different icon. When you have viewed all of the icons, click on the button until the desired icon appears and then click on the OK button to save your selection.

After you return to the Program Item Properties dialog box, click the OK window button to complete the operation. Your new icon appears in the desired program group window. To activate the program, just double-click on your icon in the same way you start any of the other applications running under Windows!

Moving a Program Icon

Before we complete this section, let's review two topics: moving and deleting a program item. To move an icon from one program group to another, open both windows and size them so that they appear on the screen simultaneously. Click on the icon to be moved and drag it across the screen. When the icon outline is positioned in a clear spot in the new program group window, release the mouse button.

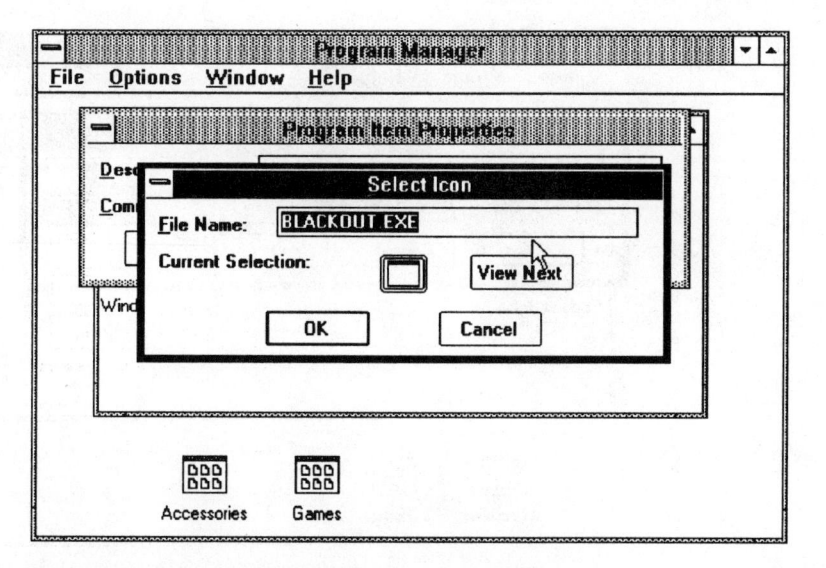

Figure 9.4. Select Icon Dialog Box

Deleting an Icon

To delete an icon, select it and then select the Delete command from the Program Manager's File menu. When a dialog box appears to confirm that you want to delete the application, select the OK button. The icon disappears.

Modifying an Icon

You can also modify an icon, its description, and other aspects of the icon (including the icons provided by Windows) by clicking on the icon once to select it and then activating the Program Manager File Properties... command. This brings up the Program Item Properties dialog box (Figure 9.5) for the selected application. Use this dialog box to change the icon information. For example, if your computer contained programs at installation time that Windows recognized, you may see an icon called Non-Windows Applications. You can change this description to something shorter, such as Non-Win Apps.

Whenever you run an application, Windows creates a default environment for your program to run in. This may be fine for a large program, such as a word-processor or spreadsheet program, but it's a waste of computer memory for a small program. To prevent wasting memory, you can use an application called the PIF Editor.

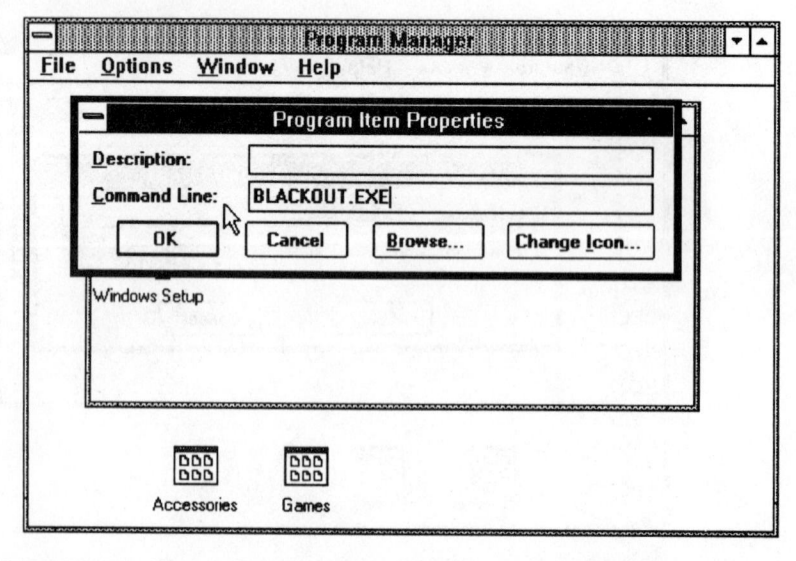

Figure 9.5. Program Item Properties Dialog Box

Working with PIFs

Recall that PIF stands for Program Information File. When you run a DOS program, Windows determines how the program should be executed—and that's where the PIF comes into play. This file provides important technical information such as:

- How much memory the application requires.
- Whether the application should be run in a window.
- Whether the application should be run in the background.
- Whether the video mode for the application is text or graphics.
- The optional parameters used to run the application.
- The start-up directory for the application.
- Whether the application modifies a communication port.

If you run a program that doesn't have an associated PIF, Windows uses default settings that work for most programs. The advantage of using a dedicated PIF for each application is that the PIF allows you to customize the runtime environment for your application and improve its performance. The drawback to using PIF files is that you need to provide technical information about your application.

Some DOS programs come with their own PIFs so that they run under Windows. Windows also provides predefined PIFs for some of the more popular DOS programs. If you use an application that has its own PIF, you can easily install the PIF by following these steps:

1. Make sure the application is correctly installed on your hard disk. To perform the installation, follow the instructions provided with the application.
2. Copy the PIF provided with the application to your Windows directory.
3. Start Windows and double-click on the Windows Setup icon in the Main group window.
4. Select the Set Up Applications... command from the Options menu.
5. Select the disk drive where the application is stored by clicking on the Setup will search pull-down box provided with the dialog box shown in Figure 9.6.
6. Click the OK button.
7. Select the application you want to add in the menu box (Figure 9.7), and click the Add-> button.
8. Click the OK button.

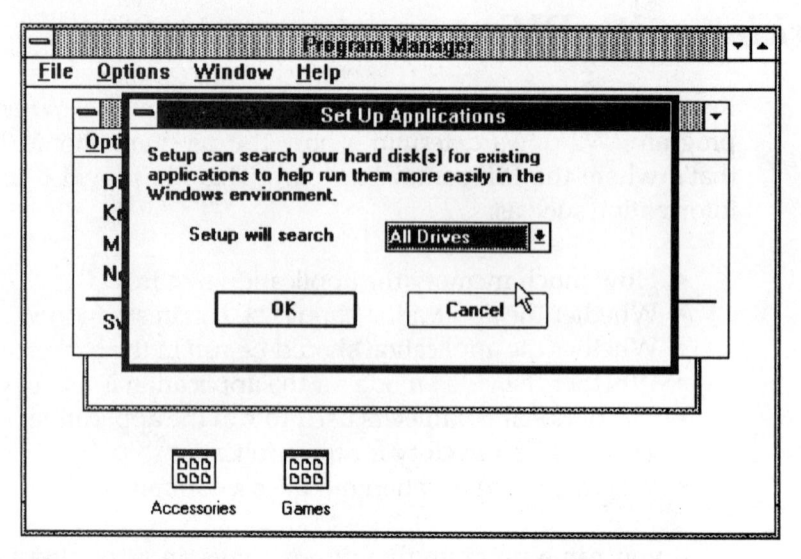

Figure 9.6. Set Up Applications Dialog Box

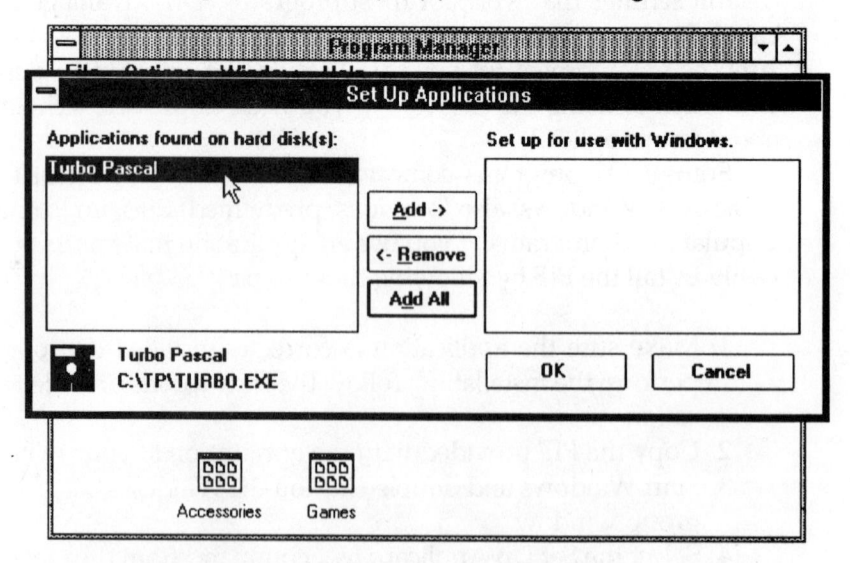

Figure 9.7. Selecting a Non-Windows Application

Using the PIF Editor

When you open the Accessories program group, you see an icon labeled PIF Editor. Activate this application to create a new Program Information File for a program.

Working with Non-Windows Applications

Figure 9.8 shows how the PIF Editor window looks when you run Windows in Standard or Real mode. The top line requests the program filename. (This entry should include the directory path information.) The next data box requests the window title that will display in the title bar. (If your application uses the entire screen, this information isn't useful because no title bar will be visible. Some non-Windows applications, however, can be run out of a window, so provide this information just in case.)

Use the Optional Parameters text box to provide information that would normally follow the program name on the command line. For example, Microsoft Excel automatically loads a specific spreadsheet file if the spreadsheet filename is typed on the DOS command line after the command filename EXCEL. If you execute this command at the DOS prompt:

EXCEL Budget

Excel starts up and loads in the spreadsheet file named Budget. To set up the PIF for the same result, type the text EXCEL into the Program Filename text box and the text Budget into the Optional Parameters text box.

If the parameter information is likely to change each time when you run the application, enter a question mark in the box. Windows will prompt you when the application program is to be invoked.

Use the Start-up Directory box to define a default directory that is different from the directory where the program resides. For example, assume that the

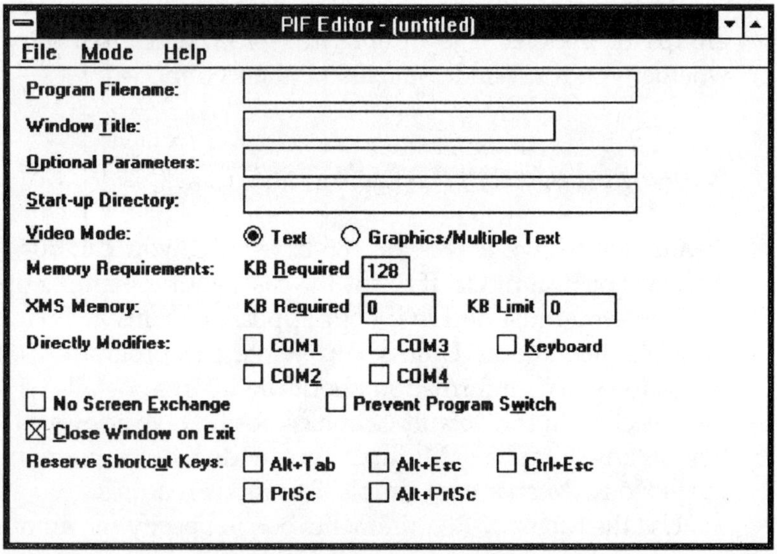

Figure 9.8. PIF Editor Window

EXCEL program is usually kept in the EXCEL subdirectory, and that your worksheet files are stored in a separate directory, WORKFLS. In this case, you would specify C:\EXCEL\EXCEL.EXE for the program filename, and you might specify C:\WORKFLS for the start-up directory.

---

1. What information do you enter into the text boxes Program Filename, Window Title, and Optional Parameters to run the application named WORD, which is stored in the directory C:\APPS? When the application starts, it should run in a window called MS WORD 4.0, and it should load in the document file NOTES.DOC (which is stored in the directory C:\APPS\WORD\DOCS).
2. Enter a ? in the Optional Parameters text box. What happens?
3. True or false? All non-Windows applications must run in a window.

---

1. *(a) Program Filename - C:\APPS\WORD*
   (b) Window Title - MS WORD 4.0
   (c) Optional Parameters - C:\APPS\WORD\DOCS
2. *Windows prompts you for the name of a parameter before it starts to run the application.*
3. *False.*

After you've filled in all of the data boxes, you can choose from several groups of options. The options that you select will vary depending upon whether you run Windows in 386 Enhanced mode.

Non-386 Enhanced Mode

If you don't have a 386- or 486-based PC, you can run Windows only in Standard or Real mode. If this is the case, your remaining options are limited.

First, you must decide if your application runs in Text mode or Graphics/Multiple Text mode. Unless you wrote the program yourself or you have access to specific information about the internal details of the program, leave this selection in the default Graphics position. Windows asks for this information because Graphics/Multiple Text mode requires more memory to simulate the video RAM area than simple Text mode requires.

Use the Memory Requirements box to specify the amount of memory that must be available in the normal 640K DOS area for the program to operate successfully. It's usually best to leave this option at the default value of 128K unless you know that the program requires more memory. Windows gives the program all available memory in the 640K partition anyway, so this is usually not very important. The XMS memory check boxes apply only to programs designed to directly utilize Extended Memory in PCs that don't have 386/486 microprocessors. Again, unless you run an application that specifically wants this additional memory (such as high-end database manager programs), leave this option at the default values of zero.

If your application directly accesses one or more hardware ports or the keyboard, click on the appropriate boxes to tell Windows which hardware components are off limits when your application runs.

Select the check box associated with the No Screen Exchange to tell Windows that you won't be copying information from that screen into the Clipboard application. By selecting this option, you reduce the amount of memory consumed by the program. Use the Prevent Program Switch option to save additional memory by telling Windows that the only way to return to Windows after this application runs is to terminate the execution of the application.

The Close Window on Exit option tells Windows that whenever you exit the application (which normally would return you to the DOS prompt), Windows should close the window automatically and return you to the Windows environment. This option eliminates the chore of typing EXIT each time you leave a window.

Use the bottom section of the window to reserve certain key combinations used by Windows, so that your application can use them instead. Leave these boxes blank unless you have a conflict. If that occurs, select the appropriate check box.

386 Enhanced Mode

The PIF Editor window for 386 Enhanced mode actually looks simpler than the one for Real and Standard mode (Figure 9.9). Actually, it provides a second page with many more options, which you access by clicking on the Advanced... button at the bottom of the window. Before we look at the advanced options, let's discuss memory requirements.

When the PIF Editor opens a new PIF file, it sets the KB Required option to 128 and the KB Desired option to 640. These numbers refer to the amount of conventional memory that should be allocated to your application. The KB Required option tells the minimum amount of memory that Windows must have available before it can start the application. The default of 128K is a reasonable compromise; many DOS applications (excluding large word processors or database programs) fit in 128K.

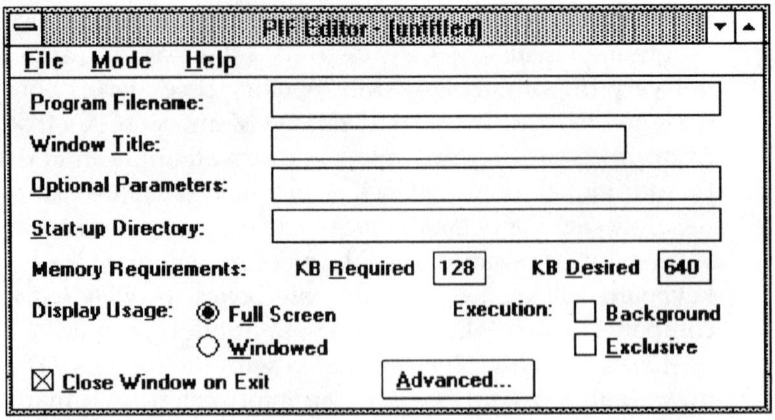

Figure 9.9. 386 Enhanced Mode PIF Editor Window

The second box specifies 640K for the KB Desired option. This is your opportunity to tell Windows the maximum amount of conventional memory that should be provided to this window. If 640K is available, Windows allocates that much to the window (which keeps other tasks from using the memory). In cases where you run only a specific application in a window, you may wish to reduce the KB Desired figure to the maximum amount of memory that the application can use. This leaves more memory available for other windows. In the next section, we'll provide an example that reduces these numbers to a very small amount.

The next option, called Display Usage, allows you to specify if the application should have the full screen to itself, or should operate in a window with all of the other applications. Select Full Screen to allow an application to operate the same way that it would if Windows were not present. This option is particularly desirable if the application can write to any text location in a 25-line by 80-character field.

The Windowed option is excellent for use with applications that insert new lines near the bottom of the screen and allow old information to scroll off the top of the screen. The main disadvantages of running an application in Windowed mode are that the application can't access the mouse (Windows keeps control), and the application consumes more memory than when running in Full Screen mode. These may be small penalties compared to the advantages of running in a window.

To the right of the Display Usage options appear two check boxes that show how and when the application in the window executes. If you click on the Background option, Windows occasionally diverts execution time to this application when another nonexclusive application is running in foreground.

This option is particularly important when the task in this window is performing a real-time function, such as communicating with another device through a port or waiting for a particular event to occur. If you don't select the check box, the task becomes completely dormant when another window is active.

The second option, Exclusive, specifies how execution time should be partitioned when this window is the active one. If you select this option, this task prevents any other Windows task from running (even if the Background option of the other task is marked with an "x"). Actually, this approach is quite valid for seldom used tasks that are very computer intensive. For example, you may have a computer program that implements a simple model of the national economy based on certain inputs. You may wish to start the program under Windows, but you want it to run as quickly as possible because you need the data before you can continue the analysis you were performing in another window. Use the Exclusive execution option so that nothing interrupts the execution of the model.

Use the last option in the window to tell Windows what it should do once the application returns to DOS. If you select the check box next to Close Window on Exit, Windows automatically closes the window when the application program terminates. If you also select the Full Screen option, the screen reverts to the Windows environment automatically. (This feature can be extremely useful if you want to create your own "pop-up" program within Windows: You can start up a sequence of events by double-clicking on an icon, and then have everything disappear once you are finished.) On the other hand, if you want to run several programs in an unpredictable order, or you need to look at intermediate results, don't activate the Close Window on Exit option.

Advanced PIF Options

Notice the button labeled Advanced... located at the bottom of the PIF Editor window. Figure 9.10 shows the Advanced Options dialog box that appears if you click this button.

The first section in the dialog box allows you to set Background and Foreground Priorities. (In reality, these should be called execution-time points.) Both boxes can receive numbers in the range of 0 to 10000.

Windows adds the Foreground Priority number for the foreground application and the Background Priority values for the various background applications together. The foreground application receives a percentage of the total available execution time, represented by its Foreground Priority number divided by the sum of the priorities. Each background application receives a percentage of the total available execution time, represented by its Background

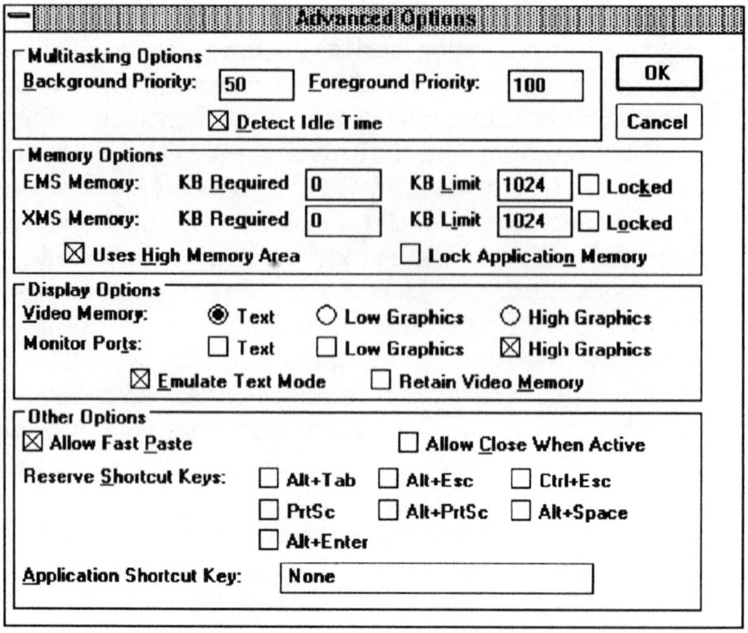

Figure 9.10. Advanced Options Dialog Box

Priority number divided by the sum of the priorities. This sharing of execution time occurs if the Exclusive option isn't selected in the PIF file of the foreground application.

The Detect Idle Time option allows Windows to steal resources from the foreground application whenever it thinks that the foreground task is waiting for input from the user. For example, imagine that you're typing a letter using Windows Write. Unless you're an extremely fast thinker, you probably type a few sentences and then stop for a minute or two while composing the next set of sentences in your mind. While the computer is waiting for your next set of keystrokes, it can run other applications in the background (for example, send additional characters to a printer). When you select Detect Idle Time, Windows can best utilize the total execution time available. Of course, if you find that a particular application runs slowly under Windows, disable this option and try the program again. It may be that Windows is being fooled into thinking that an application is idle when it actually is doing something useful.

The next set of options are grouped under the title Memory Options. If you run normal DOS applications (those that run in 640K of regular memory or less), then don't modify any of these options. If you run a memory-hungry application that tries to use more than 640K, read the user's manual for the application for more detail about what it wants to use.

Working with Non-Windows Applications

The next set of options is called Display Options. Use the Video Memory option to select between Text, Low Graphics, and High Graphics. Text mode is the least memory-hungry mode; it implies that all communications to the screen consist of the usual printable characters (including the "funny" symbols used by some programs to implement boxes around text, and so on). The second mode, Low Graphics, assumes that you use graphics images similar to those provided by a CGA card. Select the third option, High Graphics, if you expect to generate full-blown EGA/VGA graphics in the window.

The Monitor Ports options tell Windows to track the screen hardware because your application is bypassing the DOS calls and writing directly to hardware. You will know that you have this problem if you move to a different window, return to this application, and find that the screen has inexplicably changed or is garbled. You can tell Windows to monitor only for Text mode, for CGA-style Low Graphics, or for EGA/VGA High Graphics. Don't activate these options for a given window unless absolutely necessary, because the monitoring operation consumes additional computer execution time and slows down your applications programs.

Use the last two options in the box, Emulate Text Mode and Retain Video Memory, to fine-tune your application. Select Emulate Text Mode (which is normally set on) to allow your application to display text more quickly. If your application won't run or you have troubles with screen operations (garbled text, cursor not operating properly, and so on), disable this feature and see if the problem goes away. Select the Retain Video Memory option to tell Windows not to release the extra video memory if your application shifts from a higher memory-consumption mode (such as EGA or VGA graphics) to a less memory-intensive mode (such as text-only mode). Some programs allow you to switch automatically from one mode to another; by activating this option, you can be certain that your application won't stop due to insufficient memory because of a change in video mode.

The last check box contains several miscellaneous options. Allow Fast Paste is actually more of an inhibit than an enable option. If you don't select this option, Windows uses a slower method of pasting information from the Clipboard into the application. If you select the option, Windows attempts to analyze the program that you're running, and uses the Fast Paste technique only if it thinks your application can handle it. Disable this option if you have trouble bringing in data from the Clipboard.

The Allow Close When Active option tells Windows that it can just kill this task if you decide to exit the Windows environment with this window open. If you don't select this option, Windows forces you to exit the task in the window before you can exit the environment. If the tasks running under this PIF can open and modify files, leave this option off. Although DOS usually closes all files associated with an application automatically, there is a finite probability that something could go wrong (resulting in data loss). When it comes to data files, methodical and conservative techniques always pay off.

The Reserve Shortcut Keys option tells Windows to ignore the keystroke sequences selected and allow the command to go through to the application running in the window. This allows you to resolve conflicts where both Windows and the application program use the same command for different purposes.

Use the Application Shortcut Key to convert the application in this window into a "pop-up" program. To use this feature, you must specify a keystroke combination using either the Alt or Ctrl keys. For example, if you select Alt+7 as the shortcut, this window will immediately pop-up active whenever you press this combination of keys. The only disadvantage is that this combination of keys becomes reserved and can't be used in any other application. Be careful when defining shortcut key sequences to make certain that you never have two separate windows with the same shortcut!

A Custom Directory Program

Now that you know how the DOS Prompt application works and how to use the PIF Editor to create a custom process, let's look at an example. If you use Windows a great deal, you'll discover that trying to find a file using the File Manager can get tedious if you don't remember the name of the file or its extension (type). Our example is an extremely simple tool that you activate by double-clicking on a new icon and providing the directory information. This tool allows you to quickly find a file in any directory on any drive.

Figure 9.11 illustrates a simple batch file, called DIRP.BAT, which is invoked when you select the icon. The first line is a DOS command that turns off the display of batch commands to the screen. The second line does the actual work; it invokes the DOS directory command called DIR. The /P appended to the command is an option switch that requests that only enough information be displayed to fill one screen at a time. This "page" option means that DOS

```
echo off
dir/p %1
pause
```

Figure 9.11. Simple Batch Program

displays (at most) 23 file entries on the screen. The 24th line displays a message such as "Press any key to continue...", and on the 25th line, the cursor sits at column 1. After you've viewed the first page, you can see the subsequent pages by pressing a keyboard key. (The space bar is often favored for this task.) Each time you press the key, the next page appears. This process repeats itself until the last page is reached. The PAUSE command in the last line in the batch file is discussed in the following paragraph.

To make this application work as a simple pop-up task, select the Close Window on Exit option for the associated PIF. Unfortunately, when the DIR command displays its last page of information, it returns control to DOS. When control returns to DOS, Windows grabs it, decides that you have exited your program, and closes the window! We want to read the contents of the last (or perhaps the only) page of output from DIR, so we've added the PAUSE command at the end of the file. This command is normally used to give the user a chance to take some action that requires time. It simply stops the batch file execution and displays the "Press any key to continue.." message. When you press any key, DOS tries to execute the next statement in the batch file (if there is one). In our case, no statement appears after the PAUSE command, so the batch file completes. This returns execution to DOS, and then you're back in the Windows environment again.

After you've created the batch file, you need to create a PIF file to invoke it. Open the Accessories group and double-click on the PIF Editor icon. For the Program Filename, type in the path information and the name of the batch file you created. For Window Title, select whatever you want to appear below the icon (try DIR/P). For Optional Parameters, insert a question mark only.

Whenever this PIF is activated, Windows asks for parameters to be passed to the application. You can then provide a full path specification to the directory that you want to see, and provide either a full filename or a file specification, including wildcards. The information is passed to the batch file, where DOS inserts it in place of the %1 symbol on the DIR/P line. This gives you flexibility to specify any directory and file combination using one icon.

Leave the Start-up Directory field blank, and leave all of the other options in their default state. Save the file using the File Save As.. option. (This option will give the PIF file the same name as the batch file, but you can change the name if you wish.)

After you've created and saved the file, exit the PIF Editor. Double-click on the group icon where you want the new icon to appear and open the group window. While the title bar for the desired group is active, select the File New option from Program Manager. When a dialog box asks whether you want to create a new Program Item or a new Program Group, select the default (Program Item) by clicking on the OK button. A Program Item Properties window appears and asks for a description and a command line. For the description, type the text that you want to appear below the icon. For the command line, provide the full path description and the name of the PIF file (including the period followed by the letters PIF). If you want to select a special icon, click on the Change Icon... button. When you're done defining item properties, click on the OK button to create the icon and set everything up.

A new icon now appears in the selected group. When you double-click on the icon, a dialog box asks for additional parameters. If your Windows files are in a directory called C:\WINDOWS, enter C:\WINDOWS*.* and press the Enter key or click on the OK button to start the application. You will see several screens of directory information before you're returned back to the Windows environment.

If you've gotten this far successfully, you may wish to create other tools that are particularly useful to you. You may also want to experiment with providing this tool with different parameters, such as PATH*.EXE, to see only a particular type of file in a directory. Of course, the techniques discussed in this chapter are also extremely useful for running normal .EXE and .COM files. You can even use these techniques to invoke the GWBASIC interpreter that most likely came with your computer. By being able to automatically invoke a simple BASIC program from Windows, you have the ability to perform extremely sophisticated or complex operations. You will discover that your only real limitations are your PC's memory and how much time you have to devote to developing these tools. The techniques described in this chapter allow you to customize Windows in an optimal way for your needs.

Now that we've taught you how to set up your own DOS tools, let's briefly review some useful DOS commands. (If you're an experienced DOS user, skip this section. It's provided for Windows users who don't understand the capabilities of DOS.)

Basic DOS Commands

The Disk Operating System (DOS) on your machine is a rather powerful software package. Entire books have been written about how to use the features of DOS, so we only cover a few of the more important features here. Table 9.1 lists the most often-used DOS commands.

The only commands listed in Table 9.1 that can remove information are DEL and FORMAT. DEL removes a file from a specified directory. The usual way to use DEL is to move to the target directory using the CHDIR command (which you can abbreviate as CD). Next, verify the existence of the file you want to delete by typing DIR and the full filename (including the extension).

Table 9.1. Commonly Used DOS Commands

Command	Description
CHDIR	(Change directory) This command can be abbreviated as CD.
CHKDSK	(Check disk) Shows how much of a drive contains stored files and how much space is available.
CLS	(Clear screen) Erases everything on the screen, and locates the DOS prompt at the top-left corner of the screen.
COPY	Copies a file to a new file. You can use this to copy a file from one directory to another.
DEL	Deletes a file from the specified directory.
DIR	Displays the contents of the specified directory.
FORMAT	Formats a disk so that it can hold information.
MKDIR	(Make directory) Creates a new subdirectory.
REN	Renames a file.
TYPE	Copies the contents of a file to the screen.

To delete the file, simply type DEL, the full filename, and press the Enter key; the file is immediately removed.

You can think of the FORMAT command as the equivalent of washing down a blackboard: You remove all trace of what was present before. Some versions of FORMAT only reformat floppy disk drives, but others allow you to destroy the contents of your hard disk. To format new floppy disks, issue a command such as:

FORMAT A:

The program then tells you what it will do, asks you to insert the floppy disk into the drive, and tells you to press any key to start the formatting operation. When it completes formatting the floppy disk, it asks you if you want to format another. If you answer with a y, insert another floppy and press any key to repeat the operation. Get into the habit of always specifying the drive where the disk media will be formatted. If you make a mistake when you invoke this program, press Ctrl+C to cancel it!

The easiest way to use the COPY command is to move to the directory where you want to create a new copy. Then, type something like:

COPY C:\XYZ\MYFILE.ATR

where C:\XYZ represents the path of the source directory, and MYFILE.ATR represents the full filename of the existing directory. DOS creates an exact copy of the specified file in the current directory. Instead of typing a full filename, you can use the asterisk wildcard to copy an entire group of files at one time. For example, replace MYFILE.ATR with *.BAT to copy all of the batch files from the source directory into the current one. Replace MYFILE.ATR with BLANK.* to copy all files called BLANK from the source directory to the current one. This last option comes in handy with programs where the main program file is ABC.EXE, the help file is called ABC.HLP, and so on.

The TYPE command allows you to send the contents of a file to a screen. It's usually best to only TYPE files of attribute BAT or TXT. This command never causes serious problems, but you can confuse the screen software if you TYPE a file that contains machine commands. If you ask DOS to type an .EXE or .COM file, nonsense symbols may appear on the screen and the machine may beep many times. Press Ctrl+C several times to regain control of the machine. You may also have to reset the PC by pressing the reset button, or turn the computer off for a couple of minutes and reboot it. Even most word-processor files aren't compatible with the TYPE command because of the data-compression algorithms they use to save file space.

Again, this is a very brief explanation of some of the DOS commands, and many commands have been left out. If you want to learn more about DOS, read the documentation that came with your machine, or find a good introductory book about DOS at your local bookstore or library.

Summary

In this chapter, you were introduced to the powerful features provided by Windows to access the DOS environment. You learned how to customize the attributes of a particular window using the PIF editor, and how to create your own icon-activated applications to run non-Windows programs and batch files.

In the next chapter, we'll return to Windows and review some of the simpler applications available in the Accessories program group.

Exercises

Use these exercises to work more with non-Windows applications.

What You Should Do	How the Computer Responds
1. Create a PIF file for a DOS application that you already have on your hard disk.	1. The PIF file is assigned the same name of the file, with a different extension. When you later double-click on the icon for the program, the PIF file tells Windows how to run the application.
2. Include an optional parameter for your PIF file.	2. When the program runs, the parameter starts the program.
3. Start the DOS Prompt application and issue the DIR command.	3. A listing of the files and subdirectories in the current directory displays.
4. Use the TYPE command to display a text file.	4. The file is scrolled on the screen.
5. Issue the EXIT command.	5. You return to the Windows environment.

What If It Doesn't Work?

1. If you don't have enough hard disk space, Windows can't load the DOS Prompt application.
2. If you try to type a file that is not a text file, you'll see control characters on the screen.

10

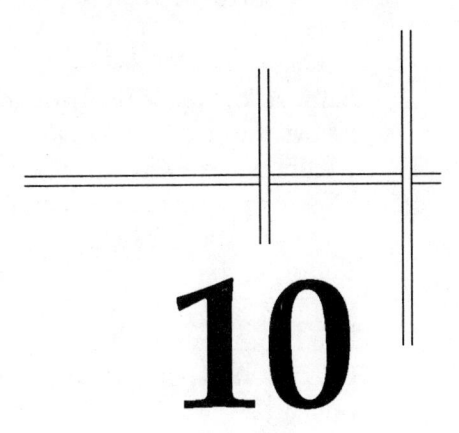

Using Desktop Accessories

Up to this point, we've only explored the major components of Windows, such as the Program Manager, the Control Panel, and the File Manager. Windows also provides a useful set of accessory applications to help you perform tasks ranging from creating and editing notes to recording your schedules and appointments. In this chapter we'll discuss each application in detail, and show how these applications can be used together.

After you complete this chapter, you'll know how to:

- Display the clock
- Use the Notepad application to create text files
- Use the Calendar application to track your important appointments
- Use the Calculator application to perform simple and scientific calculations
- Use the Cardfile application to set up a card index system

Working with Clock

The Clock application is probably the easiest accessory to use. When activated, it displays the time by using your PC's system time (which can be changed from the Control Panel). (This technique is explained in detail in Chapter 6.)

To display the clock, double-click on the Clock icon in the Accessories group window. You can change the appearance of the clock by using the

Settings menu, which provides two options: Analog and Digital. Figure 10.1 shows the clocks displayed with each option. Notice that the Analog clock is a traditional clock with hour, minute, and second hands. If you activate the Digital option, you see a green digital display on a black background.

The handy feature about the clock is that you can click on the minimize button at the top-right corner to shrink it to a working icon! When shrunk, it still displays the correct time. Don't use this feature if you have a real clock handy because the desktop clock steals some computation time from the rest of the system. This may not be very important if you only run a word processor, but can become more important if you use the full capabilities of your PC.

Using the Notepad

The Windows Notepad makes it easy for you to suspend an application that you're running, such as Excel, and compose a note. In fact, Notepad is intended to be a simple, easy-to-use editor. It creates simple text files similar to those created by the EDLIN program provided with DOS. Because the files it creates are simple ASCII files, you can print or view them with any text editor. These are some of the tasks you can perform with Notepad:

- Compose notes and save them.
- Edit text files created with Notepad.
- Search for text in a file.
- Print a text file.
- Copy sections of text files and paste them to other text files.

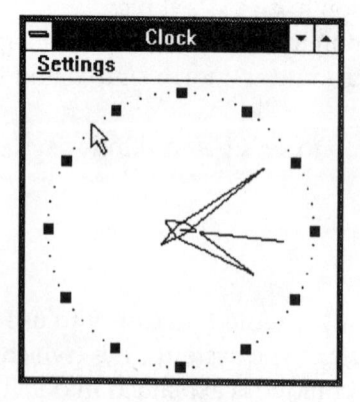

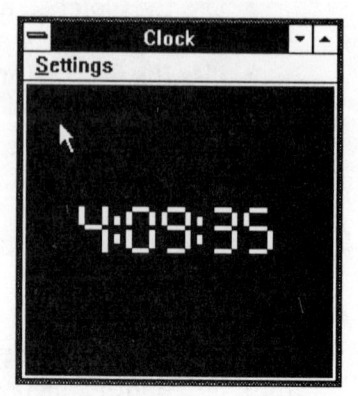

Figure 10.1. The Two Clock Styles

Starting Notepad

As with all of the applications we'll explore in this chapter, Notepad is stored in the Accessories group window. To start Notepad, open this window and double-click on the Notepad icon. Figure 10.2 shows the Notepad window that appears. Notice that a blinking, vertical-bar cursor displays in the top-left corner of the editing area. If you click on the File menu, you see the usual set of options such as New, Open..., Save, and so on.

To begin using Notepad, simply type in text that displays to the left of the blinking cursor. Use the arrow keys or the mouse to perform navigation operations, such as moving the cursor to the left or down. When you are done creating a text file, save it by activating the Save As... command from the File menu. When the dialog box appears (Figure 10.3), type the filename into the Filename text box and select the OK button. By default, Notepad uses the extension .TXT to save its text files.

After you've saved your text file, the Notepad window's title changes to reflect the name of the saved file. For example, if you save a file using the name REPORT1.TXT, the window title is Notepad - REPORT1.TXT. After a text file has been created, you can change it and save the changes by selecting the Save command from the File menu.

Figure 10.2. The Notepad Window

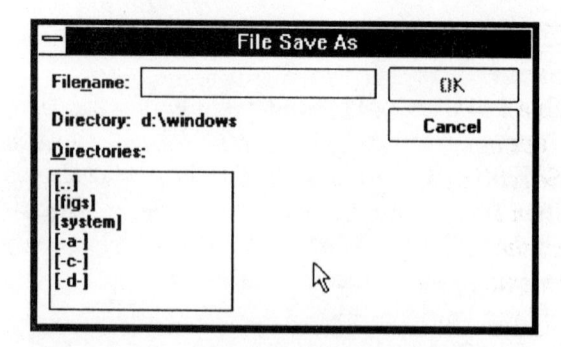

Figure 10.3. File Save As Dialog Box

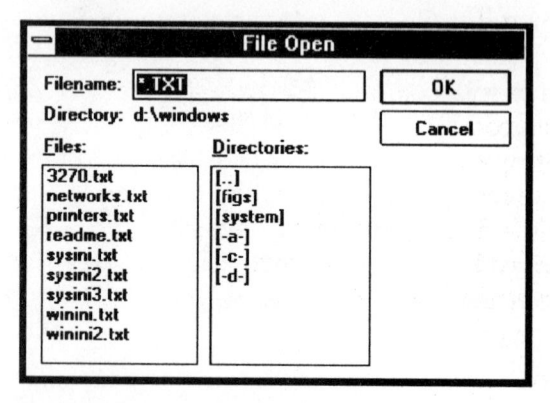

Figure 10.4. File Open Dialog Box

Opening an Existing Text File

If you've previously created a Notepad file, or you have an existing text file created by another text editor, you can open the file in Notepad by selecting the Open... command from the File menu. This action brings up the dialog box shown in Figure 10.4. Notice that this dialog box is similar to the File Open dialog boxes provided with other Windows applications. The Directories menu list allows you to select a directory, and the Files list provides a listing of the text files available in the currently selected directory. To open a file, either type the filename into the Filename text box, or click on one of the files provided in the Files list. Select the OK button to complete the operation.

1. Create a Notepad text file named NOTES1.TXT.
2. Add some text to the file.
3. Save the file and quit Notepad.

1. (a) *Start Notepad by double-clicking on its icon.*
   (b) *Select the Save As... command from the File menu.*
   (c) *Type in the text NOTES1.TXT in the Filename text box.*
   (d) *Select the OK button in the File Save As dialog box.*
2. *Position the cursor anywhere in the window and type in text.*
3. *Select the Save command from the File menu, and select the Exit command from the File menu.*

Editing Text

As we mentioned, you can easily perform a number of editing operations, such as copying, cutting, and pasting text, with Notepad. To perform any editing operation, first select (highlight) the text you want to change by dragging the mouse across the text to be marked, or moving the vertical bar to the left of the first character to be selected, holding down the Shift key, and using the arrow keys on the keyboard to move the cursor until the last desired character is highlighted. Release the Shift key when you've completed your selection operation.

Tip To select all of the text in a Notepad file, activate the Select All command from the File menu. This feature allows you to replicate several paragraphs or pages at once, without having to select the first character and then move down the document using the arrow keys.

The Edit menu provides the basic editing commands. The first command, Undo, removes the latest editing operation performed. If you use this command several times in a row, only the first invocation has any effect.

The easiest way to remove a block of text is to first highlight the text and then select the Cut command. Cut removes the selected text and places it into a temporary area (the Clipboard). You can now insert this text as many times as desired using the Paste command. Each insertion occurs at the present cursor location. Another way to repeat a block of text is to select it and then activate the Copy command. This moves an image of the selected text into the Clipboard without removing it from the screen. The Clipboard can only hold one selection at a time; a second Cut or Copy command overwrites the previous contents of the temporary buffer. If you highlight a section of text and then activate Delete, the text is removed permanently. To delete one character at a time, position the cursor to the left of the character and press the backspace key.

Basic Navigation Keys

Instead of using only the mouse to navigate in a text file, you can use the Home, End, Ctrl+Home, and Ctrl+End to go to the beginning of a line, end of a line, beginning of a document, and end of a document, respectively. You can also use Ctrl+Left Arrow and Ctrl+Right Arrow to skip a word at a time to the left or the right, respectively.

Using the Word Wrap Feature

If you're using Notepad to create a file of short notes, begin typing when the window appears. If you're creating a longer document, the text that you enter may go past the right edge of the window, out of view. In such a case, you can do one of two things: Press the Enter key when you get to the end of a line to insert a hard return, or select the Word Wrap option from the Edit menu.

When you activate Word Wrap (a check mark appears next to this option when the menu is expanded and the option is selected), Notepad always makes the text fit inside the window. If you continue typing past the end of the current line, Notepad moves the words that don't fit down to the next line. If you later resize the window, your text reflows to reflect the window's new size. The main advantage of this feature is that you can make your text fit inside a window's border without changing how the text is stored in your file, because the text is stored as one continuous line.

Searching for Text

While you're editing a text file, you can search for specific text by using the Find... command in the Search menu. This command brings up the simple dialog box shown in Figure 10.5. Enter the character, the word, or the phrase you want to search for in the Find What text box. By default, any text in the file that matches the text you enter is found. To search for text that matches the exact upper- and lowercase format that you type in, select the Match Upper/Lowercase option. For example, to search for the text "Seattle," type Seattle into the text box and select the case option because your text starts with an uppercase letter.

Normally, Notepad starts its search at the current position of the text cursor and continues until it finds a match or reaches the end of the file. If the text you are searching for can't be found, the dialog box shown in Figure 10.6 displays. To search backwards in a file, select the Backward option.

Using Desktop Accessories

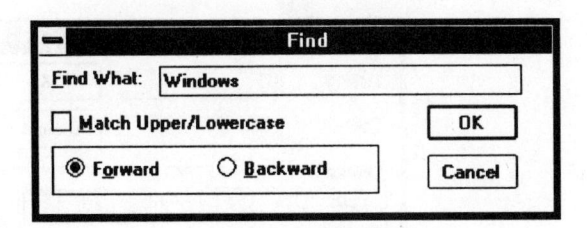

Figure 10.5. Find Dialog Box

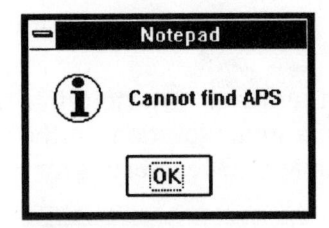

Figure 10.6. Notepad Dialog Box

Once a search has been performed successfully, you can repeat it by selecting the Search Find Next option or pressing the F3 key.

Tip Notepad doesn't allow you to perform a search-and-replace operation. If you need this feature, you'll have to use a word processing application, such as Write.

Setting Up a Page

The Page Setup... command in the File menu brings up a dialog box (Figure 10.7) where you specify the top, bottom, left, and right margins for your printed text files. Notice that each of these margins is represented in inches. To change a margin, select the appropriate text box and type in a new value. Keep in mind that fractions of an inch are represented to the right of the decimal point. For example, 1/2 of an inch is represented as 0.5.

The Page Setup dialog box also allows you to define header and footer information for each page. The Help menu provides a brief list of options available for either one. These header/footer controls are specified by two-character control codes. For example, when &l, &c, and &r precede the title information, Windows knows that you want the information printed left-justified, centered, or right-justified (respectively). The control code &p marks the location where the page number is placed, &d does the same for the date,

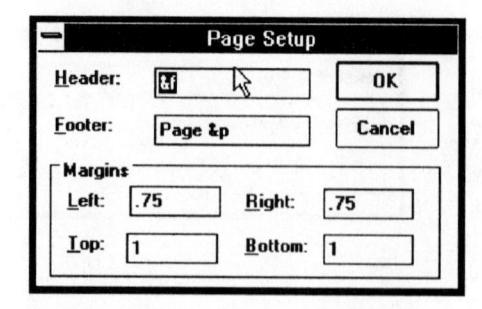

Figure 10.7. Page Setup Dialog Box

and &t causes the current time to print. The &f control specifies the printing of the filename at a given location. In the default configuration, Notepad limits you to approximately 37 characters for the title.

1. Set up a Notepad document so that it has a 1/2-inch left and right margin, a 3/4-inch top and bottom margin, and a header that displays the current date.
2. What text should be entered in the Header text box to print page numbers on each page?

1. *Display the Page Setup dialog box by selecting the Page Setup... command from the File menu. Enter the following information:*

    Header: &d
    Left: .5
    Right: .5
    Top: .75
    Bottom: .75

2. *&p*

Printing a File

After you set up your page configuration, print a text file by selecting the Print command from the File menu. A message box informs you that your file is being sent to the printer. The printed file appears exactly as it appears on the screen.

Using the Time/Date Feature

The Time/Date option inserts the current time and date at the present cursor position. You can automatically invoke this option by pressing the F5 function key or selecting the Time/Date command from the File menu. This feature allows you to keep a time log so that you'll know how you spend your time while working with your computer. Each time you use Windows, you can bring up Notepad, select the Time/Date command, and type in a note about your work.

Using Multiple Files

One of the more interesting features of the Windows environment is that you can Cut (or Copy) data across applications. This means that you can cut or copy some text from an application such as Cardfile, Terminal, Write, or Calculator, and insert it at the current cursor position in another application (such as Notepad) by simply invoking Paste. Be careful not to wipe out a previous cut operation when you move from window to window.

Using the Calendar

We introduced the Calendar application briefly in Chapter 5 to show you how to set an alarm. This application actually provides a useful daily appointment book and a monthly calendar from 1980 through 2099. We'll return to the Calendar to show you how to use its other features.

Starting Calendar

To start the Calendar, open the Accessories window and double-click on the Calendar icon. The untitled Calendar window (Figure 10.8) appears. Notice that this application provides the standard menus such as File, Edit, and Help, which are similar to those found in other applications. In addition, the menus View, Show, Alarm, and Options allow you to perform operations, such as setting an alarm or viewing different calendar dates and months in order to schedule appointments.

    The Calendar window displays an appointment page for each date in one-hour time intervals. This format is called the *Day view*. At the top of the appoint-

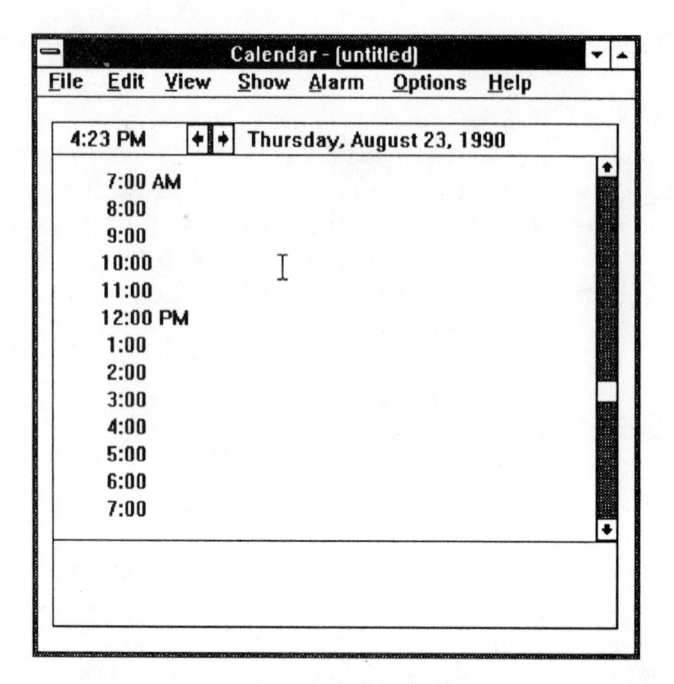

Figure 10.8. Calendar Window

ment page, a status bar provides the current time, scroll arrows, and the current date. Use the arrows to scroll through appointment pages. Click on the left arrow to see the previous day, or click on the right arrow to see the next day.

The appointment page area below the status bar contains the text for your appointments. Click to the right of each hour time interval to display the text cursor, and then type in a single-line message. For example, to remind yourself about a sales meeting in New York at 10:00 A.M. on September 21, select this day using the arrow buttons in the status bar, and then type in the text "Sales meeting in New York" at the 10:00 time slot.

The last component of the daily Calendar window is a scratch pad area where you can leave notes to yourself. To access this scratchpad area, press the Tab key or click in the rectangular region below the appointment page.

Changing the Calendar Format

To change the Calendar window so that you can see an entire month instead of a single day, select the Month option from the View menu, or press F9. The Calendar window changes to the format shown in Figure 10.9. Notice that the current date is highlighted and marked with the symbols ><. To view previous

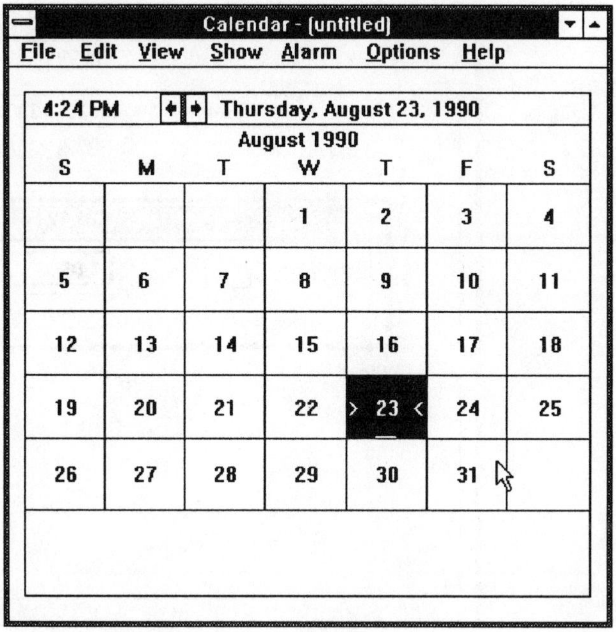

Using Desktop Accessories

Figure 10.9. Calender's Month Format

and future months, click on the left and right arrow buttons on the status line that contains the date and time. You can also select a specific date by using one of the options in the Show menu.

When viewing the Month display, you can access the daily appointments page for any particular day by clicking on the desired day, and then pressing the F8 key to bring back the Day display. As a shortcut, double-click on the desired day.

Selecting an Appointment Date

The Show menu allows you to immediately view today's appointments by selecting the Today option. You can also see the display for the previous day or the next day or month (depending on which calendar format you are viewing) by selecting Previous or Next. The shortcut keys for these options are Ctrl+PageUp and Ctrl+PageDown.

You can also activate the Date... command to enter a specific date to be viewed. When you select this command, the Show Date dialog box appears (Figure 10.10). Type the date you want to display into the Show Date textbox. When you select the OK button, Calendar moves to the date you selected.

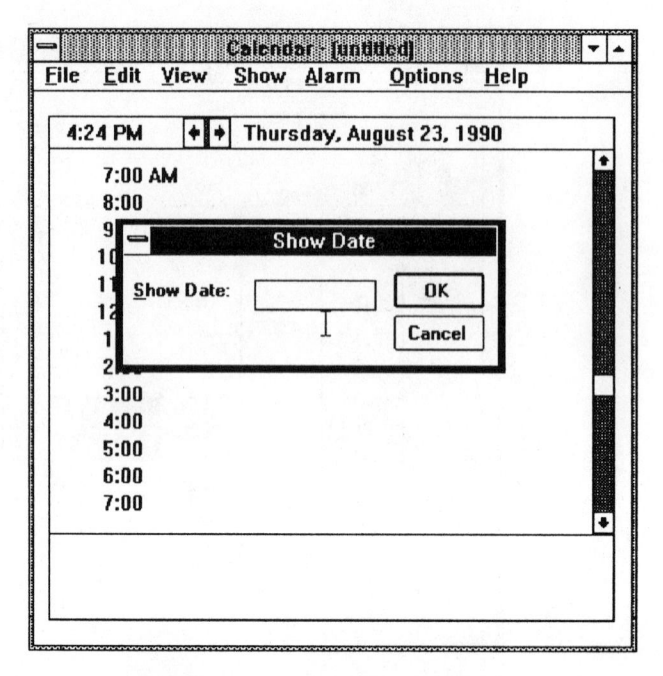

Figure 10.10. Show Date Dialog Box

Setting Time Slots

By default, an appointment page lists time slots in one-hour intervals. The problem with this arrangement is that not every activity schedule will correspond with the 12 hours of a day from 7:00 A.M. to 7:00 P.M. Fortunately, Calendar allows you to add, change, and delete time slots.

To alter the time slots in a Calendar page, use the commands in the Options menu: Special Time..., and Day Settings.... Use the Day Settings... command to select the time interval between entries on the day page, and to select between a 12- and a 24-hour format for the displayed times. Use it also to specify the default time for the first time entry on the day page. When you select this command, the dialog box shown in Figure 10.11 appears. Notice that you can set the time interval to 15, 30, or 60 minutes. To change the number of hours displayed in an appointment page, select one of the options for the Hour Format group. The last option, Starting Time, provides a text box where you type the first entry on the appointment page.

Use the Special Time... command to add a special time slot. For example, you may specify a 60-minute default interval for entries on a page, but you may want to mark a teleconference scheduled for 2:40 in the afternoon. Use the Special Time dialog box (Figure 10.12) to enter 2:40 P.M. (or 14:40 if you're

Using Desktop Accessories

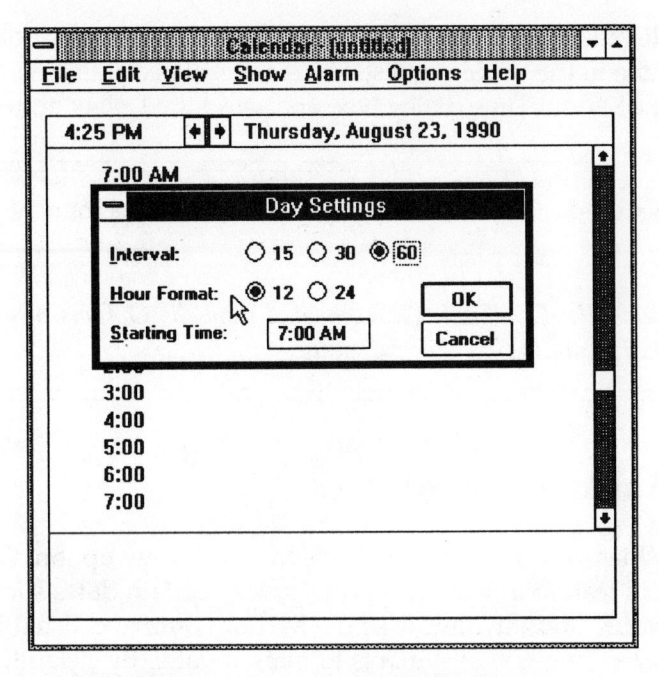

Figure 10.11. Day Settings Dialog Box

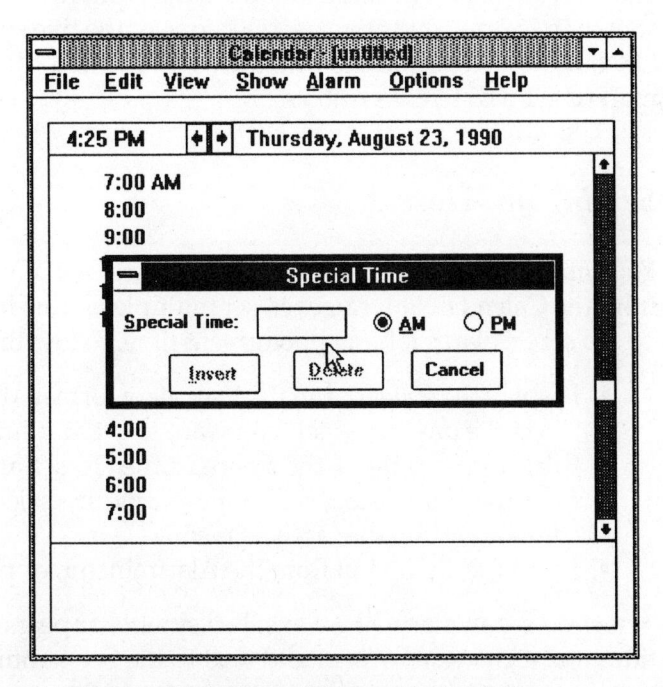

Figure 10.12. Special Time Dialog Box

defaulting to 24-hour time). Click on the Insert button to add that particular time in the usual day list. To remove a special time slot later, enter the time in the Special Time dialog box, and select the Delete button.

☑ Set up the Calendar to display times on an appointment page in 24-hour formats.

Select the Day Settings... command from the Options menu. Click on the 24 option button in the Hour Format group.

Marking Special Days

When you use the Calendar's Monthly view option, Calendar provides a special feature to help you keep track of certain dates such as birthdays, anniversaries, and paydays. Use the Mark... command listed in the Options menu to select one of five symbols to mark a date. (By default, the Month view marks the current date with the > < symbols.) To mark a different day, select the date and activate the Mark command from the Options menu. When the dialog box shown in Figure 10.13 appears, select one of the five symbols and then click the OK button. Figure 10.14 shows a calendar in the Month view that has dates marked with different symbols.

Setting an Alarm

You can use the Alarm feature to set an alarm for any day and time accessible from the Calendar. You can even set multiple alarms for one day.

To set an alarm for an appointment time, follow these steps:

1. Display the Calendar in the Day view format. (Press the F8 key.)
2. Select the day for which you want to set an alarm.
3. Click to the right of the desired time. To set an alarm for a time other than the ones listed, add a new time by selecting the Special Time... command from the Options menu.
4. Select the Set option from the Alarm menu, or press F5.

After you set an alarm, the alarm bell symbol appears next to the appointment time, and a check mark is placed next to the Set command. Figure 10.15 shows an appointment page with an alarm set for 10:00 A.M.

Using Desktop Accessories

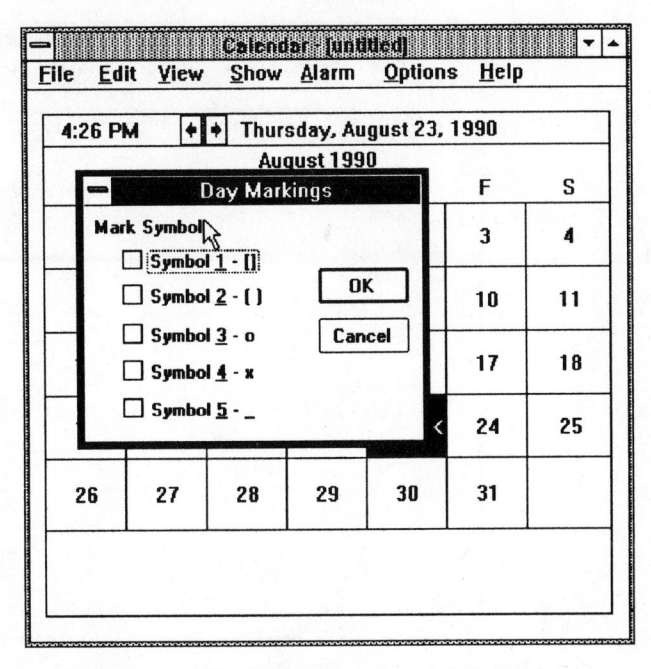

Figure 10.13. Day Markings Dialog Box

Figure 10.14. Month View of the Calendar

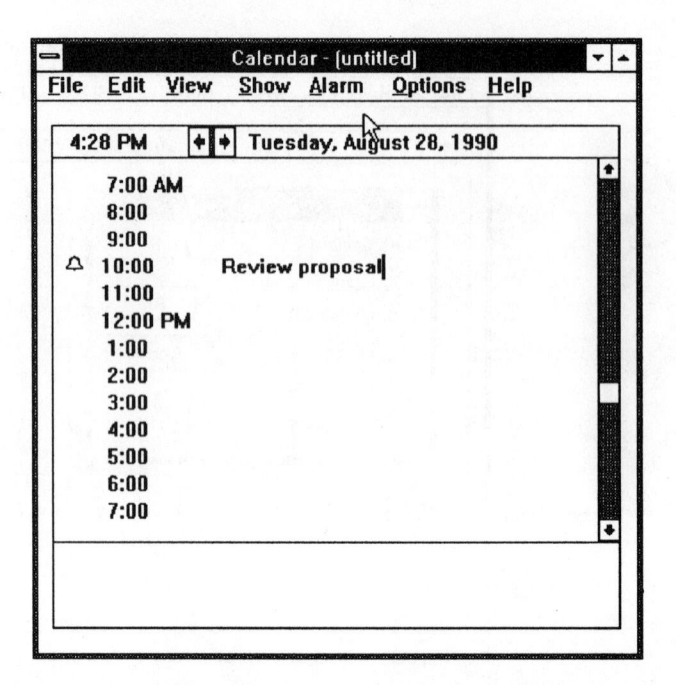

```
                    ┌─────────────────────────────────────┐
                    │ ▬      Calendar - (untitled)    ▼ ▲ │
                    │ File  Edit  View  Show  Alarm  Options  Help │
                    ├─────────────────────────────────────┤
                    │ 4:28 PM    ← →  Tuesday, August 28, 1990 │
                    │     7:00 AM                          ↑ │
                    │     8:00                              │
                    │     9:00                              │
                    │ ♤  10:00      Review proposal│        │
                    │    11:00                              │
                    │    12:00 PM                           │
                    │     1:00                              │
                    │     2:00                              │
                    │     3:00                              │
                    │     4:00                              │
                    │     5:00                              │
                    │     6:00                              │
                    │     7:00                            ↓ │
                    │                                      │
                    │                                      │
                    └─────────────────────────────────────┘
```

Figure 10.15. An Appointment Page with the Alarm Set

If the alarm goes off while you're using Calendar, a dialog box reminds you about the appointment. If you're using another application, you hear the alarm chirp and may see the calendar icon blink. Click on the icon to view a dialog box that displays the information from the line in the calendar page that set off the alarm.

Once the alarm goes off, it continues to flash and beep until it's turned off. To turn off the alarm, display the Calendar window. When you see the Alarm dialog box, click the OK button to turn off the alarm.

Tip | If you want to remove an alarm, click to the right of the time set for that alarm and select the Set option from the Alarm menu. The check mark next to Set disappears to indicate that the alarm is no longer set.

Alarm Options

You can also customize an alarm to sound early by 0 to 10 minutes. You can also enable or disable the audible alarm by clicking on the box next to the Sound label. To access these features, select the Alarm Controls... command from the Alarm menu. A dialog box appears (Figure 10.16) with the options

Using Desktop Accessories

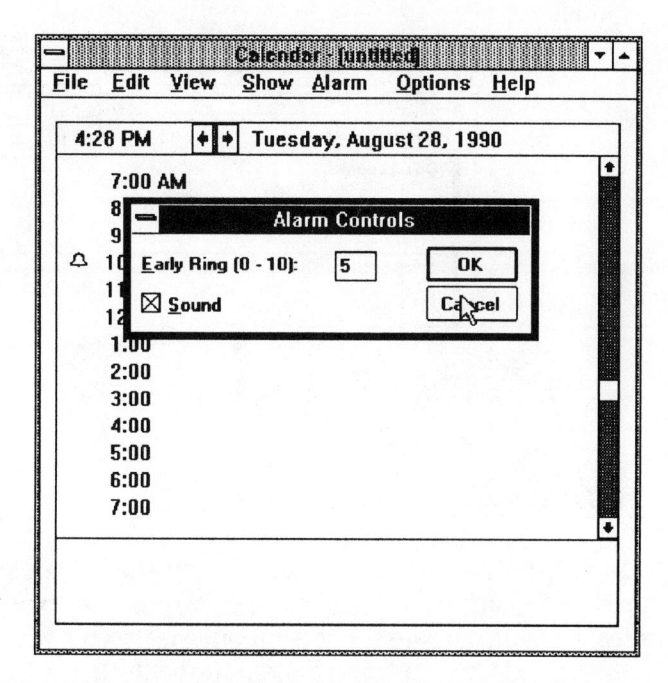

Figure 10.16. Alarm Controls Dialog Box

Early Ring and Sound. To make an alarm go off earlier than its actual set times, enter a value from 1 to 10 in the Early Ring text box. If you disable the Sound checkbox, your alarms will not make a sound when they go off.

Creating and Saving Calendars

You can create and save different calendars for different activities. Thus, you can have one calendar for business appointments and another for personal activities.

When you first use the Calendar, the window displays with the filename (untitled). After you set appointment dates, save your calendar by selecting the Save As... command from the File menu. This command displays the dialog box shown in Figure 10.17. (Notice that this dialog box is similar to the File Save dialog boxes provided with other applications.) To save your calendar, type a filename into the Filename text box. Calendar uses the extension .CAL to store calendar files, so provide this extension with your filename.

After you save a calendar file, you can open it later by selecting the Open... command from the File menu. When the standard File Open dialog box displays, select a .CAL file.

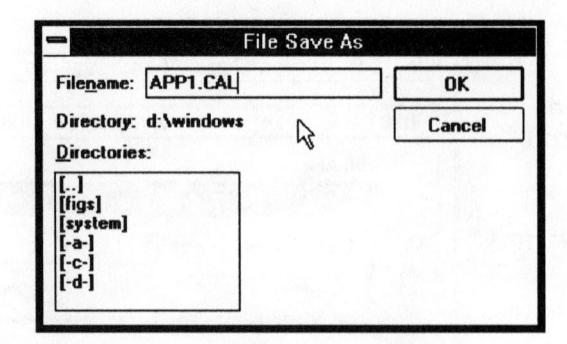

Figure 10.17. File Save As Dialog Box

Printing a Calendar

You can print your appointments using the Print... command from the File menu. This command displays the Print dialog box shown in Figure 10.18. Enter the starting date for the appointments you want to print into the From text box, and enter the end date into the To box. For example, to print your appointments from December 12, 1990 to January 15, 1991, type 12/12/90 into the From box and 1/15/91 into the To box. Click OK to start the printer. (The printer that is currently active is used by the Print... command.)

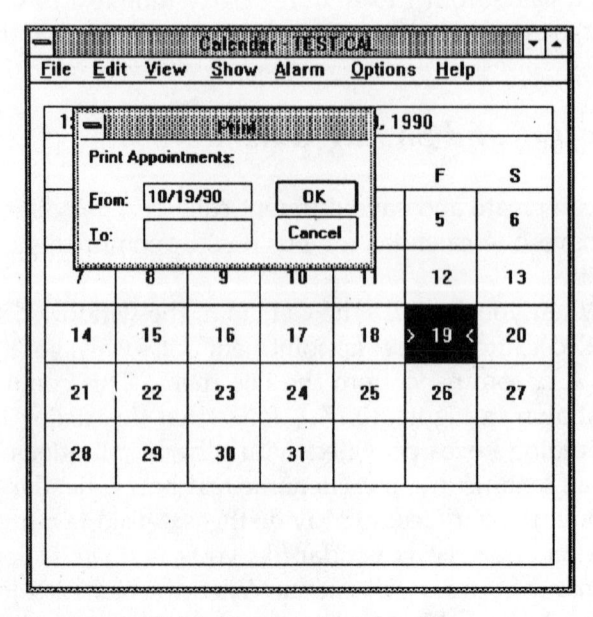

Figure 10.18. The Print Dialog Box

Working with Calculator

You can perform both simple and complex calculations by using Windows' powerful Calculator accessory.

Starting the Calculator

To open the Calculator, double-click on the Calculator icon in the Accessories group window. The Calculator window (Figure 10.19) appears with three menu items (Edit, View, and Help), a basic single-line calculator display, and a set of calculator buttons. If you know how to use a hand-held calculator, you'll find this accessory very easy to operate.

The Calculator provides two operating modes: Standard and Scientific. For basic operations such as balancing a checkbook or calculating quarterly taxes, the Standard mode provides all of the features you'll need. If you need to perform more complex operations, such as logarithmic of trigonometric functions, use the Scientific mode. The calculator window shown in Figure 10.20 provides an extensive set of operator buttons and controls so that you can display and process numbers in different base systems. We'll explore this calculator in a little more detail later.

Setting up and Using Your Keyboard

If your keyboard has a typical numeric keypad, you'll find that the basic calculator functions are easy to access. To use the numeric keypad, set your

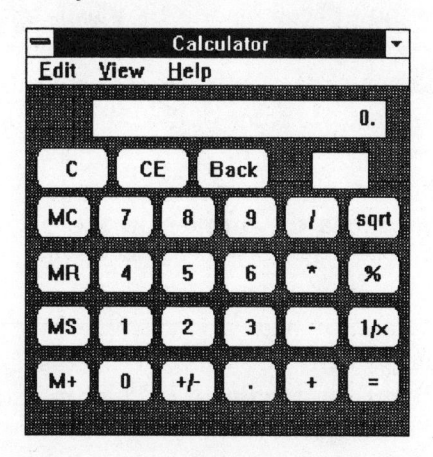

Figure 10.19. Calculator Window

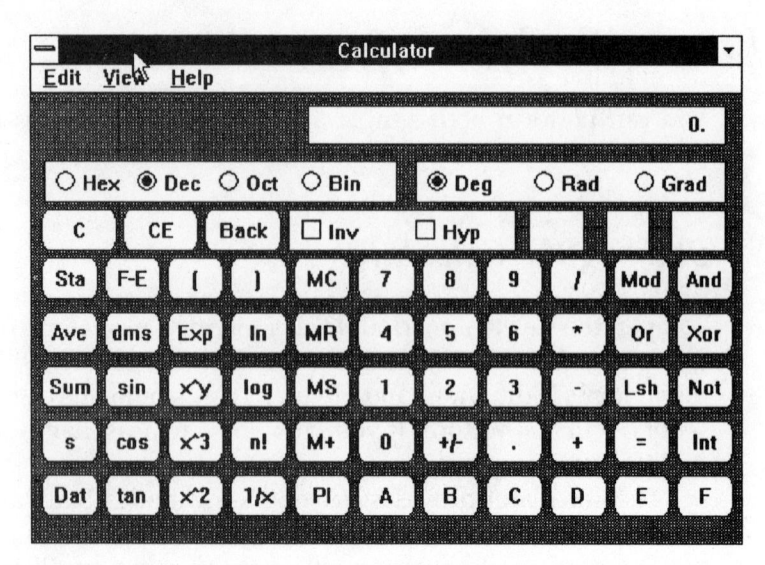

Figure 10.20. The Scientific Calculator

keyboard into Numeric Lock mode. If you don't have an LED that lights up to tell you your keyboard mode, activate the Calculator application and press one of the number keys on the numeric keypad (not the numbers along the top row of the regular keyboard area; those always work). If the number you pressed appears in the box at the top right of the calculator, your keyboard is in Numeric Lock mode. If nothing happens, press the Num Lock key (usually at the top-left corner of the keypad area) and repeat the process.

Use the keypad area to enter numbers and perform the four standard functions of addition, subtraction, multiplication, and division (the asterisk represents multiplication, and the slash represents division). The Enter key at the lower-right corner of the keypad activates the equal-sign button on the screen (which tells the Calculator to compute the answer).

You can activate some of the other calculator functions from the keyboard. For example, pressing C is the same as activating the MC button on the screen—it clears the internal memory location. The M keyboard key, like the MS button, sends the number in the display box on the Calculator to the internal memory location. Pressing the P key activates the M+ button, which adds the number in the display box to the current value in the internal memory location. The R key activates the MR button, and recalls the contents of the internal memory location to the display box.

Other keys also activate calculator buttons. Pressing the % key on the keyboard (hold down the Shift key and press the key above the T key) is the same as clicking on the % key on the screen. The use of this percent function is not intuitive. If you want to calculate 30 percent of 600, you have to enter the following keystrokes:

600*30%

You can also press the @ keyboard button to calculate the square root of the number in the display box. Press the Delete button on the keyboard to clear the display box so that you can start a new calculation.

Performing a Calculation

In the Standard calculator mode, you perform calculations using the same technique that you use with a hand-held calculator: Enter a number, select an operation (such as multiplication or addition), enter another number, and select the = key. For example, to calculate how much you save on a $12,000 new car purchase if the dealer gives you a %12 discount, enter 12,000, click on *, enter 0.15, and then click on =. The result appears in the single-line display. If you make a mistake while following these steps, select the C button to clear the calculation. Table 10.1 summarizes the basic mathematical functions that can be performed using the standard mode.

Table 10.1. Basic Mathematical Operations

Keyboard	Button	Operation
+	+	Addition
-	-	Subtraction
*	*	Multiplication
/	/	Division
%	%	Calculate percent
@	sqrt	Square Root
R	1/x	Calculate reciprocal
F9	+/-	Change the sign of a value
=	=	Perform a calculation
Delete	CE	Clear the currently displayed number
Esc	C	Clear the current calculation

1. Multiply the numbers 275 and 2097.
2. Calculate the square root of 900.

---

1. *(a) Type in the number 275.*
   (b) Select the * button.
   (c) Type in the number 2097.
   (d) Select the = button. The result is 57675.
2. *Type in 900 and select the sqrt button. The result is 30.*

Working with Memory

Take a close look at the Standard mode Calculator and notice the set of buttons in the first column labeled MC, MR, MS, and M+. These buttons access the memory features of the Calculator. When you put a number into memory, an M appears in the box directly below the display. To store a value, enter the number and select the MS button. If you already stored a number in memory and you want to add the number in the display to the stored value, select the M+ button. You can use this technique to easily keep a running total. Once a number has been stored, you can recall it at any time by selecting the MR button. If you want to clear the memory, select the MC button. When the memory is empty, the M no longer appears in the memory-status box. If you want to replace a number in memory with another number, simply enter the new number and select MS.

Using Calculated Results

You can Cut and Paste numbers between the Calculator and the Clipboard application. (Both operations are controlled through the Edit pulldown menu.) This allows you to move numbers between Windows applications without writing them on paper and reentering them in the target application. Using Windows, you transfer the results of calculations in the same way that you transfer text between applications.

To use this feature, calculate the value you want to use, and select the Copy command from the Edit menu (or press Ctrl+Ins). The value stored in the Clipboard can be pasted into another application at any time.

The Scientific Mode

The Standard mode is sufficient for most of the basic calculations that you'll need to perform. If you need to perform more complex operations, such as trigonometric functions, statistics, or logarithms, access the Scientific mode by selecting the View Scientific option from the View menu. Figure 10.21 shows the Calculator in the scientific mode. Notice that this Calculator provides all of the components of the Standard mode Calculator, such as the single-line display, memory buttons, numeric buttons, and standard operator buttons. In addition, you'll find an extended set of operator buttons for performing scientific calculations.

If you're accustomed to working with a scientific calculator capable of operating in various base-number systems, and you can perform statistical, trigonometric and logical operations, you'll find this calculator easy to use. To help you get acquainted with the Scientific mode, we'll discuss a few of its basic features.

Using Number Systems

The Standard mode Calculator only supports the decimal number system. The Scientific mode Calculator, on the other hand, converts numbers from one

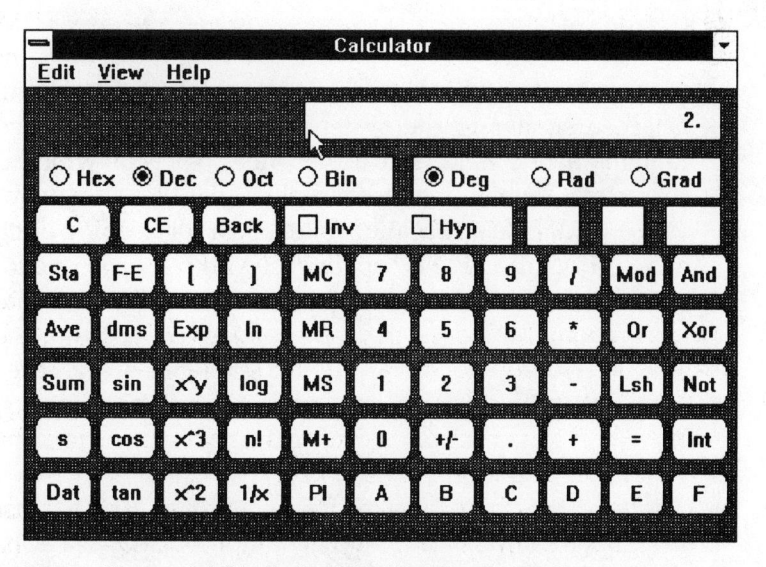

Figure 10.21. Scientific Mode of the Calculator

system to another, such as binary to hexadecimal. The four number systems supported are presented in Table 10.2, along with a column called Keyboard Select to show which quick key selects each of the number systems.

Once you've selected a number system, you can enter numbers and perform calculations using the operator buttons. Keep in mind that the numbers entered must be appropriate for the selected number system. For example, the calculator won't allow you to type the number 234 into the binary system because only 1s and 0s are valid.

To convert a number from one system to another, follow these steps: Type in the value to convert, and select the button for the new number system.

Performing Statistics

The Scientific mode also provides features that let you perform statistics with the Calculator. To use this feature, select the Sta button to display the Statistics Box window (Figure 10.22). At the bottom of the window, four buttons display for performing statistics operations. The RET button switches you back to the Calculator. LOAD instructs the calculator to display the selected number in the Statistics Box window. CD deletes the selected number in the window, and CAD deletes all numbers in the Statistics Box.

Using Cardfile

As you may recall, the Cardfile application allows you to build a limited database similar to the system you might keep on index cards. Each card contains a title field and eleven lines, each of which can contain up to 40 characters. You can search for a particular title line, word, or phrase anywhere on the card. This application is excellent for keeping electronic mail/telephone books. (Each card file is separate, so you can keep one for friends and another

Table 10.2. The Scientific Calculator's Number Systems

Number System	Sample	Keyboard Select	Button
Binary	101100	F8	Bin
Octal	245623	F7	Oct
Decimal	129980	F6	Dec
Hexadecimal	A56EB0	F5	Hex

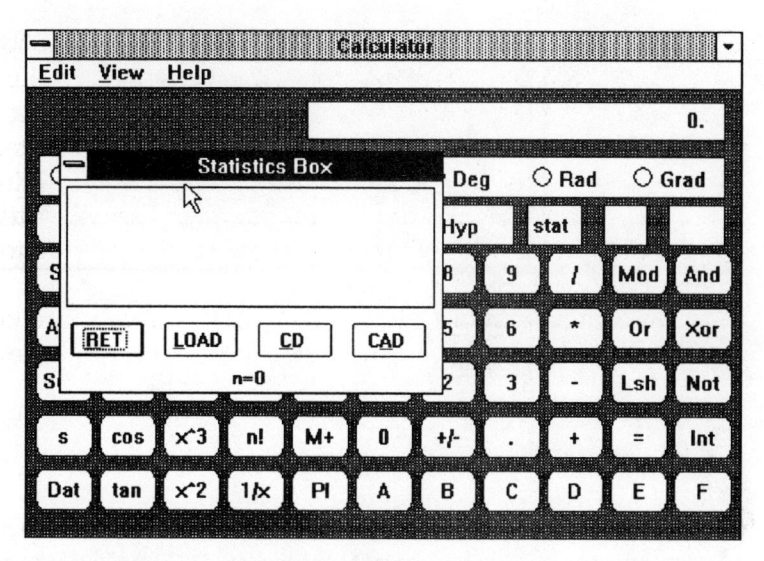

Figure 10.22. Statistics Box Window

for business contacts). Another interesting feature of Cardfile is that you can use it to keep pictures. This application is completely consistent with Windows' attempt to match as closely as possible what people do with the paper versions of these tools.

Starting Cardfile

To start Cardfile, double-click on the Cardfile icon stored in the Accessories window. Figure 10.23 shows the Untitled Cardfile window that appears, containing a blank card. Directly above the card appears a status line that indicates the view option selected. The default view is called *Card View*. The status line also contains a left and right scroll arrow so that you can easily select other cards. The status line also contains a card count. When you first start Cardfile, the card count is set to 1.

The index card itself contains an index line and an information area. The index line is used to store a word or phrase so that you can quickly identify a card. Enter the text or the graphics for a card into the information area.

Creating a Card System

To create a new set of cards, consider which information you plan to place on the cards and in what order. Imagine that you want to create a card file of your

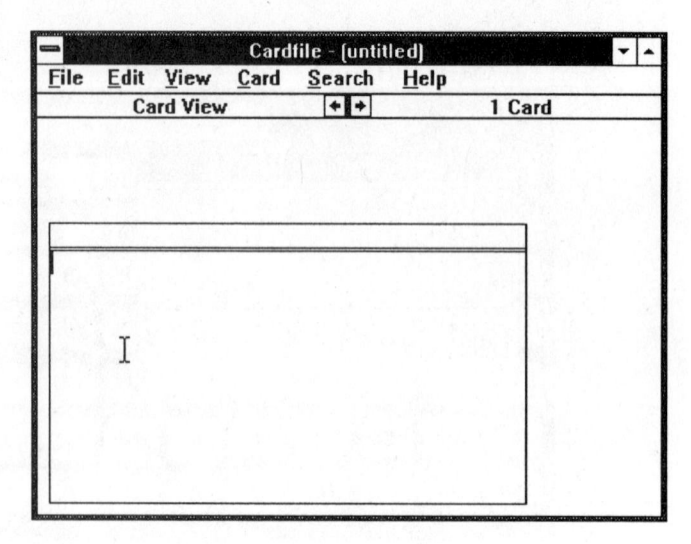

Figure 10.23. Untitled Cardfile Window

ten-year collection of computer magazines that you intend to read when you retire (thirty years from now!). Since this collection is the first of a series of cards that will cover the large stacks of magazines in your garage, place the title of the magazine on the index line, and add the date and volume number on that line also. Use the body of the card to list the feature articles and other points of interest for a particular issue.

To create this record-keeping system, you don't have to retype the name of a magazine 120 times—instead, you can create a template card that you can then duplicate many times. Double-click on the index line to bring up the Index dialog box (Figure 10.24). (If a card already has a filled index line, this dialog box allows you to alter the contents of the line.) Enter the information into this line. For the sake of our example, assume that you entered:

PC TECHNIQUES Vol. 1 No. 1

into the Index Line text box. (Keep in mind that you have to keep the index line brief because each line is only 40 characters wide.) Click on the OK button to save the information. At this point, a single card appears in your window, with the index line containing the template information.

If you want any information to appear repeatedly on your cards, add it now before you begin making duplicates. As with other Windows applications, you can edit text with the mouse or the keyboard. Click the mouse cursor where you want the information to appear (or use the keyboard arrow keys to position the cursor) and begin typing. Once you've typed your first card exactly the way you want it, activate Edit Copy (or use the shortcut key

Figure 10.24. Index Dialog Box

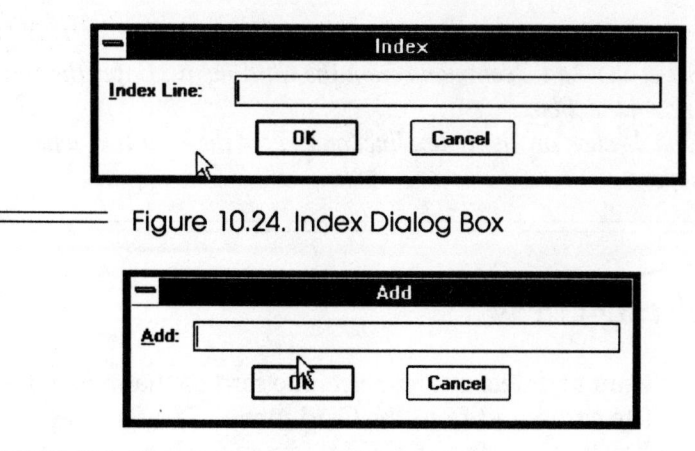

Figure 10.25. Add Dialog Box

sequence Ctrl+Ins) to duplicate the card. At this point, you can duplicate the card several times to create a set of "preprinted" blank cards to fill in later.

Tip You can also duplicate a card by bringing the card to the front of the stack and selecting the Duplicate command from the Card menu. The new card is then added to the front of the stack.

To complete a card, click on the left or right arrow button on the line below the menu bar to bring a new card to the front of the stack. Next, press the F6 function key to bring up the Index dialog box. Click on the location that you want to modify and insert the desired information. Use the Delete and Backspace keys to remove the undesired characters. Be careful to not start typing until you move the cursor over, or Windows will think that you wanted to type in a new line and will wipe out the previous contents!

Adding Additional Cards

To add a new card to a set, select the Add... command from the Card menu, or press F7. The Add dialog box (Figure 10.25) provides a text box where you can type in an index line for the new card. After you select OK, the new card moves to the front of the stack so that you can add information to it.

1. Add a card, and give it the index title New Magazines.
2. Change the index line to New Magazines—1990.

1. *Select the Add... command from the Card menu. Enter the text New Magazines in the Add text box.*
2. *Double-click on the index line, and enter the new text when the Index dialog box appears.*

Deleting Cards

If you want to delete a card, select the card so that it is in front, and then select the Delete command from the Card menu. Cardfile presents you with a query dialog box to verify that you want to remove the card.

Editing Options

The Edit menu provides all of the operations for modifying the contents of your cards. The Undo command removes the most recent editing operation. The Cut, Copy, and Paste commands work the same way as the same commands in Notepad. The Index... command (which can be activated by pressing the F6 function key) allows you to edit the contents of the card on the front of the stack.

Restoring a Card

While you're working with a card, it's easy to add or change information that you don't want to save. Cardfile provides a Restore command that restores a card to its original condition. To use this feature, select the Restore command from the Edit menu. This command only works when the card remains at the top of the stack. When you move on to another card, the changes become permanent.

Pasting a Picture

Another feature that you'll want to take advantage of is Cardfile's capability for adding graphics to a card. Normally, cards display in a text only mode and you can add only text information. When you select the Picture option in the Edit menu, you switch Cardfile to a graphics mode so that a picture can be pasted to a card.

Adding a graphics picture involves the use of another application, such as Paintbrush or Excel. Use that application first to create a picture or a chart, and then paste the image to the Clipboard. Next, start Cardfile, select the card where you want the graphic image to appear, and make sure that the Picture option is selected. To add the graphics, select the Paste command from the Edit menu. You can then drag the mouse or use the arrow keys to position the image on the card.

The pasted image always displays in black and white. If it's larger than the card, the picture is cropped. After a picture is pasted, you can add text by selecting the Text option from the Edit menu and positioning the text cursor on the card. The text that you type in appears on top of the graphics image.

Saving, Opening, and Merging a Card Set

When you've created all of the cards for a set, use the Save or Save As... commands from the File menu to store the card set on the disk. (The Save As... command must be used if you haven't yet saved a card set.) When you save a card set, it's stored as a special file with the default extension .CRD.

You can open the saved card file by using the Open... command from the File menu. This command brings up the standard File Open dialog box, so that you can easily locate the file you want to open.

One of the more unique features of Cardfile is that it allows you to merge different card files. When you select this option, the File Merge dialog box (Figure 10.26) requests the filename to be merged with the currently opened file. Provide the directory and file information (or provide the directory information, and use a file wildcard such as *.CRD) so that you can view the appropriate files in a selected subdirectory. Once you select a file, click on the OK window button to complete the operation.

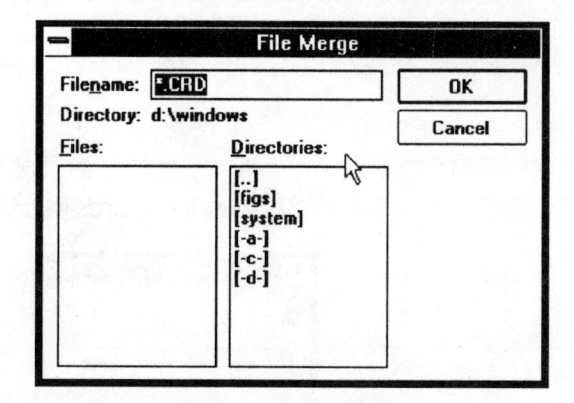

Figure 10.26. File Merge Dialog Box

Tips for Viewing Cards

Cardfile organizes your cards by alphabetical order of the index lines. To alphabetize the current set of cards (especially useful after a merge operation), select the List option in the View menu. The cards disappear and are replaced by an alphabetized list of the index lines (Figure 10.27). Use this handy option to scroll down the list to find a particular card and select the Card option from the View menu. The card highlighted in the List window appears as the top card on the screen, and all of the cards around it are no longer alphabetized.

Searching for a Card

Use the Search menu to find information quickly in your card stack. Select the Go To... command (shortcut key is F4) to bring to the top of the stack the first card with an index line matching the information you provide in the Go To dialog box (Figure 10.28). Use the Search Find option to find a match with

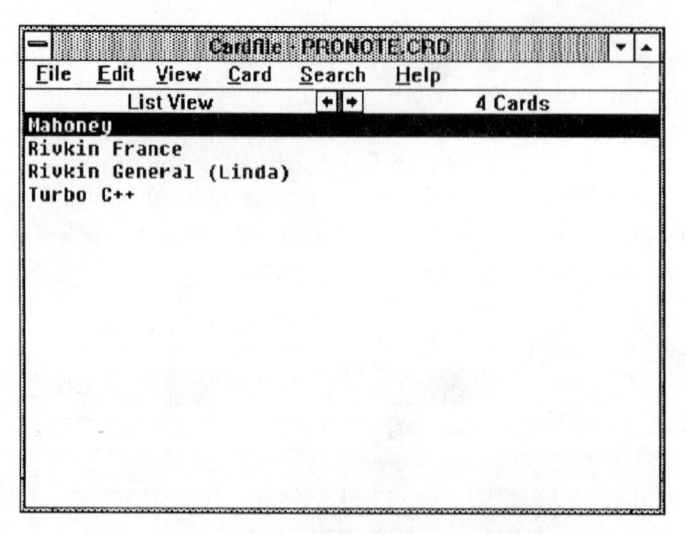

Figure 10.27. Viewing Cards in a List

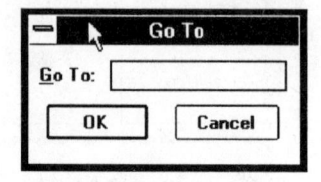

Figure 10.28. Go To Dialog Box

information in the body of the card (as opposed to just the index line). Select the Find Next option (shortcut key F3) to repeat the search specified in the Find option and quickly search through multiple matches to find the one you want.

Using a Calling Card

As an added bonus, you can use Cardfile to tell your PC to dial a phone number for you. To use this feature, follow these steps:

1. Highlight the phone number you want to call.
2. Select the Autodial... command from the Card menu.
3. Check the phone number in the Autodial dialog box (Figure 10.29) to make sure it's correct.
4. Enter a prefix (if one is required for your phone system) and select the Use Prefix check box.
5. Click the OK button to dial the number.

In order for this feature to work properly, make sure that your computer has a Hayes-compatible modem installed. To check your modem settings, select the Setup button in the Autodial dialog box. Use the dialog box shown in Figure 10.30 to configure the baud rate, the port, and your phone type (pulse or tone). If you encounter problems when calling a number, make sure these settings are correct.

Summary

In this chapter, you've been introduced to the main accessory applications of Windows. You learned how to view the system time in different formats, how to create and print notes, how to perform calculations, and how to create a cardfile system to organize important information.

In the next chapter, we'll explore the three main Windows applications: Paintbrush, Write, and Terminal.

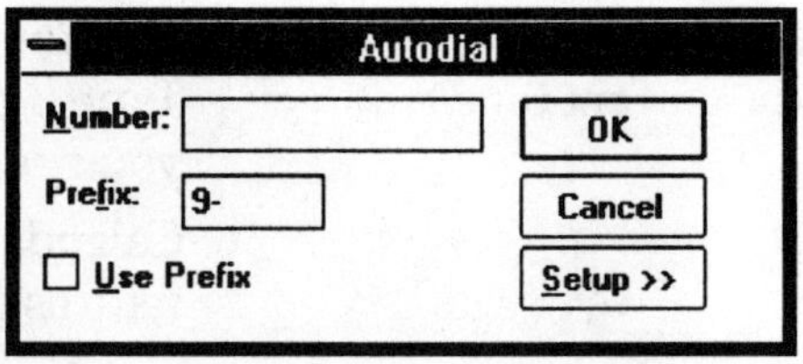

Figure 10.29. Autodial Dialog Box

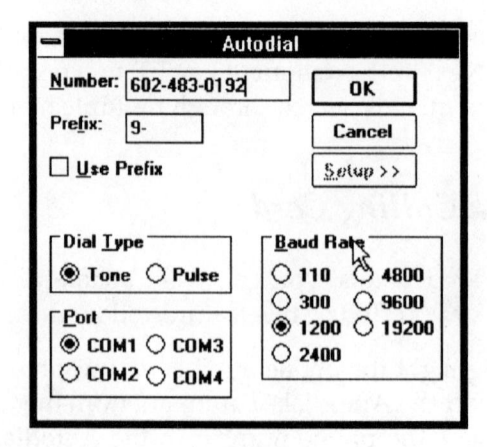

Figure 10.30. Setting Communications Parameters

Exercises

Use these exercises to master the main accessory applications.

What You Should Do	How the Computer Responds
1. Start Clock, display it in the analog format, and reduce it to an icon.	1. The clock displays in the lower-left corner, keeping the correct time.
2. Start Notepad, and open a file by selecting a .TXT file with the File Open dialog box.	2. The file opens and the window's title changes to reflect the name of the file.
3. Search for text in the file, using the Find dialog box.	3. If the text you search for is found, it's highlighted; otherwise, a dialog box warns you that the text can't be found.
4. Quit Notepad.	4. Control returns to the Program Manager.
5. Open the Calendar, and set an alarm to go off in 5 minutes. (Look at the clock icon to determine the current time.)	5. The alarm icon displays next to the time set. You may have to use the Special Time... command to add the time slot you need.
6. Minimize Calendar.	6. Calendar turns into an icon, and control returns to the Program Manager.

7. Start Cardfile and create a few index cards.

7. If you use the application for five minutes, the alarm that you set goes off.

What If It Doesn't Work?

1. If your computer's system clock is set to the wrong time, Clock won't display the correct time.
2. If you don't have a .TXT file, the File Open dialog box won't list any

11

Working with Desktop Applications

This chapter is dedicated to the three major Windows applications: Paintbrush, Write, and Terminal. Paintbrush is a graphics program that allows you to create and manipulate all sorts of pictures and graphical information. If you have a printer that supports graphics (such as a dot-matrix, ink-jet, or laser printer), you can easily print the pictures you create. Write is a powerful word-processing program that you can use to create documents that contain both text and graphics. The Terminal application allows you to use a modem to communicate with other computers and on-line communication systems.

We'll begin with Paintbrush and then explore Write and Terminal. Along the way, we'll show you how to import Paintbrush drawings in Write to create a newsletter. After you finish this chapter, you'll know:

- How to use the basic drawing tools provided with Paintbrush
- How to create and save pictures
- How to use Write
- How to combine text and graphics using Write
- How to configure Terminal to connect with other computers
- How to transfer and receive files using Terminal

Notes about Using Paintbrush

Because Windows supports many displays and graphics cards, it's impossible to cover all of Paintbrush's modes of operation. In this book, we assume that you're running Paintbrush with a color VGA display. If you use different display hardware, some of the options we cover aren't available to you. For example, if you use a system that only displays specific colors, the discussion about adjusting the Paintbrush colors won't apply. We'll try to keep our coverage of Paintbrush as general as possible.

Starting Paintbrush

To start Paintbrush, open the Accessories group window and double-click on the Paintbrush icon. Figure 11.1 shows the untitled window you'll see when the application starts. In addition to the usual Windows items, Paintbrush provides three additional sets of tools along the left and the bottom of the viewing area. To the left are the various drawing and painting tools available for creating and modifying pictures. At the bottom of the viewing area appears a group of colored squares, located at the right of a black square surrounded

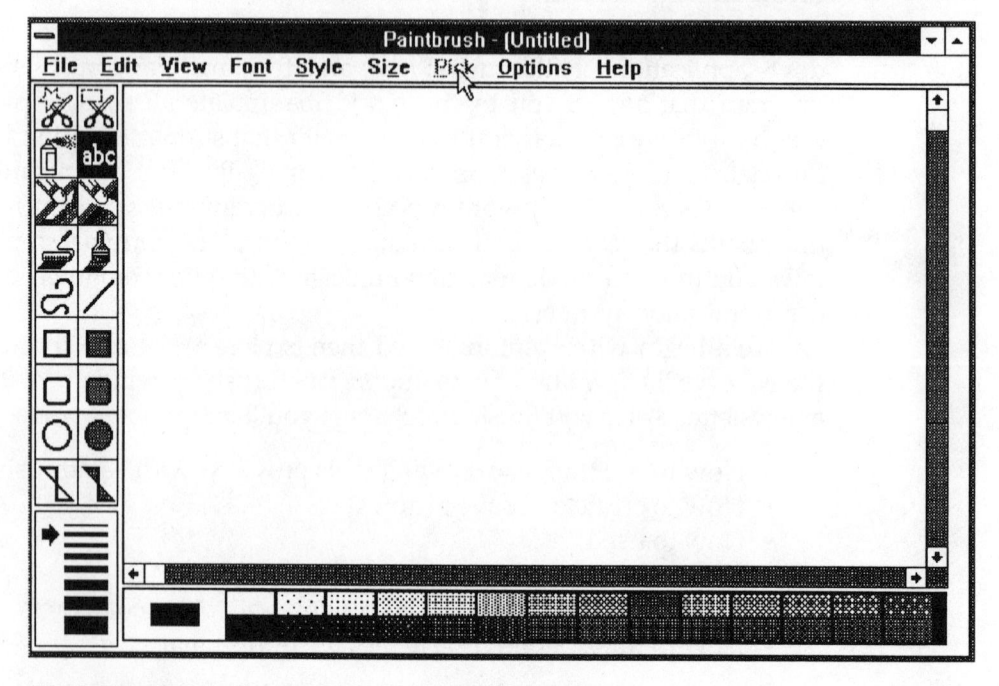

Figure 11.1. The Paintbrush Window

by a white square. This region defines the color palette. In the lower-left corner is a group of horizontal lines of varying widths, which define the line widths available for drawing lines, boxes, and curves.

Basic Techniques

Paintbrush is an intuitive tool. Once you understand some simple operating principles, you'll quickly create pictures and diagrams. At the same time, Paintbrush is the most complex Windows application because it offers numerous tools that you must master before you can use the application's basic capabilities.

We'll discuss the basics first so that you can begin to familiarize yourself with the drawing tools, and then move on to more advanced topics.

Although all of the Windows applications are designed to be used with both the mouse and the keyboard, you'll find that you need a mouse in order to fully use the drawing tools.

Defining a Drawing Region

Before you begin creating pictures with paintbrush, first define a drawing region by selecting the Image Attributes... command from the Options menu. Figure 11.2 shows the dialog box that is displayed. You can specify an image area in units of inches, centimeters, or pixels. The default setting is 6.67" for the width, and 5.00" for the height. You can also select whether you want your image displayed in Black and White or Colors. Select the options you desire and click the OK button. Next select the New command from the File menu to start a new work area.

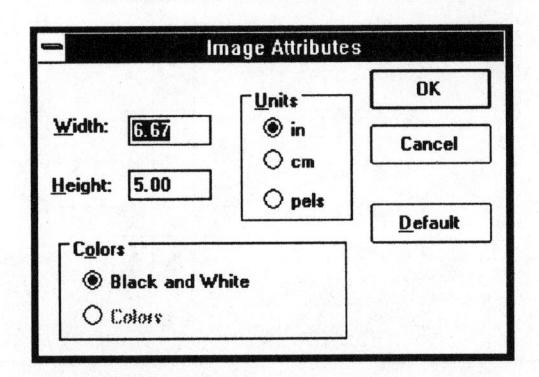

Figure 11.2. Image Attributes Dialog Box

✔ Start Paintbrush by double-clicking on the Paintbrush icon.
1. Define a new image area without selecting the New command. What happens?
2. Define an image area that is too large. What happens?
3. Move the mouse cursor inside the drawing area. How does the cursor change?

1. *The image area doesn't change.*
2. *A warning dialog box tells you that you won't have enough disk space to save your image.*
3. *The cursor is represented as a small dot.*

Introducing the Paintbrush Tools

Figure 11.3 illustrates the Paintbrush toolbox area and identifies the various tools available. The items along the top row, called Scissors and Pick, extract parts of a picture by removing the picture or making copies of it. These options

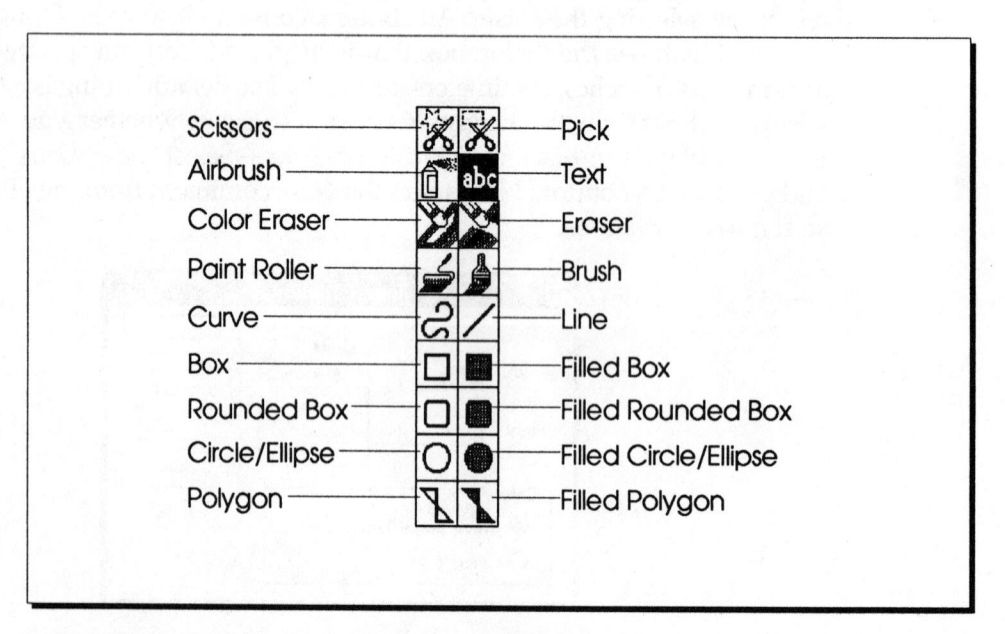

Figure 11.3. Paintbrush Toolbox Area

Working with Desktop Applications

are the equivalent of highlighting text with the mouse, and then using the Cut and Paste commands to remove and insert text. The spray-can icon represents the Airbrush tool, which allows you to "fade" one color over another, just as you would with a real airbrush.

Use the Text tool to enter text on your drawing with various sizes of letters and different fonts. The Color Eraser and simple Eraser erase portions of an existing drawing. The Paint Roller tool fills an area with a particular color or pattern; the Brush paints the current foreground color on the visible window. The Curve and Line tools create controlled curves and straight lines (respectively) on the screen between two defined points. (The Curve tool is especially handy if you're not skilled at drawing smooth freehand curves using a mouse.) Finally, the Box, Rounded Box, Circle/Ellipse, and Polygon tools create closed objects. As indicated, these region-drawing tools come in two flavors: filled and unfilled..

Selecting Drawing Tools and Colors

To select each drawing tool, click on the appropriate icon. To select the line width, move the mouse cursor to the line representing the desired width and click on it; the arrow on the left side moves to that line to confirm your selection.

To select the foreground color, move the mouse cursor to the desired color and click on it. The small black box near the line-width area changes to the selected color. The background color (represented by the larger box that surrounds the foreground color box) can be selected by moving the mouse cursor to the desired color and clicking on it with the *right* mouse button. The background color box changes from white to the new selection. For now, leave the background white.

You can completely erase the drawing area by activating the New command from the File menu (Ctrl+N). This feature is handy when you experiment with the various tools.

---

1. Select the smallest drawing line.
2. Select the Line tool, and move the cursor inside the drawing area.
3. Press the Shift key and drag the mouse in a downward motion. What does the Shift key do?
4. Release the Shift key and drag the mouse.
5. Draw a box.

1. *Click on the top line in the Line Styles box. An arrow appears to the left of the line to indicate that it's selected.*
2. *Click on the diagonal line icon. The cursor changes to a crosshair.*
3. *A vertical line is drawn. The Shift key forces the tool to draw a line horizontally, vertically, or diagonally.*
4. *You can now draw any type of line.*
5. *Click on the box icon and drag the mouse to draw the box. If you hold down the Shift key, the box is drawn as a square.*

The Closed Shapes and Standard Tricks

Let's start by drawing concentric circles to form a target. Go down to the color palette and click on the red color to select it as the foreground color. Move the cursor to the left of the viewing area and select the Filled Circle tool (the one that is shaded-in). Now move the cursor toward the top-left part of the screen, and press the left button while dragging the mouse toward the lower-right corner of the screen. The shape on the screen appears to change between a circle and an ellipse (Figure 11.4).

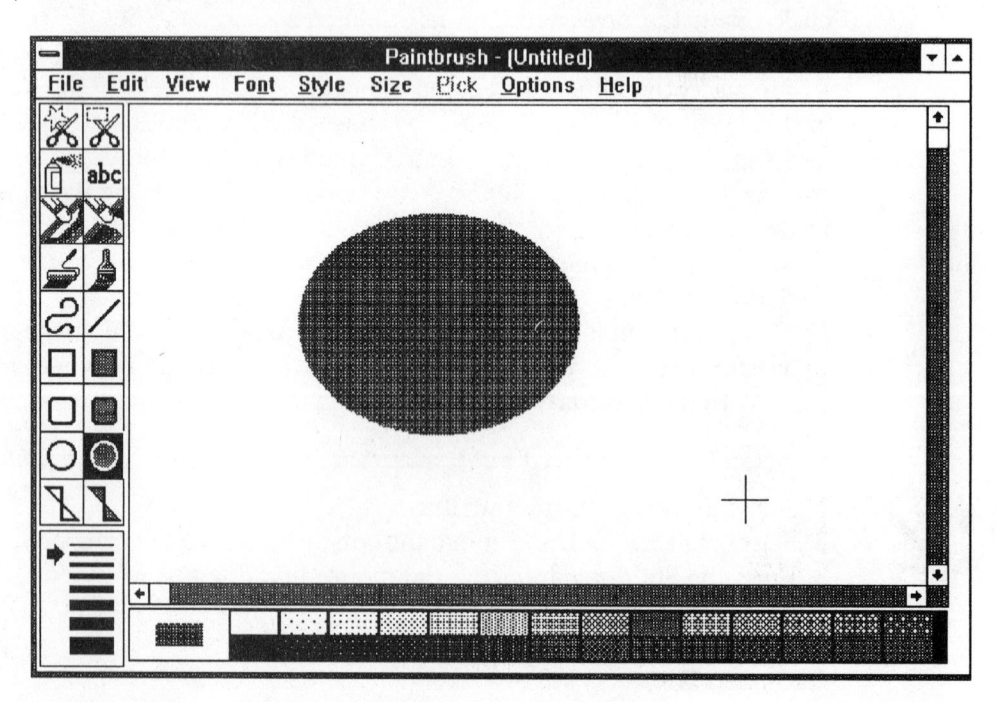

Figure 11.4. Drawing an Ellipse

Working with Desktop Applications

While you hold down the mouse button, you can move the cursor around the screen and make the shape dance around. Before you release the left mouse button, press the Shift key. The tool now draws only circles. (If you release the Shift key, the tool alternates again between circles and ellipses.) When you have a circle of the desired size, release the left mouse button to finish the operation. (If you're using the Shift key, release the mouse button before releasing the Shift key.) The circle outline is filled-in with red.

Next, go to the color palette and click on the black color sample to select black as the foreground color. (White is still the background color.) The Filled Circle option is still active, so move the crosshairs to a point in the upper-left side of the red circle, and click and drag again toward the lower-right side. Hold down the Shift key again to create a smaller circle inside the larger red one. (Don't worry that the circles aren't concentric; this isn't important in this example.)

When you've drawn a circle inside the red one, release the mouse button to freeze the shape and fill it in with black (Figure 11.5). Look carefully—around the black circle is a thin band of white! This occurred because Paintbrush always draws an edge around the filled objects, using the background color. The width of the edge is defined by the line width selected at the lower-left corner of the screen. If you don't want this edge to be drawn, make the back-

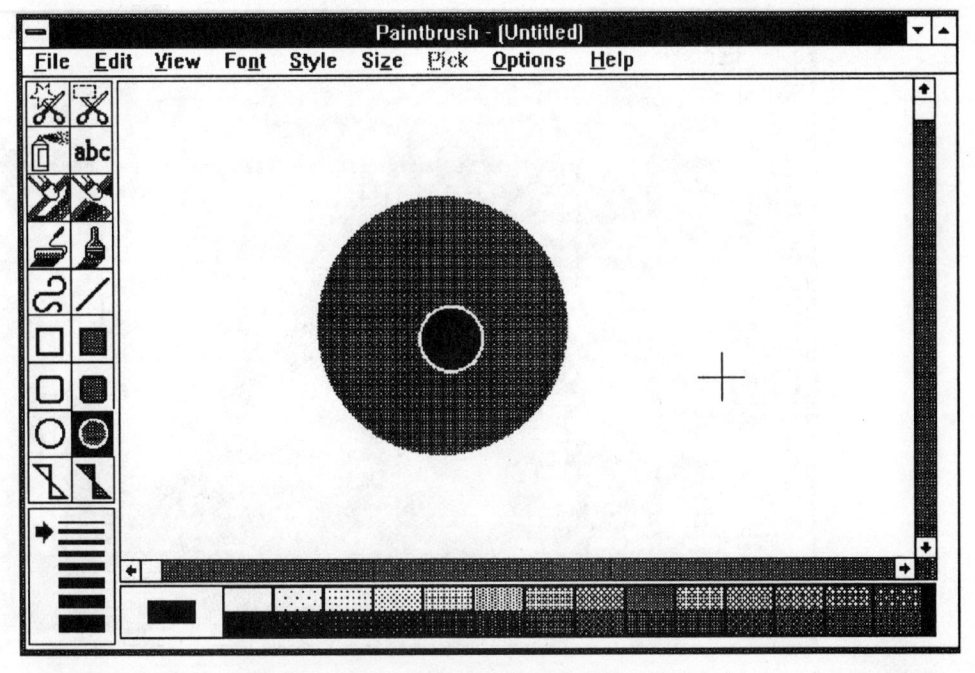

Figure 11.5. Drawing Two Circles

ground color the same as the foreground color before you draw the object. To do so, move the mouse cursor to the proper sample box in the palette and click with the *right* mouse button. The foreground/background color box next to the line-width selector turns to one color, with only a thin rectangle in a different color to indicate the boundary between the foreground and background area. Experiment with this by making the foreground and background colors red, and then drawing a small circle inside the black one.

Using The Roller Tool

You should now have a large red circle, containing a smaller black circle bordered by a white edge. (It doesn't matter whether you drew the third circle or not.) Select red for the foreground color and select white for the background again. Move the mouse up to the menu bar and select View Zoom-In (or use the Ctrl+Z shortcut). The Mouse cursor turns into a transparent rectangle when you move it inside the viewing area. Move this rectangle to the top of the black circle so that the white edge divides the rectangle into approximately equal-sized pieces. When the rectangle reaches the right location, click the left mouse button to expand the region (Figure 11.6).

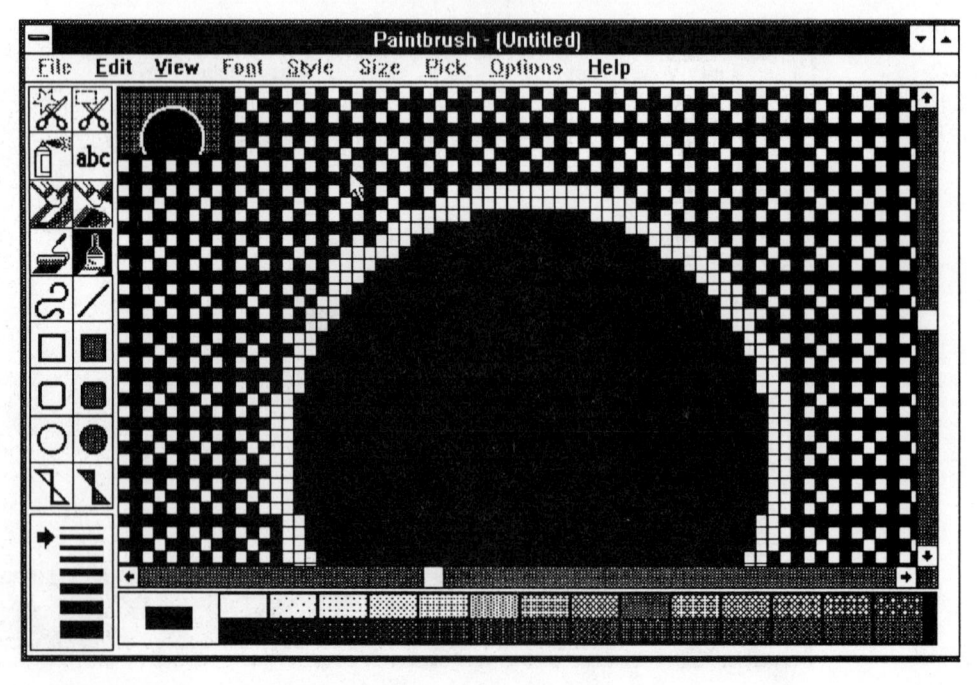

Figure 11.6. Zooming an Image

Working with Desktop Applications

When the circles disappear, a magnified version of the contents of the rectangle fills the viewing area. (You have now zoomed-in on the region represented by the rectangle.) To see how the normal-sized picture looks, look at the rectangle in the upper-left corner of the viewing area. A large white arc crosses the viewing area; the area above is red and the area below is black.

Move the mouse cursor to the Paint Roller icon and click on it once. When you move the mouse into the viewing area, the mouse cursor changes into the Paint Roller icon. This icon has a point that comes down toward the lower-left side of the icon. Position the icon so that the point is inside one of the white squares that make up the arc in the main viewing area. When you click the left mouse button to perform a fill operation, all of the white squares in the main area (and in the miniature version in the top-left corner) change to red (Figure 11.7). Now activate the View Zoom-Out (or use the Ctrl+O shortcut) to return to the normal screen (Figure 11.8). Notice that the only part of the white edge that is altered is the area that was visible in the zoom window. To change the rest of the white arc to red, position the point of the Roller tool inside the white arc. Click the left mouse button to activate the fill operation again.

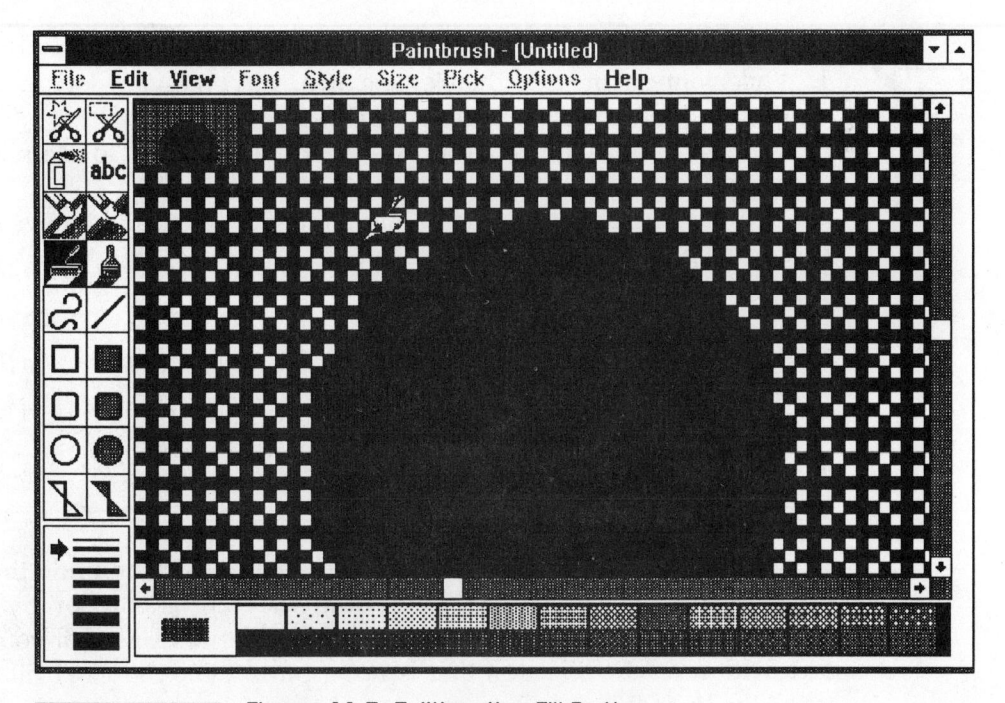

Figure 11.7. Editing the Fill Pattern

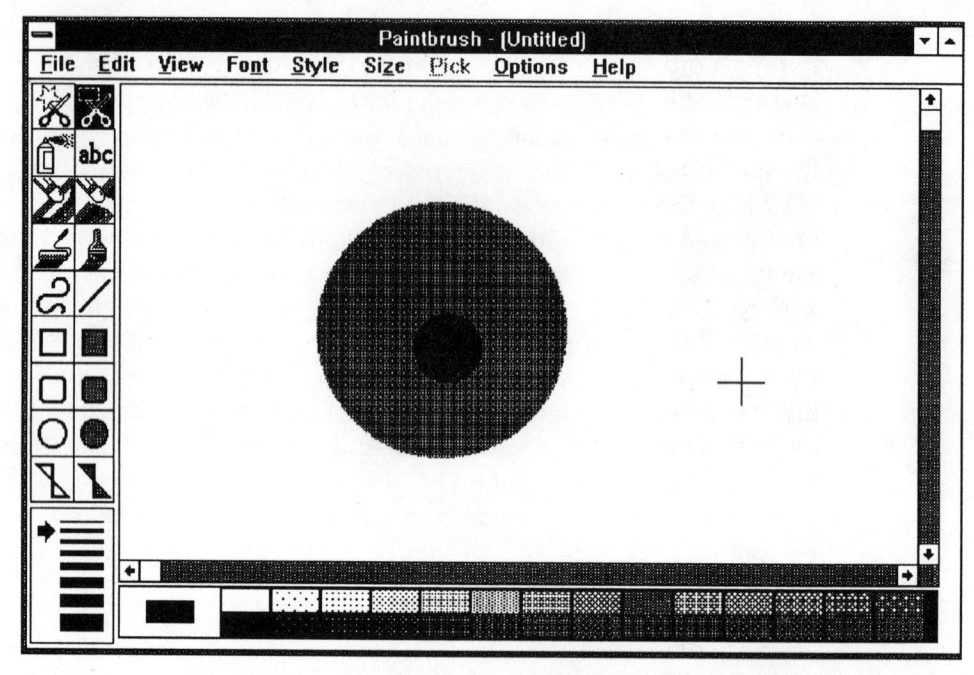

Figure 11.8. The Corrected Image

1. While your picture is in the viewing area, select the View Picture command from the View menu. What happens?
2. How many times can you select the Zoom In command to zoom in on your picture?
3. Select the Cursor Position option from the View menu, and move the cursor inside the drawing area. What happens?

1. *The picture expands to fit the entire screen. Click the mouse to return to the drawing window.*
2. *Only one time.*
3. *A window displays to show you the cursor position in units of pixels.*

If you filled in the wrong area in your picture, you can undo the damage by selecting the Undo command from the Edit menu, or by pressing Alt+Backspace. A couple of warnings are in order here. First, if you fill in an area with a palette selection that is not a pure color, you can't fill it in later using the Paint Roller, and you may need to use one of the other tools to fill in the area with a different color. The only way to be really certain if a color is pure or a mix is to create a splotch of it elsewhere on the screen, and then zoom in on it. If all of the squares in the zoom window are the same color, the color is pure. If not, Windows has mixed two or more colors to produce what you thought was a solid color.

The second warning is that the Roller can "flow" out of the area you intended to fill. If this occurs, simply select the Undo command to restore the screen to the way it was before the Roller operations were started. When you activate the Roller tool, Paintbrush begins with the selected square and changes it to the new color. It then tests each adjacent square to see if it is the same color as the original square. If a match occurs, that square is also changed to the new selection. This process repeats until either an edge of the window is reached, or all of the squares of the original color connected by similarly colored squares to the first square are changed.

Drawing Tips

If you're drawing a closed object (circle, square, polygon) and you decide to cancel it, click on the right mouse button before releasing the left mouse button. The elastic object disappears and the crosshair cursor returns.

The trick for creating a circle rather than an ellipse (pressing the Shift key) also applies for the Square/Rectangle tools. By pressing the Shift key, you force squares, rather than rectangles, to be drawn.

Using the Polygon Tools

The Polygon tools are different from the other tools because you must first define the shape of the object. Assuming that you have the usual white background in the viewing area, select red as the foreground color and dark blue as the background color. Click on the filled-in Polygon tool and move the mouse toward the viewing area; the familiar crosshair icon appears. Click on some point in the upper-left part of the screen, and drag the cursor toward the lower-right corner of the screen. (Don't release the left button until the second endpoint reaches the correct position.) Paintbrush draws a line from the first point on the screen to the current cursor position.

Next, move the cursor to the upper-right part of the screen, and click the left button once to draw a line to that location from the endpoint of the first line. Now move the cursor to the lower-left corner of the screen, and click again to define a line that crosses the first one. Double-click the left mouse button to close the object. You now see an object that vaguely resembles a red bow tie, as shown in Figure 11.9. This object has a red border whose width is defined by the line-width selector in the lower-left corner of the screen. You'll have an opportunity to experiment more with this object in the next section.

Tip | While drawing a polygon, you can double-click at any time to close the object. If you hold down the shift key while drawing the polygon, only straight or diagonal lines (45 degrees) are drawn.

The Eraser Tools

Paintbrush provides two separate erasers: the normal type and the Color Eraser. When you activate either eraser and move the mouse cursor to the viewing area, the cursor turns into a square. You can control the size of the square through the line-width selector at the lower-left part of the window. (Figure 11.10 shows the largest eraser available, erasing a picture.) Both erasers operate on the principle of replacement of a color with the currently selected background color. Drag the properly sized eraser over the area to be changed. By releasing the button, you can reposition the eraser for another pass. The two

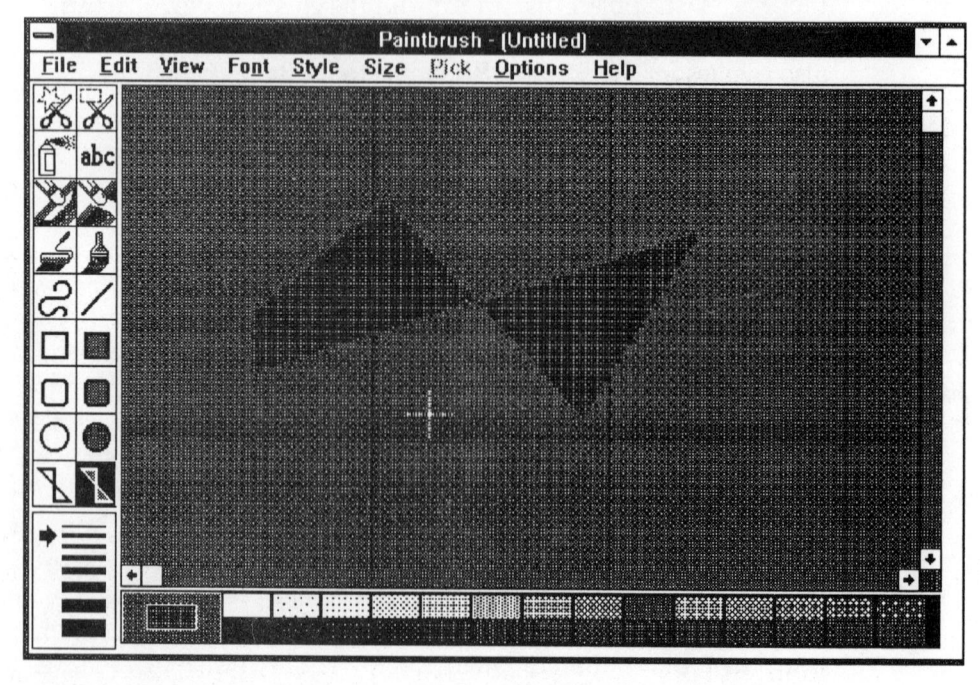

Figure 11.9. Drawing a Polygon

Working with Desktop Applications

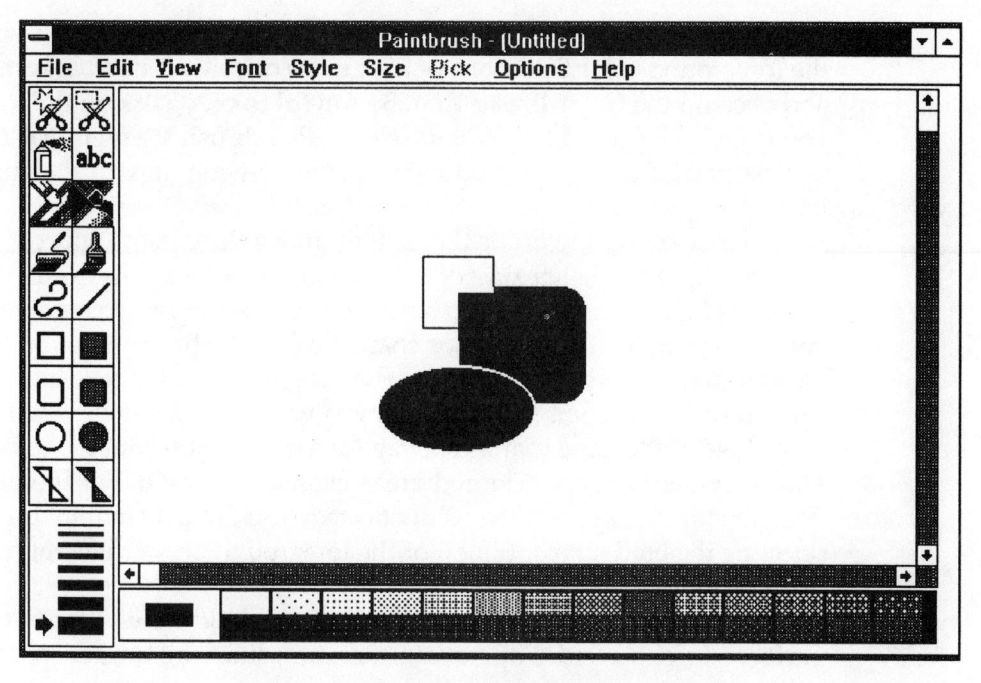

Figure 11.10. The Largest Eraser Available

tools differ only in their color replacement technique.

The normal eraser changes all of the areas it sweeps to the selected background color. It doesn't convert the swept area back to the background color of the viewing area; instead, it converts the area to the color currently shown as the selected background color. Thus, if you still have a blue background selected from the previous drawing example, you can draw a blue stripe on a free area of the screen by selecting the normal Eraser tool, moving the cursor to a blank area in the viewing area, and dragging the icon. To perform a normal eraser function, select white as the background color. When you drag the eraser across an area, the selected area appears white.

Using the Color Eraser

The Color Eraser selectively changes one color to another by replacing the current foreground color with the current background color. The best way to illustrate this is to modify the polygon created in the previous section. (If you altered the object, you may wish to erase the entire screen by selecting New from the File menu. Select the No button if the dialog box asks you if it should save the previous drawing.)

Once you see the red object with the blue border on the screen, select red as the foreground color. Select one of the greens or yellows as a background color, and click on the Color Eraser icon. Be careful to only click on the icon once: If you double-click on the icon, you select a Paintbrush shortcut that changes all occurrences of the foreground color in the viewing area to the currently selected background color!

After selecting the Color Eraser tool, move the cursor (which should be a square shape) to the left side of the viewing area. Drag the erase cursor from left to right across the viewing area and across the red shape. Only the red areas swept by the eraser cursor change color; the blue border and the white background are unaffected. Leave the foreground color red, but change the background to brown. Move the cursor (within the viewing area) to a point above one of the large triangles. Drag the erase cursor from top to bottom and observe what happens: The red areas change to brown, but the green stripe from the previous pass remains unaffected. You can also modify the border by selecting the border color (blue) for the foreground and a different color for the background.

One last trick about the eraser tools: If you hold down the Shift key while performing either erase operation, the erase lines are created parallel to the sides of the viewing window.

---

1. Draw some objects on the screen, and double-click on the eraser icon. What happens?
2. Draw two objects on the screen, and fill one in purple and one in red. Set the background color to blue. Select blue as the foreground color and purple as the background color. Double-click on the Color Eraser tool. What happens?

---

1. *A dialog box asks you if you want to save the current image. If you select the No button, your drawing image is cleared.*
2. *All of the blue areas in the drawing change to purple.*

Drawing Lines and Curves

Paintbrush provides four separate tools for drawing types of lines. All of these tools draw images in the viewing area using the currently selected foreground color and line width. The first one is simply called Line. It works like the Polygon drawing tool, but it doesn't require that the object be closed. To use

Line, move the crosshair cursor to the point where the line is to begin, and drag the cursor in the direction that you want the line to take. A flexible line appears and connects the starting point to the current cursor point.

If your computer has a reasonably fast processor and a high-resolution display, you can move the cursor in a circular pattern around the first point so that the flexible line follows the movement without much lag. As with the other tools, you can make perfectly vertical or horizontal lines by holding down the Shift key while performing the drag operation. When you're satisfied with the length and inclination of the line, release the left mouse button to anchor the end point.

The Curve tool operates in a similar manner as the Line tool and allows you to curve a line. Anchor both endpoints as you would for the Line tool, move the cursor to some point on or near the line (but away from the endpoints), and click and drag the cursor. The flexible line curves in the direction you're dragging the cursor. Once you've moved the curve to the right location, release the left mouse button. If you want a simple curve, move the cursor to the second endpoint and click on it. Figure 11.11 shows some of the types of curves you can create.

To make an "S" curve, move the cursor to the other end of the line, and then click and drag to deform it in the other direction. If you wish to cancel

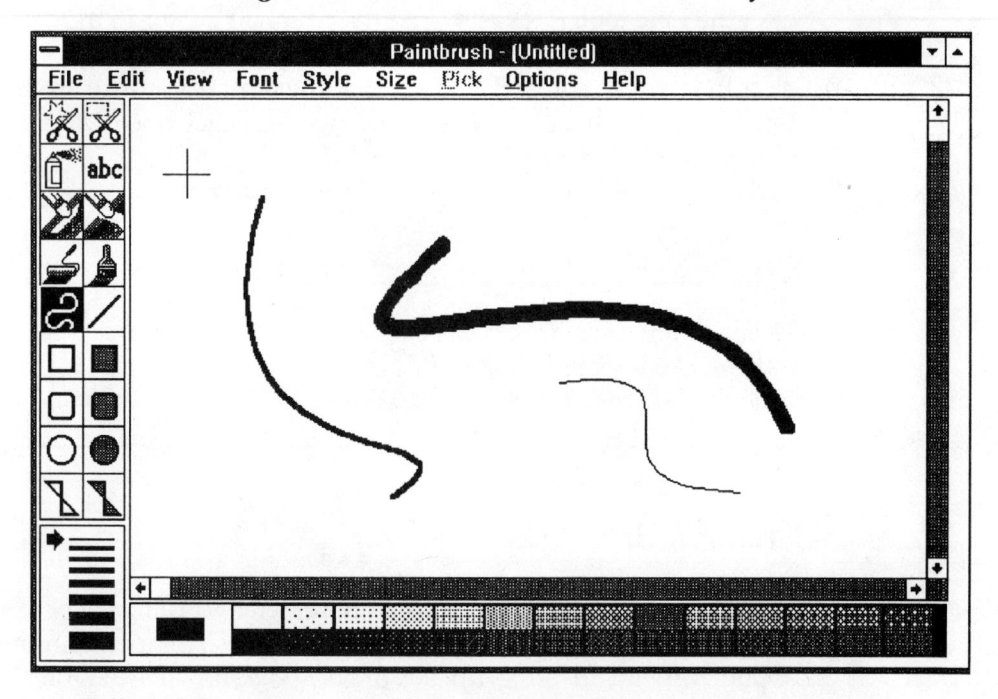

Figure 11.11. Some Curves Created Using Paintbrush

and start over at any point in this operation, press the right button once to cancel the line. If you release the mouse button for the second time and decide that you don't like the shape of the line, immediately activate the Undo command from the Edit menu to delete the line.

The Brush tool acts exactly as its name implies: as a paint brush. Simply select the desired color and brush width, and move the cursor to the desired starting location. Press the left mouse button and drag to an end point. If you click the mouse without dragging it, a dot appears, as if you've dabbed the brush at only one point on the canvas.

As with the other tools, holding the Shift key while drawing creates vertical and horizontal lines. You can also use this feature to draw "L" shaped lines. For example, when you hold down the Shift key and move the cursor to the right, a horizontal line appears. Once the horizontal line begins to appear, move the cursor at a diagonal until it reaches the desired end point of the "L" shaped line. Release the Shift key while still holding down the left mouse button. Paintbrush draws a perpendicular line from the current cursor position to the first line. In fact, you can even use this technique to draw "T" shaped lines.

1. Select the Line tool. Click and drag the crosshair cursor in the drawing area. While you're dragging, click the right button. What happens?
2. Select the Curve tool, and double-click the crosshair cursor in the drawing area. Move the cursor to a second position and click once. Move it to a third position and click again. What happens?
3. Hold the mouse button down on the third click and drag the mouse. What happens?

1. *The line disappears.*
2. *A curved, closed shape is drawn, like the shapes in Figure 11.12.*
3. *You will be able to reshape the closed, curved figure.*

Selecting a Brush Shape

If you enjoy the "Old English" look of hand-lettered calligraphy, you can use Paintbrush to create it electronically. Select the Brush Shapes... command from the Options menu to bring up the dialog box shown in Figure 11.13. This

Working with Desktop Applications

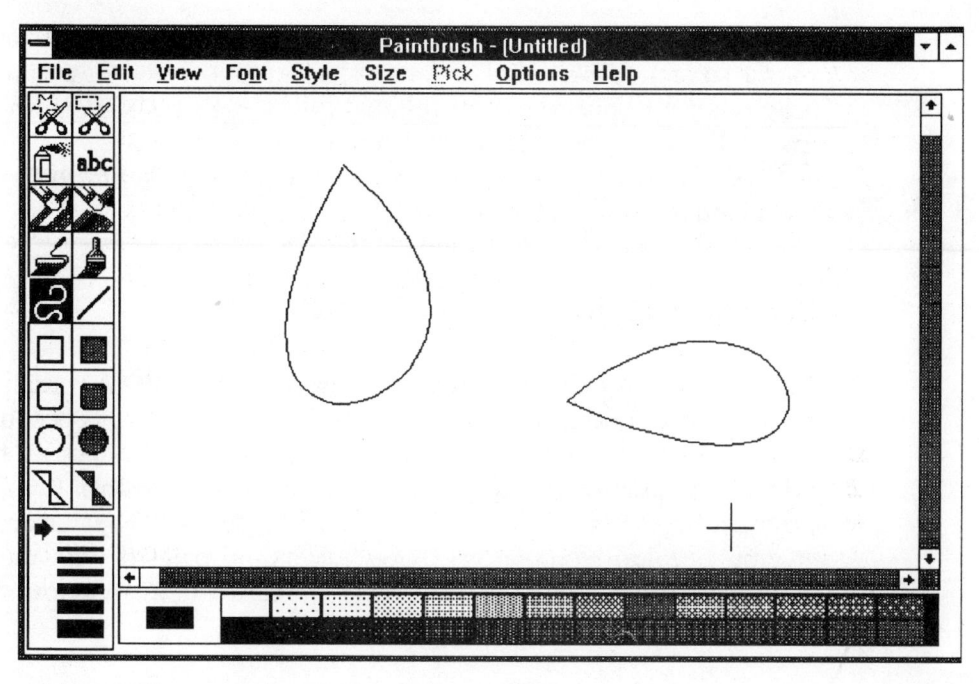

Figure 11.12. Closed Shapes

command allows you to select various brush shapes. If you click on the shape that goes from the lower-left to the upper-right and then click on the OK window button, the inclined line becomes a cursor. Now, press the left mouse button to begin your character strokes. Select different line widths to change the width of the brush. You can make perfect vertical and horizontal lines using the Shift key option.

If you want guide lines to help you control size, select an unused color and draw your guide lines with it. (Use the Shift key to make the lines perfectly parallel.) Select the color, shape and brush size for your lettering and draw the

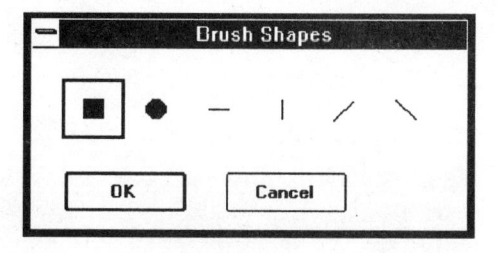

Figure 11.13. Brush Shapes Dialog Box

characters. When you're done, select the color for the guide lines as the foreground color, and select white as the background color (assuming that the background for your letters is white). Activate the Color Eraser and use it to remove the guide lines without disturbing your fancy letters!

Experiment with the various brush shapes to decide which ones are best suited for a given operation.

The Airbrush Tool

The last tool in the drawing and painting category is the Airbrush. This tool uses the foreground color to cover an area with a random concentric pattern similar to that observed from a can of spray paint. If you click on the mouse and move it quickly, only a sprinkling of paint dots is visible. If you drag the Airbrush cursor very slowly, the area becomes completely saturated with the foreground color. Figure 11.14 shows a window painted with the Airbrush tool. The line width selector at the lower-left corner of the window defines the size of the spray pattern.

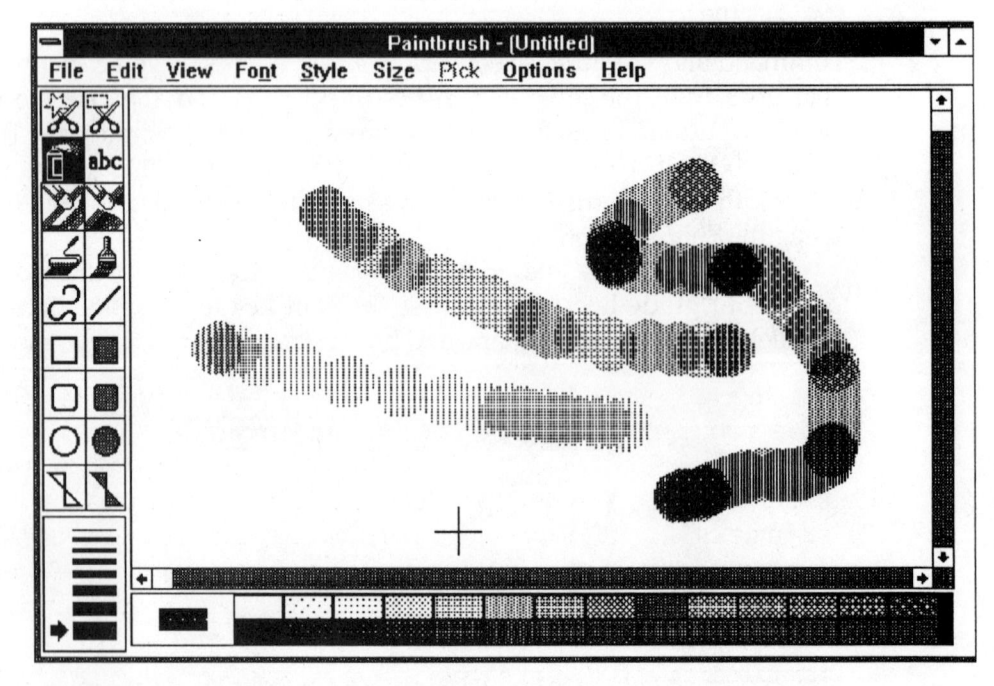

Figure 11.14. Window Painted with the Airbrush Tool

> ✓ Experiment with the Airbrush tool to change the size of the brush spray.

Change the size by selecting a different line width from the palette in the lower-left corner.

Scissors and Pick

Scissors and Pick are extremely useful when you plan on doing anything that is repeated, or you include drawings in your Write documents. Scissors and Pick generally work in the same way: use them to select a graphics area so that it can be moved, duplicated, or sent to the Windows Clipboard for use by another application.

Select Pick to define a rectangular cut perimeter. This is quite handy when you work with objects that have a substantial amount of separation from other objects. If the area that you wish to cut contains some background objects that you want to leave in place, don't use Pick. Instead, choose the Scissors tool.

Use the Scissors tool to define an elaborate perimeter around the area to be cut. This is ideal for extracting an irregularly shaped object. The only requirement is that you must drag completely around the object to the point where you began the cut operation.

Both tools define a dashed line that allows you to verify what is to be cut. The cutting perimeter is defined by moving the mouse cursor to the beginning location, pressing the left mouse button, dragging the mouse to define a closed cutting perimeter, and releasing the left mouse button. Pick works like the unfilled rectangle tool, and Scissors works similarly to Brush. Figure 11.15 shows an image area selected with the Scissors tool.

When you release the left mouse button to perform the cut operation, you have several options. You can select the Cut command from the Edit menu to move a copy of the object into Windows Clipboard, and use the Paste command to bring in multiple copies of the object. Another option is to simply drag the item to a different part of the screen. If the background of the object is the same color as the currently selected background, you can move the object transparently: the object can overlay other objects on the screen so that the objects underneath are visible. If the currently selected background color is different from the background on the screen, Windows repositions the object and fills in the blank areas within the cut perimeter using the current background color.

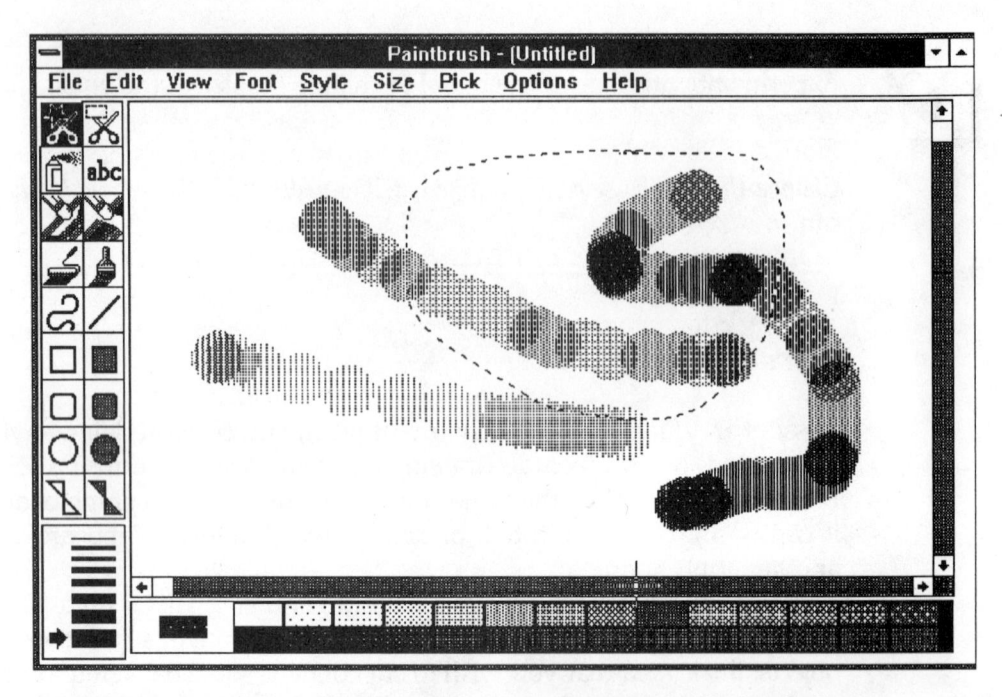

Figure 11.15. Image Area Selected with the Scissors

To move an object, first define a cut perimeter using either tool. Next, move the mouse cursor inside the cut perimeter, press the left mouse button, and drag the object across the screen to the new location. If you want to use the Cut and Paste commands to make multiple copies, define the cut perimeter and activate Cut; the object disappears from the window. Activate Paste to bring the object back (usually to the top-left corner of the viewing area). Move the mouse cursor to the center of the object (as defined by the dashed cut perimeter) and drag it to the new position. If you're not happy with the object position, move the cursor inside the dashed perimeter, press the left mouse button again, and move the object. When you're satisfied, move the mouse cursor outside of the dashed area and click the left mouse button once to paste it down. (The dashed perimeter disappears.) If you want more copies, activate Paste again, move the cursor to the middle of the object, and drag the new copy to the proper location.

The Text Tool

The last tool is the Text tool, which you can use to insert various styles of text anywhere in the drawing area. Select the Text icon, move the mouse cursor to

Working with Desktop Applications

the Font entry on the menu bar, and click on it to view a list of the fonts available. Figure 11.16 shows some of the fonts available on a VGA display. (Your list may be different if you have a different type of display.) A check mark appears to the left of the name of the currently selected font. Click on the name of the desired font to change the selection. The Size menu indicates the point sizes available for the currently selected font. Only the sizes that appear as solid numbers are available; the shaded values indicate other standard sizes that may be available with other fonts. The available size selections change with each font, so always check this option when you change fonts. The last appearance option associated with text is Style.

Unlike the previous options, you can select different style options at the same time. The main options in the Style menu are Normal, Bold, Italic, and Underline. Outline or Shadow are treated as mutually exclusive options, separate from the other three. Bold makes the letters appear to have been drawn with thicker lines. Italic slants the letters and makes each letter a bit narrower. (It was originally invented to pack more letters into a line.) The Underline option draws a line under each letter. You can select these options in any combination.

The Text tool offers one additional option: Color. You can draw characters in any solid foreground color. (Solid colors are those in which all pixels are the

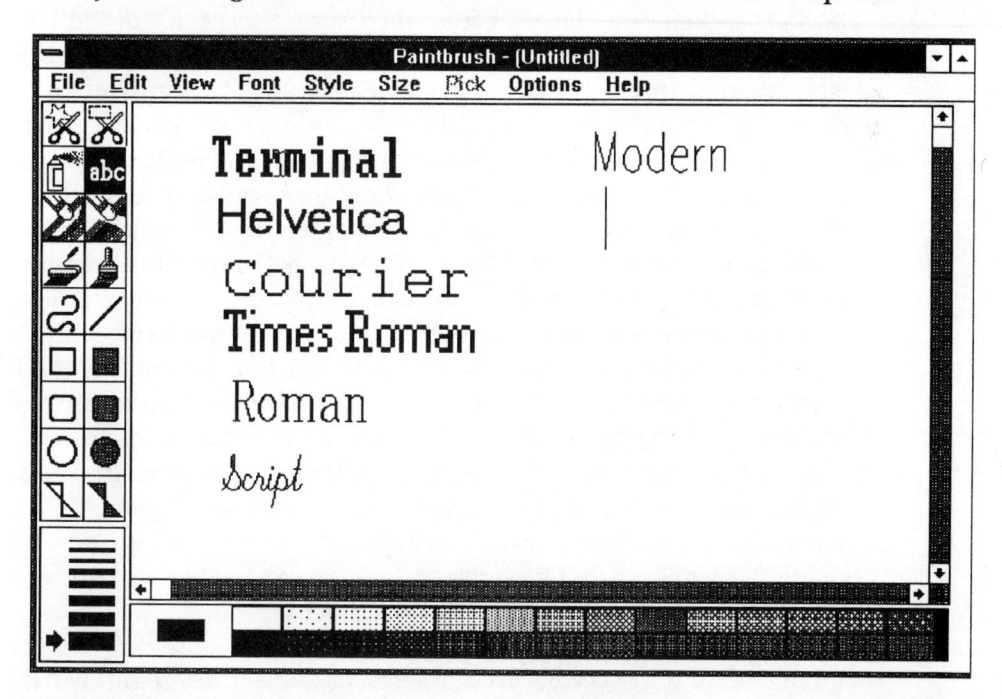

Figure 11.16. Some Fonts Available on a VGA Display

same color.) Although you may not be able to print these colors, this option can be quite useful for creating presentations, or for capturing images on film.

1. What is the minimize font size available for the Helvetica font? What is the maximum size?
2. Which fonts are available in every size?
3. Type in some text and change its font size. What happens?
4. Type in some text and select the Undo command. What happens?

1. *Select Helv from the Font menu, and then open the Size menu. The minimum size is 15 points, and the maximum is 80 points.*
2. *Roman, Script, and Modern.*
3. *As long as you don't reposition the cursor after typing the text, you can change its size. You can also use this technique to change the style of the text.*
4. *Nothing. This command is not supported with the Text tool.*

The Outline and Shadow options only work when the currently selected background color is different from the background color of the viewing area. Outline draws a band of color around the outside and the inside of each letter. The color of this band is the currently selected background color. Shadow draws an outline of the letter using the current background color, so that the letter is shadowed as if a high-intensity light source is shining on it from over the viewer's right shoulder. To best view these options, leave the foreground color as either black or blue, and select green or red for a background color. The Normal, Outline, and Shadow options are mutually exclusive. Selecting Normal also resets the other options.

Once you've made your selections, move the mouse cursor to the viewing area and position it where you want the text to appear. Click the left mouse button to make the vertical bar cursor appear. Begin typing text; if you make a mistake, use the backspace key to remove the characters to the left of the cursor, one at a time. If you type past the right side of the view window, Paintbrush won't beep or otherwise warn you, and ignores the additional letters. To get around this deficiency, move the viewing window to the right using the scroll bar and type the additional text, use the Pick or Scissor tool to cut the words and place them in their proper position.

If you need a guide line to help you position the text, first draw a horizontal line of an unused color from the existing text to the right. Perform the clip operation and position the text so that it is on top of the line, at the proper horizontal distance from the previous text. When the operation is completed, use the Color Eraser tool to remove the guide line without disturbing the text.

When you select a different tool, click the mouse button, use a scroll bar, or resize the window, Paintbrush pastes down the characters that you typed. At that point, the Backspace key no longer removes characters. To reposition or remove the text, use the techniques described earlier in this chapter.

Using Write

Write is a reasonably sophisticated word-processing program that imports graphics from the Paintbrush program. Write also allows you to select from various character fonts so you can create professional-looking materials for presentations and reports.

In many respects, Write operates just like Notepad: The basic techniques for entering and editing text are the same. Write also provides a number of powerful features that you won't find in Notepad, such as paragraph formatting, tab control, full text headers and footers, and the capability to import graphics.

Starting Write

To start Write, double-click on the Write icon in the Accessories group window. The Untitled application window shown in Figure 11.17 appears. The window provides a title, seven menu items, scroll bars, Minimize and Maximize buttons, the Control menu, and a status bar in the lower-left corner that indicates the current page number. A blinking vertical bar cursor and a star symbol also appear within the work area. The vertical bar cursor marks the place where text appears when you start typing. The star symbol indicates the physical end of the file. As with most Windows applications, Write starts up ready for you to use immediately. When you type several lines of text, Write performs automatic word-wrap to the next line if you attempt to type past the right side of the window. You can also control where a line of text appears by pressing the Enter key each time you wish to start a new line.

Using the Ruler

To take advantage of Write's formatting capabilities, use the ruler (Figure 11.18) displayed by selecting the Ruler On command from the Document menu. By

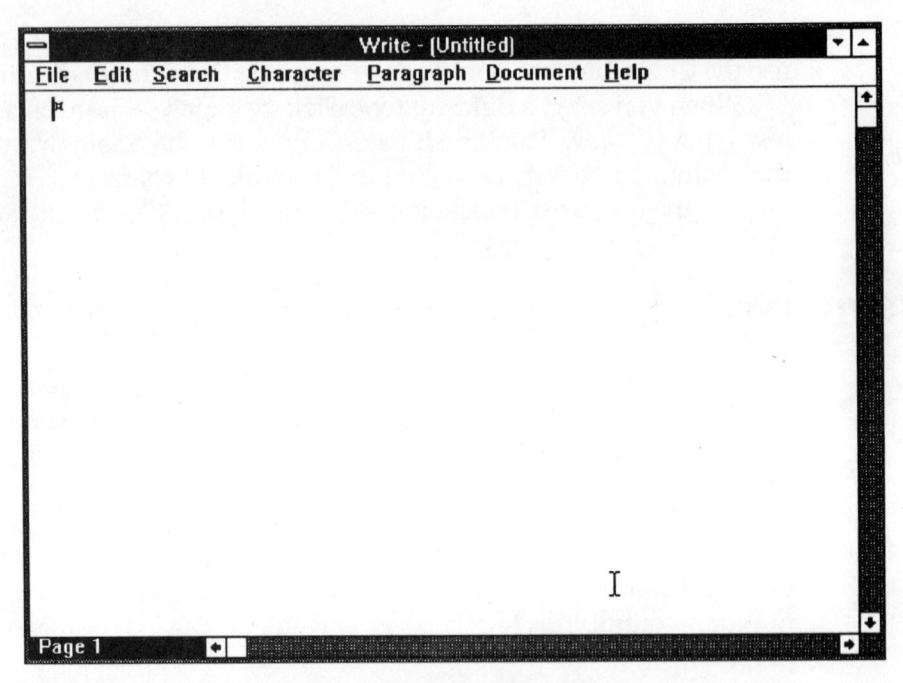

Figure 11.17. Write Window

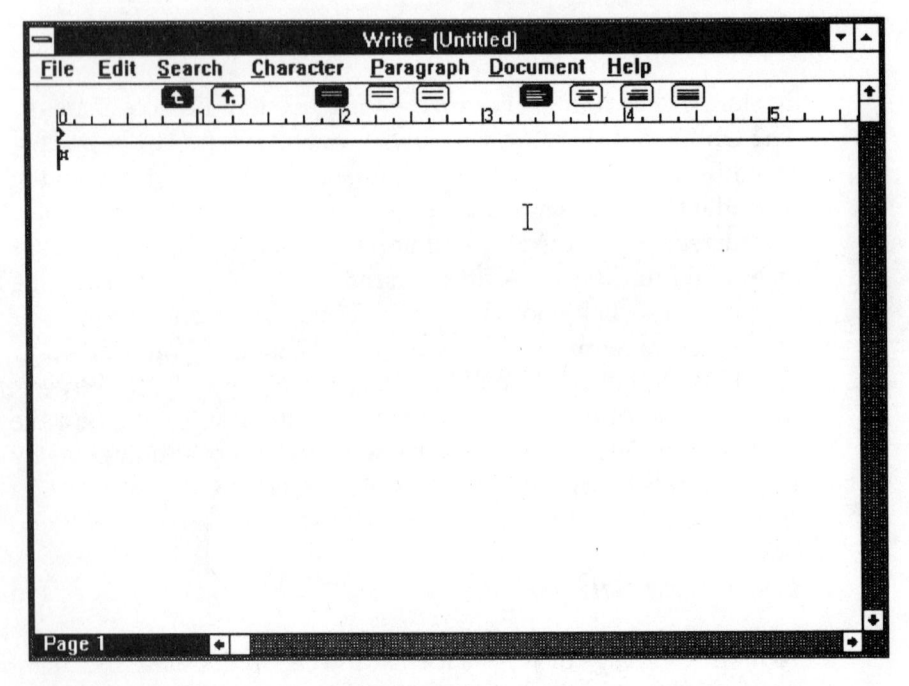

Figure 11.18. The Ruler

default, the ruler displays in units of inches. You can change it to centimeters by selecting the Page Layout... command from the Document menu, and selecting the cm option button. Directly below the ruler, a left-pointing arrowhead marker indicates the left margin. When you scroll the window, an arrow points in the other direction to indicate the right margin. Embedded in the left margin marker is a small dot that represents the indent marker. To left-indent a paragraph, mark it and slide the indent marker.

In addition to the margin indicators, the ruler contains icons for setting tabs, spacing text in a paragraph, and aligning text in a paragraph. Use the first two icons from the left to set tabs. The icon with a dot sets a decimal-aligned tab, and the other icon sets a left-aligned tab. Use the third through fifth icons to single space, 1 1/2 space, or double space a paragraph, respectively. Finally, use the last four icons to left-align, center-align, right-align, or justify a paragraph of marked text. We'll examine the steps for setting tabs and formatting paragraphs next.

Run Write and display the ruler by selecting the Ruler On command.
1. Scroll the window to the left. What is the default setting for the right margin?
2. Change the right margin to 5".
3. Type in a few sentences and double space your text.
4. Center-align the text.

---

1. *The Right margin default is 6".*
2. *Click on the right margin marker, and drag to the 5" mark.*
3. *Highlight the text you entered, and select the fifth icon from the left on top of the ruler.*
4. *While the text is still highlighted, select the seventh icon.*

Setting up A Document

Before you type multiple pages of text into a document or print the document, you'll want to make sure it's formatted properly. You can perform several formatting operations with Write such as:

- Defining left and right margins
- Defining top and bottom margins
- Defining the measurement system for a document (inches or centimeters)
- Indenting paragraphs

- Setting page numbers
- Setting paragraph line spacing
- Setting paragraph alignment
- Repaginating
- Creating headers and footers

To set up a document, display the Page Layout dialog box (Figure 11.19) by selecting the Page Layout... command from the Document menu. Page Layout allows you to set the starting page number, the margins, and the measurement system. After you make the desired entries, click OK to set up your document. The selections that you make here affect your entire document.

Formatting Paragraphs

Using either the ruler or menu commands, you can easily format one paragraph, multiple paragraphs, or an entire document. In this section, we'll cover the different options available for formatting paragraphs. To change the formatting of a single paragraph, position the cursor at any point within the paragraph and select the desired formatting option (such as left-alignment). To change multiple paragraphs, highlight the paragraphs with the mouse or the keyboard.

Placing Tabs

The easiest way to place a tab is to display the ruler, mark your text, click the Tab icon, and then click on the desired position on the ruler. Continue this process to place multiple tabs along the ruler. Once the tabs are on the ruler, you can drag them to reposition them. Figure 11.20 shows a ruler with multiple tabs. Keep in mind that only the text you have marked is affected by the

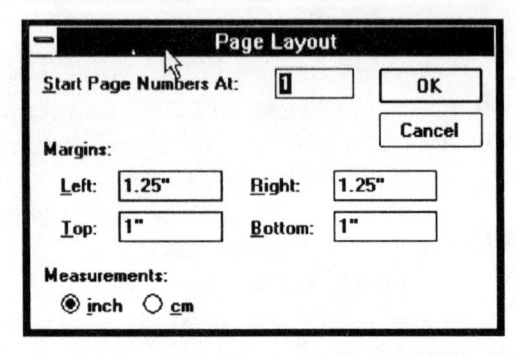

Figure 11.19. Page Layout Dialog Box

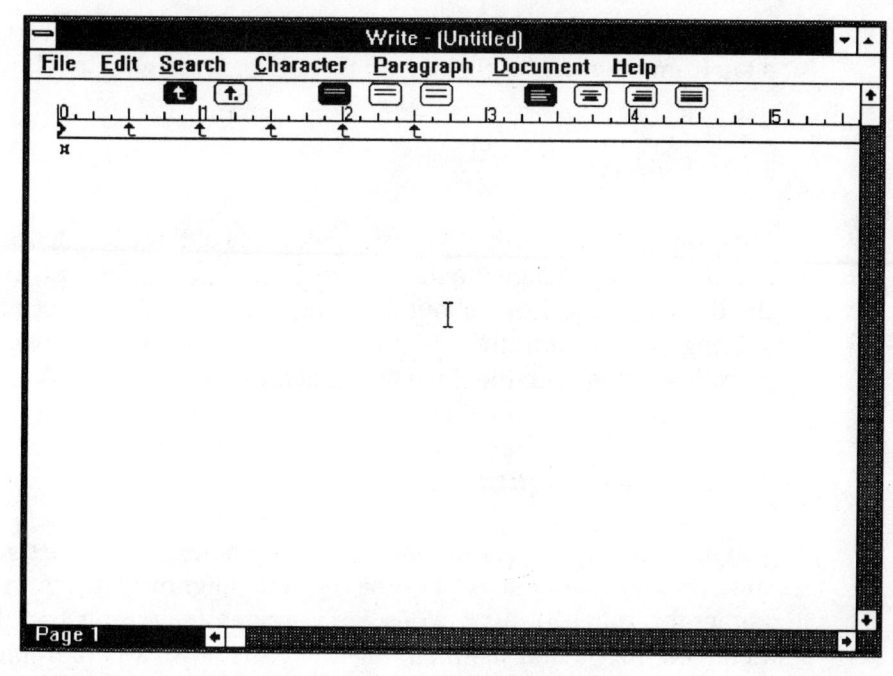

Figure 11.20. Ruler with Multiple Tabs

tabs. If you want to tab an entire document using one set of tabs, mark the document by placing the cursor at the beginning of the document and pressing Ctrl+Shift+End, and then place your tabs using the ruler.

You can also set tabs by selecting the Tabs... command from the Document menu. This command brings up the dialog box shown in Figure 11.21. Twelve tab boxes are provided so that you can enter a tab setting in units of inches. To set a decimal tab, select the Decimal check box directly below the desired tab. After you add the tabs you want, click OK to return to your document.

The Tabs dialog box can also be used to remove tabs. To clear all of the tabs, select the Clear All button. To remove one or more tabs, double-click on

Figure 11.21. Tabs Dialog Box

the desired tab boxes and press Delete to remove the value. You can also delete a tab from the ruler by clicking on the tab and dragging it below the ruler.

Line Spacing

Paragraphs can be formatted easily using one of three line spaces: single, 1 1/2, and double. To change the line spacing, click on a paragraph and select one of the three spacing icons above the ruler. You can also select one of the three spacing options from the Paragraph menu. Figure 11.22 shows text in a document formatted with the three line-spacing styles.

Paragraph Alignment

Aligning a paragraph is similar to setting a paragraph's line spacing—click on the paragraph, and select one of the four alignment icons in the ruler. The Paragraph menu also provides four options for setting the alignment: Left, Centered, Right, and Justified. Figure 11.23 shows a paragraph that is center-aligned.

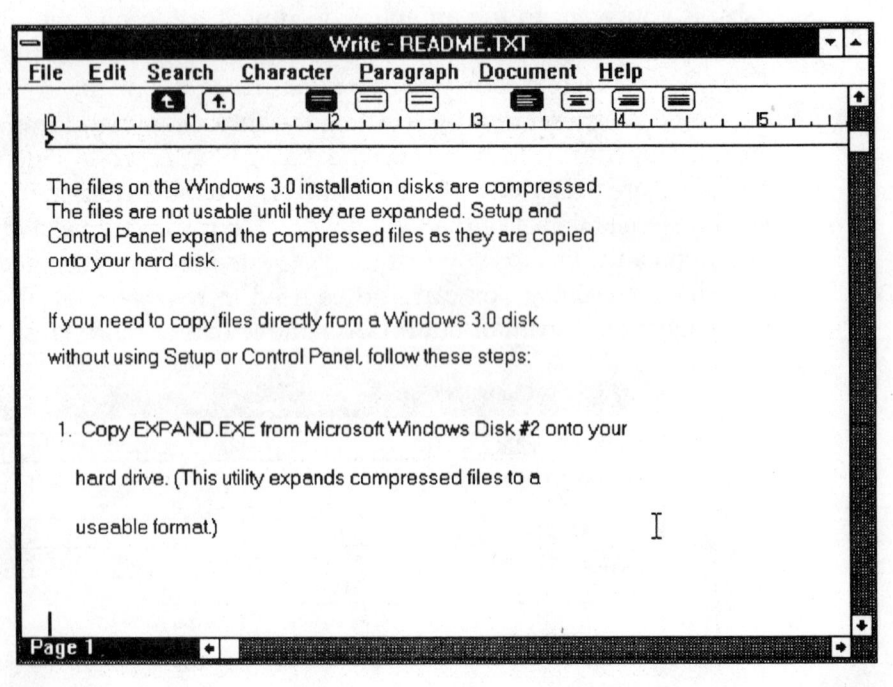

Figure 11.22. Text Formatted with the Three Line-spacing Styles

Working with Desktop Applications

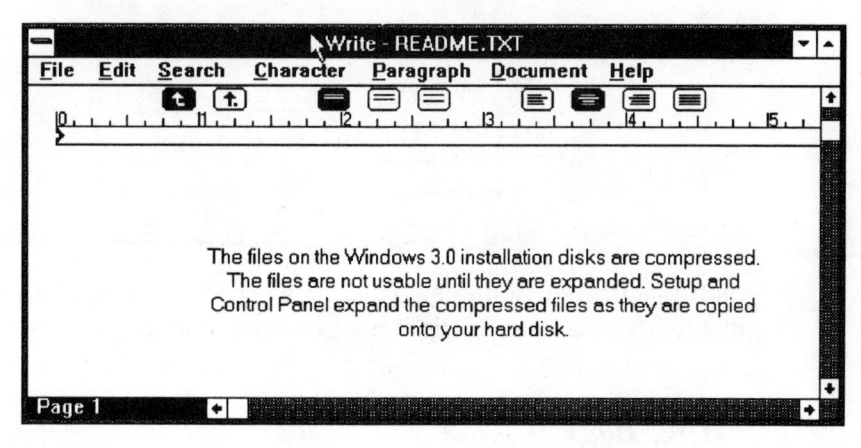

Figure 11.23. A Center-aligned Paragraph

Indenting Paragraphs

The easiest way to set paragraph indentations is to click on the paragraph and drag the indent marker on the ruler. (Remember that the indent marker is represented as a small dot.) Figure 11.24 shows a paragraph indented using this technique. In this case, the first line is indented to the right.

You can also indent paragraphs by using the Indents dialog box (Figure 11.25). To display this dialog box, select the Indents... command from the Para-

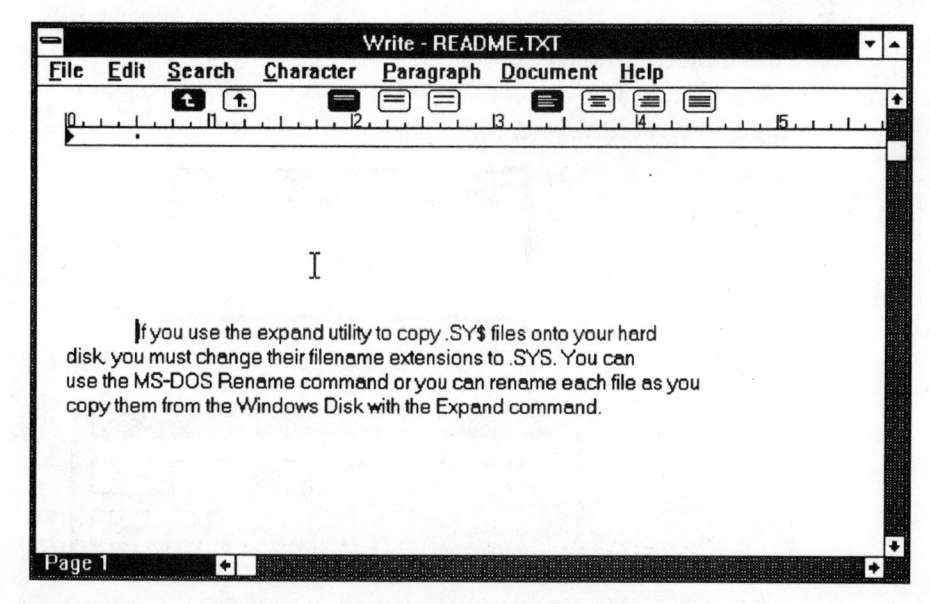

Figure 11.24. An Indented Paragraph

Figure 11.25. The Indents Dialog Box

graph menu. Use the three text boxes to specify indentations for the left margin, the first line, and the right margin of the paragraph.

Setting Page Breaks

Before printing a document, make sure that all of your page breaks are in the right place. Write doesn't provide a print view mode so that you can view page-by-page how your document will print, but you can repaginate your document and manually check or change each page break. To use this feature, select the Repaginate... command from the File menu. When the dialog box (Figure 11.26) appears, select the Confirm Page Breaks check box and click OK. Write shows you each page break, and then prompts you with the dialog box shown in Figure 11.27 so that you can confirm the break or change it. Select the Up button to move the page break up one line, or select the Down button to move the break down one line.

A manual page break can also be set from the keyboard. Position the cursor on the line where you want the break to occur and press Ctrl+Enter. The single dotted line appears representing the manual page break. To remove a page break at any time, highlight the dotted line and press the Delete key.

Figure 11.26. Repaginate Document Dialog Box

Figure 11.27. Repaginating a Document

Tip | Write displays a manual page break with a single dotted line, and an automatic page break with a double chevron.

Creating Headers and Footers

When you print your documents, you can include a header or a footer on each page. A *header* is a line or more of text placed at the top of each page. A typical header is the name of the document and a page number or date. A *footer*, on the other hand, is a line of text placed at the bottom of each page.

To create a header, select the Header... command from the Document menu. When the dialog box and Header window (Figure 11.28) display, type text into the window and use the ruler to set margins. If you want the header to display a page number, select the Insert Page # button in the Page Header dialog box. Use this dialog box also to specify where the header should appear (distance from the top of the page) and whether the header should be placed on the first page. When you are done defining the header, select the Return to Document button.

After you create a header, you can remove it at any time by selecting the Header... command, and then clicking the Clear button to erase the Header window.

You create a page footer using the same technique just presented for headers. The only difference is that you must first select the Footer... command from the Document menu. As Figure 11.29 shows, the Footer window and the Page Footer dialog box looks just like those provided for creating a header. When you finish entering text for the footer, select the Return to Document button.

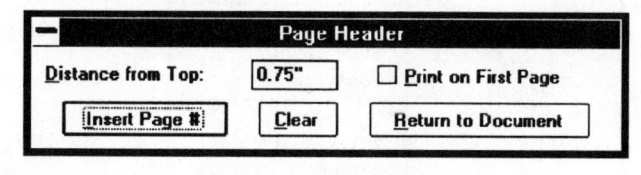

Figure 11.28. Page Header Window

Figure 11.29. Page Footer Dialog Box

1. Create a header that displays "Annual Budget" with the page number and date.
2. Create a header that displays the name of the file.

---

1. (a) Select the Header... command.
   (b) Type in the text Annual Budget.
   (c) Tab over, type in Page No:, and click Insert Page #.
   (d) Tab over again and enter &d.
   (e) Click Return to Document.
2. (a) Select the Footer... command.
   (b) Type in &f.
   (c) Click Return to Document.

Using Fonts and Styles

Open the Character menu shown in Figure 11.30 to see the options for formatting characters and selecting font styles. The first group of options allows you to change the style of text to bold, italic, underline, superscript, and subscript. When you select a style option, a check mark appears to the left of the style. By default, Write sets all type to the Normal style. You can change the style by

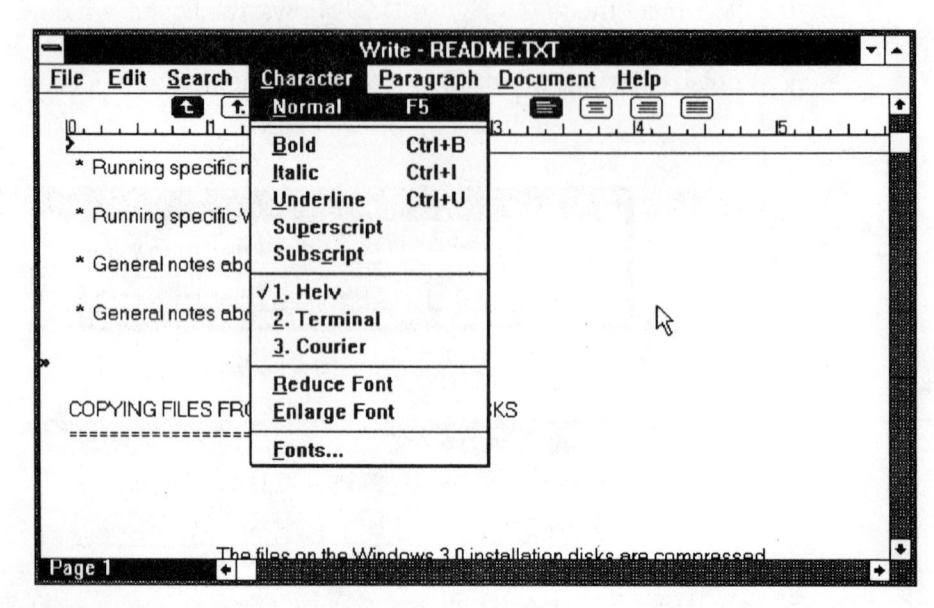

Figure 11.30. Character Menu

marking the text and then selecting one or more of the options. For example, you can set type as bold and italic. If you are working from the keyboard, you can easily change the style of text using one of these keyboard shortcuts:

Bold	Ctrl+B
Italic	Ctrl+I
Underline	Ctrl+U

Figure 11.31 shows lines of text displayed in different formats.

In addition to changing styles, you can select fonts with the Character menu. Figure 11.30 shows the three font styles listed in the menu: Helv, Terminal, and Courier. To select a different font, activate the Fonts... command. When the dialog box (Figure 11.32) appears, select a font and a point size, and click OK.

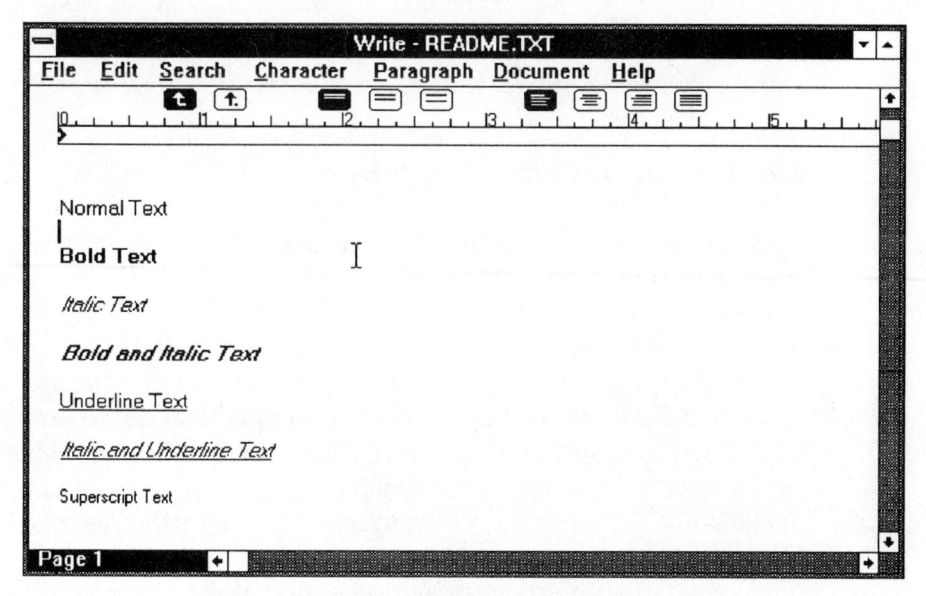

Figure 11.31. Text in Different Formats

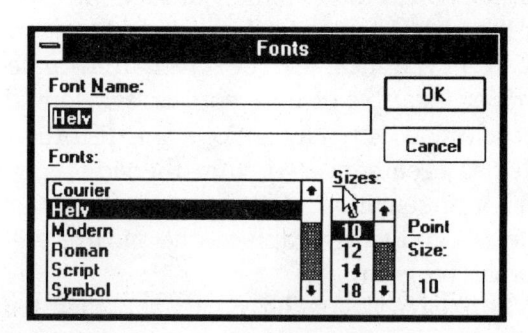

Figure 11.32. Fonts Dialog Box

> Type some text into the Write window and highlight it.
> 1. Set the text as 12-point Script.
> 2. What changes in the Character menu after you set your text to Script?
> 3. Select Normal in the Character menu. What happens to your text?

1. *(a) Open the Character menu.*
   (b) Select the Fonts... command
   (c) Click on the Script entry in the Fonts menu.
   (d) Double-click on 12 in the Sizes menu.
2. *The Script font is listed in the menu.*
3. *Nothing. The Normal option does not change the font—it only changes the type style. The type was not in bold, italic, or otherwise altered, so it doesn't change.*

Combining Text and Graphics

You'll now learn how to import a simple graphics object into a Write document. After the graphics has been imported, you'll be able to add text.

Begin by drawing a simple object using Paintbrush (a square inside another square is fine for this example). Clip the object using the Pick tool, and then select the Cut command from the Edit menu to place a copy of the picture in the Clipboard. If you want to keep the object, you can retrieve a copy again using the Paste command. If you're done with Paintbrush, either double-click on the control box or select the Exit command. If you want to keep Paintbrush active while working with Write, minimize Paintbrush to an icon before calling Write.

Whatever your screen preferences, start Write. After you've typed a few lines of text, press the Enter key at least once to move the cursor to a new line below the text. Select Paste from the Edit menu. The picture that you sent to Clipboard now appears on the screen immediately below the text! Figure 11.33 presents an example of how your screen should look. Depending upon your printer selection, you may notice some distortion in the picture. (It may appear as if it has been squeezed from the sides.) This distortion results from the internal representation of the page information in Write. If your printer is capable of producing graphics, the picture will appear just as it did in the Paintbrush program.

Write always inserts the picture at the left-hand margin. To move it toward the right (to center it on the page), follow these steps:

Working with Desktop Applications

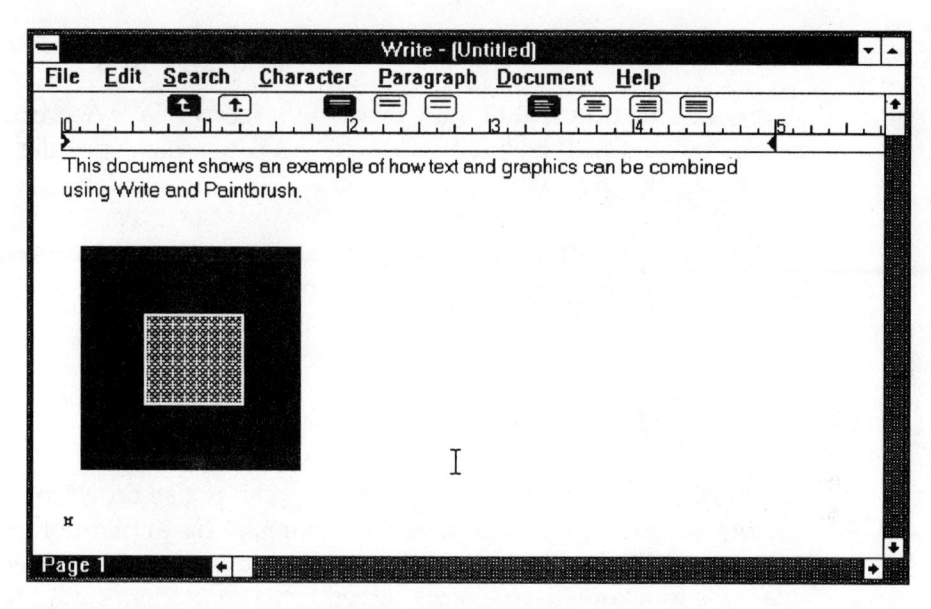

Figure 11.33. Placing a Graphics Image

1. Click on the picture with the mouse, or use the up and down arrow keyboard keys to select the picture. (The picture highlights in reverse video when it's selected.)
2. Activate the Move Picture command from the Edit menu to release the picture from the page. (A dotted square appears around the picture.)
3. Move the mouse cursor without clicking the left button to move the picture to the new location. (You can also use the left and right arrow keyboard keys to do this.)
4. When the picture is properly positioned, click on the left mouse button or press the Enter key.

You can also change the size of the picture by selecting it (so that it's highlighted) and activating the Size Picture command from the Edit menu. Next, move the mouse cursor (without clicking the left mouse button) to the center of one of the sides of the dashed square that surrounds the picture. Once the box cursor touches the dashed box, the cursor attaches to it and moves the side either in or out to adjust the size of the square. To change both the height and the width of the object, move the box cursor to a corner of the dashed box and adjust two sides at the same time. Once you are satisfied with the proportions of the sizing box, click the left mouse button or press the Enter key. Write redraws the picture to fill the sizing box. If you don't like the way your picture was resized, immediately select the Undo command to revoke the sizing operation.

Saving Files

To save a Write document for the first time, select the Save As... command from the File menu. Use the File Save As dialog box to assign your file a name. This dialog box also provides three check boxes so that you can save the file as a backup file, a text-only file, or a Microsoft Word file. If you save the file as text only, you'll lose the formatting features you've used. After you save the file for the first time, you can save it after changes are made by selecting the Save command.

Using Terminal

You might be surprised to discover that Windows also provides a full-featured telecommunications program, called Terminal. This application allows you to connect up with another computer or network, such as CompuServe or an on-line bulletin board. To use Terminal, you need a modem connected to a serial port, such as COM1. If you don't have this equipment installed, make sure to get a modem and hook it up with a null modem cable if you want to use Terminal to communicate with other computers.

Starting Terminal

To start Terminal, open the Accessories window and double-click on the Terminal icon. The application window (Figure 11.34) contains a menu bar with the following menu items:

File	Provides the set of commands for opening, saving, and printing files
Edit	Provides the basic editing commands
Settings	Provides the options for configuring communication settings
Phone	Provides commands for dialing and hanging up
Transfers	Provides commands for transferring and receiving files
Help	Provides commands for accessing Help information

If you have experience using a communications program, you'll find Terminal easy to use. If you are unfamiliar with communication programs, you should consult a book that covers the basics.

Working with Desktop Applications

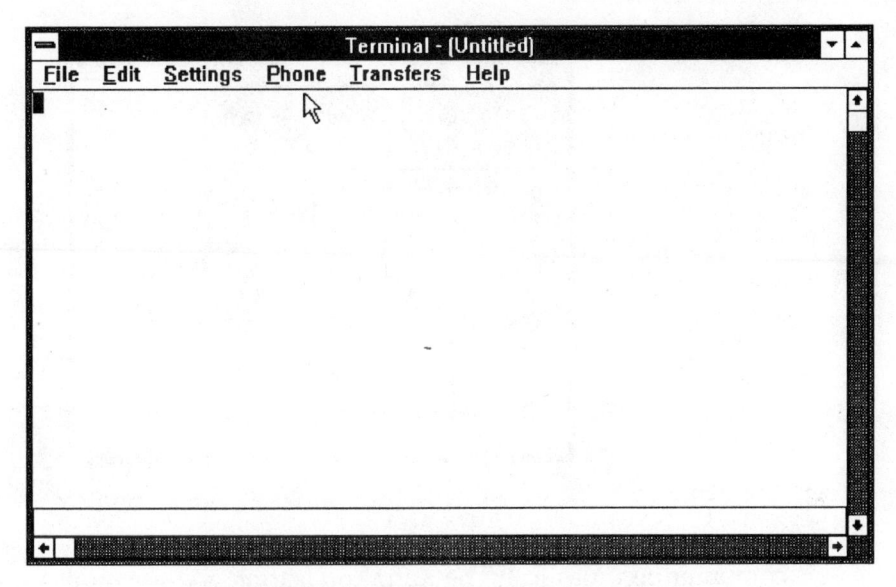

Figure 11.34. The Terminal Window

Setting Up Communication Parameters

Before you dial up and connect with another computer, make sure that your system is configured properly. You need to know the settings for the baud rate, data bits, stop bits, parity, and flow control: the *communication parameters*. If you don't know what these settings are, refer to an introductory book on telecommunications.

After you define your communication parameters, select the Communications... command from the Settings menu. When the dialog box (Figure 11.35) displays, check each communication parameter to make sure that the correct values are selected. For example, if you use a 1200-baud modem, select the 1200 option button in the Baud Rate group. The most common settings for the baud rate are 300, 1200, and 2400. (The baud rate is the rate at which data is transferred between two modems.)

The Data Bits option specifies the number of data bits in each packet sent between two computers. Usually this setting is assigned a value of 7 or 8. The Stop Bits option specifies the time interval between transmitted characters, and is typically set at 1.

The Parity option specifies the technique used for checking your data when it's being sent. If you use 8 data bits, set the parity to None. The Flow Control option specifies what will happen if the buffer receiving data at your

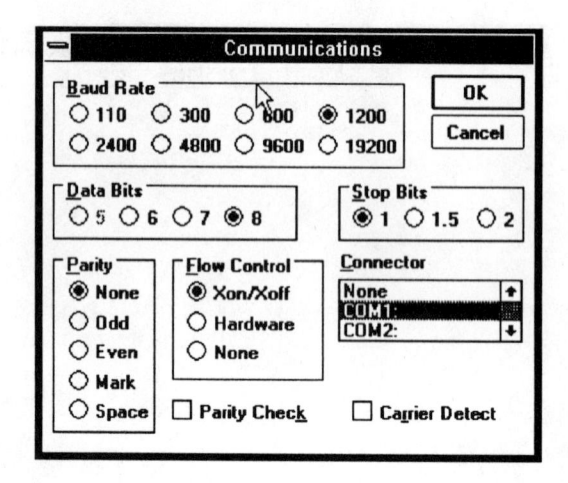

Figure 11.35. Communications Dialog Box

computer becomes full. The Xon/Xoff setting is the standard setting that tells your computer to pause so that it can clear its data buffer. When it's ready to receive more data, your computer sends a message to the computer you're communicating with.

The Connector option is the most important option to check because it specifies which serial port your modem is connected to. Make sure that one of the COM ports (such as COM1 or COM2) is selected.

When you're done selecting the communication parameters, click the OK button. If your modem is not connected or turned on, the warning dialog box shown in Figure 11.36 appears. If this occurs, double-check that everything is turned on and connected properly, and select the OK button again.

Tip | You can save all of the settings you select so that you won't have to reconfigure Terminal each time you use it. We'll show how to save your settings later.

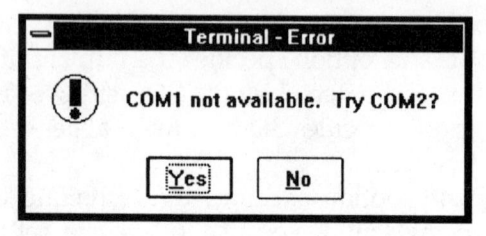

Figure 11.36. Terminal Error Warning Dialog Box

Setting up Your Terminal

Before you dial a number, set up your terminal by selecting the Terminal Emulation... command from the Settings menu. The dialog box (Figure 11.37) displays with three options. If you are connecting to another PC or a standard on-line service (such as CompuServe), select the TTY (Generic) option. The other two options enable your computer to emulate a terminal (such as the DEC VT 100) when connecting your PC to mainframe computers.

To set up the terminal settings, select the Terminal Preferences... command from the Settings menu. The dialog box shown in Figure 11.38 displays. The first group of options, Terminal Modes, allows you to select how your terminal displays data. Select the Line Wrap check box if you want incoming characters to wrap on your display. (If you don't select this option, you may lose characters that extend past the right edge of the screen.) The Local Echo option allows you to echo the characters that you type in. Because some computers automatically echo characters back to you after they are sent, you may see duplicate characters on the screen. If this happens, deselect this option. The Sound option turns on your system bell.

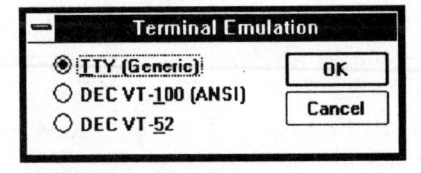

Figure 11.37. Terminal Emulation Selections

Figure 11.38. Terminal Preferences Dialog Box

When transmitting and receiving data, you may want to convert a carriage return character into a carriage return/linefeed combination so that your data displays correctly. The options for converting carriage returns are found in the CR -> CR/LF group. Select Inbound to convert the data you receive, and Outbound to convert the data you send.

Selecting a Modem

Most PC-based modems are designed to be Hayes-compatible, and this is the default configuration for Terminal. If you have a different type of modem installed, select the Modem Commands... from the Settings menu and then select the appropriate modem. Figure 11.39 shows the four options provided in the Modem Default group. After you select the correct option, click the OK button.

Selecting a Number

After you set the basic parameters and terminal preferences, you're ready to dial a number and connect with another computer. Select the Phone Number... command from the Settings menu. When the dialog box (Figure 11.40) displays, use the text box line called Dial to enter a phone number (and an area code if required). You can use parentheses and hyphens to separate the parts of the number. To insert a delay between numbers, use a comma. Each time Terminal encounters a comma when dialing a number, it pauses for 2 seconds before dialing the next digit. Here are a few examples of valid numbers:

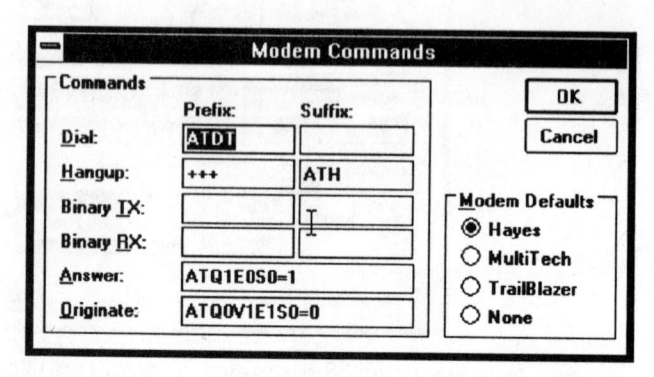

Figure 11.39. The Four Modem Default Options

Working with Desktop Applications

Figure 11.40. Phone Number Dialog Box

(602)483-2165
1-800-922-7541
9,455-3223
8,,402-351-8754

In addition to entering a phone number, you can set three options: specify a timeout value, choose to have your number redialed if it can't be connected on the first try, and have Terminal signal you when it connects. For the first option, Timeout If Not Connected In, you can enter a value to increase the number of seconds Terminal waits for a connect signal. When a number is dialed, Terminal waits until it times out or it receives a connect symbol. By default, Terminal's timeout limit is 30 seconds. If you think more time is needed to make a call, change the timeout value.

If you are calling a system that is hard to connect to, such as an on-line bulletin board, select the Redial After Timing Out option. This option tells Terminal to keep dialing the number until it connects. If you also select the Signal When Connected option, you can go off and do other things and Terminal will beep when it connects.

Making the Call

When you select the Dial command from the Phone menu, Terminal begins dialing the number. If you didn't provide a number yet, the Phone Number dialog box asks you for the number. If your modem has a speaker, you'll hear your number as it is being dialed.

What If You Can't Connect

Hopefully, your computer will connect on its first try. If it doesn't connect and you suspect that your communication parameters are not set properly, return to the Communications dialog box by selecting the Communications... command from the Settings menu. If your computer doesn't connect, here are some possible reasons why:

- Your modem might not be turned on.
- Your computer might not be hooked up to the modem with a null modem cable.
- You might not have selected the correct modem in the Modem Commands dialog box. (To check this, select Modem Commands... from the Settings menu.)
- You might be dialing the wrong number.
- You might have selected the wrong COM port.
- You might have selected the wrong baud rate.

Transferring a File

Once you have connected, you can transfer a text or binary file by selecting the Text Transfers... or Binary Transfers... command from the Settings menu. Use these commands to set up Terminal to send a text or binary file. If you send a text file, the Text Transfers dialog box provides three options for how you want to send your data: Standard Flow Control, Character at a Time, and Line at a Time. If you are sending a binary file, use the Binary Transfers dialog box to select Xmodem/CRC transfer or the Kermit transfer. After you select the transfer options, send the file by selecting the Send Text File... or the Send Binary File... command from the Transfers menu. A dialog box displays so that you can transfer the file. Select the desired file, and click the OK button.

Receiving a File

The process of receiving a file is similar to the process of transmitting one. First, select the appropriate file transfer settings using the Text Transfers... command in the Settings menu. Receive the file by selecting the Receive Text File... or the Receive Binary File... command from the Transfers menu. While your computer receives the file, a status bar displays at the bottom of the Terminal window to show you the status of the transfer operation.

✓ Use Terminal to connect to a computer or an on-line bulletin board. Send a text file, one character at a time.

Select the Text Transfers... command from the Settings menu. Choose the Character at a Time option button, and click the OK button. Select the Send Text File... command from the Transfers menu, select the file, and click the OK button.

Disconnecting

After you finish your communication session with another computer, hang up by selecting the Hangup command from the Phone menu. Before you select this command, make sure that you've logged off the remote computer you connected to. Otherwise, the remote computer might still think that you're connected.

Saving Terminal Settings

To save your communication settings before exiting Terminal, select the Save As... command from the File menu. When the standard File Save dialog box displays, type in the name of a new file. Terminal uses the extension .TRM to store its terminal settings. When you later start Terminal, you can select the Open... command to load in the settings that you saved in a previous session so that you can later use them.

Summary

In this chapter, we've taken a close look at the three key Windows applications: Paintbrush, Write, and Terminal. We learned how to use Paintbrush to create pictures and make alterations using the basic drawing and painting tools. In our exploration of Write, we learned how to format documents and import pictures from Paintbrush. Finally, we explored the communications program, Terminal, to learn how to connect to other computers in order to transfer and receive files.

Exercises

Use these exercises to learn more about Paintbrush, Write, and Terminal.

What You Should Do	How Your Computer Responds
1. Start Paintbrush by double-clicking on the Paintbrush icon.	1. The Paintbrush application displays with the Untitled window.
2. Select the largest line size available.	2. The line size pointer moves to the last line size in the palette.
3. Select the box drawing tool, and move the cursor inside the drawing window.	3. The box icon is highlighted, and the cursor changes to a crosshair.
4. Hold down the Shift key and click and drag the mouse.	4. A square is drawn.
5. Select the Scissors selecting tool, and draw a region around the box.	5. A dashed line appears around the box, and the cursor changes to an arrow.
6. Click and drag the mouse.	6. The box moves around on the screen.
7. Select the Cut command.	7. The box is deleted.
8. Exit Paintbrush.	8. Control returns to the Program Manager.
9. Start Write.	9. The Write application window appears.
10. Open a text file or a .WRI file.	10. If you open a text file, Write converts it to its own internal format. A .WRI file is opened without any conversion.
11. Mark the entire file by pressing Ctrl+Shift+End.	11. The entire document is highlighted.
12. Justify the text.	12. The text appears justified between the default left and right margins.
13. Position the cursor in the document and select the Paste command.	13. The Paintbrush image that you cut is displayed.
14. Exit Write without saving your document.	14. Control returns to the Program Manager.
15. Start Terminal.	15. The Terminal application window appears.
16. Set the communication parameters, using the Communications dialog box.	16. If your modem is installed correctly and you selected the correct options, Terminal is ready for you to call a number.
17. Dial a number by selecting the Dial command.	17. A dialog box displays so that you can enter a phone number.
18. After you connect, hang up by selecting the Hangup command.	18. Terminal hangs up the modem.
19. Exit Terminal.	19. Control returns to the Program Manager.

What If It Doesn't Work?

1. If you don't have a mouse installed, you won't be able to select the drawing tools in Paintbrush.
2. If you don't have a modem installed correctly, you won't be able to select the Dial command.

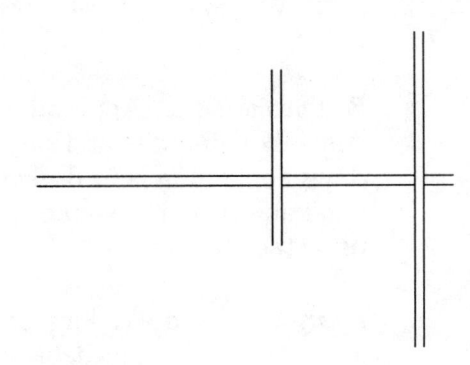

Glossary

Active Window—The screen area that represents the currently running application program. The active window can be recognized by the highlighted title bar. If several windows are open, the active window appears on top of the windows (when the windows are displayed in Cascade mode). All alphanumeric input from the keyboard goes to the active window.

Active Printer—Any printer device driver installed and designated as active in the Printers application of the Control Panel. An active printer can include output to a device driver that is directed to a file.

Applications Program—(sometimes referred to as an *Application*) An independent computer program that performs a function. The two broad categories of applications programs are Windows applications and non-Windows applications. The first are programs (such as Calculator and Write) written specifically to run in the Windows environment. The second term refers to programs written to run under DOS. Non-Windows applications can be installed for easy access in the Windows environment, using the PIF Editor application.

ASCII File—Files that contain only normal numeric codes representing letters, numbers, punctuation marks, and so on. ASCII files can be created using the Notepad Application or the EDLIN program provided by DOS. ASCII files are the easiest files to transfer with a modem because no special processing is required.

Background Tasks—Applications not directly associated with the active window. Any task reduced to an icon can be regarded as being in *Background*. If a Windows application is in Background, it still executes. Generally, non-Windows applications don't execute in Background unless you set a different option using the PIF Editor.

Binary Files—Applications program files that end in .EXE or .COM are examples of machine-readable binary files. Binary files can be transferred by the Terminal applications program if the computer on the other end uses one of the standard communications protocols.

Bitmap Files—Files (usually ending in .BMP) created by the Paintbrush application and used to save picture information. Bitmap files contain color information for each individual pixel in the picture, so they can get very large.

Cascading Windows—Option allowing several windows to remain open on the screen at the same time, where the active window overlays (is placed in front of) the inactive (background) windows. The alternative to Cascading windows is Tiling.

Check box—A small square used to activate/deactivate a feature in a dialog box. When an "X" appears in the check box, the feature to the right of the box is active. The state of a check box can be changed by clicking on it with the mouse.

Click—A common Windows action, where the mouse cursor is moved to an item and the left mouse button is pressed and released once.

Clipboard Application—Application that manages the temporary storage area for either textual or graphics information. It's used as a buffer to move information between Windows-compatible applications.

Close—Refers to an application that has been terminated. When a window is closed, the application stops running, and all disk files and other resources are released to DOS. Closing a window is different than minimizing (or shrinking) a window to an icon. A minimized window continues to run, but the output is not readily visible.

Command Button—A colored area on the screen that starts a specific operation when the user clicks on it. The OK and Cancel buttons are examples.

Control Box—A small colored square (containing a small horizontal line or dash) at the top-left corner of every window. Double-clicking on the control box closes the window; single-clicking on the box displays the Control menu.

Control Menu—Menu that typically appears when you click on an icon once or you click on the control box of an existing window. From the Control menu, you can shrink a window to an icon, expand an icon to a window, and close the window. Other options may be available depending upon the application.

Copy—A Windows operation where a section of text or a picture is copied from the current application into the Clipboard application. This operation is nondestructive; the picture or highlighted text in the active application is not removed or otherwise modified.

Current Directory—The area on your disk where files are to be found or saved. Windows always allows you to create files in other directories by accepting full path specifications when saving or searching for a file.

Cut—An operation that transfers a highlighted section of text, or a selected graphics object, from the active application to the Clipboard. Unlike the Copy command, the Cut command actually removes the object from the current application. The Cut operation can be very useful when reorganizing paragraphs in a document, or when moving graphics items in a picture.

Data File—Any disk file that contains information to be used by an application. Data files of type .WRI contain the letters and other commands associated with documents created with the Write application. Files of type .BMP contain graphics information for pictures created using Paintbrush.

Default Printer—The printer to which Windows automatically sends the information when you print a file with the Print option of the File menu. The default printer is selected using the Print Manager window.

Dialog Box—A special window that appears whenever Windows wants you to provide confirmation of an action or additional information.

Directory—A special DOS file that allows you to organize files stored on a disk.

Double-Click—An operation performed by moving the mouse cursor to an item on the screen, and then pressing and releasing the left mouse button twice in quick succession.

Drag—An operation performed by moving the mouse cursor to an item on the screen, pressing the left mouse button, and moving the mouse to a new location while holding down the mouse button. Once the dragged item is in the desired location, release the left mouse button to complete the operation.

Drop-Down Menu—Refers to any of the menus available from the menu bar. Clicking on the individual title or category (such as File or Help) causes Windows to expand the item into a group of menu items, which can be selected with the mouse or keyboard.

Extended Memory—Memory above the base 640K. Extended memory is most commonly found on PCs that utilize 80286, 80386, or 80486 microprocessors.

Font—A collection of letters, numbers, and other symbols with a distinctive appearance. The Write and Paintbrush programs allow you to select different fonts to improve the appearance of your creations.

Full-Screen Application—Applications designed to run in an area of 25 rows and 80 columns. Most non-Windows programs are full-screen applications.

Group—A collection of applications in a separate window. Groups are created to combine various files and programs used together.

Group Icon—A small picture item that can be expanded into a Program Group window to show the various items that it contains.

Handshake—A term often used in communications applications. When applied to Terminal, it refers to the establishment of a controlled interaction between the PC running Windows and a remotely located computer system such as a bulletin board.

Highlighting—The procedure where the background color of a section of text is changed to indicate that the text is selected. This is most commonly seen in the selection of an active window (the title bar is highlighted), and in the selection of text to be operated on by Cut and Copy commands.

Icon—A small picture on the screen that signifies a particular application, operation, or program group. Double-clicking on an icon of a previously minimized program expands the icon into a window, and also makes it the active window.

Inactive Window—Any window visible (not converted into an icon) without a highlighted title bar. The application in this window may still run for a brief period of time.

Insertion Point—The point where new letters entered at the keyboard appear on the screen. In most text-oriented applications, the insertion point is identified by a blinking vertical bar cursor.

List Box—Used in dialog boxes. At first glance, it may look like a pull-down menu. The difference is that a List Box typically begins as a one-item box with a down arrow box to the right of it. If you click on the down arrow, the box expands to show the available options. If the List Box contains more options than can be conveniently displayed in the window, there are scroll arrows and a scroll box along the right-hand side to allow you to view all of the available options.

Maximize Button—A small colored box located near the upper-right corner of a window, containing an up arrow. When you click on this button, the window expands to use up the entire screen.

Menu Bar—A horizontal bar below the Title Bar, which contains keywords representing various drop-down menus.

Network—The specialized hardware and software that allows several PCs and other computers to communicate with one another and to share expensive peripherals, such as laser printers. Windows supports the software protocols of several of the most popular network vendors.

Non-Windows Application—A program created to run under DOS, that doesn't adhere to the design rules of Windows. These programs can still be run under Windows if they don't perform unusual operations, such as direct writes to PC hardware.

Open—An action that applies to a data file or a Windows icon. When applied to a data file, the particular application attempts to retrieve information from a previous session. When applied to an icon, the icon is expanded to a window so that the Window's contents can be viewed.

Parallel Port—A special hardware interface used to send information to printers, called parallel because data is sent out on eight data lines at the same time. The alternative port type is a *Serial Port*.

Paste—The operation of transferring information from the Clipboard application to the currently active application. The Paste command can be used repeatedly to bring multiple copies of the text or graphics into the Clipboard.

Pathname—Refers to a full description of the location of a file. The pathname conventions are defined by DOS, and consist of the disk drive letter followed by a colon, a backslash, and the names of the various directories that must be followed to reach the destination directory. (These directory names are also separated by backslashes.) No spaces are allowed within a pathname.

Program Information File (PIF)—Files created and maintained with the PIF Editor application. These files contain specific information about the requirements and preferences of application programs to be run under Windows. PIF files are usually created by the user to facilitate the use of a particular non-Windows application under Windows.

Pixel—The smallest graphics unit on a display.

Print Queue—A list that indicates the order in which jobs will be sent to a particular printer. (The jobs are temporarily stored on disk as data files while waiting to be printed.) Print queues can be managed via the Print Manager application.

Printer Driver—A specialized program provided by either Microsoft or the printer manufacturer. The program translates Windows printer commands to commands that can be understood by a specific printer. These commands control letter shape (different fonts) and other modifications (bold, italics, underline, etc.).

Protected Mode—A special hardware/software mode of the 80386 and 80486 microprocessors that allows easy addressing of large amounts of memory, and permits protection of one program from another. Windows prefers this mode because it allows the system to use PC resources to the maximum extent possible.

Read-Only File—A file marked so that it cannot be easily erased or altered. To edit or remove such a file, you must first go into File Manager to change the file attribute from Read-Only to Read-Write.

Real Mode—The hardware/software addressing mode associated with early microprocessors, such as the 8088 and 8086. It's the most limited memory model of the Intel microprocessor line, and places serious limitations on Windows.

Restore Button—A small colored box in the upper-right-hand corner of a window when it has been expanded into a full screen. The box contains a down-arrow. When the user clicks on the button, the window returns to its normal size.

Scroll Bar—A long, thin rectangular box with a colored box at each end containing the image of an arrow. A small square glides along the length of the rectangle to indicate relative position within the list or window. This technique is used when the information to be displayed (both text and graphics) exceeds the available area. Scroll bars can appear both horizontally and vertically.

Select—The operation of clicking a particular item or group of items so that they become highlighted. These items can now be manipulated as a group. Items can also be selected from the keyboard by using the arrow keys.

Serial Port—RS-232 communications port that your computer provides for connecting to other peripherals, such as printers and modems.

Shortcut Key—A special combination of keyboard keys pressed down at the same time, causing Windows to perform a desired action. In the Windows environment, shortcuts usually involve the use of the Alt, Ctrl, or Function keys.

Text File—See *ASCII File*.

Tiling Windows—The alternative way to display several windows on the screen (see *Cascading Windows*). In tiling, several windows display side by side on the screen (room permitting).

Title Bar—A horizontal rectangle at the top of each window, which contains an identifying name or title. The title bar for the active window is always highlighted.

Volume Label—The unique DOS name that references a disk.

Windows Application—A program designed to run specifically in the Windows environment. Such applications usually take advantage of data transfers using the Clipboard, and can still execute successfully when not the active task.

Word Wrap—A technique supported by most of the text-oriented tools in the Windows environment (such as Notepad, Cardfile, and Write). When you type past the right-hand margin of the window, the application immediately relocates the next word at the left edge of the next line.

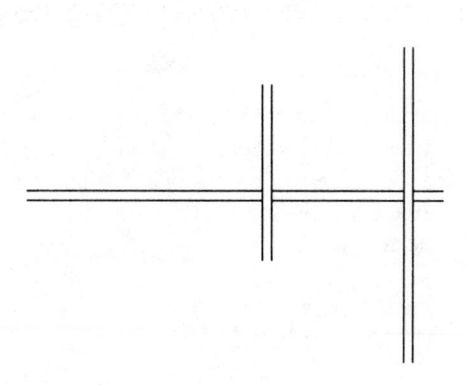

Index

A

About Windows dialog box, 102
Activating icons, 60
Active printer, 315
Active window, 10, 315
Add dialog box, 261
Airbrush tool (Paintbrush), 286
Alarm, 120-122, 248-250
Alarm Controls dialog box, 251
Application window, 55-56
Applications program, 315
Appointments (Calendar), 245
Arrange Icons command, 98-99
ASCII text files, 191, 315
Auto Arrange option, 97
Auto-repeat rate, 147
Autodial dialog box, 265

B

Background tasks, 316
Binary files, 316
Bitmap files, 316
Bold format, 301

Browse dialog box, 88
Brush shape (Paintbrush), 284
Brush Shapes dialog box, 285

C

Calculator
    and Clipboard, 256
    keyboard, 253-255
    memory, 256
    number systems, 257-258
    overview, 253
    scientific mode, 257
    starting, 253
    statistics, 258, 259
    using, 255-256
Calendar
    alarm options, 250-251
    appointment date, 245
    changing the format, 244-245
    creating and saving calendars, 251
    overview, 243
    printing, 252
    setting alarm, 120-122, 248-250
    special days, 248

starting, 243-244
time slots, 246-248
Card View, 259
Cardfile
    adding cards, 261
    Calling card, 265
    creating a system, 259
    deleting cards, 262
    editing options, 262
    overview, 116-119,258
    pasting a picture, 262
    restoring a card, 262
    saving, opening, and merging, 263
    searching, 264-265
    starting, 259
    starting a Cardfile, 119-120
    viewing multiple cards, 120
    viewing tips, 264
Cascade and Tile options, 98
Cascading menus, 18,62
Cascading windows, 316
Change Attributes command, 190-191
Character Menu, 300
CHDIR, 231
Check box, 68-69,316
CHKDSK, 24,231
Click, 316
Clipboard, 5,316
Clock, 235-236
Close, 316
Close command, 64
Closed Shapes (Paintbrush), 274
Closing a window, 56-57
Closing dialogs, 74
CLS, 231
cm option button, 293
Color eraser (Paintbrush), 281
Colors
    creating a color scheme, 130-131
    Custom, 131-133
    option, 127
    overview, 128-130
    Selection window, 129
COM ports, 306

Command buttons, 68,316
Communication parameters, 305-306
Communications dialog box, 306
CONFIG.SYS, 27-28
Confirm Mouse Operation dialog box, 179
Control box, 317
Control Menu
    commands, 64
    icons and dialogs, 65
    options, 84-85
    overview, 10,63-64,317
Control Panel
    Colors, 128-130
    Date and Time, 133-134
    Desktop, 134-140
    Fonts, 140-143
    International settings, 143
    keyboard, 147
    mouse, 147-148
    Network options, 149
    overview, 4,125-127
    ports, 149-151
    printers, 152-154
    sound, 154-155
    starting, 127-128
    386 options, 155-156
COPY, 231
Copy
    and Move, 92-93
    dialog box, 183
    Diskette dialog box, 194
    Port settings, 151
    Program Item dialog box, 92-93
Copying disks, 193-194
Copying files and directories, 181-183
Create Directory dialog box, 188
Creating
    Cardfile system, 259
    directories, 187
    headers and footers (Write), 299
    your own applications, 215-218
Current directory, 317
Custom Colors, 132
Cut, 317

D

Data Bits option, 305
Data file, 317
Date and Time, 127, 133-134
Day Markings dialog box, 249
Day Settings dialog box, 247
Day View, 243
Default printer, 317
DEL, 231
Delete command, 94
Delete dialog box, 184
Deleting
    directories, 187
    files and directories, 183-185
    icons, 218
Desktop
    dialog box, 134
    option, 127
    overview, 44
    pattern, 135
    setting, 134-140
Desktop Accessories
    Calculator, 253-258
    Calendar, 243-252
    Cardfile, 258-265
    Clock, 235-236
    Notepad, 236-243
    overview, 235
Desktop Applications
    overview, 269
    Paintbrush, 270-291
    Terminal, 304-309
    Write, 291-304
Detect Idle Time option, 226
Dialog Boxes
    About Windows, 102
    Add, 261
    Alarm Controls, 251
    Autodial, 265
    Browse, 88
    Brush Shapes, 285
    check boxes, 68-69
    closing, 74

    command buttons, 68
    Communications, 306
    Confirm Mouse Operation, 179
    Copy, 183
    Copy Diskette, 194
    Copy Program Item, 92-93
    Create Directory, 188
    Day Markings, 249
    Day Settings, 247
    definition of, 317
    Delete, 184
    Desktop, 134
    drop-down list boxes, 73
    File Copy Operation, 182
    File Merge, 263
    File Open, 238
    File Save As, 238, 252
    Find, 241
    Fonts, 109, 141, 301
    Format Complete, 196
    Format Diskette, 195
    Image Attributes, 271
    Include, 176
    Indents, 298
    Index, 118, 261
    International Settings, 143
    Keyboard, 147
    list boxes, 72-73
    Menu option, 70-71
    Mouse, 148
    Move, 180
    New Program Object, 216
    Notepad, 241
    option buttons, 71
    overview, 18, 65-66
    Page Footer, 299
    Page Layout, 116, 294
    Page Setup, 242
    Phone Number, 309
    Ports-setting, 150
    Print, 252
    Print to File, 208
    Printer Setup, 115
    Printers, 152, 201

Program Group Properties, 95
Program Item Properties, 91, 216, 218
Repaginate Document, 298
Run, 97
Search, 101, 185
Select Icon, 89, 217
selecting options, 66-67
Set Up Applications, 220
Show Date, 246
Sort by, 175
Sound, 154
Special Time, 247
Tabs, 295
Terminal Error Warning, 306
Terminal Preferences, 307
text boxes, 71-72
View Other, 173
Warning, 67-68, 113
DIR, 231
Directories, 160
Directory, 317
Directory Tree window, 165
Disk maintenance
    copying, 193-194
    formatting, 194-196
    overview, 193
DOS
    commands, 230-232
    Directory, 159-161
    Prompt application, 213-215
    prompt, 5
Double-click, 9, 317
Drag, 9, 318
Drawing lines and curves, 282
Drop-down list boxes, 70, 73
Drop-down menus, 16-18, 318

E

Edit command, 64
Edit menu, 110
Editing a document, 108-111
Editing a program item, 91
Equipment requirements, 8

Eraser tools (Paintbrush), 280
Exiting Windows, 96
Exiting Write, 115-116
Extended memory, 318

F

FIFO queue, 200
File and directory information
    copying, 181-183
    finding file size, 171-172
    overview, 171
    sorting files, 174-175
    using a filter, 175-177
    viewing by categories, 174
    viewing information, 172-173
File attributes, 190
File Copy Operation dialog box, 182
File Details option, 172
File Manager
    changing attributes, 190
    copying, 181-183
    creating and deleting directories, 187
    deleting, 183-185
    Directory requirements, 161-162
    Directory Tree window, 165-167
    disk maintenance, 193-196
    DOS Directory, 159-161
    file and directory information, 171-177
    launching applications, 190-191
    moving, 178-181
    navigation shortcuts, 169-171
    overview, 4, 159, 163
    printing files, 191-192
    renaming, 187-190
    searching, 185-187
    selecting, 177-178
    shortcut keys, 170
    starting, 163
    viewing, 167-169
File menu
    activating an application, 96
    Copy and Move, 92-93
    creating a Program Group, 87-88

creating a Program Item, 89
Delete command, 94
editing a Program Item, 91
exiting Windows, 96
including a document name, 90
moving with the mouse, 93
New command, 86-87
Open command, 91
overview, 85
Properties command, 94-95
Run command, 96
File Merge dialog box, 263
File Open dialog box, 238
File Save As dialog box, 238,252
Files and directories
copying, 181-183
creating, 187
deleting, 183-185,187
moving, 178-181
renaming, 187-190
searching for, 185-187
selecting, 177-178
size of, 171-172
Find dialog box, 241
First-in first-out queue see FIFO
Fonts
and styles (Write), 300
definition, 318
dialog box, 109,141,301
option, 127
selecting, 140-143
Footers, 299
FORMAT (command), 231
Format Complete dialog box, 196
Format Diskette dialog box, 195
Formatting disks, 194-196
Formatting paragraphs, 294
Frame, 10
Full-screen application, 318

G

Graphical User Interface see GUI
Graphics/multiple text mode, 222

Group, 318
Group icon, 318
Group selection, 100
Group window, 78,81-82
Groups, 78
GUI, 2-3,19

H

Handshake, 318
Headers and footers (Write), 299
Help
buttons, 38
Control buttons, 38
for more help, 39
Menu, 36-38
Menu options, 37,101-102
overview, 35-36,100
printing help information, 39-40
searching for, 38-39
Help Menu options, 37,101-102
Highlighting, 318
Hot key, 36

I

Iconizing a window, 52-53
Icons
activating, 60
definition, 318
deleting, 218
modifying, 218
overview, 2,11-12,57-58
Program Item, 57
selecting and moving, 59,217
Image Attributes dialog box, 271
Inactive window, 319
Include dialog box, 176
Indents, 297
Indents dialog box, 298
Index dialog box, 118,261
Insertion point, 319
Installation (Windows 3.0)
changing, 29-31

help system, 35-40
non-Windows applications, 28-29
overview, 19-22
printer, 23
procedures, 23-28
quitting Windows, 34-35
side effects of, 29
starting Windows, 31-34
Installing printers, 152-153
International option, 127
International Settings
Currency and numbers, 146-147
Date, 144-145
dialog box, 143
overview, 143-144
Time, 145-146
Italic format, 301

K

Keyboard
dialog box, 147
option, 127
setting, 147
shortcut sequence, 17,301

L

Launching applications, 190-191
Line spacing (Write), 296
List box, 70,72-73,319

M

Maximize
a window, 49
button, 52,319
command, 64
Memory
options, 226
virtual, 8,29
Menu
bar, 10,16-18,60,319
bar system, 60

box, 70
Cascading, 18,62
Character, 300
Control, 10,63-65,317
Drop-down, 16-18,318
Edit, 110
Edit pull-down, 118
File, 85
Help, 36-38
Option dialogs, 70-71
Options, 97,204
overview, 60-62
Print Manager Control, 84-85
Print Manager File, 85-96
Print Manager Help, 100-102
Print Manager Options, 97-100
Print Manager Options, 204-207
Pull-down, 60
special commands, 62-63
system, 85
View, 206-207
Window, 98
Minimize
button, 52
command, 64
on Use, 98
MKDIR, 231
Modem, 265,304,308
Modem Default options, 308
Modifying an Icon, 218
Monitor Ports option, 227
Mouse
cursor, 9
dialog box, 148
double-clicking, 9
option, 127
overview, 9-10
pointer, 9
setting, 147-148
Move command, 64
Move dialog box, 180
Moving
a window, 51
files and directories, 178-181

Index

icons, 59
  Program Icons, 217
Multiple printers, 203-204
Multiple windows, 53
Multitasking, 4

N

Network
  option, 127
  Options Setting, 149
  overview, 22,319
New command, 86-87
New Program Object dialog box, 216
Next command, 64
Non-grouped files, 178
Non-Windows applications
  Basic DOS commands, 230-232
  creating applications, 215-218
  DOS prompt application, 213-215
  options and limitations, 212-213
  overview, 211,319
  PIF Editor, 220-230
  PIFs, 219-220
  running, 211-212
Notepad
  dialog box, 241
  editing text, 239
  multiple files, 243
  navigation keys, 240
  opening an existing file, 238
  overview, 236
  printing, 242
  searching for text, 240-241
  setting up a page, 241-242
  starting, 237
  time/date, 243
  word wrap, 240

O

Open, 319
Open command, 91
Operating modes, 7-8

Option button, 70-71
Options Menu
  Arrange Icons command, 98-99
  Auto Arrange, 97
  Cascade and Tile, 98
  group selection, 100
  Minimize on Use, 98
  overview, 97,204
  Print Manager, 204-206
  using a Network, 205-206
  Window menu, 98

P

Page breaks (Write), 298
Page Footer dialog box, 299
Page Layout dialog box, 116,294
Page Setup, 241-242
Paintbrush
  Airbrush tool, 286
  basic techniques, 271
  Brush Shape, 284-286
  Closed Shapes, 274
  Color eraser, 281-282
  defining a drawing region, 271
  drawing lines and curves, 282-284
  drawing tips, 279
  drawing tools and colors, 273
  Eraser tools, 280-281
  overview, 270
  Paintbrush tools, 272-273
  Polygon tools, 279-280
  Roller tool, 276
  Scissors and Pick, 287
  starting, 270
  Text tool, 288-290
Paragraphs, 296-297
Parallel port, 319
Parent, 160
Parity, 305
Paste, 64,320
Pathname, 320
PC network, 22
Phone Number dialog box, 309

PIF Editor
    386 Enhanced mode, 223-225
    advanced options, 225-228
    custom directory, 228-230
    non-386 mode, 222-223
    overview, 6, 218, 220-222
    window, 221
PIF see Program Information File
Pixel, 136, 320
Placing graphics, 303
Polygon tools (Paintbrush), 279
Ports
    option, 127
    RS-232, 149
    serial, 149
    setting, 149-151
Print dialog box, 252
Print File Size option, 206
Print Manager
    intercepting print jobs, 207-208
    multiple printers, 203-204
    Options menu, 204-206
    overview, 4, 199-200
    selecting, 200-201
    starting, 202-203
    View menu, 206-207
    window, 202
Print queue, 320
Print to File dialog box, 208
Printer
    active, 315
    default, 317
    dialog box, 152, 201
    driver, 320
    installing, 23, 152-153
    option, 127
    removing, 154
    Setup dialog box, 115
Printing
    a document, 114-115
    Calendar, 252
    files, 191-192
    Help information, 39-40
    Notepad, 242

Program Group, 87-88
Program Group Properties dialog box, 95
Program Information File (PIF), 212, 320
Program Item, 81, 89
Program Item icon, 57
Program Item Properties dialog box, 91, 216, 218
Program Manager
    Control menu, 84-85
    File menu, 85-96
    Group windows, 81-82
    Help menu, 100-102
    keyboard and mouse, 82-84
    menu system, 85
    Options menu, 97-100
    overview, 4, 77-81
Properties command, 94-95
Protected mode, 320
Pull-down menu, 60

Q

Queues
    definition, 320
    FIFO, 200
    Network, 206
Quitting Windows, 34-35

R

Read-only file, 320
Real mode, 7, 222, 320-321
Removing
    printers, 154
    font files, 141
REN, 231
Renaming, 187-190
Repaginate command, 298
Repaginate Document dialog box, 298
Reserve Shortcut Keys, 228
Resizing windows, 48-51
Restore button, 49, 321
Restore command, 64
Reversi, 6
Roller tool (Paintbrush), 276

Index

Root directory, 160
RS-232 port, 149
Ruler, 291
Run command, 96
Run dialog box, 97

S

Saving
    a document, 111-113
    terminal settings, 311
    Write files, 304
Scientific mode (Calculator), 257
Scissors and Pick (Paintbrush), 287
Scroll
    arrows, 13
    bars, 13-14, 321
    box, 13, 47
    window keys, 48
    windows, 46-47
Search
    dialog box, 101, 185
    Entire Disk, 186
    Results window, 186
Searching
    for files and directories, 185-187
    for help, 38-39
Sectors, 194
Select Icon dialog box, 89, 217
Selecting
    an application window, 55-56
    Colors, 131
    files and directories, 177-178
    Fonts, 140-143
    icons, 59
    non-grouped files, 178
    Print Manager, 200-201
    with the keyboard, 56
Serial port, 149, 304, 321
Set Up Applications dialog box, 220
Setting alarm, 248-250
Setting the Desktop
    Border widths, 139-140
    Cursor, 138-139

    desktop pattern, 135-136
    Icon spacing, 139
    overview, 134-135
    Wallpaper, 136-138
SETUP, 24-28
Shortcuts, 169-171, 321
Show Date dialog box, 246
Size command, 64
Size Picture command, 303
Sizing
    boxes, 15
    icons, 15
    windows, 49
Slider, 47
Solitaire, 6
Sort By dialog box, 175
Sound
    dialog box, 154
    option, 127
    setting, 154-155
Source diskette, 193
Special Time dialog box, 247
Standard mode, 8, 222
Starting Windows 3.0
    options for, 32-33
    overview, 31-34
    with an application, 33-34
Statistics (Calculator), 258, 259
Switch To command, 64

T

Tabs (Write), 294
Tabs dialog box, 295
Task list, 55
Terminal
    communication parameters, 305-306
    modem, 308
    overview, 304
    Preferences, 68
    Preferences dialog box, 307
    saving settings, 311
    selecting a number, 308-309
    setting up your terminal, 307

    starting, 304
Terminal Error Warning dialog box, 306
Text box, 70,71-72
Text file, 321
Text mode, 222
386 Enhanced Mode
    setting Options, 155-156
    overview, 8,212
    option, 127
Text tool (Paintbrush), 288
Tiling windows, 321
Time, 133-134
Title bar, 10,14-15,321
Tree directory, 160
TYPE, 231

U

Underline, 301
Update Net Queues, 206

V

View menu, 206-207
View Other dialog box, 173
Viewing a Directory, 167-169
Virtual memory, 8,29
Volume label, 321

W

Warning box, 95
Warning Dialog boxes, 67-68,113
Window menu, 98
Windows (screens)
    application, 44
    cascading, 316
    closing, 56-57
    document, 44
    iconizing, 52-53
    maximizing, 49
    moving, 15-16,51
    multiple, 53-54
    overview, 10-11,44-46
    resizing, 15-16,48-51
    scrolling, 46-48
    tiling, 321
Windows 3.0 Skills
    closing a window, 56-57
    Control menu, 63-65
    desktop, 44
    dialog boxes, 65-74
    icons, 57-60
    menus, 60-63
    overview, 43
    selecting a window, 55-56
    window (screen), 44-54
Windows Setup, 5
Word wrap, 240,322
Write
    document setup, 293-294
    fonts and styles, 300
    formatting paragraphs, 294
    headers and footers, 299
    indenting paragraphs, 297
    line spacing, 296
    overview, 291
    page breaks, 298
    paragraph alignment, 296
    Ruler, 291
    saving, 304
    starting, 291
    tabs, 294
    text and graphics, 302